Argentina's Economic Growth and Recovery

This book examines the causes of the economic and political crisis in Argentina in 2001 and the process of strong economic recovery. It poses the question of how a country that defaulted on its external loans and was widely criticized by international observers could have succeeded in its growth and development despite this decision in 2002. It examines this process in terms of the impact of neo-liberal policies on the economy and the role of development strategy and the state in recovering from the crisis.

The book places the Argentina case in the theoretical framework of neo-liberalism and state performance. It examines the origins of the crisis in the 1990s, the crisis and political collapse itself, and the efforts to overcome immediate poverty and social disruption in 2002. It then reviews the record of the government of the late President Nestor Kirchner from 2003 to 2007 and the efforts of the government of President Cristina Fernandez de Kirchner to continue reform and recovery despite the coming of the global financial crisis of 2008.

The book identifies four key strategic choices, which help to explain Argentina's success:

- national priorities and preferences were more important than global priorities set outside the country;
- the importance of regional cooperation within Latin America;
- the re-assertion of the role of the State; and
- the government's objective should be to reduce poverty and inequality.

These four choices have defined Argentina's strategy since 2003. They are also useful for other developing countries and for the international community to consider in other crises, including the current global economic crisis, Greece, Ireland, and Spain, as well as the need for reform of the conventional advice of the International Monetary Fund (IMF) and the World Bank.

Michael A. Cohen is Director of the International Affairs Program at the New School University, New York, USA.

Routledge studies in the modern world economy

1 **Interest Rates and Budget Deficits**
A study of the advanced economies
Kanhaya L Gupta and Bakhtiar Moazzami

2 **World Trade after the Uruguay Round**
Prospects and policy options for the twenty-first century
Edited by Harald Sander and András Inotai

3 **The Flow Analysis of Labour Markets**
Edited by Ronald Schettkat

4 **Inflation and Unemployment**
Contributions to a new macroeconomic approach
Edited by Alvaro Cencini and Mauro Baranzini

5 **Macroeconomic Dimensions of Public Finance**
Essays in honour of Vito Tanzi
Edited by Mario I. Blejer and Teresa M. Ter-Minassian

6 **Fiscal Policy and Economic Reforms**
Essays in honour of Vito Tanzi
Edited by Mario I. Blejer and Teresa M. Ter-Minassian

7 **Competition Policy in the Global Economy**
Modalities for co-operation
Edited by Leonard Waverman, William S. Comanor and Akira Goto

8 **Working in the Macro Economy**
A study of the US labor market
Martin F. J. Prachowny

9 **How Does Privatization Work?**
Edited by Anthony Bennett

10 **The Economics and Politics of International Trade**
Freedom and trade: volume II
Edited by Gary Cook

11 **The Legal and Moral Aspects of International Trade**
Freedom and trade: volume III
Edited by Asif Qureshi, Hillel Steiner and Geraint Parry

12 **Capital Markets and Corporate Governance in Japan, Germany and the United States**
Organizational response to market inefficiencies
Helmut M. Dietl

13 **Competition and Trade Policies**
Coherence or conflict
Edited by Einar Hope

14 **Rice**
The primary commodity
A. J. H. Latham

15 **Trade, Theory and Econometrics**
Essays in honour of John S. Chipman
Edited by James C. Moore, Raymond Riezman, James R. Melvin

16 **Who benefits from Privatisation?**
Edited by Moazzem Hossain and Justin Malbon

17 **Towards a Fair Global Labour Market**
Avoiding the new slave trade
Ozay Mehmet, Errol Mendes and Robert Sinding

18 **Models of Futures Markets**
Edited by Barry Goss

19 **Venture Capital Investment**
An agency analysis of UK practice
Gavin C. Reid

20 **Macroeconomic Forecasting**
A sociological appraisal
Robert Evans

21 **Multimedia and Regional Economic Restructuring**
Edited by Hans-Joachim Braczyk, Gerhard Fuchs and Hans-Georg Wolf

22 **The New Industrial Geography**
Regions, regulation and institutions
Edited by Trevor J. Barnes and Meric S. Gertler

23 **The Employment Impact of Innovation**
Evidence and policy
Edited by Marco Vivarelli and Mario Pianta

24 **International Health Care Reform**
A legal, economic and political analysis
Colleen Flood

25 **Competition Policy Analysis**
Edited by Einar Hope

26 **Culture and Enterprise**
The development, representation and morality of business
Don Lavoie and Emily Chamlee-Wright

27 **Global Financial Crises and Reforms**
Cases and caveats
B.N. Ghosh

28 **Geography of Production and Economic Integration**
Miroslav N. Jovanović

29 **Technology, Trade and Growth in OECD Countries**
Does specialisation matter?
Valentina Meliciani

30 **Post-Industrial Labour Markets**
Profiles of North America and Scandinavia
Edited by Thomas P Boje and Bengt Furaker

31 **Capital Flows without Crisis**
Reconciling capital mobility and economic stability
Edited by Dipak Dasgupta, Marc Uzan and Dominic Wilson

32 **International Trade and National Welfare**
Murray C Kemp

33 **Global Trading Systems at Crossroads**
A post-Seattle perspective
Dilip K. Das

34 **The Economics and Management of Technological Diversification**
Edited by John Cantwell, Alfonso Gambardella and Ove Granstrand

35 **Before and Beyond EMU**
Historical lessons and future prospects
Edited by Patrick Crowley

36 **Fiscal Decentralization**
Ehtisham Ahmad and Vito Tanzi

37 **Regionalisation of Globalised Innovation**
Locations for advanced industrial development and disparities in participation
Edited by Ulrich Hilpert

38 **Gold and the Modern World Economy**
Edited by MoonJoong Tcha

39 **Global Economic Institutions**
Willem Molle

40 **Global Governance and Financial Crises**
Edited by Meghnad Desai and Yahia Said

41 **Linking Local and Global Economies**
The ties that bind
Edited by Carlo Pietrobelli and Arni Sverrisson

42 **Tax Systems and Tax Reforms in Europe**
Edited by Luigi Bernardi and Paola Profeta

43 **Trade Liberalization and APEC**
Edited by Jiro Okamoto

44 **Fiscal Deficits in the Pacific Region**
Edited by Akira Kohsaka

45 **Financial Globalization and the Emerging Market Economies**
Dilip K. Das

46 **International Labor Mobility**
Unemployment and increasing returns to scale
Bharati Basu

47 **Good Governance in the Era of Global Neoliberalism**
Conflict and depolitization in Latin America, Eastern Europe, Asia and Africa
Edited by Jolle Demmers, Alex E. Fernández Jilberto and Barbara Hogenboom

48 **The International Trade System**
Alice Landau

49 **International Perspectives on Temporary Work and Workers**
Edited by John Burgess and Julia Connell

50 **Working Time and Workers' Preferences in Industrialized Countries**
Finding the balance
Edited by Jon C. Messenger

51 **Tax Systems and Tax Reforms in New EU Members**
Edited by Luigi Bernardi, Mark Chandler and Luca Gandullia

52 **Globalization and the Nation State**
The impact of the IMF and the World Bank
Edited by Gustav Ranis, James Vreeland and Stephen Kosak

53 **Macroeconomic Policies and Poverty Reduction**
Edited by Ashoka Mody and Catherine Pattillo

54 **Regional Monetary Policy**
Carlos J. Rodríguez-Fuentez

55 **Trade and Migration in the Modern World**
Carl Mosk

56 **Globalisation and the Labour Market**
Trade, technology and less-skilled workers in Europe and the United States
Edited by Robert Anderton, Paul Brenton and John Whalley

57 **Financial Crises**
Socio-economic causes and institutional context
Brenda Spotton Visano

58 **Globalization and Self Determination**
Is the nation-state under siege?
Edited by David R. Cameron, Gustav Ranis and Annalisa Zinn

59 **Developing Countries and the Doha Development Round of the WTO**
Edited by Pitou van Dijck and Gerrit Faber

60 **Immigrant Enterprise in Europe and the USA**
Prodromos Panayiotopoulos

61 **Solving the Riddle of Globalization and Development**
Edited by Manuel Agosín, David Bloom, George Chapelier and Jagdish Saigal

62 **Foreign Direct Investment and the World Economy**
Ashoka Mody

63 **The World Economy**
A global analysis
Horst Siebert

64 **Production Organizations in Japanese Economic Development**
Edited by Tetsuji Okazaki

65 **The Economics of Language**
International analyses
Edited by Barry R. Chiswick and Paul W. Miller

66 **Street Entrepreneurs**
People, place and politics in local and global perspective
Edited by John Cross and Alfonso Morales

67 **Global Challenges and Local Responses**
The East Asian experience
Edited by Jang-Sup Shin

68 **Globalization and Regional Integration**
The origins, development and impact of the single European aviation market
Alan Dobson

69 **Russia Moves into the Global Economy: Breaking Out**
John M. Letiche

70 **The European Economy in an American Mirror**
Barry Eichengreen, Michael Landesmann and Dieter Stiefel

71 **Working Time Around the World**
Trends in working hours, laws, and policies in a global comparative perspective
Jon C. Messenger, Sangheon Lee and Deidre McCann

72 **International Water Treaties**
Negotiation and cooperation along transboundary rivers
Shlomi Dinar

73 **Economic Integration in the Americas**
Edited by Joseph A. McKinney and H. Stephen Gardner

74 **Expanding Frontiers of Global Trade Rules**
The political economy dynamics of the international trading system
Nitya Nanda

75 **The Macroeconomics of Global Imbalances**
European and Asian perspectives
Edited by Marc Uzan

76 **China and Asia**
Economic and financial interactions
Edited by Yin-Wong Cheung and Kar-Yiu Wong

77 **Regional Inequality in China**
Trends, explanations and policy responses
Edited by Shenggen Fan, Ravi Kanbur and Xiaobo Zhang

78 **Governing Rapid Growth in China**
Equity and institutions
Edited by Ravi Kanbur and Xiaobo Zhang

79 **The Indonesian Labour Market**
Shafiq Dhanani, Iyanatul Islam and Anis Chowdhury

80 **Cost-Benefit Analysis in Multi-level Government in Europe and the USA**
The case of EU cohesion policy and of US federal investment policies
Alessandro Ferrara

81 **The Economic Geography of Air Transportation**
Space, time, and the freedom of the sky
John Bowen

First published 2012
by Routledge
2 Park Square, Milton Park, Abingdon, Oxon OX14 4RN

Simultaneously published in the USA and Canada
by Routledge
711 Third Avenue, New York, NY 10017

Routledge is an imprint of the Taylor & Francis Group, an informa business

British Library Cataloguing in Publication Data
A catalogue record for this book is available from the British Library

Library of Congress Cataloging in Publication Data
Cohen, Michael A., 1944–
Argentina's economic growth and recovery/Michael A. Cohen.
p. cm.
1. Argentina–Economic conditions–21st century. 2. Argentina–Economic policy–21st century. 3. Financial crises–Argentina. I. Title.
HC175.C6112 2011
330.982'072–dc23
2011026478

ISBN: 978-0-415-59480-6 (hbk)
ISBN: 978-0-203-14452-7 (ebk)

Typeset in Times
by Wearset Ltd, Boldon, Tyne and Wear

Argentina's Economic Growth and Recovery

The economy in a time of default

Michael A. Cohen

Routledge
Taylor & Francis Group
LONDON AND NEW YORK

99 **Singapore, the Energy Economy**
From the first refinery to the end of cheap oil, 1960–2010
Ng Weng Hoong

100 **China–India Economics**
Challenges, competition and collaboration
Amitendu Palit

101 **Case Studies on Chinese Enterprises**
Edited by Donglin Xia

102 **Argentina's Economic Growth and Recovery**
The economy in a time of default
Michael A. Cohen

Contents

Acknowledgments

This book is dedicated to Margarita Gutman, my *compañera*, wife, colleague, and teacher, who introduced me to her country and encouraged me to discover its history, wonderful and perplexing qualities, and contradictions.

During this journey we have lived together through the impending crisis, the end of Convertibility, the events of 2001, and the long process of recovery. From the dark days of 2001–2002 to the season of hope from 2003 to 2008, through the coming storm of the global crisis, and its aftermath in 2011, the country and its economic performance has mystified many external observers, particularly in the non-Spanish-speaking world. With each day's dramatic developments, I found myself asking more and more questions, and Marga encouraged me to learn more, to write about Argentina, and to place it within my own professional experience of working in many developing countries for over 40 years. Her own deep commitment and infectious excitement about research and writing was a major factor in my writing the book. Without her love and support, this book would not have been written.

As I read the economics and social science literature on Argentina and Latin America in English and Spanish, I became convinced that the story of Argentina's recovery needed to be included in the wider debates and discourses about development, neo-liberalism, and development strategy. The decisions of Argentine governments following the crisis and their largely successful results have demonstrated that many of the fundamental assumptions of the international community and academic observers require further examination and revision. Most external observers of Argentina believed that the country's default on its external debt closed the door on recovery and future growth. As the book demonstrates, this was not the case.

I believe that too much of the recent literature on Latin America seeks to categorize governments, leaders, and political strategies without understanding what actually occurred in individual countries. Having worked for many years in Africa, South Asia, and East Asia, I was struck by the frequency of facile generalizations about Latin America and the relative absence of detailed country case studies, particularly of specific historical periods.

While the book focuses on Argentina, it seeks to bring in a wider literature and to link the Argentine case to comparative, global experience. My anthropologist friend, Arjun Appadurai, asked me, "What is it a case of?" I do not think the book fully answers that question, but it does examine a historically unique set of political and economic choices which has allowed the country to recover from the crisis.

The process of recovery, however, has not been easy. Argentina is a society of great political and social tension, extraordinary personal and social ambition, and deep anxieties. The crisis of 2001 reflected all of these and yet its recovery has also permitted the public acknowledgment of a terrible past in which unspeakable crimes were committed in the name of the state. Seeing the pictures of disappeared young people on the pages of *Pagina 12*, decades after their disappearance, reminds me every day of the very great human costs of the struggle for social justice and democracy in Argentina.

Learning about a country inevitably requires many teachers. In Argentina, I have been very fortunate to have benefitted from many people whom I now consider my friends: Oscar Tangelson, Martin Abeles, Berardo Dujovne, Sylvia Hirsch, Alberto Croce, Adriana Clemente, Roberto Doberti, Enrique Oteiza, Andres Borthagaray, Pablo Jacoby, Jaime Sorin, Jorge Arguello, and many others.

In New York I have benefitted from the opportunities created by the Observatory on Latin America (OLA), which brought many Latin American leaders and public officials to the New School, as well as leading North American commentators. I would like to thank Julien Studley for his continuous and generous support of the OLA. Hearing first-hand the views of the late former President Nestor Kirchner, President Cristina Fernandez de Kirchner, President Tabare Vazquez, then-presidential candidate Ollanta Humala, Alicia Barcena, Hector Timerman, Juan Manuel Abal Medina, Marco Aurelio Garcia, Heraldo Munoz, Jorge Arguello, Joseph Stiglitz, Paul Krugman, Greg Grandin, Jose Pablo Feinmann, and many others has provided helpful insights about these issues. I have also benefitted from discussions with two Argentine colleagues in New York, Alberto Minujin, Senior OLA Fellow, and Bernardo Kliksberg, Senior Advisor at UNDP, and my colleague, Sakiko Fukuda-Parr at the Graduate Program in International Affairs (GPIA) at the New School.

The book has also benefitted from the assistance provided by graduate students in the GPIA, particularly Bart Orr, Mitch Cook, and Christina Lappas. Christina helped assemble missing data, provided inputs for Chapter 9, and helped in the final formatting of the manuscript.

I am grateful to the New School for granting me a sabbatical in the spring of 2008 to work on the first draft of this manuscript in Buenos Aires and for providing an institutional framework in which I could write.

I would also like to gratefully acknowledge the helpful comments of an anonymous reviewer who suggested placing the Argentina story within the theoretical framework of the literature on state performance. This suggestion led me to return to a comparative and theoretical literature which I believe has enriched the book.

Writing this book was both a personal and family experience. My father, Seymour Cohen, a biochemist and now a historian, taught me the value and pleasure of hard work and, by example, the continued excitement of life-long learning. His own continuing work in his 90's reminds me that learning can be a vital and central activity of our lives. My mother, Elaine, a sculptor, taught me during her life the importance of possibility—that unusual and positive things could happen if we would only suspend our skepticism and doubt and learn to listen, observe, and support the efforts of others.

My adult children, Nicole and Jonah, together with Jonah's wife Katherine, have continually encouraged me in my professional pursuits. Nicole has been particularly insistent that I work on this book. My new and extended family in Argentina, including Juan Manuel and Iraci, Andres and Valeria, and Bruno, their children, and my brother-in-law Alberto Gutman has constantly reminded me that these issues are not abstractions but have real consequences for my own family and particularly for my grandchildren: Serena, Franco, Lukas, Anabella, Adrian, and Guilia. I am grateful to them for explaining their country to me.

Finally, trying to understand Argentina has been informed above all by Marga, and her work on "porvenir", or the world to come. Believing in and anticipating the future is one of the strongest motivations we can have to work today, to understand, to value, and to improve. In the end, this is best done not alone, but together.

Prologue

This book examines the process of finding alternative policies for economic and social development in a country in crisis. It covers the economic and political experience of Argentina from 1998 to the end of 2008, a period between the early days of the country's economic and social crisis and the onset of the worst global economic crisis since the Great Depression. The book presents the origins and unfolding of the country's dramatic collapse in 2001–2002, its surprising recovery through 2008, and the subsequent conflicts and obstacles to economic and social reform that emerged in 2008. The experience of Argentina in this decade is a journey from despair to hope and achievement, to growing concern, and perhaps to a new sense of realism about expectations and state responsibility in a world of global uncertainty.

This narrative and analysis of Argentina's experience is framed by three important issues, which have antecedents in both social science and economic theory and in the historical practice of the management of economies and societies. These are: the meaning of neo-liberalism and the results of the Washington Consensus, the role of the state and society in economic development, and the quality of institutions and the determinants of state performance in this process. Each of these issues has had enormous impact on the experience of Argentina, but also in determining how other states in Latin America and the world at large have managed their economies and state–society relations during the process of transformation. More importantly, these three issues are also closely woven together and are interdependent. If an ideology is adopted that explicitly limits the role of the state, it should not be surprising that state performance is not as powerful in affecting economic and social outcomes as it might otherwise be. Similarly, if the state's role is limited, then there is little reason to build and sustain institutional capacity to identify and solve problems.

Understanding the theoretical and practical debates surrounding these three issues and their interactions helps to explain what has happened in Argentina and to place that experience into a broader comparative analytic framework. The interest here is not only academic, but also to identify aspects of this experience that can be useful to other countries as they seek to improve the welfare of their peoples in an epoch of globalization and rapid change.

An important component of this study, therefore, is about the power of ideas and how they affect public choices about strategy, policy, and institutional design. In the end, ideas also determine how outcomes are understood, by what criteria outcomes are evaluated, and, finally, how the efforts of individuals, groups, and institutions are judged. Understanding the present—or even the recent past—depends heavily on how much we understand the past: the origins of perceptions and various forms of knowledge, the motivations of actors, the impact on those affected, and how experience comes to determine the design of social action in its broadest terms.

The intellectual stakes of such an inquiry are, therefore, considerable, particularly in a period of global turmoil and rethinking about the value of economic and political theories. The continuing global crisis, which began in 2008, has made it more important than ever to truly understand what can happen in a crisis, how countries and economies can recover from crises, and how insights from these experiences can contribute to the development of new theory and practice.

This story of the Argentinian crisis, therefore, is also a case study of the impact of wider global forces and how ideas come to affect nations and their people. Explaining the developments in one country in this period requires understanding this broader context and how historical forces, within and outside Argentina, have combined to define what were understood as available options in politics, economic development, and social policy in the country. The choices among these options and their consequences have proven to be dramatic. Throughout its history, Argentina has experienced deep and often momentous changes in its politics, economy, and society, leading many observers to bemoan a country of unachieved potential, disappointment, and of exceptionalism.[1] Argentines tell many jokes about themselves, like other Latin Americans, they see Argentines as apart, as different. But placing Argentine experience—both highs and lows—into a wider context can help us to understand how and why that experience has been more extreme than in many other countries. It can also help to situate that experience in the wider experiences of the community of nations and thus assist other countries to avoid some of the dilemmas and problems that Argentina faced.

This book, therefore, does not only look backwards. Rather, its intention is to understand the country's recovery and growth after the economic and political crisis of 2001–2002, the conflicts and obstacles that emerged in this process, and to look ahead as the subsequent governments seek to identify sustainable paths for the medium and longer term amidst the global environment of economic crisis. Only by locating current theoretical and policy debates in a longer national, and indeed global, historical trajectory can present choices and conflicts be more deeply understood.

The recent history of policy choices in Argentina can only be understood if it is placed within the temporal framework of the fall of the Soviet Union and the collapse of the socialist countries of Eastern Europe in the early 1990s. These events were followed by an extraordinary triumphalism by politicians, journalists, and many academics in the West who argued that the collapse of socialist economies demonstrated that capitalism was a stronger economic system and that the ideas and theories of capitalism had proven to be more sustainable and resilient over time. A 70-year experiment in Russia had ended and now the world should accept that capitalism was the only alternative economic system, and the role of the state should be circumscribed, weakened, and subordinated to the efficiency of the market. It is ironic that the very process of *glasnost* and *perestroika*, or "opening up" in the East was followed by an immediate intellectual closing down and the strong assertion in the West that the search for alternatives was over. Neo-liberalism was the dominant ideology and framework for economic and social progress.

Western triumphalism took many forms; from the assertion of the *End of History*[2] by Francis Fukuyama, celebrating the end of the Cold War, to the journalistic positivism of Thomas Friedman in *The Lexus and the Olive Tree*,[3] that all countries—rich and poor—were part of a single process of globalization in which private enterprise had triumphed over state-promoted development. Despite the vast evidence of differences around the world—from the poverty of rural Africa to the slums of Latin American and Asian cities—Friedman extended his argument to declare that *The World is Flat*[4] and that, under the process of globalization, everyone had equal chances for knowledge, prosperity, and self-respect.

This perspective on globalization was quickly challenged in many arenas, most notably in a book entitled *Globalization and its Discontents* by Nobel laureate Joseph Stiglitz,[5] in which he sharply criticized the IMF for its role in undermining the capacity of developing countries to sustain their economic growth and development in the face of pressures from the global economy. Stiglitz has rebutted the view of Friedman, saying that the world is most assuredly not flat. This critique is examined in detail in Chapter 1.

The critique also took the form of demonstrations against globalization and the Bretton Woods institutions in the streets of Seattle, Washington, Genoa, and Quebec. Indeed, another book with the same title, by Saskia Sassen,[6] looked at how vastly increased migration flows in Europe and elsewhere demonstrated that there was widespread unhappiness with the geographical distribution of opportunity around the world. In the first ten years of the new century there are literally hundreds of books, which criticize the alleged benefits of globalization and specifically its actual economic and social consequences.[7] John Gray has noted that celebrations of the neo-liberal triumph of global capitalism were a misreading of economic history.[8]

All of these debates were also conditioned by the attacks of September 11, 2001, and its consequences as the arguments about "the clash of civilizations" as formulated by the late Samuel Huntington.[9] Neo-liberal thinking was accompanied by neo-conservative insistence on the need to mount "a war on terror." Countries were encouraged by the United States to join in the wars in Iraq and Afghanistan as litmus tests of their commitment to "democracy" as defined in part as acceptance of the status quo which meant the hegemony of the United States as the world super power in the aftermath of the Cold War.

Global theories about the clash of civilizations were also challenged by closer analysis of the sources of conflicts within countries. New interpretations of rising national ethnic conflicts also emerged, such as by Arjun Appadurai, in his book, *The Fear of Small Numbers: Essays on the Geography of Anger.*[10] The process of both theoretical and empirical "push back" against global interpretations of political, social, and cultural forces by individuals, groups, cultures, and, indeed, nations has demonstrated that history has not ended. Indeed, the study of conflicts and the debates about so-called "failed states" has also led to deeper reflection about the importance of state–society relations in determining state performance.

This alternative view has been dramatically strengthened since the onset of the global financial crisis in 2008 as all countries began to question the dominant neo-liberal economic paradigm. In fact, after a bipolar world since 1945, and the end of the Western triumphalism after the end of the Cold War, for many, the real debate about alternative models about politics, economics, and society has just begun.

It is within this unfolding history of the present that change in Latin America and Argentina must be understood. Latin America has not escaped either the legacy of the Cold War or the debates about globalization of the 1990s. It has traversed a period in which dominant institutions in the United States and Europe celebrated "the return to democracy" in Latin America following the military dictatorships and political instability of the 1970s and 1980s and the acceptance of the market-based economic reforms of the 1990s. The neo-liberal notions of a "Washington Consensus," a set of economic policies largely applied to Latin America, as presented in Chapter 1, implied that the origin of, and legitimacy for, policy choices for Latin American lay outside the region, in Washington.[11] But they also have roots in the historic swings of the pendulum in thinking and power between state and market as explained by Karl Polanyi.[12] The decisions of the 1990s thus have their roots in reactions to the presidencies of Juan Peron, Arturo Frondizi, the military period of 1976–1983, and Raul Alfonsín.

In the 1990s, the apparent growth of Latin American economies was heralded as a result of these policies, yet it was also clear that market-led economic growth was not reducing either the poverty or inequality for which the region has been known for several decades. This downside to neo-liberal policies was largely ignored by economic policy-makers. One of the most striking examples of this narrow vision was the book by Chilean economist Sebastian Edwards, published for the World Bank in 1995, which for seven chapters celebrated the impact of market-based reforms, yet reported in Chapter 8 that poverty and inequality had increased in every Latin American country during this period.[13] Fifteen years later, Edwards published another book in which he criticized Latin American governments for their economic management, blaming them for not having fully implemented these reforms.[14]

Despite the certainty of the neo-liberal arguments of Fukuyama, Edwards, and many others discussed in Chapter 1, these perspectives were largely rejected by most voters in most Latin American countries from 2002 to 2010. Massive democratic change in political leadership occurred in the region from 2002 to 2010, with 11 of 14 countries electing progressive governments in the hope of finding alternative and more socially just policies than those of the Washington Consensus. In 2005–2006 alone, some 80 percent of eligible voters or about 250 million people in ten countries voted in new governments in what has been referred to as a "democratic fiesta."[15] Rather than choose candidates defending the status quo, voters elected new political leaders: a union leader in Brazil, women in Chile, Argentina, and later Brazil, an indigenous leader in Bolivia, and politicians identified more with the Left in Ecuador, Uruguay, Nicaragua, in 2008, Paraguay, and in 2009, El Salvador. The case of Venezuela is different, but Hugo Chavez's popularity and political base, before he sought even more power and an unlimited term in late 2007, demonstrated dissatisfaction with previous governments and growing poverty and social disparity in a country rich with oil revenues. All of these leaders share the belief that part of their responsibility is to protect their countries from the volatility and uncertainty of the global economy. It should be noted that this was not the case in all countries, with voters in Colombia, Peru, and Mexico supporting more conservative candidates.

This almost region-wide political change has been termed "Latin America's turn to the Left" by the North American and European media who have largely failed to examine in any depth what were the economic, social, and political conditions which led to such a massive and shared political orientation among voters in so many countries. The media have focused on Hugo Chavez and less frequently on the policies, programs, and obstacles facing individual leaders, such as Luiz Inácio Lula da Silva and Dilma Vana Rousseff in Brazil, Michelle Bachelet and Sebastian Piñera in Chile, Evo Morales in Bolivia, Nestor Kirchner, and Cristina Fernandez de Kirchner in Argentina.

This regional context, therefore, is part of the experience of Argentina. If Argentina's adoption of the ideas and policies of the Washington Consensus was rapid and complete during the early 1990s, it occurred within an official regional consensus that this was the correct direction for the country. It should be noted too that much of the country's capacity to politically oppose these policies had been decimated during the dictatorship of 1976–1982 when 30,000 people disappeared and many more left the country. Argentines had learned the high personal cost of public criticism of government policy. Acceptance of these policies, therefore, was not challenged in any organized way.

Agreement on economic policy, however, began to weaken in the second half of the 1990s as unemployment and debt increased, and fiscal pressures became serious political problems. External volatility after the Tequila Crisis in Mexico in 1994, the Asian financial crisis in 1997, and later events in Russia and Brazil all contributed to an increasingly risk-averse external environment in which the financing of Argentina's debt became more costly. As shown in Chapter 3, this situation deteriorated sharply in 2000 and 2001 and led to an economic and political collapse of Argentina in December 2001. This book explains this collapse in greater detail as a peculiarly Argentine phenomenon, but it also should be understood in its regional context. The early stages of recovery are presented in Chapter 4.

Within this wider and dynamic perspective of Latin American political and economic change, the case of Argentina also deserves special attention because its choices have been so explicit and its changes so dramatic. In almost 20 years, Argentina has changed from its policy orientation and politics of the 1990s where it was widely considered the "poster child" of the IMF, to its economic and political crisis and collapse in 2001, to its recovery and rejection of the advice of the Washington Consensus by the Kirchner administration after 2003, to the political reaffirmation of Kirchner's policies in the 2007 election of Cristina Fernandez de Kirchner as the first democratically elected woman president of Argentina, and to a new period of intense political conflict amidst a global economic crisis. The government of Cristina Fernandez de Kirchner almost immediately ran into serious difficulties both externally and domestically, raising provocative questions about whether its reformist agenda was predestined to face opposition from strong interests in the country and even whether some aspects of President Nestor Kirchner's earlier success had created the basis for subsequent opposition.

This book examines the tensions and the contradictions of how and why Argentina was able to recover from the crisis of 2001–2002 and maintain a steady path of economic growth for more than five years up to 2008. If it was true, as many argued in late 2001 and through 2003, that defaulting on its debt would permanently undermine and limit any possibility of economic growth, how did Argentina manage to grow at such world-class rates, rivaled only by China and India in the last few years? How did it manage to reduce poverty and inequality to some significant degree during this period, while dramatically reducing unemployment? How did it manage to assert its independence from the International Monetary Fund by prepaying its outstanding debt of US$9.7 billion in 2006, yet at the same time, become the largest borrower from the World Bank and the Inter-American Development Bank in 2007? The answers to these questions also help to clarify some of the academic debates about neo-liberalism, state performance, and the role of institutions in development.

While Argentina has undeniably benefitted from the growing demand for commodities from China, high prices in the world markets for soya and other oils, and other favorable global economic conditions, it has nonetheless managed to also increase industrial production and expand its urban economic base through what the World Bank has termed "a demand-led recovery."[16] How did the government use increased revenue from agricultural exports to expand social expenditures? And what proved to be the political and economic limits to such a strategy?

While these macro-economic achievements have been important, what are perhaps more telling are the many micro-indicators of reactivation of the economy and social life since late 2001. From the crisis of December 2001—and the *cacerolazos* or street demonstrations of 2002—the economy and social life returned to "normal" for many people, at least until the political conflicts erupted between the government and the rural sector in March–May 2008 as noted below. While it is true that millions of people fell below the poverty line in 2002, and for many the climb back to a decent income was slow and very difficult, both the urban and rural populations of Argentina experienced rapid improvements in their incomes and employment through 2007. This improved quality of life was reflected in the accelerating demand for goods and services, in vacations, consumer durables, in real estate purchases, and in a wide range of consumption items, which has also fueled inflation. If traffic grew exponentially in Buenos Aires, so too did taxi fares. Rapid recovery at low prices did not go unnoticed by the world at large whose tourists have been attracted initially by bargains but also high value in Argentina. The country's foreign tourists reached millions in 2007, with 12,000 tourists disembarking from cruise ships in Buenos Aires in January 2008 alone.

This period of recovery and growth was severely disrupted in March 2008 with the four-month rural protest against increases in government taxes on rural exports such as soya, corn, sunflower oil, and wheat, and the continuing political turmoil in 2009. Government efforts to continue to redistribute the profits from high world prices for these agricultural exports met resistance first from big farmers, including many multi-national companies who control large shares of total agricultural production in Argentina, and later also from smaller producers. The "*campo*" or rural sector cut roads throughout the country intermittently for three months and stopped the transport of essential foods to urban centers, adding further to inflation but also fueling wider opposition to the government. This process went through several rounds of negotiations, competing large public demonstrations of support for the two sides, and eventually the submission of the proposed measures for congressional approval. The measures were defeated in the Senate in July 2008, with the deciding vote being cast by the Vice-President, Julio Cobos, against his own government. This episode demonstrated the importance of political management of economic policy and the consequences of clumsy official responses to the claims of both rich and poor rural interests. It also augured a continuing period of political weakening of the government.

Many Argentine observers noted in 2008 that somehow Argentina had managed to convert an unparalleled opportunity, with record-high world prices for the country's agricultural exports, into a political crisis, which threatened political stability and economic growth. This was true, but it also offers an instructive case of the limits of redistribution of income even by a recently democratically elected government. The issues of state performance and institutional weakness came into sharp focus during 2008.

Despite the problems with "*el campo*," Argentina's achievements have been notable, particularly when considered in terms of the country's situation at the end of 2001 and throughout 2002. Yet these achievements have also occurred under the shadow of unresolved default on its external debt, with substantial outstanding debt to members of the Paris Club, including the United States, France, Germany, and Japan. It also faced judgments in the International Center for

Settlement of Disputes over losses to the French company, *Suez*, which claimed substantial losses resulting from the devaluation of the Argentine peso in 2001, and a minority of holders of Argentine bonds in the United States and Italy who did not accept the 2004 offer of the government to pay off the bonds at 25 percent of their face value. Most significantly, this shadow advanced just prior to feeling the impacts of a growing global financial crisis starting in the United States in 2008.

Argentina thus achieved *recovery and growth during a time of default*, in fact the largest default in world economic history—a time during which many people thought that the country might "fall off the face of the planet" or in which poverty and deprivation might hit historic levels. One journalist evoked the image of the film, *A Year of Living Dangerously* to describe Argentina's risky position in 2002. A person in the street commented in early 2002 that, "We have lost our future."[17] A Colombian newspaper ran the headline, "Argentina: Welcome to Latin America" in 2002, yet five years later Argentina had outstripped Colombia and most other countries in the region in terms of the magnitude of its growth. Official reaction to this economic rebound was reflected in the surprise and praise for Argentina by leading international personalities, including Dominique Strauss Kahn, Managing Director of the International Monetary Fund in 2007, George W. Bush, President of the United States, in 2004 and 2007, Robert Zoellick, President of the World Bank in 2007, Angela Merkel, Chancellor of the Federal Republic of Germany in 2007, and many others.

This book presents this complicated story, with its contradictions and unanswered questions, in the hope that the Argentinian experience can suggest a wider range of policy and institutional choices, which may be available for other countries as well. Recovery over five years is significant, but as many young entrepreneurs in Buenos Aires presciently asked in 2007, how long would it continue? Questions about the conditions for sustained growth and improved welfare of Argentines were again raised during the rural crisis of 2008 when multinational commodity producers and Argentine farmers opposed government efforts to tax large and growing profits for use in social expenditures and, of course, as the global economy lurched towards global recession in 2008. If supporters of the government asked in mid-2008 how poverty and inequality could be further reduced if the rural sector was allowed to retain its enormous profits, this question changed in the face of a global downturn: how could Argentina cope with yet another set of economic pressures and maintain its balance?

These domestic questions about state performance, macro-economic management, and the impact of institutional weaknesses have once again interacted with the broader global and international context. How can a national government manage risk and uncertainty in a globalized economy? How much can Argentina depend on the demand for soya and other goods from China and other countries? How do the decisions of Argentina affect the growing world demand for food and energy? Is it true, as argued by a Swedish newspaper in 2002, that Argentina has a nineteenth century definition of wealth based on agricultural commodities and that it needs to modernize this definition to include knowledge, science, and technology? If this was a valid criticism in 2002, is it still a criticism in a world of shifting commodity prices in 2008?

This book, however, suggests that the continuing story of Argentina is of deeper and wider significance as well. If the country's acceptance of neo-liberal market-based reforms in the 1990s occurred in the global environment after the end of the Cold War, it also suggests that the process since the crisis of 2001 demonstrates that history has not ended at all. Indeed, the country, along with many of its regional neighbors and partners in MERCOSUR, has only now begun the complicated task of identifying a set of policies that can contribute towards building the kind of country and society in which poverty, inequality, and social exclusion can be reduced.[18] To achieve these goals within a democratic environment, with social justice, and following the rule of law, has already proven to be a large challenge. How can state performance be strengthened so as to manage political conflicts during the process of reform? To what extent can the painful experience gained from recovering from the crisis of 2001–2002 remind individuals and political groups that the personal and national costs of paralyzing conflict, economic and political collapse, and painful recovery are just too high to sustain again and, therefore, there really is no alternative but to continue to struggle for progress while maintaining democratic institutions?

Finally, the end of the writing of this book occurred at the same time as the unexpected death of Nestor Kirchner on October 27, 2010. The former president's passing brought enormous expressions of public grief into the streets of Buenos Aires and into the Casa Rosada where his body lay in state, accompanied by President Cristina Fernandez de Kirchner, members of his family, his political supporters, and a stream of Latin American presidents coming to pay their last respects to a major political leader. While it is premature to fully assess his legacy, this book provides one account of the period of his leadership and impact. The book demonstrates that while ideas such as neo-liberalism and the role of the state have been crucial in the recent historical trajectory of Argentina, the role of personal political leadership is also central in explaining the origins and implementation of strategic decisions.

1 The emergence of neo-liberalism in Latin America

Situating the Argentine experience

One of the central objectives of this book is to locate the Argentine experience within three broader theoretical and policy debates about the economic and social development process in developing countries. These debates concern the significance of the neo-liberal framework known as the Washington Consensus for economic management in Latin America, the role of state performance in the development process, and the role of institutional capacity as a critical component of state performance. This introductory chapter examines the first of these issues in order to frame the narrative and analysis that follows and also to distinguish the experience of Argentina in relation to other countries in the region and beyond. The debates about state performance and institutional capacity are presented in Chapter 2. As noted earlier, these three issues have proven to closely inter-connected.

Setting the context of economic history

The adoption of neo-liberal economic policies in Latin America during the 1990s can only be understood within the broader context of the often tumultuous history of economic and political change in Latin America during the twentieth century. This history is one of power struggles and conflicts between landed aristocracies and urban workers, middle classes and recent rural migrants, labor and capital, and state and civil society. The economic and social policies of individual countries reflect these struggles and also contribute to them. The region is the most unequal continent, with great differences between rich and poor, and the struggle for resources, opportunities, inclusion, and social mobility is a constant theme of this history. Neither the array nor relative power of these political forces remains static, so the history of the region is one of instability of policies and institutions. Ideas change and so does the capacity of institutions to implement them.

In 1998, the British economic historian, Rosemary Thorp, captured the changing and cyclical character of thinking about Latin American economies and development performance in the following observation:

> Today's conventional wisdom for Latin America heralds export-led economies fueled by technical innovation, but in 1900, the same idea was in

> vogue. The social cost of excluding poor and marginalized people is singled out as a crucial issue today, while only two generations ago exclusion was so thoroughly woven into the fabric of Latin America that it was simply accepted. The focus now is on the shortcomings of import substitution industrialization, in the process seemingly wanting to forget it was once reasonably considered to be the pillar of progress upon which a modern Latin America would be built.[1]

The adoption of a particular development strategy and set of policies, however, is not just an outcome of the evolution of changing circumstances, but also about the shifting theoretical ideas and framework supporting those strategies and policies including their origins, the experience of their application in other places, and how and through what channels do the ideas themselves travel and eventually are adopted. This chapter, therefore, seeks to explain the adoption, performance, and consequences of neo-liberal policies in light of the region's economic and political history. These shifts in thinking can also be understood in terms of the broader historical changes and shifting pendulum of views about the relative primacy of the state and the market as explained by historian and philosopher Karl Polanyi.[2]

The understanding of this recent economic and political history is itself both enormously enriched and confused by the myriad interpretations of analysts, leading public figures, and the media, as well as by external observers and international institutions. Telling the story and identifying its implications for present policy and politics therefore is an enterprise with high stakes. Recently published books and institutional reports demonstrate that the debates about appropriate economic policies are hot, much contested, and actively present in current political struggles in many countries.[3] The politics of the chosen historical narrative is present in the media on a daily basis.

At the start of the twentieth century, Latin America had a population of 70 million people, 75 percent of whom lived in rural areas. By 2000, the population had reached 500 million, with 66 percent living in cities and towns. In 1900, some 75 percent were illiterate; by 2000, 87 percent were literate. Population growth accompanied massive economic growth as well. Tables 1.1 and 1.2 show the gross domestic product (GDP) growth for Latin American countries for different periods from 1900 to 2008 Despite this growth, at the beginning of the twentieth century, 40 percent of the Latin American population was poor.[4]

The first decades of the twentieth century saw rapid economic growth, fueled by trade, European immigration to Argentina and Brazil, and institutional development. Many countries celebrated the first 100 years of independence from Spain. The 1920s was a period of institutional innovation: central banks were created and customs and tax collection agencies established. It was a time of the consolidation of capital in industry and manufacturing, as well as by an urban middle class. This process varied across countries, but it created the basis of significant political struggle throughout the 1930s and through World War II.[5] Twenty years later, new development institutions began to appear: planning

Table 1.1 Average GDP growth, 1900–1996

Country	*1900–1913*	*1913–1929*	*1945–1972*	*1971–1980*	*1981–1989*	*1990–1997*	*1900–1996*
Argentina	6.3	4.1	3.4	2.5	1.9	3.0	3.3
Brazil	4.1	5.1	4.4	6.6	2.4	6.1	5.5
Chile	3.6	3.7	3.0	3.6	5.4	3.6	3.3
Colombia	4.4	4.9	3.8	5.0	4.0	4.9	4.7
Mexico	3.4	1.4	4.2	5.5	1.5	5.2	5.0
Peru	4.5	5.3	5.3	3.4	0.4	3.7	3.9
Venezuela	2.3	9.2	5.7	4.7	2.2	4.2	5.9

Source: Thorp, 1998. *Progress, Poverty And Exclusion: An Economic History of Latin America in the 20th Century*, p. 2.

Table 1.2 GDP growth, 1971–2009 annual rates of variation

Country	*1971–1980*	*1981–1989*	*1990–1997*	*1998–2003*	*2004–2008*	*1990–2008*	*2009*
Argentina	2.8	–1.0	5.0	–1.3	8.4	4.2	–6.6
Brazil	8.6	2.3	2.0	1.5	4.6	2.5	–0.2
Chile	2.5	2.8	7.0	2.7	4.8	5.0	–1.5
Colombia	5.4	3.7	3.9	1.1	5.3	3.4	0.4
Mexico	6.5	1.4	3.1	2.9	3.5	3.1	–6.5
Peru	3.9	–0.7	3.9	2.0	7.6	4.3	0.9
Venezuela	1.8	–0.3	3.8	–2.7	10.1	3.3	–3.3

Source: United Nations Economic Commission for Latin America and the Caribbean (ECLAC), 2010, *Time for Equality*, 2010, p. 53.

ministries, development banks, and industrial development institutions. The first half of the twentieth century was also one of incorporating new economic and political forces into society, including labor, which became an increasingly important political force.

Unlike Europe and Asia, Latin America came through the 1939–1945 period without the physical and institutional destruction of its economies, but it did strongly feel the economic and political impact of the World Wars and the Great Depression, with a drop in demand for its exports, higher prices for its manufactured imports, and changing levels of protection of its trade. While there were differences in the position of Latin American countries towards the war against fascism, Latin American economies had continued to grow following the 1930s and the subsequent growth in global demand for goods, services, and raw materials, which accelerated after 1939.

Ideological conflict became important in the postwar period in many countries, with arguments about the role of the state, the need for land reform, and how to address the well-established differences in income and wealth between a landed upper class and rapidly growing middle and lower classes. Even though these historic debates predated the Cold War in countries such as Guatemala, Brazil, Chile, or Argentina, these economic issues quickly became politicized internally through the growing activity of groups across the ideological spectrum.[6] They were also internationalized by the Cold War perception of the United States that more social and distributive views of economic policy would take Latin American countries towards socialism and the Soviet Union, thereby providing the justification for active intervention in all countries in the region.[7]

Taking a broad view, Latin American economies grew substantially but very unevenly during the first half of the twentieth century, with high levels of volatility depending heavily on the changing global economic environment. These twists and turns resulted in processes and patterns of growth that generated and exacerbated many conflicts and unresolved problems. A central and continuing question concerned the quality of economic growth itself and how its benefits were distributed. Indeed, the highly unequal pattern of economic growth from the late eighteenth and nineteenth centuries and the concentration of wealth and land in many countries had provided the foundation upon which export-led economies continued to grow, diversify, and consolidate during the twentieth century. This form of growth was built on monopolies and land ownership patterns inherited from the colonial period. Indeed, powerful landed elites were able to avoid paying taxes and thereby also limited the redistributive power of the state.[8] This distribution of wealth and income also had a major impact on the evolving character of political systems in the region as rural elites struggled with urban middle classes for political power.[9]

The growth of Latin American economies, therefore, was not a smooth process. The region experienced extraordinary instability of prices and incomes over time, with major consequences for macro-economic performance and the welfare of national populations. While Latin American economies grew at over 4 percent through the twentieth century, they experienced intense periods of instability even before the debt crisis and post-1980, growth of the global economy.[10] Some of this instability resulted from the weak performance of national financial systems, and later by the interaction of these institutions with global markets. There is an extensive literature on the economic instability of individual countries, particularly Argentina, Brazil, Chile, and Mexico, but other countries also experienced wide swings in their growth.[11] This is well-illustrated in Table 1.3 on the levels of growth over various periods in the region.

Postwar economic growth: 1950–1980

The post-World War II period saw a continuity with patterns in the 1930s as the state was expected to play a growing role in economic development and in protecting individual countries from the growing impact of the world economy. This led to the adoption of import substitution strategies in most countries, including the biggest economies: Argentina, Brazil, Chile, Colombia, and Mexico. These strategies were well articulated by Latin American economists such as Raul Prebisch, who argued in a 1951 report of the United Nations Economic Commission for Latin America and the Caribbean (ECLAC) that, "Two World Wars in a single generation and a great economic crisis between them have shown the Latin American countries their opportunities, clearly pointing the way to industrial activities."[12] Latin America could not depend on the stability of the global economy. Moreover, despite patterns of trade and foreign investment, the economic gains from technological innovation in the industrialized countries actually remained in those countries, while those gains at the periphery did not generate local benefits. He concluded that there was a need to actively promote local innovation and investment as central components of industrial development strategy and a means to substitute local production for imports, a strategy that became widely known as "import substitution."[13] Other leading Latin American economists such as Celso Furtado also supported this view. Their intention was to protect growing national industries from international competition in order to allow the growth of employment, productivity, and technology, and to keep incomes and profits within national economies. The period of 1945 to 1973 saw a growing role for the state in many Latin American economies in promoting industrialization.[14]

These policies were successful in many respects during the late 1940s and 1950s. Many governments accepted their responsibilities in supporting industrial development and productivity, while also trying to expand their provision of welfare through education, health, housing, infrastructure, and social security systems. The emphases of these policies differed across countries, with Juan Peron adopting strategies for industrial development and creation of a welfare state for a growing working class in Argentina, while Brazil, for example, placed more weight on technological development in its industrial strategy. In both cases, however, as discussed in more detail below, the state was assumed to have a central and active role.[15] This role included the state as a major source and channel of funds for investment in support of industrial development, increasing

Table 1.3 Phases of productivity growth, 1900–1990

Quality of growth	*Argentina*	*Brazil*	*Chile*	*Mexico*	*Venezuela*
Early high growth, unstable	1900–1913	1900–1920	No data	1900–1910	No data
Period of relatively slow growth, high instability	1914–1950s	1921–1947	1908–1938	1910–1940	1926–1950
Accelerating stable high growth	1950s–1974	1947–1980	1938–1972	1940–1981	1950–1977
Deceleration with increased instability	1975–1990	1986–1990	1972–1990	1982–1990	1977–1990

Source: Thorp, op. cit., p. 16.

capacity in various sectors, and orienting consumption, all of which contributed to the rapid growth of employment and the development of a large urban labor force.[16]

The key central feature of the import substitution strategy was the high level of nominal protection given to the products of domestic industries. For example, in 1960, the average protection given by the government of Argentina to its industries through tariffs and duties was 131 percent of the value of imported products, while Brazil's average was 168 percent, both of which contrasted sharply to the protection within the then European Economic Community at 13 percent.[17] From 1945 to 1973, Latin America's GDP grew at 5.3 percent annually, not surprisingly with manufacturing becoming the engine of growth, expanding at 6 percent per year, reaching 26 percent of GDP by 1973. By the late 1960s, state enterprises represented 15 percent of total investment. In 1966, ECLAC estimated that there was a 36 percent increase in industrial output attributable to import substitution for Argentina, Brazil, Chile, Colombia, and Mexico between 1929 and 1960. When Brazil was excluded, the number rose to 43 percent.[18]

The macro-economic results of import substitution strategies were excellent for this period, but they were short-lived. Incomes and employment grew at rapid rates, reflecting high rates of capital formation within economies, which were also becoming increasingly urban. This period of economic growth was accompanied by the urban transformation of many countries, such as Argentina, Brazil, Colombia, and Mexico, as shown in Table 1.4. Rural to urban migration in search of employment was high, accompanied by high urban fertility rates. The result was increasingly productive economies, with growing urban economic activities, but also growing urban problems such as squatter settlements and deficits in infrastructure. Indeed, subsidies for urban-based industries contributed to migration and the urban growth process.[19]

When confronted by changes in the global economy, the success of import substitution policies in Latin America was not sustainable. The growing role of trade in the global economy during the 1950s and 1960s, the rise of Taiwan, Japan, as well as the commercial reach of industries from the United States, brought serious competition for many Latin American industries, from steel to shoes, plastics, machinery, and pharmaceuticals, among others. Latin America could produce, but, with high costs and technology, which was becoming obsolete, it could not compete. Some Argentine analysts wrote of this period, "Import substitution led to rapid development of the industrial sector, but exports did not expand much, and over time this was at the core of the economic stagnation that marked the eventual collapse of that development model."[20] Within the region as a whole, by the mid-1950s many multi-national subsidiaries were entering Latin American markets, allowed in by governments wanting foreign investment and technology to sustain and improve productivity. This process displaced many domestic firms in sectors producing consumer durables.[21]

Governments such as Argentina and Brazil had imposed high tariffs on these imported products and had provided direct subsidies in order to protect domestic industries but this strategy was expensive and ultimately not financially sustainable.

Table 1.4 Urban demographic growth in Latin America (compound rate in percentages)

Country	*1900–1930*	*1930–1950*	*1950–1970*	*1970–1995*
Argentina	3.1	1.8	1.7	1.5
Bolivia	1.0	1.1	2.2	2.3
Brazil	2.1	2.4	3.0	2.1
Chile	1.3	1.7	2.3	1.6
Colombia	2.2	2.0	3.1	2.5
Costa Rica	1.6	2.4	3.9	2.8
Cuba	2.8	2.1	2.2	1.0
Dominican Republic	2.6	2.6	3.2	2.7
Ecuador	2.5	2.5	2.9	2.6
El Salvador	2.0	1.3	3.1	2.1
Guatemala	2.3	2.4	3.2	2.8
Haiti	2.2	1.2	1.6	2.1
Honduras	2.8	2.1	3.1	3.1
Mexico	0.8	2.4	3.1	2.4
Nicaragua	1.6	2.2	2.8	3.3
Panama	1.9	2.8	2.9	2.5
Paraguay	0.9	2.5	2.4	3.2
Peru	1.0	1.6	2.5	2.6
Uruguay	2.2	1.2	1.0	0.7
Venezuela	0.9	2.2	3.8	2.9
Latin America	1.8	2.1	2.7	2.2

Source: Thorp, op. cit., p. 16.

As these protections were withdrawn, a process of de-industrialization occurred, leading to significant disruptions in national and local economies, with conflicts with organized labor over wages, then workers losing their jobs, and eventually a transformation of industrial structure. These economic conflicts also fueled opposition to national governments and a political polarization between those benefitting from greater openness to global trade and those hurt by economic displacement.

A response to these pressures in both Argentina and Brazil was the adoption of a state-driven strategy known as "developmentalism," which had three major components:

1. A policy of vertical import substituting industrialization which focused on priority basic industrial sectors such as steel, energy, chemicals, machinery, vehicles, and capital goods.
2. An expansion of capital accumulation through foreign private and public sources of capital.
3. The expanded involvement of the state in directing the development effort.[22]

In contrast to the national populist regimes of the late 1940s, such as Peron's government in Argentina, which favored horizontal industrialization with an emphasis on consumer goods, the developmentalism of Brazil favored vertical industrialization through development of heavy industry. Kathryn Sikkink explains in her excellent 1991 comparative study of developmentalism in Argentina and Brazil that national populism was a demand-driven economic model, whereas developmentalism was an investment-driven model. The former was more inward looking than the latter, which looked outward for sources of finance.[23] The national populism economic model placed more emphasis on small industry and consumer goods, which the populist coalition demanded. It was less enthusiastic about foreign borrowing. This approach very much characterized the first Peron government after 1945 as a prototype of national populist economic policies, including the refusal by Argentina to join either the International Monetary Fund or the World Bank. The government also believed that increased wages would increase the demand for domestic consumer goods, thus stimulating expansion of domestic industry.

Developmentalism emerged from the theories and practice of import-substitution in the late 1950s, with President Arturo Frondizi in Argentina and President Juscelino Kubitschek in Brazil agreeing in parallel on the need for a strong state effort to lead and promote development. The challenge was twofold: invest and accumulate. Investment should occur in industrial sectors, which could provide the foundation for future growth. This included building capacity in technology, infrastructure, and basic industries such as energy, chemicals, engineering, and manufacturing.

The development strategies of both Frondizi and Kubitschek focused on production, not distribution. Growth could be unbalanced, as suggested by Hirschman, as accumulation of capital was the requirement for the subsequent development of other sectors, such as education or health. Sikkink notes that developmentalism was not a redistributive model. "It was not justice, it was the need for technical-economic transformation."[24] This process of capital formation, therefore, required a positive investment climate and the opening up of domestic markets for foreign investment with the support of state incentives for private investment. The process of opening up trade and the financial sector was to go much farther in the neo-liberal strategies of the 1990s, but developmentalism of the late 1950s was the theoretical and policy framework, which undermined the autarchy, implied by the earlier theories of import substitution. It was an initial opening up to the penetration of international capital, which increased both in magnitude and impact from 1960 onward.

The economic strategy of developmentalism also placed the state in a central role in the development process, a subject that will be addressed in Chapter 2. Sikkink notes that both Frondizi and Kubitschek admired the policies of President Franklin Delano Roosevelt and the New Deal.

While the shift from import substitution towards developmentalism is frequently described as an economic process, it should also be understood as a major re-alignment of political power. Organized labor lost power as protection of domestic production began to come down, first with individual factories closing and then whole industries disappearing, leaving the workers without jobs and shifting political power to the often foreign managers of capital in a changing global and national economic landscape. Arceo and Basualdo describe this process as "transformation," using Gramsci's term, noting that the political parties were also co-opted in this process, not because of ideology but for material reasons.[25]

Table 1.5 shows the changes in Latin American trade patterns from the height of the import substitution period to a decade later.

This period was also one of "emerging disequilibria," with growing fiscal deficits.[26] Local production declined, with consequent effects on public revenues and trade balances. The need for the government to stabilize the economy began to provide the justification for entering into an agreement with the IMF, which it did in December 1958. The stabilization program, which focused on controlling inflation, directly contradicted Frondizi's developmentalist program.[27] The president's aspirations for a developmental vision were directly undermined by his own ministers, who were appointed to maintain stability. In fact, Frondizi lost much of his political support and this led to a military coup in March 1962. The Brazilian government was also overthrown by generals seeking to install "order" in an increasingly conflictive political situation.

Despite its political weakness, the developmentalist strategy in Argentina produced some positive results, notably a big expansion of petroleum production from 1958 to 1962, growth in steel production, automobile manufacturing, and expansion in the petrochemical industry. Nonetheless, with deteriorating trade balances, uncompetitive prices for their products in world trade, and increasing labor problems, Frondizi's approach had not received much support from industrial groups.[28]

In contrast to Argentina, developmentalism in Brazil had a much more enduring influence on the country's developmental path. The strength of the Brazilian state and closer elite relations with public policies resulted in the adoption of elements of a strategy, which continue to this day. Brazil focused on heavy industries in the 1960s and the economic policies of the military regime from 1964 to 1985 was not so different from Kubitschek's developmentalist orientation.[29] Argentine political scientist Guillermo O'Donnell wrote that the Argentine state had been highly affected by the struggle with societal forces, while, in contrast, the Brazilian state was more tied to the Brazilian elite and had greater authority.[30]

Developmentalism was caught between the two objectives of transformation through investment and stabilization. Stabilizing the economy meant cutting

Table 1.5 Shares of manufacturing and exports in GDP: Latin America (% of GDP, 1970 prices)

	1945	*1955*	*1965*	*1975*	*1985*	*1995*
Manufactures	19	21	23	26	24	23
Exports	16	10	9	6	9	14

Source: Thorp, op. cit. p. 160.

public expenditure and thereby reducing employment. With domestic industries unable to compete, they closed, exports declined, and imports grew. This process led to political conflicts with labor and a growing polarization between the interests of labor and capital.

These problems worsened considerably during the 1970s. As the demand for imports increased, Latin American countries found themselves in foreign exchange problems, particularly after the oil crisis after the 1973 Middle East war and rapidly increasing oil prices. Foreign exchange shortages then made Latin America overly eager to borrow from banks in the United States, Europe, and Japan, leading to the 1980s debt crisis, where most Latin American countries could not service their debts, particularly those with floating interest rates. Latin American debt grew enormously, as shown in Table 1.6.

The 1980s is frequently referred to as "the lost decade" for Latin America. This period was characterized by a much-reduced rate of economic growth compared to earlier periods, fiscal crises, dramatically reduced public expenditures, inflation, and rising poverty and inequality. The macro-economic volatility of the 1960–1985 period resulted in uncertainty, reduced investment and trade, and a greater dependency of Latin American countries on the global economy. In contrast to the period of import substitution, Latin America had proven to be highly vulnerable to changes in energy prices, interest rates, and global market conditions.

With continued high rates of population growth, the face of Latin American countries changed dramatically. Life expectancy had gone from 29 years in 1900, to 47 years in 1950, and later to 68 years by 1990. Even though the average life span had more than doubled, Latin America was still 40 years behind the United States, which had reached 68 years in 1950. Rapid demographic increase led to a high demand for urban employment and, in the absence of formal sector employment, to more informality.[31] By 1970, Argentina had had

Table 1.6 Growth in Latin American debt, 1970–1985

Year	*External debt stocks (current US$ billion)*
1970	31.31
1975	78.27
1976	97.62
1977	128.98
1978	159.53
1979	193.81
1980	238.60
1981	290.15
1982	326.97
1983	354.04
1984	368.52
1985	379.19

Source: World Bank, World Development Indicators 2009.

the largest percentage in Latin America of its labor force in the urban formal sector, some 66 percent. At the same time, only 5 percent of its urban households lived in absolute poverty, compared to 35 percent in Brazil, and Colombia with 38 percent.[32] This picture was to change, however as, by 1994, 12 percent of Argentine urban households were below the absolute poverty line.[33] Rural poverty was much worse, with 19 percent for Argentina, 73 percent for Brazil, and 68 percent for Peru and Panama.

These patterns had worsened considerably during the debt crisis of the 1980s. While the world economy had expanded after the 1973 oil shocks, Latin American debt skyrocketed. Money was flowing out of Latin America, with capital flight to the United States reaching US$160 billion by 1983, and debt owed to North American banks at US$209 billion.[34] Despite promises to the contrary, Ronald Reagan did not cut the US deficit, with the result that real interest rates continued to rise, thereby exacerbating Latin American debt. In fact, from 1981 to 1982, real rates of interest increased from –6 percent to +14.6 percent in 1982. Thorp notes that the debt crisis was felt in four ways: the prices of imports increased and exports declined, interest rates increased, developed countries fell into recession, and Latin American experienced an abrupt turnaround in finance from abroad. The case of Argentina is instructive: for its debt rescheduling, Argentina paid 219 percent more in 1982 than it had paid in 1981.[35]

A very significant indicator of this process was the rise in inequality, which Giovanni Andrea Cornia, explains in the following terms:

> During the "lost decade" of the 1980s, inequality in Latin America was affected by the 1982–1984 world recession, the debt crisis, a large decline in commodity prices, and the recessionary adjustments introduced to respond to these shocks. Altogether, the 1980s were characterized by regressive distributive outcomes and, during this period, income inequality fell only in Colombia, Uruguay, and Costa Rica out of 11 countries with reliable data.[36]

He attributes this pattern to five factors: sluggish growth slowed job creation, more informal employment, formal sector wages grew more slowly than GDP per capita, minimum wages fell in relation to average wages, and the skill premium widened.[37]

The crisis and adjustment in the 1980s: the emergence of neo-liberalism and the Washington Consensus

It is within this historical context that the neo-liberal recommendations for financial stabilization and economic liberalization were made to Latin American governments in the early 1980s. These recommendations grew incrementally, initiated after the 1982 Mexican debt crisis, when Mexico required a major bailout from the United States Treasury and the Bretton Woods institutions. Through the 1980s, the policy package, which became known as structural adjustment, began to take shape. Its logic had an internal consistency, which started from the assumption that if countries could not pay their external debts, they needed to "adjust" their economic and fiscal "structure" so that waste was eliminated, budgets were balanced, and no additional debt was entered into. In economic terms, the recommendations assumed that policies, which relied on market signals, were more likely to avoid "distortions" in prices and, thereby, were more efficient in the use of capital and labor. "Getting the prices right" was understood as fundamental to a market-based economic strategy.[38] These prices included shifting the rural–urban terms of trade towards the rural sector, thereby encouraging production and exports, and reducing urban subsidies for food, energy, infrastructure, and social services.[39]

This approach involved major economic reform, justified externally in terms of the large debts of Latin American countries and their alleged inability to find sustainable development paths in the growing global economy. In specific terms, the reform package included the following:

- Fiscal discipline, meaning more balanced budgets with reduced fiscal deficits and fewer needs for domestic and foreign borrowing;
- A redirection of public expenditure priorities toward fields offering high economic returns;
- Tax reform (to lower marginal rates and broaden the tax base);
- Interest rate liberalization;
- A competitive exchange rate;
- Trade liberalization;
- Liberalization of inflows of foreign direct investment;
- Privatization of public services and public enterprises;
- Deregulation (to abolish barriers to entry and exit); and
- Secure property rights.[40]

These measures were clearly intended to give the market a major role in economic decision-making, taking decisions for resource allocation away from governments and allowing them to be made by private companies and economic actors. They also clearly reflected the growing disappointment of the 1980s with the efficacy of the state as an institutional actor, not just in the economy, but in society as a whole. This view reflected the ascendancy of the conservative thinking of Margaret Thatcher and Ronald Reagan, but also of a revisionist view of the state among developing country policy-makers as well. One particularly articulate statement of this was by Shahid Husain, then Vice-President of the World Bank, when he said that, "Twenty years ago we believed that government could be efficient, compassionate, and just. Today we no longer believe that to be the case."[41] This type of international assessment opened the door for many changes in policy and also to the recommendation that public services in many countries would be more effectively provided by private enterprises.

What is clear is that the Washington Consensus policies in fact represented a different model of economic growth and development for Latin America. ECLAC noted in 2010 that:

> During the period of reforms, policy-makers of the countries of the region were guided by the over-arching assumption that companies and sectors adapted better and produced more efficiently when markets were liberalized and resources could shift freely to more competitive activities.[42]
>
> Countries used policy tools to overcome "the unwanted effects of these macroeconomic policies in the real economy: development banks, State ownership of main natural resources, public investment policies to strengthen production linkages, pro-active industrial policy, and technology development."[43]
>
> In the first half of the 1990s, significant progress was made in macroeconomic stability. But long-term policies were eschewed. As the State shrank in size, industrial policy further lost legitimacy, having been discredited by poor industrial performance since the late 1970s and early 1980s. As a consequence, not only was industrial policy abandoned but, such policies came to be perceived as an obstacle to growth.[44]

As suggested above, this policy package is essentially a set of ideas about economic growth, which largely originated from institutions outside Latin America, mostly in Washington. While there were certainly many Latin American economists who believed that such reforms were needed,[45] many were in fact graduates of American and European universities and had the same policy and political orientation of their counterparts in the IMF and the World Bank.[46] Even if these "local" economists supported and indeed enacted these policies when they held government positions, the policies were largely perceived as being externally imposed and not local in origin.

Not surprisingly, this perception led to opposition in some countries even before the impacts of the policies were felt. Financial liberalization had opened the way for the arrival of foreign capital into national economies. As the share of foreign capital began to grow significantly, it became apparent that the power of local economic forces had diminished in relative terms. But those that had joined foreign capital, including many of these foreign-trained economists, or had tied their production to foreign markets, now became what was been termed "dominant sectors" in a new political economy.[47] Not surprisingly, 15 years later, after these policies had generated significant opposition, a second process of transformation occurred as a significant wave of change of governments across the region from 2002 to 2008 brought not only a shift in policies but also a major change in personnel.

Assessment of the results of reforms of the Washington Consensus

With hindsight and the experience of almost two decades, it is apparent that many of the intended results of this economic reform package were not achieved. Thorp observed that that adjustment forced countries to move from one disequilibrium to another. The balance of payments became surplus, but at huge social costs.[48] Ricardo Ffrench-Davis, the Chilean economist, noted that the accomplishments of the Washington Consensus in the 1980–1990s were lower inflation, better fiscal balances, and increased exports. However, at the aggregate level, macro-economic growth rates were definitely lower than in prior periods and they were not accompanied by sufficient reduction of either poverty or inequality.[49] Table 1.7 demonstrates that sustained productivity growth was occurring prior to the introduction of the reforms. Even John Williamson, who coined the term "Washington Consensus" in 1989, described the results as "disillusioning".[50] From 1990 to 2004, as shown in Table 1.7, GDP per capita only grew at 0.9 percent compared to 1.8 percent in United States, and 1.1 percent in the rest of the world in this period.

In a 2006 assessment of economic growth during the reform period, Jose Antonio Ocampo, a Colombian economist and former Under-Secretary-General for Economic and Social Affairs of the United Nations, noted that evaluations of moderate growth rates from 1990 to 1997 by Chilean economist Sebastian Edwards, the Inter-American Development Bank, and the World Bank had led to positive conclusions about reform.[51] However, slower rates in the period 1998–2003 led to extensive re-evaluation of the impacts of reform.[52] Ocampo remarked that the reforms had opened up economies, but that in the period 1998–2003, net financial flows to LAC actually had become negative.[53] Further, he argued that the data on positive growth in the state-led growth period (1950–1980) contradict the assertion that liberalization was correlated with growth.[54] Ocampo persuasively demonstrated that there was confusion in the policy debate about this period, which mixed up structural reforms reducing the public sector role in the economy and the need for macro stabilization policies.[55] This point was reinforced by the assertion that growth can be achieved with large differences in degrees of liberalization across countries. Indeed, weak growth in the late 1990s cannot be attributed to weak export growth because this growth

Table 1.7 Per capita GDP growth for select countries, 1971–2004 (in percentages)

Country	*1971–1980*	*1981–1989*	*1990–1997*	*1998–2003*	*2004*	*Total*
Argentina	2.8	–1.0	5.0	–1.4	9.0	2.6
Brazil	8.6	2.3	2.0	1.2	5.2	2.0
Chile	2.5	2.8	7.0	2.7	6.0	5.2
Colombia	5.4	3.7	3.9	1.0	3.5	2.8
México	6.5	1.4	3.1	2.8	4.4	3.1
Peru	3.9	–0.7	3.9	2.0	5.1	3.2
Uruguay	2.7	0.4	3.9	–2.5	11.8	1.8
Venezuela	1.8	–0.3	3.8	–2.8	17.3	1.9
Latin America						
Total	5.6	1.3	3.2	1.2	5.8	2.6
Per Capita	3.0	–0.8	1.4	–0.4	4.2	0.9
Per Worker	1.7	–1.5	0.5	–1.2	3.4	0.0

Source: Ffrench-Davis, 2005, *Reformas para America Latina*, p. 20.

was the highest ever in Latin American history, reaching about 9 percent per year.[56]

By 2005, 15 years after the designation of the reform package as the Washington Consensus, real wages were below 1980 levels. The numbers of people in poverty were higher and the rate of investment was lower than in the 1980s. And political responsibility was absent.[57] Moreover, with GDP growth the same as the growth rate of the labor force, there was little improvement in incomes and a deterioration in what Ffrench-Davis called "macro-social balances"—poverty, inequality, and employment.[58] He also noted that this period was characterized by a double divergence: a growing gap between Latin American countries and developed countries, and within Latin America, between rich and poor people. Finally, he demonstrated that these policies resulted in lower rates of gross fixed capital formation from 1970 to 2004, as shown in Table 1.8. This subject is highly significant for the story of Argentina in subsequent chapters of this book.

There have been many analyses of the impacts of the Washington Consensus and a general agreement that the policy package not only did not deliver what it promised,[59] but actually contributed to a further deterioration of the economic welfare of Latin American countries. Some have argued that a "model of no development" was in fact adopted, as social indicators declined despite modest growth in some countries.[60]

However, there are two further critiques of the neo-liberal reforms, which go deeper. The first is the well-known critique of Nobel Laureate Joseph Stiglitz, who argued in his 2002 best seller, *Globalization and its Discontents*, that the Washington Consensus policies had been driven by the International Monetary Fund. He noted that, "at the IMF, decisions were made on the basis of what seemed a curious blend of ideology and bad economics, dogma that sometimes seemed to be thinly veiling special interests."[61] Stiglitz placed the Washington Consensus at the center of the debate about the effects of globalization on developing countries. He argued:

> The backlash against globalization draws its force not only from the perceived damage done to developing countries by policies driven by ideology but also from the inequities in the global trading system.[62]
>
> The West has driven the globalization agenda, ensuring that it garners a disproportionate share of the benefits, at the expense of the developing world.[63]

Table 1.8 Gross fixed capital formation (% of GDP) 1970–2004

Year	*Average % of GDP*
1970–1982	25.6
1983–1991	19.2
1992–1998	20.0
1999–2004	19.0

Source: Ffrench-Davis. op. cit., p. 24.

> If, in too many instances, the benefits of globalization have been less than its advocates claim, the price paid has been greater, as the environment has been destroyed, as political processes have been corrupted, and as the rapid pace of change has not allowed countries time for cultural adaptation.[64]

The Stiglitz critique therefore places the neo-liberal reforms within the framework of globalization itself. It has been taken as a rallying cry by the critics of globalization. The weakness of the reforms was emphasized even further by another assessment by Acuna, Galiani, and Tommasi about the narrow thinking behind the notion of the so-called first and second generation reforms which the IMF advocated:

> The original promise of the Washington Decalogue that more market and less government would bring about better politics and economics was wrong. Economies cannot be understood or reformed independently of the political conditions and institutions in which they operate. Good governmental institutions allow bad policies to be redefined, while bad institutions cannot even assure that good policies will be maintained. Conceptually the "Washington" notion of first and second-generation reforms got the order wrong.[65]

As this book will suggest, there are many important enduring effects of neo-liberal reform, which are still to be remedied. As some of the flaws and negative impacts of the Washington Consensus became evident, efforts were made to adjust and enhance the policy package. For example, a further list of measures was later added to this earlier policy advice, in what Harvard economist Dani Rodrik has described as "the augmented Washington Consensus." These include the following policy areas which received increased attention from international institutions and academic writers on development:

- corporate governance;
- anti-corruption;
- flexible labor markets;
- World Trade Organization agreements;
- financial codes and standards;
- "prudent" capital-account opening;
- non-intermediate exchange rate regimes;
- independent central banks/inflation targeting;
- social safety nets; and
- targeted poverty reduction.[66]

This list certainly contains some important areas for reform and strengthening, but by themselves, these items do not represent a wholesale change in the development model, which the Washington Consensus policies recommended.

A similar revised reformulation of these policies was published in 2008 by The Center for Global Development and the Inter-American Dialogue under the title, *Fair Growth: Economic Policies for Latin America's Poor and Middle Class Majority.*[67] This analysis was striking because it argued that Latin American countries would have been worse off if the reforms of the 1990s had not taken place. The authors, Nancy Birdsall, former Executive Vice-President of the Inter-American Development Bank; Augusto de la Torre, Chief Economist for Latin America for the World Bank; and Rachel Menezes, Research Associate at the Inter-American Dialogue acknowledged that, from 2003 to 2007 the countries achieved higher rates of growth as they climbed out of economic crises. But they do not articulate that, implicitly, this growth also reflected the decisions of new governments to shift away from the Washington Consensus policy package. The authors do, however, admit that the reforms of the 1990s are no longer politically viable and that Latin Americans are resentful of privatization, high unemployment, low wages, and a growing percentage of their people living under the poverty line.[68]

Birdsall *et al.* concluded that:

> The market reforms of the last fifteen years may have made things worse – or at least failed to make them better.... This central problem with the reform agenda since the 1990s – the lack of any explicit inclusion of equity concerns – undermined the potential benefits of reforms for social cohesion, undercut the enthusiasm for further reform, and may have even reduced some of the benefits of reforms for growth, although the last effect is difficult to demonstrate.[69]

This observation, however, was too facile and did not acknowledge the major political costs of this almost two-decade experience and the destruction of any credibility for proposals for reform. Clearly, proposals that have been approved by governments and then later failed to work, contribute to undermining the political and institutional credibility of the state. The fact that the reform agenda "left out ... the silent majority"[70] eventually proved to be politically explosive and resulted in the "democratic fiesta" of 2005–2006, when the silent majority stopped being so silent. They remark that "in Argentina, Ecuador, and Bolivia protests led to the ousting of incumbent presidents. However it would be an exaggeration to blame their departure on the reforms."[71] This was a disingenuous comment, because the departure of these presidents was largely a result of the protests against the economic conditions for which the reforms had played a major role in creating.

Birdsall *et al.* offered a contradictory economic assessment of this period as well. For example, they praised the reforms of the 1990s while admitting that GDP per capita was only 1.5 percent per year for the decade in contrast to earlier periods as presented in Table 1.7 and as cited by Ocampo.[72] They explained regional growth since 2003, at 3.5 percent annually for the region as a whole, largely in terms of the export of commodities whose price had increased substantially in global markets: soya, corn, wheat, oils, and copper. At the same time they noted that labor productivity had grown much slower than in Asia.

They argued that dependence on exports and commodity prices increased the sense of vulnerability in the region to changes in the global economy and concluded that, "Latin America has still not found its competitive legs."[73] This assessment was obviously quite mixed. It also diverged in important ways for example, from the country assessment of the World Bank, for example, of the case of Argentina where Bank reports described country's recovery as "demand-led" in reference to domestic demand, rather than having been so dependent on exports.[74]

A further and quite significant aspect of this new assessment is that it failed to recognize the long-term impacts of the reforms. For example, Birdsall *et al.* noted that studies in the region showed that fiscal management and adjustment in the 1990s led to infrastructure compression which adversely affected GDP by more than 1 percent per year.[75] First, and probably most seriously, adjustment had a big and enduring impact on the poor in terms of jobs and services.[76] Not only did the poor feel the impact of the reforms, but also they were less able to take advantage of the recovery of the economies after 2002.[77] In addition, by reducing investment in infrastructure, the reforms further reduced the capacity of Latin American economies to later meet rising demand for goods and services. It thereby contributed to accelerating inflation in 2006–2008.[78]

In contrast to the book by Nancy Birdsall and her colleagues, Ricardo Ffrench-Davis had remarked in 2005 that the Washington Consensus reforms represented a "disingenuous neo-liberalism."[79] In its place he referred to a new "pragmatic progressivism" which characterizes the new leadership in some Latin American countries instead of a "one-size-fits-all approach" which applies to the Washington Consensus reforms. While he agreed with Birdsall *et al.* that the objective should be growth with equity, he was less defensive about the results of the earlier policy advice and hence was able to offer a more balanced view of what was likely to happen in the region.[80]

The battle to interpret Latin America's economic history in the 1990s and the effects of the Washington Consensus continues. In 2010, Chilean economist, Sebastian Edwards, published a highly defensive rebuttal of the critiques of the reforms of the 1990s. In his book, *Left Behind: Latin America and the False Promise of Populism*,[81] Edwards offers a negative assessment of Latin American economic performance and a stinging indictment of Latin American governments. He refers to Latin America as "the eternal land of the future."[82] He praises the reforms of the 1990s, but noted:

> Progress, however, was short-lived. Neither efficiency nor investment in equipment, machinery, and infrastructure increased sufficiently to sustain economic growth over the long run. Institutions were not reformed, property rights were not protected sufficiently, and there was scant improvement in the rule of law. Poverty did not decline significantly, and income distribution remained as skewed as in the past."[83]

Edwards remarked that, between 1998 and 2002, Latin America's income per capita grew on average merely 0.2 percent; during the same time per capita income grew in Asia ten times faster.[84] He explained slower growth as a result of "the reforms of the 1990s and first decade of this century (being) superficial and incomplete. (Therefore), most Latin American countries continue to this day to be inefficient and to have low productivity and a high incidence of poverty."[85] He concludes that, "Latin America, with very few exceptions, clearly suffers from fractured and incomplete economic reform."[86] While praising liberalization, Edwards blames low productivity growth on endogenous factors and not on the external environment. The sub-title of this section in his book, "The poverty of institutions and long-term mediocrity," conveys his disapproving perspective. It is also reflected in his argument that the current progressive regimes in the region are populist. He defines populism as "an approach to economics that emphasizes growth and income distribution and deemphasizes the risks of inflation, external constraints, and the reaction of economic agents to aggressive non-market policies."[87]

The ideological view of Edwards clouds his view of trends in other countries as well. For example, he urges in his book that Latin America in the period 2003–2010 should be compared with successful competitors such as Spain, Greece, and Portugal. This suggestion does not seem to have much foundation when the 2010 performance of these countries is assessed.[88] He unfortunately also praises the management of Jose Martinez de Hoz, Argentine Economy Minister during the military dictatorship of 1976–1983, without mention of the dictatorship at all.[89]

The changing impact of the global economy

The above assessments of the impacts of the Washington Consensus thus generally conclude that while the impacts were not positive, they do not agree in their diagnoses of the reasons for poor performance. An important factor, however, which should influence the assessment of the applicability of policy measures to Latin American economies, is the changing impact of the global economy itself. The period 2003–2007 generally saw high levels of economic growth across the world, ranging from very high growth rates in China and India, to somewhat lower rates in other countries. Rising global demand for commodities and higher commodity prices certainly aided those exporting countries, such as Argentina and Brazil, for whom the demand for commodities such as soya, corn, wheat, and various oils from China and other countries generated record surpluses and trade balances. Low interest rates, intended to restart a slowing United States economy in 2007–2008, have also supported this process, with excess liquidity being invested in commodity futures, thereby contributing to growing demand and rising prices.

Historically, high degrees of volatility in the global economy have contributed to the instability of financial flows to Latin America.[90] This has produced what Ffrench-Davis refers to as "asymmetric impacts" and leads to the under-use of the economic potential of Latin American countries.[91] Projects may begin but may not have sufficient resources to be completed, price changes undermine financial projections and cost estimates; and unstable market conditions undercut investment assumptions. All of these raise the issue of vulnerability of Latin American economies to big changes in either prices or interest rates and underlines the importance of having a cushion to soften impacts of such changes. One of the most functional cushions in these circumstances has been a fund of foreign exchange reserves, a subject which will be discussed in Chapter 5 in the case of Argentina. This cushion has proven to be very important for Latin American economies in the face of global economic turmoil as experienced in 2007 and 2008 as a result of the deteriorating performance of the economy of the United States.

The relative economic success of the Latin American countries during the period 2003 to 2007 also proved to be critical in helping the region cushion the impact of the global economic crisis, which started in 2008 and continued through 2011, with especially severe consequences in the United States and Europe. The financial crisis in the developed world led to a sharp drop in demand for goods and commodities produced in Latin America. The region thus experienced the global crisis as a trade shock, with a drop in the aggregate demand for Latin American exports and a drop in prices. This crisis then was transformed into a steep drop in production, employment, and eventually in public revenue, thus seeing a trade crisis become an economic and public finance crisis as well. In general, however, the region weathered these changes relatively well and quickly returned to the path of economic growth. The countries affected most seriously were Mexico, due to its proximity and interdependence with the United States' economy and those Central American countries highly dependent on North American tourism. By 2011, countries such as Argentina and Brazil, which had rejected neo-liberal economic policies, were firmly back on a path of high growth.

This chapter has sought to explain the continuing changes in the economies of Latin American countries and in the strategies and policies that have been adopted by governments to manage and sustain economic growth. The story presented here is controversial and not a happy one for the millions of Latin Americans who have experienced declining welfare at various periods over the last century. While there has been economic growth, the number of poor households in the region has increased dramatically. Moreover, the situation has become more complicated as well, with the region more dependent on its relationships with an active and unstable global economy. This is the context for understanding the crisis and recovery in Argentina.

From this perspective, it is important to understand some of the perceptions of Latin America in the early years of the twenty-first century. One important perspective is presented in the book, *The Political Economy of the Possible: Beyond Free Marketeers and Revolutionaries*,[92] by Spanish economist, Javier Santiso, published in 2006, who argued that Latin American politics had changed and had become less ideological and less focused on changing the framework of society, economy, and politics, and more directed towards managing smaller problems and achieving lesser objectives. Santiso, Chief Economist of the

Organisation for Economic Co-operation and Development (OECD), wrote of the "end of the future" as a dimension of this politics, with the short term replacing the long term as the time horizon for action and expectations. Implicit in this argument were several key premises:

- that the big framework issues were in fact resolved to everyone's satisfaction;
- that the model of economic growth and development was effective in providing the incomes, jobs, goods, and services which are needed by Latin American populations;
- that the distribution of benefits from growth and development was acceptable, despite the existing and widening gaps between rich and poor in many Latin American countries; and
- that the "political economy of the possible" was sufficient to manage the risks and uncertainty of change in the medium and long term.

This argument also accepted the basic prevailing de facto definitions of justice and political institutions in countries which have long been characterized by an absence of consensus and, indeed, by intermittent violence and armed conflict to support political agendas. The argument was, in effect, a sophisticated defense of a status quo, which was adjusting to emergent needs but not changing in ways that might alter the basic distribution of economic and political power within Latin American countries. It was clothed in the language of realism and insider knowledge of the world of economic policy choices and so-called "policy space," the area in which "real choices" are possible.

The argument repeated, in a different form, the perspective of a book published earlier in 2002 entitled *Latin America at the End of Politics* by Forrest D. Colburn, an American political scientist, who extended the "end of history" argument of Francis Fukuyama to Latin America. Colburn wrote, "We have come to the end point of ideological evolution, and that the universalization of liberal democracy and the unfettered markets of capitalism are the final forms of government and economic organization."[93] Colburn observed that,

> The end of ideological contestation has lessened the sense of urgency for solving trenchant problems of poverty and social inequality.... Another worry is that liberalism in Latin America is, at least presently, unprepared to offer public solutions to serious collective problems.[94]

Despite his relative equanimity over this "end of politics," he nevertheless noted that "a number of indicators suggest that both new and old democratic regimes are under stress, their legitimacy is being questioned, and their public support is increasingly fragile."[95] He concluded his book, in the last paragraph, with the observation that,

> Latin America begins the twenty-first century with an uneasy calm. There is political peace. Political passion – with vocal concern for the public good –

> is out of fashion, appearing to be futile. However, there are abundant and trenchant problems in the region. Much cloth remains to be cut.[96]

Another intriguing and very different perspective on what has happened to Latin American societies has been suggested by Greg Grandin, a historian of Latin America at New York University, who developed the argument that the legacy of the Cold War in Latin America—through the experiences of military repression of political, social, and economic conflicts in many countries and the harsh abuse of human rights—has been a definition of democracy that is largely devoid of economic and social content. He suggested that, in the face of authoritarian governments, Latin Americans have defined democracy as protection of their rights in confronting state power.[97] Election of those most likely to protect their rights has become the priority.

This issue, addressed in subsequent chapters, converged with mass unhappiness with the results of the economic policies followed by Latin American governments during the neo-liberal period of the Washington Consensus in the 1990s. The results were the national elections, which took place in the region from 2002 to 2011, where most countries defeated incumbents and elected new progressive leadership committed to finding alternative economic policies.

2 State performance and institutional capacity in development

As noted in Chapter 1, in addition to the theoretical and policy importance of understanding neo-liberalism in terms of its impact on Latin American and Argentine development performance, the two other theoretical and policy issues to be addressed in this book are the issue of state performance itself and the role of institutional capacity in determining state performance. While the book focuses on the Argentine experience, an assessment of that experience needs to be placed within a broader analytic and comparative framework, which allows the reader to evaluate the achievements and disappointments of Argentina in relation to the performance of other middle-income developing countries. This chapter will address those issues.

Frameworks for assessing state performance

The historical and political debates about the role of the state in development go back at least to the debates of ancient Greece and Rome about what are desirable forms of government and society in which individuals and the society at large can prosper. Central to these debates has been the notion of democracy as a desirable form of governance in which popular representation and participation is an essential ingredient for decision-making about the most important questions affecting the collectivity. The role of the decision-maker, whether monarch or elected leader, military ruler or dictator, has been frequently discussed in terms of the "efficiency" of authoritarian leadership versus the transactional and political costs of democratic societies.

For the purposes of this book, the debates about state performance will be presented in their post-World War II form around three central issues: first, the debates and social science literature about what kinds of states are able to best promote "development" per se, which will be elaborated below; secondly, how understanding of the role of state has been heavily influenced by theoretical and indeed ideological notions about the relative roles of state and market in determining social and economic progress, and thirdly, how these ideas themselves have evolved and shifted over the past 50 years in Latin America, thus affecting how states have been redefined and reorganized over time. This latter evolution also necessarily involves understanding the changes and discontinuities in state–society relations during this period, particularly the effect of military interventions and dictatorships.

States and development versus states and markets

The study of development performance in the post-World War II period has focused heavily on the organization of the economy, largely in the comparison between state-controlled and market economies. This debate became part of the theoretical and political confrontation between Marxist and market economic thinking since the nineteenth century and later accentuated after the Russian Revolution of 1917 and embodied in the Cold War. Beyond the heavily ideological debates between East and West, there was also extensive comparative analysis of the economic performance of countries and regions across the developing world.

Reviewing country performance across regions from the post-independence period in Africa after 1960 up to the 1990s, there were some rather startling comparisons. For example, in 1960, India and Korea had the same GDP per capita and Ghana was richer than both, but 30 years later, Korea was the 11th largest economy in the world, with per capita income close to US$14,000, compared to around US$800 in India and Ghana—much less. Africa had clearly been unable to grow, as its 1990s GDP numbers remained at 1970 levels in most countries. Latin America had also stagnated, having grown significantly from 1950 to 1980, but having succumbed to the debt crisis of the 1980s and the so-called "lost decade." The only standout performer was East Asia, at least up to 1997 and the East Asian financial crisis. While China is part of East Asia, it was nonetheless treated as *sui generis* and not usually included in the positive characterization of East Asian development.

These dramatically different development results provoked many comparative debates, particularly at the beginning of the 1990s and the collapse of the Soviet Union and the end of the Cold War. In the environment of Western triumphalism over the "success" of the free market economy over socialism, the government of Japan supported a study of the "East Asian Miracle" by the World Bank to demonstrate the essential and central role of the state in promoting economic development in East Asia.[1] While the financial crisis of 1997–1998 demonstrated that some state regulatory functions over the financial sector in Thailand, Korea, and other countries had failed and resulted in major financial and economic collapse, it also underlined the importance of the role of the state at a time when the "public sector" was clearly on the defensive in all regions, as suggested by the wave of privatization of public services that was occurring in both developed and developing countries at that time.

The story of Latin American economic performance presented in Chapter 1 suggests that, as in other regions, the role and perception of the state also changed at various times in the post-World War II period. As discussed later in this book, the differences in economic performance between countries became manifest in the degree of divergence in GDP per capita and other indicators between countries. Growing divergence has been well documented in studies of the East Asian countries[2] as well as in broader comparative studies of late-industrializing developing countries from other regions and in detailed case studies posing these comparative analytic questions.[3]

These issues were also examined by the international financial institutions starting in the late 1980s, as their focus became increasingly macro-economic through the emphasis on structural adjustment. While the concern for adjustment grew out of the macro-economic imbalances resulting from the oil price hikes of the 1970s and the resulting debt crises of the 1980s, starting with Mexico in 1982, the focus on the importance of economic policies logically led to examination of the institutions responsible for executing them. Three strands of thinking emerged. First, the World Bank's macro-economic and sectoral adjustment programs involved proposed changes in institutional roles and regulatory functions, including reducing the size of the public sector under the guise of fiscal contraction. While the quality of the World Bank analyses of macro-economic and sectoral institutions varied considerably across countries, they consistently had a strong normative orientation and content, particularly with regard to public sector reform, and increasingly had a simplifying "one-size-fits-all" character.[4]

A second strand concerned understanding the meaning of governance as a broader concept than government, including acknowledging the role of civil society institutions in governance.[5] This represented a significant shift from the earlier, more limited, focus of the development institutions on the role of community participation in project design and implementation.[6] This work on governance evolved over the 1990s and ended up being heavily focused on the issue of corruption in developing countries.[7] This was unfortunate because corruption is only one specific problem within the larger set of issues of how societies are governed and what roles they might play in the development process. In the end, corruption, while significant, distracted attention away from important political and institutional questions related to development performance.

The third strand of thinking concerned the explicit role of the state in relation to the market. Unfortunately, this more narrow focus reflected the heavy and growing ideological emphasis of the World Bank and the IMF by the late 1990s. For example, the World Development Report of 2001 argued that development performance and the reduction of poverty depended largely on the adoption of market-friendly development policies.[8] This overly simplistic view clearly was a result of the political atmosphere of the time in which the collapse of the Eastern bloc was perceived as a failure of state-managed economies. While a popular view in Washington and European capitals, there were many empirical problems with this conclusion: among others, it contradicted the historical record of development performance of countries, as suggested in Chapter 1. For example, as noted earlier by well-known economists such as Jose Antonio-Ocampo or Ricardo Ffrench-Davis, the emphasis on liberalization in the policy package of the Washington Consensus was not ultimately proven to contribute to higher growth rates. Furthermore, explanations, which were solely based on the efficiency of markets, could not explain the extraordinary growth experience of China or state-market interactions in Japan and later Korea.

Nonetheless, in the analysis of the role of the state in development in the 2002 World Development Report, *Building Institutions for Markets*, published by the World Bank,[9] the report is slanted towards subordinating institutions to strengthening the functioning of markets, rather than address the broader issue of the role of the state and institutions in development. This report was symptomatic of a larger and more important debate about whether the focus of governance should be to enhance growth or to enhance markets, clearly different objectives.

The debate over this distinction was addressed in some detail by the economist, Mushtaq H. Khan in 2007, in an empirical study of the relative performance of countries following these different strategies of governance. Khan explained the problem in the following manner:

> There is an important empirical and theoretical controversy between liberal economists, who constitute the mainstream consensus on good governance and statist and heterodox institutional economists, who agree that governance is critical for economic development, but argue that theory and evidence shows that the governance capacities required for successful development are substantially different from those identified by the good governance analysis. The economists in favor of good governance argue that the critical state capacities are those that maintain efficient markets and restrict the activities of states to the provision of necessary public goods to minimize rent seeking and government failure…
>
> In contrast, heterodox institutional economists base their argument on case studies of rapid growth in the last fifty years. This evidence suggests … that states that did best in terms of achieving convergence with advanced countries had the capacity to achieve and sustain high rates of investment and to implement policies that encouraged the acquisition and learning of new technologies rapidly. The institutions and strategies that achieved these varied from country to country, depending on their initial conditions and political constraints…[10]

Khan describes market-enhancing versus growth-enhancing governance strategies in some detail. While the market-enhancing governance strategy is clearly close to the World Bank 2002 World Development Report (WDR) model, the growth-enhancing governance strategy bears some notable resemblance to the "developmentalism" approach adopted by Presidents Frondizi of Argentina and Kubitschek of Brazil in the late 1950s, as described in Chapter 1. Khan notes that from 1950 to 1980 there was a major focus in many states towards growth enhancement and improving the efficiency and impact of resource allocation, but that this focus was not accompanied by much attention to government capabilities per se.[11] The resulting poor performance of states, as demonstrated by indicators such as high fiscal deficits or high levels of protection, led to a call for reform towards market-enhancing policies for governance, as best exemplified by the Washington Consensus. As suggested earlier, however, this line of analysis could not explain the "miracle" of the performance of the East Asian countries.

Khan's empirical study of these two alternative governance strategies uses World Bank and Institutional Reform and the Informal Sector (IRIS) data sets and comes to the following important conclusions about the differences between what he refers to as the converging (fast growing) and the diverging (slowly growing) economies:

1 There is virtually no difference between the median property rights index between converging and diverging developing countries.
2 The absence of any clear separation between converging and diverging developing countries in terms of market-enhancing governance conditions casts doubt on the robustness of econometric results of a large number of studies that find market-enhancing governance conditions have a significant effect on economic growth (Kauffman *et al.* 1999).
3 Third, for all the indices of governance we have available, the data suggest a very weak positive relationship between the quality of governance and economic growth. (This relates to fact that a large number of advanced countries have high scores on governance while the developing countries have lower scores. The direction of causality is not clear.)
4 Analysis of expected growth rates and governance strategies generates a problem of causation. (Sachs *et al.* shows that market-enhancing governance had no affect on African performance.)
5 The growth-enhancing governance argument suggests that markets in developing countries will be "relatively inefficient in transferring assets and resources to growth sectors", with long periods of losses, uncertainty for investors, thereby emphasizing the need for rapid learning. The problem of this conclusion is that to do this also requires effective governance.
6 The Asian experience shows that there is not one single set of governance requirements. For example, India did well under liberalization even if it continued to operate through older state structures, while Latin America countries did less well with the same liberalization strategies using their previous structures.
7 Growth enhancing strategies vary from place to place, with different components and results.
8 Latin America provides even more compelling evidence that a focus on market-enhancing governance alone cannot provide adequate policy levers for governments interested in accelerating growth and development [...] In terms of market-enhancing governance, Latin America, on average, scores highly, compared to other areas of the developing world. This is not surprising given its higher initial per capita incomes, much longer history of development, and relatively old institutions of political democracy [...] Yet, the combination of more developed market-enhancing governance capabilities and a more thoroughgoing liberalization did not help Latin America beat Asia in terms of economic development in the 1990s and beyond. In fact, its relative performance was exactly the opposite of what we would expect from the relative depth of its liberalization strategy and its relative

governance indicators. But in fact, the rapid liberalization of Latin America and its greater reliance on market-enhancing governance achieved results that should not be entirely surprising given our analysis. Latin American countries shifted even more rapidly to producing according to their comparative advantage, and in most Latin American countries, this meant a shift to lower technology industries and to commodity production. This has produced respectable output growth in some countries, but productivity growth has been low and living standards have yet to fully recover from the collapse suffered in the 1990s.

9 Evidence on the poor performance of import substitution strategies is supposed to explain poor overall performance, but empirical analysis shows that the evidence is weak, because high growth countries also failed to meet market enhancing governance criteria.[12]

Most importantly, Khan observes that global and generalized recommendations about governance strategies are ignoring the "initial conditions" and specific political constraints facing countries. These initial conditions are critical, as the economist, Hollis Chenery, argued in 1970 when he suggested that development strategies could not be generalized and that assessment of how well a specific development strategy had performed could only be made in terms of the initial conditions and objectives which had been set. For example, a desert country should not be assessed in terms of its wheat production, or a small island state should not be judged by the same criteria as a large agricultural or manufacturing country with substantial endowments of natural resources.[13]

In contrast to the broad and essentially unsubstantiated and highly ideological generalizations of the World Bank, a rich comparative and contextual understanding of these issues has also come from comparative studies of specific countries and/or specific sectors between countries. Some of these studies have been rooted in the sociological understandings of institutions and bureaucracy going back to the work of Max Weber. For example, the Weberian models of bureaucracy and the state have been carefully applied in the work of sociologist, Peter Evans, in his now well-known book, *Embedded Autonomy: States and Industrial Transformation*, where he sought to understand the differences in the performance of Brazil, India, and Korea in developing the informatics sector within their respective industrial sectors.

Evans starts with the assertion that:

> The state lies at the center of solutions to the problem of order [in order to avoid Hobbesian disorder. He argues,] Without the state, markets, the other master institution of modern society, cannot function.... We need predictable rules, and these in turn must have a concrete organizational structure behind them.[14]

He cites Karl Polanyi, who had concluded that: "The road to the free market was opened and kept open by an enormous increase in continuous, centrally organized, and controlled interventionism."[15] Evans observes that, "successful policies have structural foundations."[16] The state is "a historically contingent creation whose properties depend on specific institutional endowments and the character of the surrounding social structure."[17] In linking this perspective to other development thinkers, he writes:

> The underlying assumption of Weber, Gershenkron, or Hirschman is that a shared project underlies the interactions of state and society. Both industrial elites and the state are interested in transformation, neither can implement this project on their own, and each brings something to the task.[18]

This focus, and its emphasis on building the productive capacity of the economies of developing countries in the service of a "national developmental project," implies first that a primary task of the state is to lead this economic transformation. He noted, in 1995, that earlier debates about whether the state should intervene in the economy had been replaced by the question of what kinds of intervention are most effective.[19] It is remarkable that this observation contrasts so clearly with the emergent thinking of the time in the World Bank which failed to recognize that these debates were so alive. Evans also noted that, "'development' is no longer just a local trajectory of transformation. It is also defined by the relation between local productive capacity and a changing global array of sectors."[20]

While placing these debates within this historical thinking about development, Evans' major theoretical contribution was his proposal of the notion of "embedded autonomy" by which he characterized state–society relations, in which the state is sufficiently informed and engaged with specific industrial or other transformation projects possibly through various policy instruments or budgetary investment, but recognizes the autonomy of the state and the local non-state economic actors, entrepreneurs, firms, and associations of firms in making economic and financial decisions about their investments and business strategies. Explaining the differences in the historical experiences of Brazil, India, and Korea in the role of the state in the development of their respective informatics industries, he noted that the characteristics and capacities of state institutions alone are not sufficient to explain the differences in these national experiences. Rather, the role of state–society relations is also critical in conditioning how the state can operate and in turn, how industries can develop. He concluded that, "State and society are not just linked together: each helps constitute the other [...] State strategies can also create social groups whose agendas conflict with the state's original project."[21]

Evans distinguished between so-called predatory, developmental, and intermediate states, noting that they have both "different internal structures and external ties."[22] His empirical studies of Brazil, India, and Korea demonstrated these differences and how state–society relations matters in the evolution of their respective informatics industries. The key lessons from his comparative analysis are the following:

> The fate of civil society is inextricably bound to the robustness of the state apparatus [...] Sustaining or regaining the institutional integrity of state bureaucracies increase the possibility of mounting projects of social transformation.
>
> Bureaucracy is not enough. Even the most bureaucratically coherent state cannot effect transformation without a network of ties to social groups and classes with which it shares a project. Connectedness is as important as coherence and cohesion.
>
> The concept of embedded autonomy is useful because it concretizes the structural relations that lie behind the efficacy of the ideal typical developmental state.[23]

While the concept of embedded autonomy opened up the discussion through the presentation of interesting analytic categories, it was less strong in terms of its practical and policy implications. Writing about the industrial sector in Minas Gerais, Brazil, Alfred P. Montero noted the difficulty of finding the political balances required for significant change and observed that Evans had asserted that a mixture of state autonomy and embeddedness can produce economic efficiency, but he was unclear about the political balance required to do so.[24] This important comment builds on the earlier work of Barbara Geddes in her 1994 analysis of the "politician's dilemma" of finding a sustainable balance between short-term political needs and longer-term development objectives.[25] Indeed, decisions by politicians to promise one thing during their campaigns and not surprisingly to do another in office are common, as shown by Susan Stokes in her 2001 study of many Latin American cases.[26] Evans, however, also insisted upon the importance of state–society relations as a critical component of embedded autonomy and ultimately of government performance. The various forms of state–society relations will be discussed later in this chapter.

Studies since 2000 on institutional capacity in Latin America suggest that the real world is more complicated than the caricatures presented by the international financial institutions, for example between rural and urban interests or labor and capital. Anthony Pereira noted, that "Brazil may have a capitalist democracy, but its form of capitalism in the countryside is not very democratic."[27] This complexity is well illustrated in an insightful article on state reform in Brazil and the discourse on social policy by Joanildo A. Burrity and Laurence Hallewell.[28] They noted that after the Brazilian state was reformed, creating more openness to civil society organizations, there were rising expectations that more democracy would lead to material improvements in people's lives. However,

> The idea that democratization was going to bring about a general improvement in the lives of the majority gradually faded and another, more 'minimalist' vision – stability (of prices, employment, public safety, and the ability to forecast the economy and the policies of those controlling it)–took its place.[29]

In the 1990s, the government of Fernando Henrique Cardoso "was born under the sign of the 'third way,' the compromise between the discourses of neo-liberalism and social democracy." These two discourses were reflected in two different parallel processes: one, a new discourse on social policy with more independent participation by civil society in the public sphere and in government policies, and the other, the adoption of policies of economic adjustment and reform of the state.[30] The authors pointed out that when the resources of the state were exhausted by the economic crisis in the 1990s and the growing indebtedness of the public sector, more attention was focused on the specific functions of the state. This then generated a new discourse, highlighting the lack of resources, responsibility, participation, and partnership.[31] They concluded with an important analytic observation:

> The rhythm of the changes introduced during the 1990s and the early years of the new century showed a mismatch between the agenda of institutional reforms and economic restructuring (the overwhelming priority) and the agenda of social reform. This mismatch has led to a retreat from the expectations associated with the process of re-democratization."[32]

The evidence for this conclusion had been signaled five years earlier, for example, by Brazilian economists Edmund Amann and Werner Baer, when they noted that the 1990s had seen price stability and foreign investment, but little progress on reducing poverty or inequality in Brazil,[33] further confirming the regional conclusions about the impact of the policies embodied in the Washington Consensus as presented in Chapter 1.

In the real world, the actual combinations of state and market are even more nuanced. For example, the case of Chile has been caricatured as a highly neo-liberal state where the market rules, but studies of Chilean policies and institutions have revealed a much more complicated picture. Marcus Kurtz argued

> That important parts of the neoliberal explanation for Chile's development do not fit the evidence, most critically in terms of the role of public intervention or the virtues of radical trade liberalization. When successful integration into export markets occurred, public action was both substantial and crucial. Important elements of the neoliberal model, moreover, were just as often barriers to economic adjustment as promoters of it.[34]

He correctly observed that, "the question should be about what policies are most appropriate in underdeveloped countries where government and market failure are both prevalent."[35]

The Chilean case also demonstrates that the choices between policy objectives and their political costs also are not entirely consistent. For example, Patrick Barrett argued in 2001 that the *Concertación* was committed to flexible working conditions as an aspect of Chile's international competitiveness, but that this flexibility was incompatible with its objectives for equity and a well-organized and protected labor force. He noted that too much emphasis on labor flexibility may actually slow down economic growth, but that finally the *Concertación* was reluctant to challenge business.[36]

These dynamics were also present in Argentina where the Radical government of President Raul Alfonsín could not resolve the struggle over income distribution between capital and labor. Laura Tedesco wrote in 1999 that, "the neo-liberal state of the 1990s has similar characteristics to the bureaucratic authoritarian state of the 1970s. Both attempt to subordinate, politically and economically, the working class."[37] Ana Dinerstein went further, arguing that while the neo-liberal restructuring of the 1990s was in part intended to de-politicize labor, in fact the opposite occurred, resulting in the new protest movements of the *piqueteros*.[38] These issues became further complicated by the system of federalism in Argentina where provinces, and particularly governors, encouraged different fiscal and policy behavior across the provinces.[39] More generally, the case of Argentina, described in much more detail below, is a case of complicated dynamics where institutional weaknesses in the executive, legislative, and judicial branches of government interact with individual and collective behavior to produce less than optimal outcomes.[40]

Institutional capacity and state performance

As suggested in Chapter 1, ideas have a major impact on the formulation and execution of development strategies and policies. The short-lived efforts to introduce developmentalism in Argentina and Brazil in the late 1950s reflected economic and political ideas, which became political and institutional commitments by newly-elected presidents to modify the role of the state. Both presidents sought more active state intervention in the economy by certain state ministries and governmental bodies, while at the same time creating conditions, which would attract both domestic and foreign private investment. The state was to be explicitly involved in helping to build the foundations for growth, particularly through incentives and investments in domestic industries and technology. The Brazilian state proved to be much more successful than the Argentine state in formulating and carrying out this plan.[41] This result, as argued by Peter Evans,[42] was also a consequence of the nature of state–society relations in Brazil, a subject to be explored later in this chapter.

A different set of ideas was behind the neo-liberal reforms of the 1990s, which deliberately sought to reduce the size of the state. Carlos Ramio and Miguel Salvador have noted, for example, that

> The central objective of the reforms, which we label 'downsizing government,' as they were applied in Latin America, was not so much to improve the functioning of the state as to reduce it, on the grounds that it performed functions that were not considered suitable in the new ideological context [...] the focus of these modernizing initiatives was the external orientation of the state apparatus: that is, they set out to modify the state's relations with society but not its internal operations.[43]

This led to reductions in the numbers of state employees from 5 to 40 percent of the civil service[44] and necessarily also weakened the institutional capacity of the state.

There has been a significant growth of literature on institutional capacity in the public sector in Latin America, including analyses of patterns which pre-date the neo-liberal turn of the 1990s. One type of literature has been comparative studies of tax performance, for example, between Argentina and Chile. These demonstrate great differences in institutional arrangements and capacities to legislate and collect taxes.[45] Whereas Chile has had a stable and effective tax collection system, Argentina did not until the administration of Nestor Kirchner, as explained in Chapter 5.

Marcus Andre Melo has argued, for example, that Argentine federalism contributed to low taxation rates through disincentives to tax at the provincial level, incentives to give tax exemptions to attract investment, and federal bailouts.[46] Argentina has had a higher GDP per capita than Brazil for the postwar period, but the tax share to GDP is lower. Weak and unstable political leadership also contributed to low tax performance, for example, from 1955 to 1983, Argentina had 16 different presidents, with an average of less than two years in each term of office. From 1958 to 1962, the government of President Frondizi faced 35 failed coup attempts. The Province of Buenos Aires had 74 different governors from 1900 to 1984.[47]

Institutional instability and frequent changes in leadership characterize Argentine institutions more broadly, including the executive, legislative, and judicial branches of government. Levitsky and Murillo attribute Argentina's erratic development performance to this instability.[48] They note that, "during the 1990s, Argentine democracy was characterized by both unprecedented stability and persistent institutional fluidity," (reflecting shifts in positions of Peronist leaders) but Menem did not attempt to strengthen public institutions. In fact, he did the opposite, weakening the Supreme Court and privatizing many state functions.[49]

Spiller and Tommasi suggest that two sets of factors explain the policy-making process in Argentina: high democratic instability from 1930 to 1983 and constitutional structure and electoral rules, both discussed at length in later chapters. Together, these produce short time horizons and a "policymaking process that lacks the institutional mechanisms for inter-temporal agreements." As a result, there is a high instability of public policies. They found that in a study of policy stability in 106 countries, Argentina was the seventh most volatile country, with drastic shifts in policies as ministers abandoned the frameworks of their predecessors. Not surprisingly, they concluded that Argentina is a weak enforcer of its policies.[50]

Spiller and Tommasi develop these arguments in much greater depth in their book, which treats each of the political institutions in Argentina in some detail.[51] Their analysis leads to the following propositions about Argentine institutional actors and the characteristics of some of the main institutional arenas:

1 Congress is not an important policy-making arena.
2 The executive tends to have substantial leeway to take unilateral policy action.
3 Provincial political powers (especially provincial governors) are very important in national policy making.
4 There is a symbiotic interaction between national and provincial policy making that operates through political and federal fiscal channels.
5 Given the incentives of the executive of the day, of legislators, and of provincial governors, there is little investment in policy-making capacities in several spheres.
6 Fiscal federalism considerations are a factor in almost every policy issue, adding transaction difficulties and rigidities to policy making.
7 The bureaucracy is not an effective corps to which to delegate the technical implementation of policy bargains.
8 The judiciary does not provide much inter-temporal "glue" to political or policy agreements.
9 Nongovernmental actors in the policy process (such as business groups and unions), lacking a well-institutionalized environment for political exchange, usually follow strategies that attempt to maximize short-term benefits and to build in rigidities into future policies.[52]

It is beyond the purpose of this book to address these conclusions in a systematic manner. Nonetheless, the reader will see that their observations are very helpful in understanding some of the limitations of institutional capacity, which are presented in later chapters. While some of these characteristics are "structural," i.e., they originate in the Argentine Constitution. Others are behavioral and reflect how national and provincial leaders operate within these institutional parameters. The result is a significant lack of cooperation among institutional actors and a high degree of short-term thinking and political strategies, both of which have significant effects on the role of government in the pattern of development of Argentina, as shown in Chapter 10.

This assessment needs also to be understood as a result of various historical political forces in Argentina and the region more generally. For example, neoliberal notions of appropriate state functions led to rapid privatizations in Latin America during the 1990s. Argentine political scientist, Maria Victoria Murillo, argues that even with high external financial pressures for privatization, electoral competition and partisan linkages shaped the policy-making on privatization. Electoral competition affected the timing of decisions to privatize and the decision to reform, but the partisan orientation of incumbents determined the content or design of the policies.[53] This suggests that while ideologies such as neo-liberalism helped to establish the orientation of policy, national and local political and institutional processes played major roles in how privatization actually occurred.

As noted earlier in the discussion of Evans' theory of state performance, a critical component is also state–society relations. These are obviously country-specific and are the product of the interplay of historical forces which shift and express themselves differently over time. One particularly significant set of forces is what Ruth Berins Collier and David Collier have referred to as the incorporation of labor into the political system. In their study of this process across Latin American countries, they argue that during the first decades of the twentieth century the relationships between labor and the state fundamentally changed.[54] They refer to this process as being a "critical juncture" and note that the process of "incorporation meant the end of oligarchic domination and of a predominantly agrarian society in these countries." This process does not take one form, but rather results in various types of outcomes which they describe as four kinds of labor incorporation: radical populism, labor populism, electoral mobilization of labor by a traditional party, and depoliticization and control.[55]

As will be shown later in the case of Argentina, the state develops new relationships with labor at different times. Importantly, they also suggest that,

> The political arena is not simply fluid, constantly responding to socioeconomic change. Instead, because of autonomous political logic and vested interests, it may be resistant to such change over significant periods of time. Socioeconomic change is important to political outcomes, but the political arena may to some degree follow its own pattern and pace of change, that at times takes a highly discontinuous form.[56]

In their analysis of Latin American political change, the Colliers identify steps in critical junctures as being antecedents, cleavages, and legacy,[57] distinctions which are helpful in understanding historical processes. The political role of labor is central to this process, particularly in light of neo-liberal reform where, as Kurt Weyland has argued, neo-liberalism has weakened unions and generally weakened the balance between capital and labor within economies.[58] This point is also reflected in the work by Argentine political scientist, Sebastian Etchemendy, who has written about the cooptation of labor within the reform coalition of President Carlos Menem, by being given the task of managing the health care systems of workers and having made profits from these funds.[59]

Weyland observes that,

> Neo-liberalism clearly has not destroyed competitive civilian rule in the region; it has actually helped to secure the survival of democracy, as defined in minimal procedural terms. Drastic market reform, however, seems, on balance, to have limited and weakened the quality of democracy in Latin America.... Structural adjustment and its corollary, the deeper integration of Latin American countries into the global economy, have made the region more susceptible to international pressures for maintaining democracy.[60]

Institutional capacity, therefore, cannot be considered outside of the political framework of state–society relations. These relations change over time, with state capacity expanding and contracting in part as a function of what the state attempts to do, whether to enforce rules, to allocate public resources or to articulate strategies for the future, among other tasks. What this means in the case of Argentina is in large part the subject of the rest of this book.

While these country-specific problems of institutional capacity have major impacts on state performance, we also need to be reminded that they stem in part from the process of regional and indeed global diffusion of ideas about the role of the state and how these ideas take root in specific countries. In a very insightful 2005 article on what they refer to as "Latin American regulatory capitalism," Jacint Jordana and David Levi-Faur explain that these ideas come from both outside countries while also following paths of diffusion from one sectoral institution to another inside countries, with the number of regulatory authorities increasing from 43 in 1979 to 138 by 2002.[61] They also suggest that the proliferation of these agencies is not a sign of institutional strength, but rather of weakness of democracies to regulate and manage activities through democratic institutions.[62]

While the contribution of ideas by international agencies is significant, it is less important than the endogenous diffusion of ideas of regulatory capitalism within countries themselves once the ideas enter the society.[63] They describe this as a process of "social learning" in which

> Even the "willing pupils" … are essentially imitating the rich and successful countries of the "North". These countries are at the moment not only telling the poorer ones what the solutions to their problems are; they are also defining and telling them what their problems are. From this point of view, the current restructuring of the state in Latin America is another chapter in the long saga of the export of Occidental state structures to the rest of the world.[64]

As subsequent chapters suggest, the role of external advice about policies and institutions can have dramatic and often disastrous consequences for developing countries.

3 The Argentine crisis

What happened?

Origins

On December 20, 2001, Fernando de la Rua, President of Argentina, resigned from office and left the Government House by helicopter. This act symbolized the weakness of the Government of Argentina in an economic and political crisis whose origins go back over the previous three decades. Three days later, interim President Adolfo Rodriguez Saa announced the cessation of payments on Argentina's external debt. On January 3, 2002, the new President Eduardo Duhalde devalued the Argentine peso from 1:1 with the US dollar, to 3:1 and to a floating currency. Argentina was in the midst of the worst economic crisis in its history.

The story of the crisis, its causes, and its serious consequences have been the subject of many books, commentaries, and as is frequently the case, also the casting of blame in many directions. Although the economic and political history of the country has been dramatic, with many twists and turns during the twentieth century, it is clear that the crisis, which came to a head on December 19, 2001, was different and marked a turning point in the understanding not only of Argentines but of the world at large. Comparison with other financial and economic crises of the 1990s in East Asia, Russia, and Brazil underline the severity of the crisis and support the assertion that this crisis was the worst in the recent economic history of nations.

It was also a dramatic crisis of state performance. The government could not manage its international economic relations effectively and this in turn had significant domestic economic and political consequences. It could also be argued that its failure to manage the domestic economy and establish effective state–society relations precipitated the international crisis. Clearly the causation was multi-directional. As this chapter will show, the crisis itself was more than an economic crisis alone.

The economy of Argentina has always been somewhat of a puzzle. The country enjoys enormous natural wealth, land area, water, fertile soils, and has been inhabited by a population, many of whose families came from Europe in the late nineteenth and early twentieth centuries. In 1910 at the time of its centennial celebration of independence from Spain, the country had received one immigrant every two minutes, mostly from Spain and Italy, testimony to its attraction for those seeking to go to "America."[1] Immigrants arrived in a place in which the land was very productive, as Argentina became known as the bread-basket of the world, exporting huge quantities of beef and grains to Europe. Agricultural productivity was matched by rapid development of industries and services as the national government clearly pursued its national project in supporting new institutions, education, infrastructure, and many of the components of a new nation-state. Investment, rising incomes, consumption, and improved welfare were the mark of a rising new country. In this almost half century, Argentina had grown at six percent per year from 1870 to 1913, making it the fastest growing country in the world, along with Japan.[2]

Buenos Aires was called the "Paris of the South," as visitors noted its European architecture, its flourishing cultural life, and apparent modernity. This development did not occur without conflict and political tensions, between new classes struggling for political and economic power, strikes, and violence. Today, the country looks back at the beginning of the twentieth century with nostalgia as a time of unlimited hope and expectations for a bright future.

Yet despite this auspicious beginning and its abundant resources, Argentina's economy has proven to be a disappointment in many respects. For the twentieth century as a whole, the country's economy grew at about 3.3 percent from 1900–1996 and falls below the regional average. In later periods, for example, 1972–1981, Argentina had the lowest GDP growth rate of any Latin American country at 2.5 percent.[3] The author, V.S. Naipaul, in his novel, *The Return of Eva Peron*, commented that, "The failure of Argentina … is one of the mysteries of our time."[4] In 1978, Nobel Laureate W. Arthur Lewis commented that Argentina was "strikingly backward in relation to its relative riches."[5]

As later chapters will describe, the country experienced high rapid growth in the 1990s, collapse in 2001–2002, and then world-class growth from 2003 through 2008. The story is one of growth, crisis, unmet expectations, and higher levels of poverty and inequality than might be expected. This trajectory was also heavily affected by the country's interactions with the global economy over the last century.

After the impact of the slowdown during World War I, Argentina was also heavily affected by the crash of 1929 and the worldwide depression, which followed it. In fact the depression intensified the competition for wealth, income, and opportunities within the country, leading to a politics mirroring the ideological debates and organized conflicts in Europe, the mother continent. Political instability in the 1930s and 1940s continued, in what Argentine historian Tulio Halperin Donghi has called "a half century of perpetual political crises that were punctuated by military takeovers."[6] One of the legacies of this period was the increasing difficulty of the government managing its administrative functions such as revenue collection, a subject which will be discussed in later chapters. Halperin Donghi has observed that, "it was this inability (to collect taxes), rather than excessive public expenditures, that encouraged governments to avoid bankruptcy by resorting to high inflation and later to foreign borrowing for much longer than prudent."[7]

Even though the rest of the world was caught up in the rise of fascism and World War II, Argentina proclaimed itself neutral, despite entreaties to join the Allies from Britain and later the United States. The military intermittently had taken control of the country's government from the 1930s on, with civilian politics often unable to manage institutions and economic conflict for sustained periods. In the post-World War II environment, this resulted in coups and eventually the election of Juan Peron as President in 1946. Peron's mass support from an expanding urban and industrial working class led to complete dominance of the state by the Peronist Party during a period of sustained economic growth, until his overthrow in 1955.

The key political fact of this period was the process of incorporation of labor into the polity in a way in which former industrial and agrarian interests in Argentina had previously excluded these groups. This has been described as "labor populism" as a specifically Argentine mode of this incorporation process, which was also going on in many other Latin American countries at the same time, notably "incorporation meant the end of oligarchic domination and of a predominantly agrarian society in these countries."[8] Groups known as "*descamisados*"—those without shirts—were adopted by Peron and most notably by his wife, Eva Peron, known as Evita, who rallied enormous support for the regime from 1946 to 1955. What Peronism meant in part was that the state had new relationships with labor, a shift that took on many different forms in the following 50 years.

The decade of Peron's leadership was marked by the construction of a national industry protected by import-substitution policies, the expansion and distribution of public services including education, health, social security, and housing. The country could afford the establishment of a welfare state, which brought a high level of income and well-being to a relatively small population of about 25 million people living in a vast national territory. From 1936 to 1947, nearly one million people had moved from rural to urban areas. The urbanization of the population was also coupled with the urbanization of the economy. Peron supported this process and initiated a major redistribution of profits from rural producers to the urban sector, largely in manufacturing, and institutionalized in an Argentine Institute for Trade Promotion. In political terms, "Peron attacked the oligarchy but did not destroy it."[9]

This period, while remembered nostalgically, nevertheless could not escape the shifting pressures of either the postwar global economy or the Cold War. Political instability returned to Argentina in 1955 with the military overthrow of Peron, who went into an 18-year exile in Spain. The military leadership of General Aramburu and his successors attacked Peronist institutions and tried to erase reminders of the Peronist era,[10] eventually giving way to the election of President Arturo Frondizi in 1958 for what was initially a hopeful period of returning the country towards a development strategy.

However, as noted in Chapter 1, the economy was heavily buffeted by global economic pressures and was not easily stabilized. This in turn led to the overthrow of Frondizi in 1962 and a series of military governments until 1973, when

Peron returned to Argentina in very different economic circumstances. He was again elected president but he only lived for a further year. His wife, Isabel Peron, became President until the military coup of March 24, 1976, when Argentina entered almost seven years of military dictatorship, massive repression, and the deaths of 30,000 citizens through state-sponsored terrorism. Thousands more left the country to seek safety and exile outside of Argentina.

These turbulent events built on the legacy of earlier and sustained political change. Within the national government, there were 49 directors of tax administration from 1947 to 2002.[11] Comparative analysis of Latin American countries concluded that the least competent bureaucracies were to be found in Peru and Argentina before 1980, the same countries that had had the most instability and that political instability leads to low taxation performance as well.[12]

The military period had several major consequences that contributed to the crisis of 2001. First, the military government literally eliminated the voices of political opposition, which might have led to more balanced support and debate over economic policies after the return to democracy in 1983. Secondly, the military government dramatically increased the national debt.[13] Further, the management of the economy under the Economy Minister, Martinez de Hoz, involved a rapid liberalization and opening up of the economy to global trade and competition, leading to a sustained process of de-industrialization in Argentina, which contributed to rising unemployment and inequality. Thousands of Argentine factories and businesses closed during the 1980s and 1990s.

As noted above, military dictatorship and repression in the name of protecting the country against extremism not only resulted in unspeakable short-term consequences for thousands of people, but it resulted in the physical and psychological destruction of civil society and political discourse. This process must also be understood as a fundamental disruption of state–society relations and as a major factor limiting the subsequent development of consensus about public policies of all kinds.

After 1983, it also became apparent that the dictatorship period had also led to a redefinition of democracy with less attention to economic equality and an almost single focus on formal political rights. While the country has been nominally democratic since 1983—with elected presidents and legislators—the underlying and worsening economic and social problems resulting from the military period had created conditions in which two Argentine presidents were unable to complete their mandates and were forced to resign early. Indeed, an uneasy peace prevailed after the abuses of 1976–1983 were brought to trial under President Raul Alfonsín in 1984 and then later swept under the carpet by an amnesty law, which appeared to be the price of keeping the military out of politics. After the efforts of Alfonsín and up until the election of Nestor Kirchner to the presidency in May 2003, the country did little to address its violent past in terms of the prosecution of violation of human rights.

The economic legacy of the military period immediately appeared in the 1980s during the presidency of Raul Alfonsín as rising debt, fiscal crisis, and eventually uncontrolled hyper-inflation which led to Alfonsín's early exit in 1989. By June 1985 the Economy Minister, Juan Vital Sourrouille, had introduced the *Plan Austral*, intended to stabilize the economy through devaluation, a fixed exchange rate, and a drop in interest rates. This plan, however, proved unable to balance the diverse pressures of salaries, prices, foreign trade, and interest rates. Political pressures from agriculture, the unions, and disagreements among the many economic policy-makers themselves further complicated a difficult balancing act in an unfavorable economic environment, particularly as the impact of growing debt was beginning to be felt after 1982. In June 1987, the government signed an agreement with the IMF promising to further devalue the currency and to reduce the fiscal pressure on the national budget by privatizing many public enterprises.

This was the backdrop to the ascendancy and presidency of Carlos Menem, who promised in 1989 to control inflation and provide economic stability. This stability was assured after 1991 through the pegging of the Argentine peso to the US dollar and the adoption of the Convertibility Law introduced by Economy Minister Domingo Cavallo and passed on March 27, 1991. This "hard peg" allowed security for investors, savers, and led to the strong economic growth from 1991 to late 1994 when Argentina felt the impact of the Tequila Crisis in Mexico. Table 3.1 shows the dramatic improvements in economic performance during this period compared to the late 1980s.

The success of the Convertibility Law was accompanied by the adoption of many measures to further liberalize the Argentine economy, including capital and trade flows, banking regulations, which led to the arrival of many foreign banks in the 1990s, and privatization of public services from water, electricity, transportation, telecommunications, garbage collection, and mail. The Argentine privatization program, while rapid and comprehensive, raised many issues of transparency, corruption, and very uneven results. In some sectors, such as telecommunications, this led to significant and immediate improvements, while in others, such as water, improvement was much slower and incomplete.[14] Most importantly, the security of the peso tied to the US dollar attracted foreign investment from many sources, particularly from European countries such as Spain, France, and Italy, and contributed to what initially appeared as a vibrant, growing economy. Foreign investors were attracted by monetary security and the promise of an easy expatriation of profits. Spanish companies alone withdrew US$45 billion during the 1990s.[15] This period was also characterized by high levels of political support and approval of the performance of the Argentine state. The notion of a privatizing and reduced state very much corroborated the neo-liberal principles of the Washington Consensus.

This picture began to darken for Argentina after 1995 as the Tequila Crisis increased the cost of capital for servicing Argentina's debt and its borrowing to cover fiscal deficits. The artificial over-valuation of the peso also hindered the growth of Argentine exports and weakened the external account, as Argentines imported many products. A chronic trade balance deficit developed. External shocks such as the East Asian financial crisis in 1997, the Russia crisis in 1998,

Table 3.1 Economic performance of Argentina 1988–1994

	1988	*1989*	*1990*	*1991*	*1992*	*1993*	*1994*
GDP[a]	126.21	76.64	141.35	189.72	228.78	236.75	257.44
GDP Growth	–2.6	–7.5	–2.4	12.7	11.9	5.9	5.8
Inflation[b]	0.03	0.961	23.21	63.054	78.754	93.333	97.232
Inflation[c]	388.5	3,057.6	2,076.8	133.0	11.9	–1.5	2.8
Current Account Balance, % GDP	–1.234	1.34	3.301	–0.226	–2.827	–3.401	–4.266
Unemployment[d]	6.3	7.7	7.4	6.5	7.0	9.6	11.5
Exports of goods and services (% of GDP)	9.5	13.1	10.4	7.7	6.6	6.9	7.5
Imports of goods and services (% of GDP)	6.2	6.6	4.6	6.1	8.1	9.3	10.6

Sources: IMF 2010, World Bank–World Development Indicators 2011, ECLAC 2005.

Notes

a At current US$ billion.

b Consumer price index annual average (2000 = 100).

c Urban areas (ECLAC).

d GDP Deflator (annual %) – World Bank.

and later Brazil, which devalued the real in 1999, all increased the cost of capital for Argentina. This began to show up in the form of reduced investment, increased unemployment, growing poverty and inequality, difficulties in servicing debt, and in growing fiscal deficits.[16] Growing economic difficulty led to repeated requests by the Menem government for financial support to the IMF, which provided resources to its "poster child" of the 1990s. The conditions for this support, however, were repeated calls for fiscal adjustment, further market reforms such as the liberalizing of the labor market, and various tax laws and financial regulations. Menem followed most of this advice and, evoking the fear of inflation and monetary instability, continued to promise that despite the country's economic difficulties, the Convertibility Law would be maintained.

As the economy adjusted—in fact contracted—it became increasingly obvious that the government would have serious difficulties in repaying its debt, now over US$180 billion and representing 120 percent of GDP. External markets and rating agencies were conscious of this deteriorating situation, with the country's risk rating dropping by the day. It eventually fell below the risk rating of Nigeria in 1999—clearly a nonsensical comparison—but which demonstrated that, even with its physical and human infrastructure and extraordinary economic potential, global financial markets were only interested in the short-term capacity of Argentina to pay its debt.

Table 3.2 shows the rise in this stock of debt and repayments during the 1990s. Whether this alarming situation was due primarily to external factors or a result of internal economic mismanagement is a subject of extensive debate.

It is generally agreed that the Convertibility period can be divided into two stages, the first from 1991 to early 1995, when the economy expanded at a rapid pace, and a second, a deepening recession induced by the Tequila Crisis, which included changes in the labor market, further de-industrialization as many Argentine firms were unable to compete in now open markets, and a deterioration of the income distribution. Capital flows played a key role in this process, supporting growth in the first phase, and then becoming increasingly expensive and hesitant as negative signs appeared about the country's economic performance.[17]

If there was increasing international concern about the sustainability of this situation, there were also many domestic indicators of economic and social distress. Unemployment was the most obvious indicator, as the ratio of full-time employed to population began to fall to a new low in 1996, even below its 1990 level.[18] This was worsened by the influx of imported goods and the drop in the domestic demand for labor. It can also be shown that volatility in external financial markets was mechanically transmitted directly to the domestic Argentine economy, because the hard peg to the dollar meant it was impossible to adjust the value of the peso as external conditions changed.[19] The consequences of these changes in employment and declining real household incomes included school dropouts, crime, and drug use.

By 2000, Argentina's per capita income in purchasing power parity was about US$12,000, well above any other country in Latin America and only exceeded by Korea among emerging market economies.[20] The country had the highest literacy in Latin America and the lowest infant mortality, with the exception of

Table 3.2 Rise in external debt and payments, 1990–1999

Year	*Total external debt*[a]	*Debt service*[b]
1990	62,232,663	37
1991	65,405,786	34
1992	68,339,299	27
1993	64,428,005	31
1994	74,819,284	25
1995	98,464,911	30
1996	111,077,387	39
1997	126,532,392	50
1998	139,788,188	57
1999	140,344,022	75

Source: World Bank World Development Indicators 2009.

Notes

a Current US$ thousand.

b % of Exports of Goods, Services and Income.

Chile. But these aggregate numbers masked the fact that Argentina was quickly becoming a society of separate worlds.

A 1998 press article entitled, "The Distribution of Income: Each Time More Unequal," showed that the top 20 percent of the population received 53.2 percent of income, while the poorest 20 percent received only 4.2 percent. The data from the Instituto National de Estadistica y censon (INDEC) showed that the bottom 10 percent actually received only 1.4 percent of income, while the top 10 percent received 35.8 percent.[21] Table 3.3, prepared in November 1999, presents what was referred to as "the record of ten years of adjustment." The 1990s had generated important increases in income for many households, but the combination of increased inequality and differences, poverty, the numbers of people working informally, and the level of delinquency all demonstrated important problems, which differed from the self perception of Argentines in the 1950s or 1960s of their country as a prosperous, largely middle class society.

In Buenos Aires, middle- and upper-income households benefitting from economic growth under Convertibility increased their consumption with one peso equal to one US dollar. Many moved into some of the more than the then 300 new gated communities surrounding the Federal Capital District, where they developed suburban lifestyles resembling the car-dominated cultures of the United States. Their lifestyles separated them from the mass of urban and indeed national population.[22] This was reflected in the growing perception of inequality of access to infrastructure, public services, and the quality of living conditions. An analysis of public expenditures within the Federal Capital from 1991 to 1997 showed that 11.5 percent of the population received 68 percent of public expenditures, creating, in effect, "five cities of Buenos Aires" with the distribution of services by neighborhood correlating strongly with poverty, crime, and environmental quality.[23] Table 3.4 shows the wide discrepancies by neighborhood in public expenditures for infrastructure and education.

Table 3.3 The record of ten years of adjustment

Indicators	*Area*	*1980*	*1985*	*1990*	*1991*	*1992*	*1993*	*1994*	*1995*	*1996*	*1997*	*1998*
Unemployment rate	Urban Argentina	–	5.9	6.3	6.0	7.0	9.3	12.2	16.6	17.4	13.7	12.4
Informal employment	Metro BA	–	–	27.6	31.5	31.8	32.8	31.1	32.9	34.9	–	–
Per capita income (top 10%)	Metro BA	29.2	31.2	36.6	34.1	32.5	34.9	33.7	36.5	36.7	36.6	–
Per capita income (Middle 60%)	Metro BA	59.4	59.8	54.6	57.1	57.8	56.4	57.3	55.4	55.2	55.7	–
Per capita income (Bottom 30%)	Metro BA	11.4	9.0	8.8	8.8	9.7	8.8	9.0	8.1	8.1	7.7	–
Poverty	Metro BA	8.7	18.4	33.7	21.5	17.8	16.8	19.0	24.8	27.9	26.0	25.9
Extreme poverty	Metro BA	–	–	6.0	3.0	3.2	4.4	3.5	6.3	7.5	6.4	6.9
Infant mortality rate	National	33.2	26.2	25.6	24.7	23.6	22.9	22.0	22.2	20.9	18.8	–
Delinquency rate	National	80.0	141.9	172.1	148.5	154.5	164.5	182.2	204.3	–	–	–

Source: Clarín 1999.

Table 3.4 Public expenditures in the federal capital 1991–1997

Indicator	*Recoleta*	*Northeast Corridor*	*Central & Northwest*	*Far West*	*Southwest Belt*	*Federal Capital*
NBI 1991 (%)	7.1	5.3	3.4	4.9	16.7	–
NBI 1 1991 (%)	3.7	2.3	1.8	2.6	14.2	–
NBI 3 1991 (%)	1.8	1.5	1.0	1.3	4.4	–
No health coverage (%)	19.5	15.0	14.7	16.1	21.0	–
Pri. school dropouts (%)	0.0	1.0	0.8	1.3	16.6	–
Sec. school dropouts (%)	57.4	34.2	38.8	46.5	67.7	–
Education expenditure 1997 ($000)	45,748	111,616	110,071	146,135	191,256	604,826
Education expenditure (%)	7.6	18.5	18.2	24.2	31.6	100.0
Public investment infrastructure ($000) 1991–97	199,129	215,245	77,219	221,186	294,069	1,006,848
Public investment infrastructure ($000) 1991	87,699	44,571	12,380	22,680	26,450	193,780
Avg. public investment infrastructure per capita in 1991–1997 ($)	306	123	18	33	40	49
Public investment infrastructure per capita 1991 ($)	943	179	20	24	25	65
% Public investment infrastructure 1991–97	19.8	21.4	7.7	22.0	29.2	100.0
% Investment infrastructure 1991	45.3	23.0	6.4	11.7	13.6	100.0
Population 1991 (000)	93	249	619	945	1,058	2,964
% Population 1991	3.1	8.4	20.9	31.9	35.7	100.0
Number of claims due to insufficient public lighting	13	45	99	111	584	852

Source: Cohen and Debowicz, 2001.

Note

The NBI was defined according to the methodology used by INDEC in "Poverty in Argentina," (Series of Studies INDEC N1, Buenos Aires, 1984. Households with NBI are those that present at that lack at least of one the following indicators:

- Overcrowding: households that had three or more people per room.
- Housing: families that inhabited an inadequate unit (rented room, precarious construction or another type).
- Sanitary Conditions: households that did not have any type of toilet.
- School Attendance: households that had one child in school-age years that was not assisting school.
- Breadwinning Capacity: households that had four people per one employed person, in which the head of household had little education.

Within the metropolitan area as a whole, there was a growing spread of squatter settlements, where almost one million people were living without a piped water supply and in-house sanitation. This problem was raised as one of the "great pending issues for Argentina" in an article in early January 2000, where data from SIEMPRO, a program within the national Ministry of Social Development, was presented to illustrate the growing nexus of slum problems which was making metropolitan Buenos Aires similar to the slum areas of other cities in developing countries.[24] A front-page story in *La Nación* in February 2000, reported a 15 percent growth of the population in *villas miserias* in the wealthier Federal Capital of some 14,000 people in two years, reaching 100,000 persons.[25] Some of the indicators of this deterioration are presented in Table 3.5.

It is important to note that growing intra-urban inequality cannot be blamed on the global economy or on international institutions. Rather, decisions about locating water supply and fixing potholes in urban streets are local, largely municipal, decisions. Even though many newspaper articles during this period gave the impression that *bienestar* (well-being) depended largely on employment and that employment in turn depended on the global economy, this explanation was not accurate. Place matters a great deal in Buenos Aires, as in any city anywhere in the world. This will be discussed in more detail in Chapter 9.

Inequality, however, is not only an urban subject. One of the legacies of the 1990s was a growing gap between incomes in metropolitan Buenos Aires and the country as a whole. A 1999 World Bank study, aptly titled, "Argentina: Poor People in a Rich Country," assembled this data and clearly demonstrated the enormous differences in education, health, water supply, and housing conditions between different provinces in Argentina.[26] Jose Luis Machinea, then former governor of the Central Bank, wrote a commentary on these data arguing that they showed "the absence of a compensatory State,"[27] an important reference to the performance of state institutions in addressing inequality.

In the midst of this economic decline and growing social exclusion, the country had presidential elections in 1999. In response to the growing economic and social distress, two political parties, the *Union Radical Civica* and the *Frente para Un Pais Solidario* (FREPASO), formed an Alliance to take on the Peronist *Justicialista* Party in the battle for the presidency and promised to address the issues of unemployment, inequality, and exclusion. The Alliance, led by Fernando de la Rua,

Table 3.5 Growth of population, absolute and relative, between *villas miserias* and informal settlements and total growth of the GBA (1981–2006)

Area	*1981–1991*		*1991–2001*		*2001–2006*		*1981–2006*	
	Absolute	*%*	*Absolute*	*%*	*Absolute*	*%*	*Absolute*	*%*
GBA	1,146,149	16.8	715,113	8.97	573,270	6.6	2,343,532	35.68
Villas	119,559	41.1	184,302	44.9	342,074	57.51	646,935	220.03

Source: Cravino 2008.

a former Senator and Mayor of Buenos Aires, and Graciela Fernandez Mejide, won the elections, with de la Rua becoming President of Argentina on December 10,1999, with Chacho Alvarez from FREPASO as Vice-President, and Graciela Fernandez Mejide becoming Minister of Social Development. The Alliance had promised to maintain the Convertability Law but to devote more attention to the country's economic and social woes, particularly for the poor. Jose Luis Machinea was appointed as Minister of Economy with the intention of increasing the role of the state in addressing these social issues.

The Alliance, despite its political base, which extended beyond the Peronist party and unions, and its clear victory in the presidential elections, proved unable to stop the downward spiral of the economy. As the price of debt servicing increased, the de la Rua government had to borrow more from both the private sector and the IMF, with the latter agreeing only if Argentina would further cut its fiscal expenditures and accept politically unpopular measures. A particularly important episode in this process led to the resignation of Vice-President Chacho Alvarez on October 6, 2000, in protest of the discovery that bribes were being paid by the government to legislators in order to induce them to vote for legislation reducing labor regulations. This legislation had been made an important condition by the IMF for continued financial support, which the government was desperate to obtain. The resignation of the Vice-President undermined the political credibility of the government and certainly added points to the political risk index for Argentina.

All of this occurred in an increasingly conflictive environment. In July–August 2000, for example, a 14-day march was organized from Rosario, some 150 miles away, to the Plaza de Mayo in central Buenos Aires by one of the unions, to protest rising unemployment.[28] This followed a weekend article in *La Nación* entitled, "The Sad Country of Psychoanalysis and Tango," in which it was reported that only three of ten Argentines believed that the economy would improve in the coming year.[29] These findings corroborated survey data from 1999, in which 63 percent of respondents felt that their parents had lived better than they.[30] *La Nación* wrote about "the metamorphosis of Buenos Aires," commenting on the contrasts between the gated communities around the Federal Capital and the increasing numbers of people living in slums without adequate water and sanitation.[31] This situation continued over the following months, leading, for example, to a march in Buenos Aires for employment on December 20, 2000, in which the General Confederation of Labor (CGT), asked for 500 pesos per month for workers and increased government assistance for unemployed workers.[32]

IMF bailout: the *blindaje*

All of this came to a head in November–December 2000 when the government argued to the IMF that without a major package of cash to help service the debt, Argentina would come much closer to default. At the time, Argentina was being increasingly noticed in the US and European press. For example, the *New York Times* was skittish and at best inconsistent in its assessment. In an article on

November 9, 2000, entitled "Argentina, Wobbly, Clears a Borrowing Hurdle," the *Times* reporter, Clifford Krauss observed: "A wide range of Argentine economists say there is virtually no chance that the country, which has South America's second-largest economy, will default on its US$123 billion of foreign debt, suspend payments, or be forced to remove its currency's trading-rate link to the United States dollar."[33] Krauss also quoted then former Economy Minister Cavallo who said, "There is a very exaggerated pessimism outside the country with respect to the true situation in Argentina.... There is no reason Argentina cannot meet its obligations." Less than two weeks later, on November 22, 2000, Paul Krugman, the American economist and now Nobel Laureate, wrote in the same newspaper, under the title, "The Shadow of Debt," that:

> The country has gone into a slow but dangerous tailspin. A depressed economy has led to budget deficits; the need to reassure skittish investors has forced the government to cut spending and raise taxes, further depressing the economy; and rising unemployment has led to growing social unrest, making investors even more nervous.[34]

With the active political support of the Clinton Administration and Secretary of the Treasury, Lawrence Summers, the IMF agreed to put together such a package of US$39.8 billion in exchange for agreements by the government for further budgetary reform. This package was known as the "*blindaje*," or shield, and was intended to provide the government with a major share of its foreign exchange needs for 2001 and thus, allow the economy to recover without continuing to service its external debt from domestic resources. On December 19, Jose Luis Machinea, the Minister of Economy, announced that the government would approve a set of measures, which had been negotiated with the IMF over the previous several months including a presidential veto of congressionally approved salary increases for public sector employees and other spending measures, such as delaying end-of-year payments (*aguinaldos*) and some further privatization of public services. Two days later, Machinea was in New York, speaking with Wall Street investors trying to convince them that, with IMF support Argentina would be able to meet its obligations. IMF Managing Director, Horst Kohler, declared that Argentina would achieve some fiscal discipline by controlling the deficits of the provinces.[35] In fact, the IMF had relaxed its deficit targets for the first semester of 2001. In a Christmas toast to the country's journalists, President de la Rua said the "next year will be one of prosperity." A few days earlier, former Vice-President, Chacho Alvarez, had met with President de la Rua and said that his party, FREPASO, a member of the Alliance, would continue to support the government if the administration continued to pursue political reform, social welfare, and economic growth. One of the last acts of the calendar year was the sale of the *Tango 01*, the presidential plane. All of these agreements and declarations were consistent with the neo-liberal policy framework.

Reactions to the *blindaje* were generally favorable, although there were some skeptics among professional economists and bankers. For example, Jose Juan

Ruiz of Banco Santander welcomed the *blindaje*, saying that it is "a bridge of money which will allow Argentina to pass through the first semester isolated from external shocks."[36] The newspapers reported that financial people began to look at the *blindaje* with "*cariño.*" The stock market went up, the prices of Brady bonds increased, reflecting the perception that the *blindaje* would help resolve the debt problem. Daniel Marx, the Under-Secretary for Finance, responsible for debt re-financing, said that the *blindaje* would meet 90 percent of the country's foreign exchange needs for 2001.[37] The test of the *blindaje* would be if short-term interest rates for Argentine bonds would go down. March 2001 would be a key month when it would be evident if the economy had begun to grow or whether it had failed to pick up, reflecting a lack of internal confidence. The Union Industrial Argentina issued a statement saying that the *blindaje* was an opportunity but that it did not guarantee growth.[38]

This skepticism was reflected in many statements, for example, by Miguel Angel Broda, one of the leading opposition economists, who commented on a report by the Ministry of Economy that had shown that during the third quarter, GDP had dropped by 1.5 percent, instead of the 4.5 percent growth rate forecast by the government. Broda noted that there had been 30 consecutive months of recession, that national per capita income had fallen five percent since 1999, and that Argentina had the worst country performance in the world.[39] This mood was continued in *La Nación*, which noted that industrial production had fallen 5.6 percent in November 2000 compared to the same month in 1999. Further, some 60 percent of businessmen did not expect an economic improvement in 2001.[40]

An editorial by *The Buenos Aires Herald* noted:

> The 39.7 billion dollar bailout package was unveiled with great fanfare on Monday as a bumper Christmas present to the nation but it would be more accurate to see it as a supreme confession of failure. Rather than boasting that no previous government ever received such a huge sum of money, the Alliance administration should be ruefully reflecting that no previous government ever needed it—is being on the brink of default really a source of pride?
>
> The IMF finds itself in a situation where Argentina's problems are its own. That creates a strong disincentive to pull the plug on the country, no matter how poor a job it does of carrying out reforms.[41]

The Herald concluded: "While the IMF loan buys time, it is not at all clear how time will improve the situation."[42] A few days later the Herald wrote, "Most observers agree that this will be the last fresh start this government will have the opportunity to make."[43]

The government sought to moderate this criticism by offering theories of how the economy would grow. On Christmas Eve 2000, *Clarín* published an interview with Economy Minister Machinea who said that growth would come from the construction sector.[44] This would be spurred by more housing loans and reduce the unemployment in the construction sector which had reached 27 percent, double the national rate. In fact, the construction sector had declined by 12.5 percent in 2000. Machinea assured the country that the *blindaje* would open a new stage of growth. But in the same issue of the newspaper, a headline declared: "Without growth the life preserver won't work."[45] The newspaper observed that the *blindaje* would not resolve the causes of the country's long recession. It commented that people in the streets were saying that the *blindaje* made funds available, but these funds would be used to repay the external debt, and then the problems would remain. The paper also noted that Christmas sales had dropped 22 percent compared to 1999.[46]

Thus, while the government trumpeted its optimism in posters around Buenos Aires saying: "*Blindaje* 2000: Argentina Will Grow," there was considerable debate about what would actually happen. For many people servicing the debt was less immediate than the needs of poor Argentines. Hungry people began to march to demand food from supermarkets on the periphery of Buenos Aires, first in La Matanza, a very poor area housing almost two million people, and later in other cities around the country. Most of these marches were peaceful and supermarkets handed out tons of food. One of the few which refused was the US-owned Wal-Mart, which said it did not hand out food.[47]

While the *blindaje* promised relief in debt service, its *quid pro quo* with the IMF was continued fiscal adjustment and cutting of public expenditures during the first quarter of 2001. The IMF approved the release of the first tranche of US$13.7 billion on January 12, 2001. Continuing fiscal adjustment in fact meant that the government was contracting the economy and was unable to generate the tax revenues required to fund expenditures, thus again worsening the deficit. In late February 2001, the IMF released economic projections for Argentina saying that the unemployment rate would stay above 14.5 percent for 2001 and that by the end of President de la Rua's mandate in 2003, Argentina's debt would reach US$170 billion. These projections were much worse than the projections presented by Economy Minister Jose Machinea.[48] Machinea resigned a few weeks later, in early March 2001 and was followed by Ricardo Lopez-Murphy who lasted only two weeks, from March 5 to March 19, 2001, after he proposed that the government introduce charges to students attending public universities. While Lopez-Murphy was undoubtedly correct that there were groups more worthy than university students to receive scarce public subsidies, his proposal immediately brought the students into the streets of Buenos Aires. He was replaced on March 21, 2001, by the triumphant former Economy Minister Domingo Cavallo, who himself had run for president in the 1999 elections and who was commonly perceived as having an exaggerated perception of his own ability to solve economic problems.

Soon after taking office in late March 2001, Cavallo insisted that President de la Rua ask the Congress for extraordinary executive powers for his Economy Minister including spending and taxing authority. In the meantime, Cavallo used his well-developed relationships with IMF officials and Treasury officials in the US and various European capitals to ask for continued support from the IMF Board to allow IMF support to Argentina as well as permission to issue new Argentine bonds in various capital markets, particularly on Wall Street and in

London. The cajoling of the IMF by Cavallo is well-documented in several books, giving rise to extended arguments about whether the IMF had actually been "lenient" with Argentina by not stopping financial support earlier or whether it had been too "tough" in demanding fiscal adjustment, which certainly contributed to the contracting of the economy and the inability of the government to collect revenue to meet its expenditures.[49] The behavior and personalities of IMF officials such as Anne Krueger, Deputy Managing Director of the IMF, Anoop Singh, Director for Latin America, and officials as well, all became common subjects of newspaper articles and café conversation as periodic visits by IMF "missions" were received with foreboding and anticipation of further fiscal adjustment, the end of subsidies, and higher prices for consumers. On the other side, there were a group of Western-trained Argentine economists who were serving in various official positions and who were largely sympathetic to the Fund's insistence on further adjustment.[50]

The opposing sides of this argument also had considerably different views of the causes of Argentina's problems. Some blamed the rising cost of borrowing in world markets, brought on in part by the cumulative effect of the Tequila Crisis in 1994, the East Asian financial crisis of 1997–1998, Russia's crisis in 1998, and eventually Brazil's crisis in 1999, which had led to a devaluation of the Brazilian real, which improved the competitiveness of Brazil's exports and made Argentina's exports into Brazil too expensive for Brazilians. Others believed in internal factors such as Argentina's lax record of tax evasion and poor revenue collection, thus worsening the fiscal deficit. Those placing the blame within Argentina also began to criticize Argentina's political leadership and newspaper articles began to appear asking whether it was time for President de la Rua to step down, following the tradition of presidents from the Radical Party who had been unable to finish their mandates, the last being Raul Alfonsín in 1989.

There were also worries about "contagion," whether developments in Argentina would affect other economies, as in the East Asian financial crisis of 1997. This concern is captured in a *Reuters* article of July 15, 2001, entitled, "Argentina's bark seen worse than its bite."[51] Similar concerns were voiced in *The Economist*. One self-appointed advisor advised, "Dollarize Argentina, Now."[52]

In either case, however, it is generally agreed that delaying significant change of the country's economic strategy, either by abandoning the Convertibility Plan and the 1 peso: 1 dollar peg, or other measures, eventually contributed to an even more severe crisis later at the end of 2001 and through 2002–2003. The costs of delay, therefore, were significant.

The lack of clear support from the international community was reported in a lengthy story in *The Economist* on August 11, 2001, entitled, "Crunch Time: The United States needs to make up its mind about Argentina—and fast." The journal observed that the Bush administration appeared to have written off Argentina while supporting Brazil's request for assistance at the same time. It noted: "The IMF and America's Treasury even more so, have been sending hopelessly mixed signals about what support Argentina can expect."[53] A second story in the same issue was entitled: "Mixed Signals: Poor Argentina deserves better than confused messages from Washington."[54] The point of this message was also captured in a *Reuters* article about the IMF on July 12, 2001, entitled, "Fell asleep at the wheel."[55] The same day, Guillermo Perry, a World Bank economist, was quoted as saying, "Objectively speaking, there is no reason for Argentina to default. Argentina's debt is totally sustainable in the medium term."[56]

The crisis as an event

By November 2001, money was flooding out of Argentina, from savings accounts in the banking system and from liquidated investments. Public debt as a percentage of GDP had grown from 30.7 percent in 1992 to 62.2 percent by 2001.[57] Despite the government's commitments to the IMF under the conditions for the *blindaje*, revenues were unable to cover domestic expenditures. Confidence was falling rapidly as 2001 had demonstrated that even with extraordinary support from the IMF and the United States, another bailout was unlikely to be forthcoming and in any case, if it came, was unlikely to improve the situation.

Capital flight continued, with many of the richest and most informed Argentines continuing to move large sums outside the country. An article one year later even showed that government officials involved in economic management also moved some portion of their personal holdings to off-shore accounts. In 2001, some US$18 billion left the country.[58] In order to stop this hemorrhage, on December 1, 2001, Economy Minister Cavallo announced controls and restrictions on foreign exchange transactions, thereby ending the Convertibility regime, which he himself had established in 1991. Four days later, the IMF recommended to its Board not to approve another US$1.2 billion loan to Argentina to meet external payments. Two weeks later, Cavallo set a limit on bank withdrawals known as the *corralito*, which restricted people from taking more than US$250 per week out of their accounts. This drastic measure led to immediate mass protests in front of banks and to nightly *cacerolazos*, street demonstrations where people would bang pots together. This mostly middle-class protest was vociferous and widespread, sparking further demonstrations against the government. It led to Cavallo's resignation on December 19, 2001, one day before President de la Rua resigned as well. The growing protests and attacks on supermarkets during the previous week had led the president to declare a state of siege for 30 days on December 19 in response to the chaos in the streets. On December 20, 26 people participating in the protests died as the police and army sought to restore order and ended up shooting protesters.

In the dramatic two weeks that followed, Argentina had five presidents, including de la Rua. The first of these was Senate Leader Ramon Puerta, who was constitutionally next in succession to the President. Puerta was president for 24 hours and then turned the position over to Senator Adolfo Rodriguez Saa, who was designated as interim President by the Peronist Party for three months. His presidency lasted one week. During this time, Saa took the dramatic step on December 23, 2001, of suspending payment on Argentina's external debt. The country was now legally in default to its external creditors.[59] Rodriguez Saa was replaced on December 31, by Congressman Eduardo Camano, who then agreed later that day to turn over the position to former Vice-President Eduardo Duhalde. In his first speech to the nation on January 1, 2002, Duhalde said, "Argentina is bankrupt but it has a future." Duhalde's frank assessment and direct talk to the country contributed to the eventual stabilization of the situation. When asked of his chances of success in stabilizing the country and the economy, Duhalde reportedly told his wife, "ten percent." As noted earlier, on January 3, 2002, President Duhalde devalued the peso and delinked the tariffs for public services from the US dollar. Two days later, he established a new monetary framework, which included a new dual exchange rate: AR$1/US$1.40 for commercial operations and a floating rate for other operations.

The crisis, however, was much more than an economic crisis or a default on Argentina's debt. It represented a failure by the then weak Argentine democracy to address continuing political, economic, and social problems. One observer questioned the efficacy of democracy, noting that: "After almost nineteen years of democracy, it has been the framework and scenario of a long process of institutional deterioration, social exclusion, and growing inequality."[60] Yet at the same time, the period of Convertibility was perceived by many people as a time of relative stability—at least of prices and currencies. It was supported by the fear of returning to the period of the "*hiper*" or hyperinflation of 1989–1990, when prices increased from the time a person entered a supermarket to when he or she left. It represented an artificial support—at least for the middle and upper classes—for a time, even if it was not sustainable. And as mentioned above, the income distribution tilted sharply towards the rich.

Before turning to the immediate consequences of the events of December 20, 2001, it is useful to compare the economy in 2001 with its condition a decade earlier. Among the important changes was the fact that unemployment had increased from 6.3 percent in early 1991 to 14.7 percent by late 2000. Full-time employment had dropped by 1.8 percent. The only sector to generate full-time jobs was financial services. Per capita real income was nine percent higher, and average earnings of employed workers rose by less than ten percent, but the income distribution had significantly worsened, as reflected in the Gini coefficient. All of these developments, however, preceded the events of December 2001 and should be viewed as the results of the deep and worsening recession resulting from the Convertibility Plan.[61] And yet, no politicians had suggested that Argentina get out of the Convertibility framework.[62] Even though the consequences of the economic policy framework were visible, no one wanted to say that the emperor had no clothes.[63] Margarita Gutman wrote:

> It is not true that the storm arrived without warnings. Nor is it true that these explanations appeared suddenly. On the contrary, there were warnings, commentaries, opinions, and criticisms in public and private debates and publications. What was missing was a large receptive audience prepared to listen and repeat them.... This is what was missing before December 2001: an extended and intense public debate.[64]

She further argued that in fact the events of December 2001 were not a crisis, but rather a continuation of a process of 25 years. She asked, "Can it be described as a crisis if it is only the tip of an iceberg which has been growing since the mid-1970s?"[65]

Understanding what happened

Previous pages have explained the origin and coming of the crisis of December 2001. Yet, there are divergent explanations by economists who have studied the crisis. In 2003, William Cline, an American economist, described the 2001 event as a "perfect storm" and "3D collapse: default, devaluation, and depression."[66] Table 3.6 was developed by Cline to show the divergent views of 12 different studies of the crisis. Each assigns different weights to the factors explaining Argentina's collapse: fiscal problems, the role of Convertibility, external shocks, political shocks, rigidity of labor costs and regulations, and mistakes by the IMF.[67] Table 3.6 demonstrates that there was no real consensus in the diagnoses of these economists, with most assigning blame to some combination of domestic management errors, the rigidity of Convertibility, and the effects of external shocks. Among the economists, only Nobel laureate Joseph Stiglitz assigned high importance to the mistakes of the IMF, noting that IMF insistence for fiscal tightening worsened the recession by speeding the contraction of the economy.[68]

Cline himself observed that the country was vulnerable due to its large debt, its inadequate fiscal adjustment, and rigidities from an over-valued peso. Despite these vulnerabilities, the country might have avoided this 3D collapse but for "the inflammatory interaction of domestic political shocks and external credit market pricing."[69] Some economists felt that the country's historical inability to manage its fiscal balances was a key explanatory factor. Even though other economists challenged this view, it is nevertheless true that the country was unable to raise reasonably-priced funds in external credit markets. Moreover, even if public expenditures were not wildly out of line, the growing recession meant that revenues could not keep up with spending and debt service. Increasingly the sustainability of Argentina's debt payments was called into question, as growth was not sufficient to reduce debt to GDP ratios. Accordingly, external credits continued to increase the cost of borrowing.

An important policy conclusion from this fiscal analysis is that Argentina should have built a surplus of funds in the good years, before 1995, and later in the recovery period of 1996–1998. This would have reduced vulnerability to external shocks and helped to keep the price of borrowing at a lower level. Cline noted that this conclusion, however, does not absolve the IMF from the strong criticism of Stiglitz, among others, who argued that the IMF was wrong to press for fiscal contraction.[70] This criticism, for example, was well-articulated by Stiglitz in a lecture at the New School in New York in April 2002, when he asked why had the IMF sought fiscal contraction for Argentina when the managers of the economies of every developed country knew that the recipe for recession was

Table 3.6 Main causes of Argentina's economic collapse: alternative diagnoses

Economist	*Fiscal*	*Currency board*	*External shocks*	*Political shocks*	*Labor rigidity*	*IMF mistakes*
Calvo-Izquierdo-Talvi	M	M	H	–	L	N
Corrales	L	N	(H)	H	L	(H)
Hausmann-Velasco	L	H	H	L	L	N
Krueger	H	H	M	–	M	N
Mussa	H	L	M	–	L	N
Perry-Serven	H	H	M	–	L	N
Porzecanski	L	H	M	–	–	–
Pou	L	N	M	H	H	L
Powell	M	M	M	H	L	N
Stiglitz	N	H	M	–	L	H
Teijeiro	H	L	L	M	L	N
Cline	M	M	M	H	L	N

Source: Cline, 2003, *Restoring Growth in Argentina*, p. 11.

Note
Impact: H = high, M = medium, L = low, N = no.

more spending, not less. He commented that either the IMF economists were "bad economists" or there was some other agenda being pursued.[71]

Another explanation for the crisis focused on the consequences of the Convertibility Plan, which both over-valued the peso and reduced the competitiveness of Argentine exports. These results undermined the domestic economy and contributed to the country's growing debt. While the hard peg of the peso to the dollar contained domestic inflation, its other results contributed to the vulnerability of the economy to external shocks such as the need to raise foreign exchange to service the country's debt. The political possibility of devaluing the peso to spur exports was zero before December 2001. The Alliance Government of President de la Rua could not contemplate such a drastic move, which would have generated enormous middle- and upper-class opposition. The government unhappily accepted a higher country risk premium and sought to borrow externally on that basis.

It is also clear that external shocks contributed to the collapse: a stronger US dollar, the devaluation of the Brazilian real, the halt in market capital, and the surge in rates for borrowing, all played an important role.[72] Cline's overall conclusion, however, was that with these heavy vulnerabilities, the key factor which pushed the country over the cliff was political. He relied on the argument of Javier Corrales that de la Rua lost the support of his own party and that Argentina became a "state without a party."[73] The growing fissures in the Alliance, from the resignation of Vice-President Chacho Alvarez in October 2000 and the resignations of three economy ministers in 2001 all fueled the perception that de la Rua faced opposition not only from the Peronists, but perhaps more importantly from within his own Alliance of the Radical Civic Party and FREPASO. It is clear that political unraveling fueled the collapse of market confidence in the government. Given the earlier histories of presidential resignations in the face of economic crises, this process set the stage for de la Rua's resignation in 2001.

The final explanatory factor for the collapse was the role of the IMF, the leading conveyor of neo-liberal advice. As noted earlier, there are divergent views about whether the IMF was too tough or too lenient on Argentina. But there are other more specific questions, which Cline articulated well about the role of the IMF:

- Was the IMF too lenient in its conditionality before the collapse?
- Did the IMF give the wrong advice, particularly in pushing for excessive fiscal adjustment?
- Was the IMF wrong to have provided another round of financial support in August 2001?
- Did the IMF's large outstanding claim on Argentina place it in a "lender's trap" in which it cannot impose strict conditions because its own portfolio will be affected?[74]

These questions retained a continuing importance when the period of 2002–2003 is assessed as the IMF refused to negotiate a new agreement with Argentina.

On the first question, it is important to note that Argentina had had seven major IMF programs starting in 1992. Through this period the country consistently failed to meet the agreed targets. The IMF eventually and repeatedly relented in the face of criticism that the targets had been too demanding and were unachievable. It is clear that this external pressure on the IMF itself was significant, particularly after its inability to halt the East Asian financial crisis in 1997–1998. Cline argued that finally the IMF was too lenient in not insisting that Argentina build up a surplus during the high-growth years. On the all-important second question of fiscal adjustment, he disagreed with Stiglitz and said that the IMF was not too harsh in seeking fiscal adjustment.[75] He also disagrees with IMF insiders such as Michael Mussa that the IMF should not have tried to help Argentina with new money in August 2001, saying that the costs of a potential default were too high. He agreed with the then US Treasury Secretary, Paul O'Neill, who argued that some IMF disbursements might help towards restoring market confidence. He also did not agree that the IMF was in a lender's trap, because it had considerable freedom of maneuver.

Standing back from these many arguments, a few conclusions about the process of crisis and recovery itself deserve examination. Argentine economist Jose Maria Fanelli offered several general conclusions about this process, which were to be prophetic as well for the next period. These included the following:

a Although the 1989 hyperinflationary crisis did foster reforms, the Argentine case suggests that crises do not necessarily produce good-quality policies; crisis-induced institutional, distributional, macro-economic, and political disarray created path-dependence effects that severely constrained society's institution-building ability.
b After hyperinflation, it was necessary to build institutions to ensure sustainable macroeconomic fundamentals. "Convertibility" was an institutional shortcut towards the building of such institutions but it did not work."
c The characteristics of the polity influenced sustainability.
d After the demise of the reforms, not only the government's legitimacy but also that of the international players weakened. It is no wonder that the ensuing government adopted an anti-reform discourse.[76]

All of this sets the context for the next stage in this drama, which was the interregnum of President Eduardo Duhalde in 2002–2003 and his government's efforts to stabilize the economy after default and devaluation.

4 Stabilization in 2002

Stopping the free fall into poverty

Fires were burning in the streets every night in Buenos Aires in January 2002. Drivers had to avoid burning tires and demonstrations on street corners. *Cacerolazos* and marchers occupied avenues and boulevards. The summer heat was fueled by burning torches and angry people. These were some of the immediate consequences of the crisis of December 2001. The important-sounding measures, changes of occupants of high office, and the international outcry in response to default and the halt in payments for Argentina's debt all received external attention as Argentina immediately became a symbol of collapse and chaos in the world press.

But this crisis meant more than that. It was the culmination of a process of economic decline in which Argentines were forced to recognize that the way they had organized political and economic life did not work. It was psychological as much as economic, and each of these spheres interacted with and depended upon each other. How people felt—shocked, angry, depressed, in denial, and finally deeply hurt—affected how they behaved as economic and political actors. The surge of protest in the streets—some 13,000 protest marches from 2002 to mid-2003—demonstrated the need to express their feelings about the impacts of economic collapse and their opposition to government policies. The battle cry at this time was, "*Que Se Vayan Todos*"—"throw them all out," referring to the politicians.

The reaction of Argentines was not simply to be angry and to protest. It quickly evolved into many new behaviors and forms of social, political, and economic organization. This adaptive behavior emerged out of the need for survival for some—with barter clubs in Buenos Aires in which eventually about two million people participated[1]—to the creation of *asambleas* barriales,[2] or neighborhood assemblies to identify neighborhood problems and to find solutions, to the estimated 100,000 *cartoneros*, who, in the absence of other work, descended on the Federal Capital each night and collected, transported, and recycled huge amounts of refuse.[3] If national and local government institutions were not functioning properly, how could people help themselves?

The response was stunning. What emerged were new forms of micro-political behavior in a country in which, as suggested in Chapter 3, had largely seen civil society organizations wiped out during the military dictatorship from 1976 to

1982. The capacities of a well-educated population at all income levels to adapt to new circumstances were extraordinary to observe and for many, simply inspiring and a source of pride. These new forms of action co-existed with patterns of crisis management by the government, with continued criticism of Argentina by external observers and institutions, and what appears, with hindsight, to have been a set of careful decisions, which helped to move the economy towards its eventual reactivation.

This chapter presents these various parallel processes and then focuses on three major aspects of 2002: the social and economic impact of the recession, the political interactions among various players, including the unions, the *piqueteros*, and formal institutions, and the gradual improvement of the economy and particularly, the business perception of this process. These three perspectives on the events of 2002 can also be seen as shifts in state–society relations, a critical component of state performance itself, as noted earlier in Chapter 2, in the discussion of the work of Peter Evans.

What is intriguing about the governmental decisions, which were taken in 2002, and their subsequent impacts, is how they cumulatively contributed to changing Argentina from its shocked state in January 2002 to a more positive outlook by January 2003. What is apparent and needs to be stressed at the outset is that multiple simultaneous processes were going on, which helped the country to stabilize itself by the end of 2002. This is not just a story about effective politicians and economic managers, or even of cooperation between the two groups. Nor is it a story about a well-organized civil society, which stepped into the breach. Rather, it is about multiple, parallel, sometimes conflicting, but finally, complementary paths of behavior, which allowed the other to succeed as well, despite a hostile and disapproving external environment. It is this multiplicity of behaviors, which is perhaps the most unusual, and least recognized aspect of the economic and political recovery of 2002–2003.

January–August 2002: collapse and depression

As noted in Chapter 2, President Duhalde took office on January 1, 2002, with his term to extend to December 2003. He immediately announced in a speech to the Congress that he would not be a presidential candidate in 2003. He also confirmed the decision of interim President Rodriguez-Saa to default on Argentina's external debt payments. On January 3, 2002, he announced the devaluation of the peso and observed that the economic damage to the country had come from "an alliance of political power with financial power." Seeking above all to buy time and to stabilize the economy, Duhalde proposed to freeze all rents and private contracts for 180 days and to seek power for the state to fix maximum prices for essential items such as medicines and fuel. This Economic Emergency Law, including the devaluation of the peso and the establishment of the dual exchange rate, was approved by the Congress on January 5, 2002.

These measures, however, did not mollify the populace, which was struggling first without the money from their own bank accounts but also, from the impact of their currency being worth one-third of its previous value. Continuing *cacerolazos* and demonstrations in front of the Congress and in the Plaza de Mayo led the government to relax the strict 250 peso per week withdrawal limit on January 17, 2002. Two weeks later on February 2, 2002 the Supreme Court declared the limit on deposit withdrawals to be unconstitutional. On February 4, the government announced the "*pesificación*" of the economy as a whole. By February 11, the AR$1 was worth US$0.50, but it then began to drop, eventually reaching almost AR$4 to US$1 in May 2002, thereafter stabilizing to about AR$3 to US$1 by October 2003.

What is striking about this first month's efforts at stabilization is the enormous criticism of Argentina by the external media: the *New York Times*, the *Financial Times*, and European newspapers as well. The editorial boards of these global newspapers immediately blamed the Argentine political class and the governments of de la Rua and then, Duhalde. For example, the *Financial Times* wrote on January 4, 2002:

> Argentina's political and economic transition in the two weeks since President Fernando de la Rua's resignation has been badly mismanaged. The consequences for the country and the world are ominous…
>
> Contrary to a view commonly held in Buenos Aires, Argentina is not suffering a Keynesian crisis that requires stimulation of domestic demand.… The situation is aggravated by domestic capital flight, caused by the imminent collapse of the currency regime and the weak banking system.
>
> Stimulating domestic demand is not the solution. Instead, stimulating foreign demand via a competitive exchange rate and re-establishing financial stability are essential.…
>
> Without access to international finance and with a much more closed economy, Argentina should expect a substantial depreciation.
>
> Rather it should seize the opportunity to create jobs in agriculture, industry, and tourism and adopt an aggressive trade integration strategy…
>
> Argentina should not seek debt forgiveness from the International Monetary Fund, the World Bank, or the Inter-American development Bank. It should not run into arrears with these institutions either. Instead, it should gain their continued financial support as it negotiates a private debt restructuring with a large write-down.[4]

The value of this advice will be evaluated later in this book. Another European newspaper from Stockholm, *Dagens Nyheter*, placed the crisis into a much broader political and historical framework. It attacked "five myths about Argentina":

> Myth 1: The uprisings during the past few weeks were spontaneous expressions of popular opinion." The newspaper argued that looting was encouraged by the political opposition.

> Myth 2: It was Argentina's dangerous foreign debt that broke its back." The newspaper asserted that the quantity of debt compared to GDP was not so much, but simply its overvalued currency inhibited sufficient exports.
>
> Myth 3: Argentina is a rich country, and its missing prosperity is one of the great paradoxes of global politics." The paper said this view is a "folk-tale" and reflects an "antiquated nineteenth century definition of wealth based on ore, meat, and wheat, and that today the key to wealth is knowledge and technical development..." a desert with good scientists can produce more wealth than a cornucopia of raw materials. Holland, Japan, and Taiwan are rich countries. Argentina is poor.
>
> Myth 4: This sad development came about because world markets are unfair to Third World countries.... While Argentina slipped on the world market, its neighbors, whose original lot was even worse, moved forward."
>
> Myth 5: It is the IMF and the behavior of the creditors that brought Argentina to its knees. This untruth is the only one of the prevailing myths that holds a grain of truth ... the IMF helped Argentina secure new loans to back up its currency. When this venture misfired and the peso collapsed in autumn, the IMF washed its hands and changed hats to become the bankruptcy receiver.[5]

This editorial is also a good indicator of the anger in Sweden toward Argentina.

But the reactions from Europe were less important than the shift in policy of the United States vis-à-vis Argentina. the *New York Times* headlined a January 5, 2002, article, "Bush's Policy on Argentina Signals Shift in Approach." The newspaper explained that Mr. Bush had made the "decision ... to let Argentina suffer the consequences of its own economic mismanagement ... [and] Argentina had not heeded repeated warnings that its policies were leading to financial disaster." The newspaper wrote:

> Mr. Bush's aides have adopted a policy some call "tough love," meant to reverse the expectations in capitals around the world that if you are big enough, or strategically important, Washington will always find a way to prevent fiscal and political collapse.
>
> The hard line on Argentina, White House and Treasury officials say, was calculated to send the message that under the Bush administration, the United States would be a reluctant financial firefighter and that the markets should not bet on a bailout...
>
> Treasury officials in the Clinton era never shied away from dispensing a steady stream of advice to countries on the condition that they would have to meet to get Western aid. In contrast, during the Argentina crisis, Treasury Secretary Paul H. O'Neill was nearly invisible rarely commenting on the country's approaching default, or the violent protests that led to the resignation of President Fernando de la Rua.

> Mr. Bush's approach carries considerable risks. There is every possibility that Argentina's new government will abandon the free-market leanings, tight fiscal and banking controls the country embraced with the International Monetary Fund support over the last decade.[6]

The next day, the *New York Times* published an article by Mariano Grondona, a conservative Argentine journalist, entitled, "One Last Chance for Argentina's Politicians," in which he described the first days of the Duhalde administration, criticizing it before it had barely started:

> Mr. Duhalde represents the establishment that has already gotten Argentina into so much trouble ... The government is taking the economy into its hands and away from the programs required by the International Monetary Fund. The government, by following this course, will not be able to shift blame to foreign institutions; nor will it be able to count on their help.
>
> In these circumstances, simply making it through the next two years without dramatic instability would be an admirable achievement. But if the Duhalde administration fails, it is probable that Argentina will polarize into a left and right, the first in search of a Chavez and the second looking for its Fujimori – returning us to the political chaos of decades past."[7]

Together, these two articles articulate an American perspective and policy vis-à-vis Argentina as well as invoke the fear of anti-market political alternatives. It is interesting to note that neither article refers to the social and economic conditions facing the Argentine people, or to the poverty resulting from the crisis. Despite the complexity of any explanation of the role of external institutions and advice, including from the United States government, there is a sense of blaming the victim (Argentina) for the consequences of its own behavior.

This position is further supported by the American economist Jeffrey Sachs in an article entitled "Duhalde's wrong turn" published by the *Financial Times* on January 11, 2002. Sachs argued that with Argentina's history of financial crises, dollarization would have been a better alternative than devaluation or floating the currency. Sachs commented:

> I do not know of another nation with Argentina's capacity to abuse, manipulate, freeze, confiscate and periodically replace the national currency and the contracts set in it. The currency board was introduced precisely to break this record. Dollarization would have ended it decisively.

Sachs goes on to say:

> The Duhalde government has shown two very different faces in its first few days. One is rather responsible, calling on the public to accept large

> shocks and fiscal austerity as the economy reorients to a more realistic exchange rate.
>
> The other is the red-hot Peronism of the past. Mr. Duhalde himself has been a leader of this approach, claiming ominously that Argentina's collapse reflects an alliance of political power with financial power at the expense of industry during the past decade. The truth is much more prosaic: the currency board was a good effort that failed.

After further criticizing the new government's attempts to address the crisis, Mr. Sachs concedes:

> Devaluation, with the right accompanying policies, might still work. Yet, in practice, we may well be on a course marked by a flagrant violation of property rights, growing confusion and corruption, arbitrariness and escalating social unrest.[8]

After reading such strong and definite views, it is worth noting that the Mr. Sachs, who wrote this article, was the author of the shock treatment economic policies in Russia and Poland in the early 1990s, which caused half of the population of the former Soviet Union to fall below the poverty line. This perspective is very different from that of the Mr. Sachs who became a proponent of poverty reduction and the Millennium Development Goals of 2000. The contradiction is reminiscent of the description of an economist often heard in the World Bank: always certain, occasionally correct.

It is relevant to note that, the next day, January 13, 2002, the *New York Times* published another alarmist article, this time by correspondent Larry Rohter, in which he raised the specter of "contagion" of the crisis to other Latin American countries and "the spread of an old and eternally appealing political idea: resentment-based populism." Rohter observed that Bolivia, Colombia, Ecuador, and Brazil would be having elections in the following ten months and the Argentine crisis "provides ammunition for candidates who reject the notion, propagated by the United States, that there is an unbreakable link between democracy and the North American model of an open economy, a combination of which Latin Americans call neoliberal…"[9]

Three days later, this cascade of critical comment continued with an article entitled "The mess Duhalde is making" by Martin Wolf, chief economics writer in the *Financial Times*. He asserted that, "Argentina's president has turned calamity into something worse. But it is still not too late to set the country back on course." Wolf was personal and biting in his criticism:

> Eduardo Duhalde is a remarkable man. In two weeks as president, he has demonstrated why Argentina's politicians cannot be trusted with their country's economy.… The government had to reduce panic, not increase it. What we have seen has been almost the exact opposite…

Criticizing specific measures, Wolf writes:

> Still worse, in a populist gesture, the government has turned dollar borrowings below dollars 100,000 into pesos but has left dollars deposits unadjusted. This has devastating consequences for a once well-capitalized banking system. At present, analysts believe this mismatched conversion of bank assets into pesos may cost banks up to dollars 9Bn.
>
> To add insult to this injury, even though the government has committed itself to maintaining the dollar value of deposits, it knows that neither it nor the banks have the funds to meet this commitment.... [He argues that these actions will] exacerbate the recession.[10]

While the voices of external observers of the Argentina crisis are remarkably strident and angry, there were also many strident voices heard in the country itself. For example, Miguel Angel Broda, a leading economic consultant closely identified with the convertibility period of the 1990s, gave a speech in April 2002 about two possible scenarios for Argentina: one, 60 percent likely and optimistic and the other, 40 percent likely, pessimistic, and anarchic, each with different economic results. In Broda's pessimistic scenario, the peso lost its value, reaching 20 to the dollar. In contrast, his optimistic scenario required reaching an agreement with the IMF.[11] Another economist, Daniel Artana of FIEL, a conservative economic think tank, asserted that there was 100 percent lack of confidence in the government and the economy. He said it could not be worse, and predicted that the government would hand over a bad situation to its successor.[12] Outside, a prestigious Argentine Wall Street economist, Alberto Ades, said the peso would go to six to the dollar.[13]

Despite these predictions of doom, there were many other more thoughtful observations being made in the press and among the many people who were actively debating what had happened to the country. Argentine political scientist, Torcuato di Tella, noted that the country had passed a step in its evolution where people had believed that economics explained everything.[14] Recognizing the *cacerolazos*, the looting, and the anger of people, he observed that the real power of the people lay in the coming elections in October 2002, when new leadership could be put in place. If the political leadership of the country had performed badly, it should be admitted that those politicians had been democratically elected by the people. He urged that a "new coalition" be built, like the government in Chile.

Acknowledging that the crisis was more than an economic crisis was an important step. For example, even Pope John Paul II spoke during this period of the moral crisis of Argentina's political leadership.

Graffiti with the message "*Que Se Vayan Todos*", could be seen all over the country, but institutions were nevertheless beginning to work, for example, the Supreme Court which declared on February 1, 2002 that the *corralito* or freeze on bank deposits imposed by former Economy Minister Cavallo was unconstitutional. This accelerated the government's plans for the total *presificación* of the economy which was announced on February 3. This measure mandated that all dollar deposits would be transformed at the rate of 1.40 pesos per US dollar.

The intent to establish institutional stability was given a big lift in President Duhalde's announcement on February 4 to present a plan for a Federal Agreement on Reform of the Argentine Political System, reducing the numbers of elected deputies, having single chamber legislatures in the provinces, and other measures generally seeking to reduce the cost of these institutions by an estimated 800 million pesos for 2002. Plans were announced to further reduce the financial costs of judicial institutions as well. President Duhalde said that his government had to develop a new institutional framework and division among the executive, judicial, and legislative powers for the country. This framework would include reducing by 40 percent the number of political appointments at the national level, limit provincial and municipal legislative expenses, reduce number of elected officials, and reform the electoral system to allow independent candidates. On February 6, 2002, the government announced that the new constitution should result in renewing all elected officials in the 2003 elections.

These institutional measures paralleled continued economic policy measures including the presentation of the 2002 budget, which presented a panorama of extreme fiscal austerity. Taxes were increased, only interest would be paid on some small share of the external debt, ministries were cut back in terms of their budgets, both for personnel and program activities, with the overall budget deficit intended to be 72 percent of the 2001 budget.[15] The economy was expected to contract by about five percent, with an inflation rate of about 15 percent for 2002. On February 12, 2002, the *Financial Times* reported that the fall of the peso had been contained on the first day when it had been placed on floating basis.[16] This proved to be a continuing challenge during the next few months, as the peso approached four to the US dollar, eventually settling at three to the US dollar.

Despite these positive steps, the United States' Treasury Secretary, Paul O'Neill, warned Argentina that without further economic adjustment, it should not expect assistance from the IMF. He referred to Argentina as "a disorganized society where only 30 to 40 percent of the people pay taxes."[17] Speaking to 200 US businessmen at the US Chamber of Commerce, he argued that President Duhalde had to take the measures required. This constituency was worried about the $18 billion in US private investment in Argentina. O'Neill spoke insultingly about Argentina:

> If one goes to a bank and asks for a loan to use at the supermarket to buy bread, grapes, and a bottle of wine, he will be OK for a while, but later the bank will want the money to be repaid, and the country won't be able to do so because it has not created an investment machine with the borrowed money.

Two weeks later the IMF, during a month-long 14-person staff mission to the country, asked the government of Argentina to make a further fiscal adjustment of $3.5 billion pesos, focusing attention on the fiscal deficits of the provinces. The government quite correctly observed that the IMF staff had no idea of the economic and fiscal structures of the provinces and was in no position to understand what they were asking for.

The question of whether the government would attempt further fiscal adjustment in an already contracted economy made the headlines throughout 2002. While the IMF took the hard-line position that such an adjustment was a precondition for assistance, the political and even the economic rationale for such measures was clearly lacking. The last thing that most Argentine politicians were prepared to accept would be further budget cutting, particularly in a social and economic environment, with half of the population falling below the poverty line, with unemployment almost reaching 30 percent, and repeated daily demonstrations throughout the country during 2002. People wanted help, in the form of food, cash, health care, and reductions in utility prices, transport, and other expenses. In hindsight, the gap between the IMF and Argentines inside and outside government in their perceptions of what constituted an appropriate response by the government was remarkable.

Despite this wide gap, the Duhalde government persisted in seeking external aid to help cushion the shocks of devaluation and to help restart the economy. In early April 2002, the Economy Minister, Remes-Lenicov, went to Washington seeking help from the IMF and the United States. He was reproached by Paul O'Neill for not having a plan and for trying to obtain IMF support. As suggested earlier in the foreign press commentary on Argentina, the world was saying that Argentina required an agreement with the IMF before any countries would extend assistance.[18] It is worth remembering here that Anne Krueger, the IMF's Deputy Managing Director, had urged Argentina to float the peso as the best way to return to equilibrium. This was consistent with George W. Bush's statement on January 19, 2002, that Argentina should let the markets work.

By mid-April 2002, the job of Minister of Economy became untenable for Jorge Remes-Lenicov after his proposals to the Congress were rejected and, facing enormous pressure from provincial governors, he resigned in the midst of widespread public and professional debate about which policies should be followed. Both Argentine and external observers were offering a wide range of alternatives. Rudiger Dornbusch, the late MIT economist, suggested that Argentina should renounce its sovereignty on monetary, fiscal, and regulatory policies and management of its economy for a period of years, in effect turning itself over to foreign receivership as a measure to attract external financial support and to assure potential supporters than any financial aid would be well-spent. He argued that Argentina should get external financial help only if it accepted to undertake radical reform. Dornbusch referred to the case of Austria after World War I when its economy was managed by other European powers. This approach was also suggested by Peter Hakim, President of the Inter-American Dialogue in Washington.[19] In contrast, Nobel Laureate Joseph Stiglitz argued that Argentina had suffered enough from bad advice from the IMF and did not need new intervention from external institutions.[20]

In fact, President Duhalde had great difficulty finding another Economy Minister until he convinced Roberto Lavagna, a respected Peronist economist, former official during the Alfonsín Government from 1983–1989, and former representative of Argentina at the European Union in Brussels, to take the position. Lavagna was sworn in on April 26, 2002.

Clarín, the newspaper with the largest circulation in the country, headlined its Sunday Economics Section on April 28, 2002, "Roberto Lavagna: Duhalde's Last Card." The first item on Lavagna's agenda was to see how the 14 points on economic policy, which the governors had imposed on President Duhalde, could be translated into economic policies. They included, among others, managing the shifting value of the peso vis-à-vis the US dollar, seeking to stabilize prices, relaxing and managing the unpopular *corralito*, protecting public employment where possible, organizing the level and process of payments to the provinces.[21] Table 4.1 shows some of the changes in the economy in the first months of 2002, which Lavagna had inherited. A major concern was the fear of rising inflation, which some observers were estimating to be about 65 percent for 2002.

In response to this situation, Lavagna began to move in 11 important areas, which pointed the direction towards recovery.[22] Lavagna:

1 Ended restrictions on market operations for banks, for stocks and bonds, and futures.
2 Reopened currency markets with a floating exchange rate, with moderate intervention from the Central Bank.
3 Began to reform the bankruptcy and economic subversion laws (*Quiebras* and *Subversión Economica*), which differed from law in other part of the world.
4 Signed agreements with each of the provinces on their budgets, reducing past deficits in order to reach zero deficits in 2003.
5 Noted that points 3 and 4 were prior conditions for IMF support, thereby anticipating further discussion with the IMF.
6 Paid US$680 million in arrears to the World Bank, also a condition for possible IMF support.
7 Examined the nominal value of certain prices and tariffs which required adjustment after the devaluation.

Table 4.1 Changes in economy during 2002

- GDP at constant prices = 16.3% drop in first quarter
- Unemployment reached 21.5% in urban agglomerations
- Value of the dollar increased 200% (1 to 3.15 pesos)
- Total consumption down by 12.9%
- Investment fell by 36.1%
- Imports fell by 49.7%
- Exports increased by 3.2%

Source: Ministry of Economy (MECON) "The Argentine Economy during 2002 and its recent evolution." p. 1.

8 Addressed energy supply, allowing imports as well as exports upon which taxes were increased by 20 percent.
9 Introduced measured to promote exports by delaying payment of export taxes until payments had been received by exporters.
10 Addressed public expenditures, continuing tight controls, but noting that normal market functioning had begun to improve public revenue.
11 Began to address reform in the banking sector.

As suggested above, within this difficult and complex political and international environment, the Duhalde Government faced three major broad economic policy challenges: managing inflation after devaluation, finding a balance between fiscal austerity and the need for public expenditures to help restart a contracted economy, and managing the peso under a system of liberalized foreign exchange controls.[23] The risk of hyperinflation was real as domestic prices, particularly for food, increased sharply after the devaluation of the peso. The *pesificación* process had brought many new pesos into the money supply and had contributed to rising prices. This was somewhat moderated by the reduction of the money supply through the freeze on deposits and later extending term deposits. Through the year, inflation was concentrated mostly before August, with a peak in April 2002 at 20 percent for the wholesale price index and 10 percent for the consumer price index, and dropping to zero by the end of the year. In cumulative terms for 2002, the rise in prices for wholesale prices was 120 percent and 40 percent for consumer prices.[24] Freezing utility prices throughout 2002, a contentious subject treated later in this book, also helped to dampen inflation.

The second challenge of balancing fiscal austerity with the need for targeted social expenditures was politically charged. The government ended up broadening the *Jefes y Jefas des Hogares* Program of targeted cash payments to qualifying families throughout the country, eventually reaching two million people in 2003. The World Bank observed later in 2003 and further in 2005 that this program contributed substantially to providing a social safety net for the poorest households. The program grew in size until 2005, when it was discontinued. The program provided minimal amounts starting at 150 pesos per month for households and later incorporated the requirement that heads of households worked specific numbers of hours. With the exception of this public program, the new Economy Minister, Roberto Lavagna, generally withstood the intense political pressures to spend more.

The policies that were followed were a combination of fiscal restraint and some carefully targeted revenue increases. First, despite 40 percent inflation, public sector salaries were not increased. Primary spending declined, which did not help to restart the economy, but at least helped to slow down the rate of indebtedness. Revenue on exports, however, proved to be a key measure which later proved to be highly responsive to mounting volumes of exports, particularly commodities such as soya.

The third crisis, managing the value of the peso, was also difficult. The Convertibility Law of the 1990s, with the peso tied to the US dollar, had effectively eliminated the need for and relevance of monetary policy. However, the logic of devaluing the peso in January 2002 had been based on the conclusion that the economy's difficulties in the second half of the 1990s had resulted in part from an overvalued exchange rate and the inability of the country to increase its exports. Devaluation was expected to have clear and relatively quick benefits on the export side, while at the same time sharply increasing the cost of imports, with the net result of dramatically improving the country's trade balance. In fact, Argentina's imports, which had averaged US$28.1 billion from 1997 to 2000, dropped from US$20.3 billion in 2001 to US$9 billion in 2002. Exports remained at about US$25.3 billion, close to prior year averages. This delayed export response was in part tied to the unavailability of short-term credit.[25] The overall improvement in the country's trade surplus also reduced the demand for dollars for external debt. Strict foreign exchange controls in 2002 limited further capital flight, before their relaxation in 2003.

Managing the peso had been further complicated during 2002 by the issuing of currencies by the provinces. Unable to pay their bills and even the salaries of their employees, the provinces issued new currencies such as *patacones*, *lecops*, and others, which were then used in various parts of the country as legal currency. These of course challenged the Central Bank's monetary targets and judgments in managing the peso against the dollar as well. The Central Bank tried at various times to reduce money supply during the second half of 2002, but this does not seem to have worked very well. Overall, Cline notes an expansionary effect of more pesos in the economy and its effect on the reactivation of economic activity in late 2002 and 2003.[26]

As suggested above, by August 2002, there were some signs of a slowing down in the free fall of the economy and a worsening of the social situation. The three subjects which later proved to be the most significant results of 2002 were:

- the worsening unemployment, poverty, and inequality within the population;
- the new forms of politics and implicit compromise among political forces; and
- the reactivation of the economy and the businessmen's perception and expectations for 2003.

Unemployment, poverty, and inequality

As noted in Chapter 3, one of the most preoccupying aspects of the recession of 1998 to December 2001 had been increasing unemployment. Despite the many policy changes and programs intended to re-activate the economy during the pre-crisis period, they did not generate employment. De-industrialization had been severe, with some 4,600 small and medium-sized businesses closing from 1995 to 2000 alone.[27] Macro-economic slowdown was immediately felt through job losses, as in 1995 after the Tequila Crisis in Mexico, which induced a recession in Argentina and when unemployment had reached 18.5 percent.[28] Growing unemployment had also been fed by the privatization process through which 69 percent of the jobs in privatized public services (water, electricity, telephone, air and rail transport, gas, and mail services) were lost from 1985 to 1998. Some 167,500 people lost their jobs.[29]

By October 2001, total employment was four percent greater than in 1991, but by May 2002, total employment was two percent below the 1991 level, even though the country's population had grown by several million people from 1991 to 2002. Informal sector employment was up 23 percent, while industry, construction, and even domestic servants had dropped 44, 39, and 14 percent, respectively.[30] In the first four months of 2002, private companies had reduced their labor force by 83,000 jobs.[31] For example, car manufacturing dropped by 46.7 percent from May 2001 to May 2002.[32] Many of these private sector jobs were lost in cities such as Rosario, Cordoba, and in metropolitan Buenos Aires. Total unemployment by May 2002 had reached 22 percent in urban areas.[33]

By July 2002, INDEC issued a report on unemployment and job loss over the previous 12 months. It painted a picture of the labor market breaking up. Some 755,000 jobs had been lost in the 12 months period from July 2001–2002.[34] Argentina had some 3.036 million unemployed, or 21.5 percent of the active population. Underemployment had reached 18.6 percent or some 2.630 million persons. The World Bank estimated in 2002 that the rate of growth of unemployment had reached 29.3 percent, excluding the impact of the Plan *Jefes*, which was employing about two million people at very low wages at this time. The Bank reported that of the 14.3 million people in the labor force as of May 2002, only about five million had stable employment and of these, 1.7 million were in the public sector. The formal private sector had shrunk drastically, while informal activities had grown and was employing about 21 percent of the labor force.[35]

Not surprisingly, real wages fell precipitously during 2002. Real labor costs fell 30 percent from December 2001 to September 2002 and the total wage bill fell 34.5 percent. These adjustments were the mechanisms in the labor market for reducing costs and to a lesser extent, employment.[36] This change is notable, but became even more critical in the subsequent reactivation of the economy towards the end of 2002 and into 2003–2004, where the share of costs attributed to labor had dropped, adding to the negative impact of the crisis on income distribution as well.

The drop in real wages also pushed many people below the poverty line. Extreme poverty, defined as those with incomes to buy the basic food basket, increased from six to 28 percent. The World Bank noted that few countries in the world had ever experienced such a rapid rise in poverty numbers.[37] For Buenos Aires, this translated into more than half the population below the poverty line: one of every two people did not have the minimum income needed to meet their basic needs. Among this group, 22 percent of the total population did not have money for food, or the 280 pesos needed for basic nutrition. As noted earlier, this situation was deteriorating as food prices were increasing following the devaluation.

From May 2001 to May 2002, some 2.1 million persons had fallen below the poverty line. Most shockingly, looking back over the past decade, which had included high growth in the early 1990s, the share of total population in poverty had climbed from 23.8 percent in 1991 to 56.8 percent in October 2002.[38] Some 45.8 percent of all households were classified as poor. By June 2002, Argentina had become a country with the fourth highest unemployment rate in the world.[39]

This dramatic increase in unemployment had resulted in large part from the general shrinking of the economy as a whole. While the devaluation of the peso in January 2002 had certainly reduced the GDP by some 16.3 percent, the country had experienced 45 consecutive months of recession starting in July 1998, and the economy had shrunk by 20.1 percent, with a 60 percent drop in investment alone.[40] This was hastened by capital flight in 2001 as well as by the *corralito* starting in December 2001. In effect, the Argentina economy had shrunk from being close to the size of Belgium to the size of Poland or Indonesia, i.e. about $100 billion dollars which is about $2,800 per capita in comparison with Brazil at $3,700 or Chile at $5,000 per capita.[41] Monthly incomes by June 2002 were US$268.30 for adult-equivalent households in urban areas and at US$168.90 in rural areas.[42]

At the same time, the Gini coefficient, representing the distribution of income across Argentine households increased significantly from 0.488 in 1991 to 0.567 by May 2002.[43] This increased level of inequality is a result of the structural changes in the Argentine economy over the previous decade, but also the differential vulnerability of various income levels to respond to the crisis. The poorest ten percent of the population experienced a 49 percent drop in their real incomes.[44] Households not dependent on the local economy were able to do better, and, as will be discussed later in this book, those households with savings in US dollars outside the country were able to capture the three to one windfall in the value of their savings by returning these funds back to Argentina after January 2002. This further worsened the income distribution.

As noted above, one of the factors which contributed to the immediate increase in the population having fallen into poverty after December 2001 was the rapid increase in food prices and the fall in purchasing power. On average, real household incomes dropped 22 percent from September 2001 to April 2002 and then by 29 percent to September 2002.[45] This effect was experienced, like hyper-inflation, with a corresponding drop in the purchasing power of households. By the end of 2002, the percentage of the population living in poverty had reached 57.5 percent.[46]

It is interesting to note that the increase in the poverty numbers, however, also reflected the relative improvement of the situation of the very poorest people, known as "indigents" in Argentina, without any income. By September 2002, some 1.7 million persons were benefitting from the *Jefes y Jefas* Program, each receiving 150 pesos each month. This allowed the indigent numbers to drop with the poverty rate increasing from 53 to 55.7 percent.[47] INDEC concluded that there were 20 million poor people in Argentina, of whom nine million were indigent.

These numbers for urban areas are summarized below in Table 4.2.

Table 4.2 Profile of urban poverty in Argentina in 2002

	Indigent	*Moderate poor*	*Non-poor*	*Overall*
Family size	4.9	4.0	2.7	3.5
Adult equivalent family size	3.8	3.2	2.2	2.8
% Female-headed households	24.0	22.8	32.1	28.1
Average age	23.3	29.2	38.0	31.3
Years of schooling among adults aged 20 and over	7.9	9.3	11.7	10.2
Labor force participation	59.2	62.2	69.8	64.9
% Informal sector	39.0	39.5	33.2	36.3
Unemployment rate	34.9	20.7	9.7	17.8
Hours worked per week	29.1	38.6	42.0	38.7
% Working over 30 hours/week	37.8	25.9	17.5	24.6

Source: World Bank, *Argentina: Crisis and Poverty 2003: A Poverty Assessment*, p. 7.

These data also provide entry points towards understanding some of the coping mechanisms that the poor used to survive during this period. First, female-headed households tended to be less poor than male-headed households[48] in part because a considerable portion of female employment was not in the formal sector. Within households, consumption patterns changed, with reductions in the quantities of food consumed and substitution of cheaper foods. Table 4.3 shows how these patterns varied across income groups.

Interestingly, there is little evidence of increased dropouts from primary and secondary schools, but there is evidence of poor households having difficulties purchasing needed school materials. In contrast, there is a significant impact on health status. The government reported that some 12 percent lost health insurance and thus relied more on public health facilities.[49] 23 percent of families in a survey reported that at least one member of the household had lost access to health services. One indicator was the visible appearance of many people on the streets of Buenos Aires with their teeth in bad condition.

Table 4.3 Changes in consumption by income quintile

Changes in consumption patterns	*I*	*II*	*III*	*IV*	*V*	*Total*
Food						
Reduced consumption	90.4	83.1	73.2	69.0	59.1	74.9
Substituted for cheaper products	97.6	95.4	92.5	91.5	84.8	92.3
Other goods						
Reduced consumption	90.5	87.7	81.5	76.8	68.3	81.0
Substituted for cheaper products	89.5	89.3	80.4	80.2	76.6	83.2
Purchased second-hand products	51.7	40.2	34.8	33.0	24.3	36.7
Dismissed/reduced the use of domestic services	–	–	43.0	27.8	40.5	37.9

Source: World Bank 2003, op. cit., p. 19.

Government social spending

While there were very tight controls on public spending during 2002, the government reduced total expenditures, but shifted its composition towards pro-poor policies. These programs fit within a Social Emergency Program, which focused on the poor through income support, nutrition, health, education, temporary work, and community support. Table 4.4 shows these shifts from 2001 through 2002.

Within these sectors, social assistance saw an increase in food payments and conditional cash transfers through two programs: the *Programa de Emergencia Alimentaria* (272 million pesos) and *Programa Fondo Participativo de Inversión Social* (FOPAR) (16.5 million pesos). The most significant program, however, was the *Jefes y Jefas de Hogar* Program (2.248 million pesos), which had reached about two million people in 2002.[50] The World Bank concluded that the rapid expansion of the *Jefes* program explained the drop in unemployment from May to October 2002. This program in effect doubled the total public spending devoted to cash payments to needy families. Its design was based on earlier work done by SIEMPRO, which had monitored earlier social programs and had a strong analytic knowledge of what it was recommending.

Another area of public policy which had a pro-poor bias was the setting of social tariffs for infrastructure services such as electricity, gas, train and subway

Table 4.4 Shift in government spending 2001–2002

	2001	*2002*	*% Change*
Public sector			
Total spending			
Millions current pesos	96,153	91,111	–5.2
Millions 1993 pesos	91,643	57,302	–37.5
Social spending			
Millions current pesos	59,112	60,962	3.1
Millions 1993 pesos	56,340	38,341	–31.9
National government			
Total spending			
Millions current pesos	48,935	46,091	–5.8
Millions 1993 pesos	46,640	28,988	–37.8
Social spending			
Millions current pesos	28,651	29,587	3.3
Millions 1993 pesos	27,308	18,646	–31.7
% Total spending	58.55	64.19	
Targeted social spending			
Millions current pesos	3,308	6,056	83.1
Millions 1993 pesos	3,153	3,816	21.0
% Social spending	11.55	20.47	77.2
% GDP	1.23	1.70	38.2
Per poor person	240	202	–15.8

Source: World Bank 2003, op. cit., p. 28.

fares. For other sectors such as water, they were affected by first a *pesificación* of all tariffs at a 1:1 ratio (from dollars to pesos) and then by freezing tariffs and not allowing private concessionaires to increase the tariffs. While this was not good for the private stockholders, it helped Argentine households by reducing the financial burden of devaluation and the subsequent inflation in prices in foodstuffs and other basic needs such as medicines. All of these measures were of course accompanied by intense political activity and lobbying by various groups and interests.

New politics in 2002

With these dramatic economic and social changes going on, it is not surprising that 2002 also saw many new forms of political activity as well. Argentines were angry, vocal, and desperate to find ways to take control over their own fates. No longer could it be assumed that the government would or could solve problems. The year 2002, therefore, was the beginning of a political transition following the 2001 collapse of the *Allianza* government of the Radical Party and FREPASO and the discrediting of the policies of the Menem government undertaken in the name of a new form of Peronism.[51] Indeed, the Peronists themselves were in conflict, with former President Menem defending his policies of the 1990s and blaming the *Allianza* led by President de la Rua for the 2001 collapse. On the other side, President Eduardo Duhalde sharply criticized the past and was trying to stabilize the economy and society as a whole. He, in turn, faced opposition and challenges from various provincial governors who were either defending their past allegiance to Menem or were anticipating the 2003 presidential and legislative elections. These various political machinations received extensive press coverage, even though it was not apparent that they truly affected the well-being of a country in economic and social crisis. In this situation, a new party emerged, promising great equity in a new society. The party, "*Argentinos por una República de Iguales*," or ARI was led by Senator Elisa Carrio and received some left-wing support, mostly from Buenos Aires.

In parallel to the machinations of the national party politicians, there was increased real protest by social groups. Government data on monthly protests for 2002 show that there were 11,088 protests from January through May 2002, with some 612,855 participants. These protests took place all over the country, not just in Buenos Aires.[52]

One of the most notable protest groups was the *piqueteros*. Starting in the mid-1990s as a protest against rising unemployment, the *piqueteros* had become very active and present in the country's daily life, starting in 1997–1998 when they blockaded major highways and urban roads at the rate of one every few days. From 191 blockades in 1997–1998, they increased their protest considerably in 1999, up to 766 blockades, or twice a day. This quadrupled in 2001, reaching four per day or 2,992 blockades in 2001. This increased further in the first six months of 2002, with 1,609 blockades.[53]

The *piqueteros* were largely composed of three groups:

1. the *Federación Tierra y Vivienda*, a member of the *Confederación de Trabajadores Argentinos* led by Luis D'Elia, which identified itself with left-wing groups, and which had some 150,000 members and received 100,000 "*planes de Jefes*," with its principal base in La Matanza, a large poor municipality in metropolitan Buenos Aires;
2. the *Bloque Piquetero*, which grouped together several workers and community-based organizations, with 40,000 to 50,000 members, and received 30,000 "*planes*"; and
3. Anibal Veron, an alliance of unemployed workers based in various districts of metropolitan Buenos Aires.[54]

Over time, they received political recognition from the national government and in effect controlled the distribution of many "*planes*" to their members. While these groups were effectively allowed to continue their disruption of traffic and daily life around the country, they actually had little impact on society as a whole and on government policy.

The blockades of roads were also paralleled by *cacerolazos*, or pot-banging, marches during the first six months of 2002. Unlike the *piqueteros*, who were largely poor, unemployed people, the *cacerolazos* were mostly supported by the middle class, which was primarily outraged by the freezing of their bank deposits in the *corralito*. These groups did not really converge in their motivation, organization, or message. Indeed, the *piqueteros* had long felt that the middle class regarded them as an annoyance and had not recognized their legitimate demands for employment. Occasionally, there were some exceptions to this pattern, for example, on January 27, 2002, when 4,000 people cut off the Pan-American highway leading out of Buenos Aires to the north in order to protest unemployment and the *corralito*.[55]

A third phenomenon, the *asambleas barriales*, or neighborhood assemblies, also emerged with great intensity in January through April 2002.[56] People assembled in open spaces and discussed how they could manage issues affecting their own neighborhoods, as well as voicing unhappiness with the national economic and political collapse. It is noteworthy that women played a disproportionately large role in the *asambleas*. Julio Godio described the mentality of some of the participants in the asambleas as saying: "I have nothing to lose." They included all ages, the new poor, the old poor, as well as the future poor. He observed that the *barrio* was transformed from a place of residence to a place of identity and belonging, with the cry: "*Soy asambleista*!" (I am an assemblist!).[57]

But the *piqueteros*, the participants in the *cacerolazos*, and members of the *asambleas*, as well as other political groups in the country, did not seek to transform their social protest into revolutionary action. Godio notes that this reflected what he called, "the moral fatigue of the society."[58] Indeed the protest itself subsided as 2002 continued, with new signs of economic improvement and confidence in the new Economy Minister, Roberto Lavagna. The unions also fell into this pattern, with occasional work stoppages, but no general strikes were called in 2002. In fact, the unions held many congresses to decry the economic state of the country and to call for measures to improve employment. For example, a document from the Congress of the CGT includes the strong statement that: "In 1975, Argentina had 22 million people, of whom less than two million were poor; by 2001, population was 37 million, of whom 15 million were poor. Of the growth of 15 million, 13 million were poor."[59] Nevertheless, the key labor unions supported the Duhalde government.

Another noteworthy development was the establishment of a Dialogue led by the Catholic Church and the United Nations Development Program in January 2002. This dialogue offered an opportunity for diverse groups to express their dissatisfaction with the situation as well as to offer their suggested remedies.

Reactivation of the economy and expectations for 2003

As noted earlier, a growing factor in maintaining stability and reducing incipient violence was the perception that the economy was beginning to start up again. One of the most shocking indicators of the contraction of the economy had been the absence of coffee sellers and small kiosks selling candy and other items on the streets. During the months of the *corralito*, when people were limited to withdrawing 250 pesos per week from their bank accounts, and when jobs were disappearing on a daily basis, most Argentines carefully spent their scarce cash on essential items: food, rent, and transport. As a result, all those people selling "non-essential" items on the streets or in small shops simply had no customers. The contraction of the economy and the disappearance of economic transactions, which fed the demand for, and encouraged supply of, goods and services were immediately visible on every street corner.

As the situation began to change, in small and then bigger ways in the later months of 2002, this positive feeling began to raise people's expectations for 2003.[60] Articles in the press noted that the peso had stabilized with the dollar around three to one, inflation had not gone out of control, the end of the *corralito* had brought more money into the streets thereby feeding the full chain of economic supply and demand, and exports were growing slowly. The crescendo of negative external comment had stopped; even the IMF was being more discreet and less publicly critical. Economic consultants were also concluding that the fall of GDP was less than expected.

Julio Godio, however, noted the existence of a paradox: the economy was slowly stabilizing itself, but political disorder continued.[61] This disorder was expressed through debates over when to hold elections, through the continued assertion by former President Menem that he would seek re-election within the Peronist Party, and through the effective absence of either the Radical Party or FREPASO which had been discredited by the 2001 collapse.

By the end of 2002, in the predictions for the coming year, there were signs of optimism. While the data on 2002, shown below in Table 4.5, further demonstrate the depth of the fall of the economy, the country had survived one of the

Table 4.5 Severity of the 2002 recession

Country	*Year*	*GDP growth*	*Change to Exchange rate*	*Unemployment rate*	*Growth in man wages*	*Poverty rate (after crisis)*	*Change in poverty rate*
East Asia crisis							
Indonesia	1998	–13.1	70.9	5.4	–44.0	13.8	20.3
Korea	1998	–6.7	32.1	6.8	–9.8	7.6	64.4
Malaysia	1998	–7.4	28.3	3.2	–2.7	10.4	21.2
Thailand	1997	–1.4	19.2	3.7	–6.3	12.9	24
Tequila crisis							
Argentina	1995	–2.8	0.0	16.2	–1.9	27.6	22.8
Mexico	1995	–6.2	47.4	5.7	–18.5	53.3	23.7
Others							
Russia	1998–99	–4.9	60.6	13.3	N/A	N/A	N/A
Argentina	2002	–10.9	210.0	17.8	–21.9	57.5	50.1

Source: World Bank 2003, op. cit., p. 2.

most difficult years of its history. In contrast to recessions in Indonesia, Malaysia, Mexico, and Russia, the Argentine collapse had been deeper and broader.

Nevertheless, as the anniversary of the December 19 collapse and departure of President de la Rua approached, people realized that the country had survived. An index of national consumer confidence was even 13.3 percent higher than in December 2001.[62]

The title of one newspaper article in *Pagina/12* captured the sentiment: "*Los empresarios porteños opinan que estamos mal, pero vamos bien.*" A survey of 136 businessmen revealed that they thought they were better off than they had been six months earlier. Interestingly, industrialists were more optimistic than people in service sectors, reflecting the competitive advantage and benefits resulting from the 2002 devaluation. Half of the respondents thought that 2003 would be a year of recovery.[63]

With hindsight, the year 2002 had been the worst of times, with only a glimmer of hope that a recovery was on the way. In the first three quarters of 2002, growth had stopped and unemployment had grown dramatically. The economy was feeling the impact of the devaluation of the peso, which meant that prices for food and other essential goods were going up. Higher prices pushed more people below the poverty line. Expenditures were weak because individuals had their savings locked up in the *corralito* and because the government had few resources to spend.

But the key result of this situation was that local production began to meet local demand, and it was this local production, with its multiplying effects, that triggered what has been described as the first phase of the recovery.[64] Damill, Frenkel, and Maurizio argue that export prices and terms of trade cannot explain the restart of GDP growth, noting that the average price of exports was still falling in 2002 and that the terms of trade dropped further, with improvement only coming in 2003, as shown in Table 4.6. They conclude that:

> Recovery was actually bolstered by the shift in relative prices caused by the devaluation and also by an adequate set of policies that, despite its flaws and ambiguities, nevertheless succeeded in stabilizing the foreign exchange market and domestic prices and recuperating the basic macroeconomic equilibria.[65]

Table 4.6 Indicators for performance in 2002

	I	*II*	*III*	*IV*
GDP growth rate	−16.3	−13.5	−9.8	−3.6
Unemployment rate	–	21.5	–	17.8
Poverty rate	–	53.0	–	57.5
Peso/dollar*	1	2.84	3.73	3.36
Exports	5.6	−1.6	3.4	6.4
Inflation, annual variation (%)	7.9	28.4	38.5	41.0

Sources: Ministry of Economy 2002, INDEC 2003, World Bank 2003, op. cit.

Reaching agreement with the IMF

The end of the first phase of recovery was the announcement on January 16, 2003, that the government had reached an agreement with the IMF for Argentina to receive a Standby Loan until August 31, 2003, to help cover the costs of the transition back to economic growth. The total package of this loan amounted to US$16.112 billion dollars of which US$11.712 billion was to come from the IMF itself and the remaining US$4.4 billion from the Inter-American Development Bank. The IMF's portion included some US$5.112 billion reprogrammed from resources in 2002. The Fund transferred US$1.065 billion on January 17, 2003. While the agreement did not bring much new money to Argentina, Economy Minister Lavagna asserted that the agreement did help to demonstrate that Argentina was beginning to strengthen specific aspects of its economic management.[66]

The road to this agreement had in fact taken most of 2002 and was marked by many disappointments for the Duhalde government, as it had tried to demonstrate that it was taking measures to shore up the collapsing economy.[67] On March 12, 2002, for example, the vice-Minister of Economy, Jorge Todesca, had predicted an IMF agreement by April 2002, which would release US$10 billion from the previous agreement in 2000 and could amount to US$25 billion.[68] Two weeks later Economy Minister, Remes Lenicov, was predicting an agreement by the beginning of May. By the end of May, President Duhalde was saying that an agreement would be reached in three weeks. On June 1, 2002, the government paid US$3.8 billion in repayments to international organizations as a confidence-building measure. On July 15, the Economy Ministry reported that it believed it reach an agreement with the Fund in July.

On August 7, President Duhalde declared that Argentina would reach an agreement on September 7 or 8, 2002. However, this was rejected by IMF Managing Director, Horst Kohler, who, on September 5, said he was preoccupied by Argentina's delay in formulating a sustainable plan. A month later, President Duhalde said, "We will be able to sign in November." In November, he observed, "We are closer than ever." On November 15, however, Argentina failed to meet the payment date of the World Bank for US$805 million, leading the IMF to state that this failure complicated any possible IMF agreement. Guillermo Nielsen, Secretary of Finance, stated on November 20 that there was no fixed date for an IMF agreement, suggesting that it might not occur until 2003.[69] The next day, former Economy Minister, Aldo Ferrer, reminded the country, in an article in the popular magazine, *Veintitrés*, that Argentina could continue to live without an agreement with the IMF and even without paying its external debt.[70] Finally on December 28, Duhalde described 2002 as "the year we lived without the Fund."

This cycle of disappointment ended on January 15, 2003, when Lavagna announced that Argentina would not pay any of the international organizations until an agreement was reached with the IMF. In hindsight, the difficulty of this process involved much hand-wringing by the IMF and substantial criticism from many countries of the IMF and the Bush Administration's lack of support of an agreement for Argentina. Within Argentina, Duhalde asserted that the agreement provided the economic stability required for orderly presidential and legislative elections later in the year. Lavagna pointed out that difficult negotiations lay ahead for the next president.

5 Electing a new government and facing the external world

The traumatic experience of 2002 demonstrated to Argentines the close interdependence of life at home and factors in the outside world. The neo-liberal 1990s had shown that tying the peso to the US dollar and opening the country's economy to foreign private financial flows, investors, goods, and services had brought high growth and relative stability following the hyper-inflation of the late 1980s. Yet, the confidence of the 1990s was shattered in the growing recession, and finally the collapse in 2001. Many blamed this collapse on external players such as the IMF, Wall Street, rating agencies, and the US and European governments. The antagonistic relationship with the IMF throughout 2002 and the frequently-articulated attitude of the IMF that Argentina must pay for its mistakes failed to acknowledge that many Argentines were suffering from the collapse.

In the same January 17, 2003 edition of *La Nación* reporting that the agreement with the IMF had been reached, a front-page story reported that 50 percent of Argentine children under two years old suffered from anemia.[1] Almost 15 million Argentines, 40 percent of the population, were not receiving basic nutritional requirements. This study by the *Centro de Estudios sobre Nutrición Infantil* presented data showing that rising food prices and declining incomes had seriously worsened the country's food situation, particularly for the poorest sections of the population. Underweight births dramatically increased the risks of infant mortality. Pictures of malnourished children in Tucuman shown on television and published in the press earlier in 2002 had shocked the country and had impressed on many Argentines that their perception of Argentina being a first-world country was far from the reality.

The Tucuman situation had presented three problems for Argentines. First, the level of poverty and malnutrition was severe throughout the country. In news stories on November 21, it was reported that three children were dying each day of hunger or of diseases linked to poverty. This was shocking in a country that produced enormous quantities of food. Second, in the province of Tucuman alone, 359 children had died of malnutrition since the beginning of 2002, showing the location of the need.[2] Third, despite both government and civil society efforts to provide aid, institutional obstacles had stopped the delivery of food. *La Nación* had reported in November 2002 that supplies, which had arrived in the Port of Buenos Aires on August 5, 2002, were still in the port. Other reporters had discovered that aid was only being distributed in Tucuman through clientelist political party channels tied to the provincial governor, a fact which had even frustrated the then First Lady, Chiche Duhalde, who had extensive experience in managing food distribution.[3]

The Tucuman situation became highly symbolic, as some newspapers and magazines compared Tucuman to Biafra in the 1960s, an allusion that further shocked and angered many Argentines. It was in this atmosphere of unhappiness with the outside world and real immediate problems at home that the election campaigns were in full swing by February 2003—in the hot mid-summer of the southern hemisphere. The framework for the election had been worked out in lengthy negotiations with senators of various political parties in November 2002. This framework included the earlier end of the term of President Duhalde, now set for May 25, 2003, primary elections to be held on April 27, 2003, and a possible second round runoff set for May 18, 2003.

To the astonishment of many Argentines, who blamed him for the crisis, former president Carlos Menem nevertheless presented his candidacy for president. He strongly criticized Duhalde's administration and asserted that he would return to office and resolve the crisis. Other candidates, mostly provincial governors, argued that Menem's policies in the 1990s had actually created the crisis. Many people could not believe that Menem really had political support, but it was clear that significant support could be rallied around nostalgic phrases, such as "the prosperity of the 1990s." Opposing Menem were Carlos Reutemann, a popular former racing car driver and governor of the province of Santa Fe, Jose de la Sota, governor of the province of Cordoba, and Nestor Kirchner, governor of Santa Cruz province in the south of the country. While all were nominally Peronists, no primary election was held and they all presented themselves as viable alternatives to Menem.

The decision of President Duhalde to support Nestor Kirchner, a successful governor of a rich but small and distant province, proved to be decisive in legitimizing the Kirchner candidacy and focusing attention on Kirchner as the true alternative to Menem. Reutemann eventually dropped out and de la Sota's candidacy lost support. In elections on April 2003, Menem received 24 percent of the votes with Kirchner trailing with 22 percent. Since neither candidate had either won a majority of the votes or was ahead of the other by 20 percent—the two requirements for first round victory as stipulated by the Argentine constitution—a run-off was mandated between Menem and Kirchner. Soon after, Menem announced that he would not contest the run-off, following the shared analysis of the press and most political observers that he could not expect to receive more than the 24 percent he had received in the first round. He preferred to withdraw rather than dilute his claim that he had never lost an election. Kirchner was pronounced the winner by the Electoral Commission and was inaugurated as president on May 25, 2003.

New leadership

The inaugural speech of Nester Kirchner marked a turning point in the activism of the government in addressing the many consequences of the crisis and in seeking major new changes in policies and institutions. Kirchner emphasized the role of economic policy, saying: "The problems of poverty cannot be solved by social policies but rather by economic policies."[4] He argued that a sustained annual growth of 4 to 5 percent would generate jobs and allow real incomes to double in 15 years. He said that his government would follow prudent fiscal policies, improving tax collection and broadening the tax base. He spoke of "national capitalism" in which the state would play a greater role in infrastructure, housing, and health care. It is interesting to note that three years later, in 2006, the World Bank commented that: "The Government has been consistent in its pursuit of these goals and articulate in their elaboration in successive official documents and public speeches."[5]

Kirchner's views had their origins in his experience as a mayor, and later governor, of the province of Santa Cruz. These views were published prior to his election as president and are quite instructive.[6] In this book, he notes:

> The State must recover control of the macro-economic instruments and support a model of production and work.[7]
>
> The search is to combine production, work, import substitution, take advantage of technological capacity, deepen traditional exports, consolidate those which can bring large benefits, and, penetrate specific markets in the world.... We must make a big investment in public works, infrastructure works to redefine the productive profile of the country for the development of agro-food industries, tourism, energy, mining, software and new technologies as principal motors, without leaving aside support for exports of products from sectors such as textiles, shoes, wineries, or fruit.
>
> We must actively develop agro-industries. Agriculture, livestock, and all the specialties within primary sector activity needs machines, technology, innovation, development and invention, and uninterrupted research for the possibilities of primary products and the development of manufacturing linked to the countryside.[8]
>
> In Argentina we must think strategically. We must take into account that there are asymmetries in the international markets, where our products are not competitive. Therefore we must subsidize the producer ... we need industrial policy.[9]

He argued:

> In the decade of the 1990s the market and the economy disconnected from the State and politics, in a tacit acceptance of the end of history and an explicit acceptance of the theory of trickle-down ... I say that trickle-down is a theory of misery. It is true that the market organizes economically, but it does not articulate socially. We need to find "an intelligent state."
>
> I believe in a national project. I don't know why this upsets and preoccupies people so much, because the only thing I am saying is that we must construct a national capitalism in Argentina and that we must generate an alternative which permits us to mobilize society.[10]

> We are the only country in the world, along with Russia, which does not manage our own oil and oil reserves.[11]
>
> I believe firmly in a present State, repairer, protector, promoter, that recovers the control of macro-economic instruments which were weakened or disappeared during privatization and the Menem period ... if the productive system falls and there is no protection from the state, who is going to do it? Last year we saw pictures of malnourished children, a result of 26 years of neoliberal models and an absent state.[12]

These views, both about the need for industrial policy and the need for an active state, which have their intellectual roots in some of the development thinking of the 1950s and 1960s, as explained in Chapter 1, were soon to become embodied in the government's domestic and international policies and strategies. They also established new standards for the assessment of state performance. Later chapters will address how the government addressed the multiple economic challenges of poverty, unemployment, and the need to generate growth in the economy, as well as the institutional challenge of re-asserting the pre-eminence of the state itself. These proved to be continuing themes and foci of policy from May 2003 to December 10, 2007 when Kirchner's term ended.

One critical dimension of Kirchner's leadership from the outset was his careful management of public expectations. When asked about Argentina's recovery, he repeated frequently that the country was in hell and was trying to arrive at purgatory. He did not suggest that recovery would come quickly or easily, even though Argentines certainly would have been happier hearing that recovery and normality was just around the corner. He was careful but also able to take advantage of a likely recovery, which had been the experience in other countries after severe economic crises. Table 5.1 shows that many countries are able to have significant positive growth a year after the most severe year in recession, followed by moderate positive growth for the second and third years.

Table 5.1 Growth after recessions

Country, crisis year	*Year relative to crisis*						
	–3.0	*–2.0*	*–1.0*	*0*	*1.0*	*2*	*3*
Argentina, 2002	–3.4	–0.8	–4.4	–10.9	–	–	–
Indonesia, 1998	8.4	7.6	4.7	–13.1	0.8	4.9	3.1
Korea, 1998	8.9	6.7	5.0	–6.7	10.9	9.3	3.0
Malaysia, 1998	9.8	10.0	7.3	–7.4	6.1	8.3	0.4
Russia, 1998	–4.1	–3.4	0.9	–4.9	5.4	8.3	
Thailand, 1997	8.9	9.3	5.9	–1.4	–10.8	4.6	4.7
Argentina, 1995	11.9	5.9	5.8	–2.8	5.5	8.1	3.8
México, 1995	3.6	1.9	4.4	–6.2	5.1	6.8	5.0
Chile, 1982	8.7	8.1	4.7	–10.3	–3.8	8.0	7.1

Source: World Bank 2003, op. cit., p. 50.

Whether post-crisis growth is high enough to bring the country back to its pre-crisis GDP depends on many domestic and external factors. There is no hard and fast rule. But clearly, in political terms, as Kirchner articulated the issue in his public discourse, it made sense to lower, rather than raise, expectations.

It is significant to recall that in this period—from late 2002 through 2003 to the second quarter of 2004—the recovery of the economy was being led by domestic demand. As prices had stabilized, the private sector could take advantage of changes in relative prices and began to produce for the domestic market which could no longer afford so many imported items. Domestic production grew rapidly and absorbed domestic demand. Exports were still weak in this period. Real wages began to increase after the fourth quarter of 2002. Inflation slowed down and dropped to less than 1 percent for the next two years. Unemployment also dropped due to depreciation of the peso. As employment grew, it further stimulated private consumption and generated more employment and higher incomes, helping at the aggregate level to contribute to rise in real wages.[13]

The recovery in this second phase is remarkable because it was truly domestic and demand-led. Investment grew by 40.9 percent in this phase and contributed to 55 percent of the growth of GDP. Investment came from the growing profits of individual firms. The construction sector accounted for 56 percent of the investment in this phase. The other 44 percent of investment came from investment in needed capital goods.[14] The news was good, as long as the outstanding debt of the country was forgotten. It was in this context that the newly-elected president addressed this outstanding question.

Restructuring the Argentine debt

The president's views and his management of expectations also provide insights and the context in which to understand his strong and aggressive approach to the renegotiation of the Argentine debt. The importance of this issue cannot be overestimated, because the growing difficulties of managing the economy in the period 1998 to 2001 had been heavily determined by the fact that the government was sending large debt repayments to external creditors on a weekly basis. As noted in Chapter 3, on December 23, 2001, Argentina had suspended payment on about US$80 billion worth of sovereign bonds. This was widely described as the largest sovereign debt default in history.[15] The anger of the world financial community was reflected in the many press articles cited in Chapter 3. The world's bankers feared that a default of this kind would not only mean that the loans to Argentina of individual private and public banks might not be repaid, but also that Argentina could serve as a "bad precedent" for other countries facing debt repayment problems.

At the time of Kirchner's inauguration as president in May 2003, Argentina's total external debt was about US$180 billion, or about 120 percent of GDP. If the government had restarted to repay its sovereign debt as of June 1, 2003, it would have been expected to pay about US40 billion in 2003 alone. This hemorrhaging of national financial resources in 2001 eventually meant that even if all domestic public finance were used to service the debt, the country still would have been unable to meet all of its external obligations.

While Kirchner was quite clear in asserting that domestic needs had priority over paying the external debt—a position which needed relatively little public defense in Argentina—he nevertheless faced a united international community calling on the newly-elected president to honor his country's external obligations. His answer came in August 2003 when his Secretary of Finance, Guillermo Nielsen, presented Argentina's offer to bondholders in a meeting in Dubai.

The first offer to bond-holders for restructuring this portion of Argentina's debt amounted to reducing the face value of bonds by about 75 percent. This reduction, known as a haircut or *quita* in Spanish, predictably provoked an outcry from bondholders in many parts of the world, from the United States, Italy, Germany, Japan, Canada, and from Argentina itself. Some of these bondholders were retired individuals who had invested their retirement in Argentine bonds on the basis of exaggerated claims of their return without realistic assessment of their risks. Many others represented investment banks and companies who had profited considerably from Argentine bonds in the 1990s. International press comment was once again extremely angry at Argentina, with additional threats leveled at the country as a pariah unreasonably seeking to avoid meeting its legitimate and freely-entered into legal obligations. References to hunger in Argentina, such as the sad example of Tucuman, were rejected by bondholders whose only interest was to get their money back.

This reaction also came at a time when Kirchner was negotiating the extension of an agreement with the IMF. Argentina owed some US$12.5 billion to the IMF, but Kirchner refused to pay on the grounds that Argentina did not have the funds to do so, and in any case, any available funds would be used for social needs at home. The IMF sought to pressure the Argentine government, but on September 10, 2003, on the eve of his trip to New York, the Fund finally accepted the government's offer not to cancel the debt, but simply to reschedule payment. This agreement was taken as a great victory for the new president, demonstrating his bargaining prowess, and helping Argentina to regain its self-esteem.

During President Kirchner's September 2003 visit to New York to participate in the United Nations General Assembly, he was repeatedly asked if the Dubai offer was simply a bargaining position, with questioners assuming that the Argentine government was prepared to negotiate with bondholders. Kirchner firmly maintained his position, even commenting on one occasion that it was immoral for the government to repay bondholders while half of the Argentine population had fallen below the poverty line and many people were hungry. He even threatened to harden the offer.[16]

During the last months of 2003 and during 2004, the bondholders gradually began to understand that the initial offer was indeed the final offer, and that there were diminishing prospects for negotiating a more favorable settlement from the government. Groups of bondholders formed associations in the United States, Germany, and Italy. Each group sought support from their respective government and introduced legal action against Argentina in their national courts. Threats were made to legally confiscate Argentine property in these countries and to generally make foreign commercial activity extremely difficult for Argentine businessmen.

Throughout this period, the Argentine government met many of these groups, and the Wall Street firms working on their behalf, but refused to soften its position. While the bondholders began to cite the much-improved economic position of the country as a basis for seeking repayment, the government repeatedly pointed out that millions of Argentines were still living in poverty and that unemployment was still over 20 percent. This position received strong political support in Argentina, as well as from some other Latin American countries.

The government issued its formal debt restructuring proposal to bondholders in January 2005, which amounted to a reduction of about 76 percent of face value on many bonds. This offer did in fact reflect some of the demands of bondholders during 2003–2004 and was softer than the original August 2003 proposal made in Dubai. Economy Minister Lavagna noted at this time that, "it has come the moment for the markets to talk."[17] By January 2005, about US$102 billion of the country's total debt of US$190 billion was in the form of bonds and past due interest. The proposal included several different types of newly-offered bonds, including some tied to GDP performance. The value of these bonds would depend on whether Argentina's economy continued to grow. The government concluded the debt exchange in March 2005 and announced an acceptance rate of 76.1 percent of bondholders. This reduced the stock of Argentine debt from about US$191.3 billion to US$126.5 billion, as indicated in Table 5.2. This amounted to reducing the ratio of debt to GDP from 126 percent at the end of

Table 5.2 Debt stock before and after restructuring (in US$ million)

	Before exchange[a]	*After exchange*[b]
Total public debt	191.3	149.8
International organizations	30.6	27.4
Official organizations	6.9	6.5
Guaranteed loans	14.6	15.1
Provincial guaranteed bond	10.2	11.0
Bonds	123.3	60.5
Bonds issued after default	17.8	19.6
Bonds issued in debt restructuring	0.0	37.7
Bonds eligible for restructuring	102.6	0.0
Other bonds	2.9	3.2
Holdouts	0.0	23.4
Other	5.6	6.0
Total excluding holdouts	191.3	126.5

Source: World Bank, 2008, *Country Assistance Strategy* p. 84.

Notes

a As of December 31, 2004.

b As of June 31, 2005.

2004 to about 85 percent by the end of 2005. The average bond maturity also increased from about ten years to 18 years. Further it reduced repayments by about US$30 billion from 2005 to 2010.[18]

This debt reduction scheme was managed by Economy Minister Lavagna, but was widely perceived publicly as a result of President Kirchner's firm determination and hard bargaining skills. Kirchner's popularity and approval rating in Argentina soared to the high 70 percent level in mid-2005 as the results of the debt re-negotiation were made public. In its wake, however, were the 24.9 percent of bondholders who had not accepted the government's offer. These bondholders still held about US$23.4 billion in unpaid Argentine bonds and continued into 2009 to make their case in various national courts.

In its analysis of the government's debt position, the World Bank noted in 2006 that, following the debt restructuring, the government had managed to obtain finance in both domestic and international capital markets. Indeed, in a July 2005 operation, the demand was 54 percent higher than the amount issued. The position improved further in December 2005, when the government announced its intention to pre-pay its total outstanding obligation to the IMF, amounting to about US$9.7 billion. This decision came shortly after a similar move by Brazil. Both actions were perceived as strong declarations of independence from the IMF and political and economic interference, which regular supervisory IMF visits implied. This action later saved Argentina from about US$10.3 billion in debt repayments for the period 2006–2008 and also sharply reduced the country's overall debt burden, projected by the World Bank to reach about 66 percent by the end of 2008.[19]

This positive economic news continued in many forms, at both the micro and macro levels. For example, Felipe Rovera, the Brazilian president of General Motors in Argentina, commented in a newspaper interview in January 2006 that the recovery allowed him to make more investments in his company.[20] At this time, occupancy of stores in the center of Buenos Aires reached 95 percent. The Florida Street mall, whose businesses had fallen onto hard times during the crisis, was fully active again. At the macro-level, throughout 2006, the government was able to keep the dollar at a high rate, eventually reaching $3.12 on September 6, 2006, the highest rate in three years. The Central Bank kept working to maintain this high rate, but its reserves nevertheless grew, reaching over US$30 billion by the end of 2006 and about US$50 billion by the end of 2007.

This period was the third phase of the recovery. Starting from the third quarter of 2004 exports had begun to expand faster, at a rate of 11 percent to the second quarter of 2006. While the recovery of GDP growth can still be explained mostly by domestic demand, the combination of the dynamism of domestic markets and now export growth proved to be mutually reinforcing. By early 2005, Argentina's GDP had surpassed its pre-crisis maximum level and by 2006, the external sector was beginning to help. In fact, by late 2006 activity was growing at 8 to 9 percent annually.[21]

Not only did the economy as a whole improve, but its performance also dramatically changed the fiscal situation of the government. From 2001, when the fiscal deficit for the Consolidated Public Sector was 5.6 percent, the situation had turned to a surplus of 1.9 percent by 2005. A big improvement in tax revenues, coupled with restraint in public expenditures, had produced a dramatic turnaround. Over time, these increased revenues came less from valued added taxes on domestic consumption but more from taxes on high-value exports such as soya. As noted in later chapters, the general increase in tax collection contributed to the buildup of significant reserves, in fact the largest in Argentina's history.

The good news improved further. On January 17, 2007, the country's risk premium dropped below 200 points, a sharp contrast from the time of default when it had reached 7,222 points on August 7, 2002.[22] This was below the ten year low of 280 points in 1996. The economic team of the Kirchner government was brimming with confidence. In January 2007, President Kirchner sent Guillermo Nielsen and his colleagues from the Ministry of Economy to advise the government of Ecuador on its debt management strategy. This support was later publicized in a visit of the then First Lady, Cristina Fernandez de Kirchner to Quito in March 2007. At that time, Argentina's own stock of debt had dropped further, going below US$110 billion.[23] The country's overall position had remarkably improved.

This improvement largely resulted from a strategy, which asserted the priority of the domestic needs of the population and the economy, rather than the wholesale continuation of the liberalization policies recommended by institutions supporting the Washington Consensus. While the default on the debt payments was the most visible component of this policy, it was complemented by prudent fiscal management at home, including significant improvements in revenue performance, which helped to solidify the fiscal position. At the same time, increased production in the local economy resulted from changes in relative prices induced by the devaluation of the peso. These changes both helped to reduce unemployment but also generated increased tax revenues. The latter were important in allowing the government to focus more spending on the poorer segments of the population.

Benefitting from the global economy

Having restructured its sovereign debt and placed its external obligations on a more sustainable basis, Argentina found itself, by the beginning of 2006, in a highly favorable position in the global economy. World commodity prices for soya, wheat, and oils, which the country produced in great quantities, had all reached record levels. Export earnings soared, growing by 19 percent from the end of 2004 to the end of 2005, and then by 20 percent to the end of 2006. Farmers were making record profits and among the indicators of rural prosperity was the high number of Sports Utility Vehicles (SUVs) being purchased in small towns in agriculturally productive regions. Rural incomes were also increasing the demand for other consumer durables and services in towns throughout the country, thereby contributing more than just export earnings to the GDP. In fact, rural wealth was increasing the demand for goods and services in the urban economy as well.

Income growth also permitted the government to dramatically increase its tax revenues, allowing the rapid growth of foreign exchange held by the Central

Bank of Argentina. These reserves, which had been depleted during the late 1990s during repayment of external debt, and had dropped as low as US$10 billion in early 2002, were now growing faster than debt service. They reached US$50 billion by mid-2008.

Accelerating growth

In contrast to external expectations and predictions in the midst of the crisis of 2002, the economy grew at an increasing rate from 2003 to 2006, with an average of 9 percent from 2003 to the end of 2005, as shown in Table 5.3.[24] On a per capita basis, gross domestic product was 7 percent higher than in 1999. The leading sectors of growth were the financial sector (22 percent), construction (18.6 percent), and manufacturing industries (8.9 percent). Interestingly, agriculture and livestock only grew at 1.5 percent in 2006, while it had been 11.5 percent in 2005.

This aggregate growth was supported by high gross fixed investment as shown in Table 5.4.[25]

Table 5.3 GDP growth 2003–2005

Year	*GDP growth (%)*	*GDP*[a]
2003	9	129,597,103,034
2004	9	153,129,481,873
2005	9	183,193,408,941

Source: World Bank, World Development Indicators, 2009.

Note
a Current US$.

Table 5.4 Gross fixed investment, 1999–2006

Year	*Total*[a]
1999	51,074
2000	46,020
2001	38,099
2002	37,387
2003	56,903
2004	85,800
2005	114,132
2006	152,838

Source: INDEC 2006.

Note
a Millions of pesos (current prices).

This enormous growth in 2002–2003 reflects the use of installed capacity and was somewhat predictable. As consumer demand picked up in 2004, it was further stoked by investments in advertising by many multi-national companies, such as Unilever, Danone, Proctor and Gamble, and Johnson and Johnson. In fact investment in advertising increased by 26 percent in 2004 and was expected to grow at about the same rate in 2005. Table 5.5 shows this pattern of advertising expenditure as another indicator of how multipliers were fed within the domestic market.[26]

High investment rates continued in 2005–2006. In fact, the 2006 investment level was the highest in 26 years. Investment was 18.7 percent higher in 2006, twice as fast as growth of the economy as a whole. Domestic gross fixed investment was 21.7 percent of GDP, higher than any time since 1998 when it reached 21.1 percent. The link between investment and exports is shown in Table 5.6.

These high rates of investment were in turn supported by continuing high rates of private consumption, generating demand for new goods and services.

These numbers were presented by then Minister of Economy, Felisa Miceli, at the annual meeting of the Inter-American Development Bank in Guatemala City in late March 2007. While there was some skepticism about the value of official data generated by INDEC, the data were internally consistent and presented an overall picture of continued growth. As a result of this outstanding macro-economic performance, unemployment dropped sharply from 28 percent in 2002 to around 10 percent in 2007. This was a remarkable achievement. Cristina Fernandez de Kirchner repeatedly reminded crowds during the presidential election campaign from August to October 2007 when she frequently repeated

Table 5.5 Advertising expenditures

	2000	*2001*	*2002*	*2003*	*2004*	*2005*
Annual expenditures	$3.180	$2.674	$1.586	$2.394	$3.006	$3.725

Sources: Noticias 2005; Mediamap 2005.

Table 5.6 Investment and net exports

Year	*Domestic gross fixed capital investment (% of GDP)*	*Net exports (% of GDP)*
1999	18	–2
2000	16	–1
2001	14	2
2002	12	15
2003	15	11
2004	19	7
2005	21	6
2006	23	6

Source: World Bank, World Development Indicators 2010.

that when her husband had won the presidency in 2003, there was a higher number of unemployed people than there were votes for him. Not surprisingly, the share of Argentina's population living below the poverty line also dropped precipitously, from over 55 percent in 2002 to about 20 percent in 2007, as shown in Table 5.7. As of 2007, the official extreme poverty line in Argentina was roughly equivalent to US$1.3 a day, while the poverty line was US$2.8 a day.[27]

It is useful to remember that, from 2000 to 2002, the population living in poverty had grown from 12 to 22 million, while the number of extreme poor had doubled to 10.4 million, or about 30 percent of the population.[28] By the first half of 2005, the share of the population living in poverty had dropped from 55 percent to 38.5 percent.[29] By 2007, the number of people in poverty had been reduced even further, by some 15 percent. In fact, the World Bank noted in 2006 that the incomes of the poor had grown faster than the average for the population.[30]

Other macro-economic indicators were also surprising. For example, in contrast to external conventional wisdom and predictions that, following its default on its external debt and its tough position in negotiating with bondholders, Argentina would not receive foreign direct investment, Argentina actually received a higher share of foreign direct investment in relation to GDP than Brazil in 2006, according to the *World Investment Report* published by United Nations Conference on Trade and Development (UNCTAD).[31] Argentina had received about US$4.8 billion in foreign direct investment in 2006, or about 2.26 percent of GDP in contrast to Brazil, which received 1.76 percent, albeit a much larger absolute amount. UNCTAD also measured the extent of "*transnacionalición*" and discovered that Argentina had a higher index than Brazil, Mexico, China, and India, and was at the level of Spain and France. It was nevertheless behind Chile, a much smaller economy but with a longer history of openness and

Table 5.7 Share of population below the poverty line

Year	*Extreme poverty*	*Poverty*
October–1998	8	30
October–1999	8	31
October–1900	10	33
May–1901	12	36
October–1901	14	38
May–1902	25	53
October–1902	28	58
1 Sem 2003	28	54
2 Sem 2003	21	48
1 Sem 2004	17	44
2 Sem 2004	15	40
1 Sem 2005	14	39

Source: World Bank, 2006, "Project Appraisal Document 32463-AR," p. 1.

economic stability. The Report noted that while foreign direct investment is important in terms of technology transfer, most gross fixed capital formation comes from local investment, and that was certainly the case in Argentina. Some of the industries that received this external investment include mining and oil exploration, the latter being 100 percent in the hands of foreign companies, and increases in existing foreign-owned firms in manufacturing in response to the rapidly growing demand for consumer products, particularly durables, such as refrigerators and other home appliances.

Foreign direct investment was also accompanied by funds returning to the country from Argentines who brought their capital back under very favorable terms following the devaluation of 2002. Other funds represented investments by Brazilian companies and private investors buying companies and property at bargains in then crisis-stricken Argentina.

This performance contrasted sharply with earlier "expert advice," for example, as collected and published by *La Nación* in August 2006, when it argued that Wall Street investment firms, including the later to be bankrupt Bear Stearns, were concerned about the difficulties of investing in the country, such as energy problems, inflation, and interventionist policies of the government.[32] While debates about policy were certainly alive, the high growth rates of the Argentine economy were exceeded only by China and India in this period and thus nevertheless managed to attract foreign investment. Another indicator was the improved health of the local banking system, which began once again to attract private Argentine savings.

Finally, the indicators most observed were the twin surpluses: the fiscal account and the external account. By the end of 2004, the fiscal surplus had reached 4 percent of GDP and remained around 3 percent through 2008, as seen in Tables 5.8, 5.9, and 5.10. Government spending was dwarfed in comparison to increased tax collection and savings. On the external side, Argentina was earning huge incomes through agricultural and manufacturing exports, taking advantage of the devaluation, its installed capacity, and its natural advantages in the agricultural sector.

Seeking help and advice

One of the interesting components of this recovery, as presented above, is that it also involved the government reaching out to its neighbors. Despite enormous domestic problems and the considerable external hostility facing the country due to its default, the government nevertheless reached out to seek help and advice and to avoid greater isolation in the global economy. It was also well aware that a sustainable medium-term path out of the crisis was not yet clear. Poverty and unemployment continued at high levels in a country with great potential. Ideas were important in developing policies and strategies to renew growth. Also important were external resources for foreign direct investment, private and public partnerships, as well as lowered tariff barriers, which could permit Argentina to export its products and to earn valuable foreign exchange. All of this

Table 5.8 Federal public sector, balance sheet and financing (millions of AR pesos and as % of GDP)

	2005		*2006*		*2007*		*2008*	
	AR$	*%*	*AR$*	*%*	*AR$*	*%*	*AR$*	*%*
Current revenues	125,594	23.9	140,349	23.6	154,838	23.5	171,135	23.5
Current expenditure	108,355	20.6	117,592	19.8	130,895	19.9	144,076	19.8
Economic deficit/surplus	17,239	3.3	22,757	3.8	23,943	3.6	27,059	3.7
Capital revenues	156	0.0	133	0.0	116	0.0	119	0.0
Capital expenditure	9,975	1.9	13,517	2.3	14,106	2.1	15,124	2.1
Total revenues	125,750	23.9	140,482	23.7	154,954	23.5	171,254	23.5
Total expenditure	118,330	22.5	131,109	22.1	145,001	22.0	159,200	21.8
Overall deficit/surplus	7,420	1.4	9,373	1.6	9,953	1.5	12,054	1.7
Primary deficit/surplus	18,326	3.5	19,349	3.3	22,045	3.3	24,759	3.4

Source: World Bank 2008, op. cit., p. 78.

Table 5.9 Balance of payments 2001–2004

	2001	*2002*	*2003*	*2004*
Current account (% of GDP)	–1.2	8.5	6.2	2.1
International reserves, US$ bn.	14.6	10.5	14.2	18.9

Source: World Bank 2008, op. cit., p. 17.

Table 5.10 GDP growth 2001–2005

Year	*Annual growth rate*	*Per capita income*
1998	3.9	8,002
1999	–3.4	7,647
2000	–0.8	7,507
2001	–4.4	7,105
2002	–10.9	6,270
2003	8.8	6,761
2004	9.0	7,302
1S 2005	5.3	7,772

Source: World Bank 2006, op. cit., p. 2.

Note
Per capita income in 1993 AR$.

could be enormously helpful in sustaining the recovery and building the basis for that growth over the medium and long term.

The government, however, also faced the dilemma of how to explain its recovery in a way that gave reason for optimism and hope, and thereby encouraged domestic support as well as attracting external resources, but did not fail to acknowledge the continuing enormous social and economic problems faced at home. Indeed, those problems were the basis of the legitimacy of the argument for not paying its debts, at least in the short term. In a word, its narrative had to be optimistic and encouraging through its record of progress, yet strategically modest in not suggesting that it had sufficient resources to pay its debts.

Reaching out beyond Argentina itself was also complicated, because the political landscape and pace of change in Latin America had speeded up, as new progressive political leaders were elected in neighboring countries. New relationships had to be developed, trust nurtured, and new realistic assessments had to be made of the costs and benefits of working with each country. This was further complicated by the global political context, which also had changed following the attacks of September 11, 2001. While the United States was less present diplomatically than it might otherwise have been if it was not involved in wars in Iraq and Afghanistan, there was a distinct perspective from Washington and most European capitals that a "left turn" was occurring in Latin America and that this was not good. Many of the new democratically elected governments were quickly called "populist," regardless of their policies and approaches to pursuing development objectives.

This process also needs to be understood in historical terms as a result of the very troubled external relationships Argentina had had during the 1990s. Both advice and external resources from many sources, public and private, had been plentiful for almost a decade, pumping up an economy, its standard of living, but also creating its debt and vulnerability in a volatile global economy. Enthusiastic private investors had bought dozens of companies and properties in the Argentina of the 1990s, leading one analyst of Spanish investor behavior in Argentina to describe the process as "*los nuevos conquistadores*" (the new conquistadors).[33] Some US$45 billion in profits had been returned to Spain alone from Argentina in this period. This history could not be ignored, as the socialist government of Zapatero reached out to the Kirchner government in friendship.

Similarly, as suggested in Chapters 3 and 4, relationships with the IMF had placed both the country and the IMF in positions where both believed they had been wronged by the other. This relationship was important because officially acceptable relations with the IMF were necessary preconditions for official support and lending from both the World Bank and the Inter-American Development Bank. It also provided the key to the Paris Club where Argentina had outstanding debt to resolve.

In similar terms, Argentina had cordial relationships with new progressive governments in neighboring Bolivia, Brazil, Chile, Uruguay, and Paraguay, but in each case the country had also important economic interests, which directly conflicted with the political intention to build alliances and cooperation. These included the price of natural gas imported from neighboring Bolivia, Brazilian tariffs on Argentine manufactured products, honoring commitments for energy provision to Chile, or accepting the environmental consequences of paper mills in Uruguay. Each had major domestic economic costs and political consequences in Argentina as well as in the respective country. Progressive solidarity was valued, but at what cost?

This section examines some of these dilemmas in terms of their impact on attracting the support needed to restart and sustain the economy. It briefly examines some critical bi-lateral relationships, such as those with Brazil, Uruguay, and Venezuela, as well as with the United States and Spain, its regional policies in Latin America, and assistance from the World Bank and the Inter-American Development Bank. While it is not the purpose of this book to examine foreign policy per se, it is nonetheless clear that Argentina's relationships with other Latin American countries heavily influenced the formulation of domestic development strategy as well. Indeed, one of the objectives of the post-crisis government was to reduce the country's dependency upon and vulnerability to volatile external forces.

Redefining bi-lateral relationships

As noted in the Prologue, nine new progressive governments in Latin America were democratically elected from 2002 to 2008. Many of these, with the notable exception of Chile, explicitly rejected the policies of the Washington Consensus as they sought to articulate new development policies for their countries. They shared the objective of seeking to reduce poverty and inequality by implementing more distributive policies and programs. Yet the extent of their rejection of past policies varied considerably. The most notable case was Brazil under President Lula who adopted a surprisingly conservative fiscal policy, which was largely consistent with IMF advice.

However, even while not completely rejecting all prior economic policy, these governments needed to take control of the instruments of macro-economic policy to promote growth, while also developing social programs in education, health, nutrition, infrastructure such as water supply and sanitation, housing, and regional development of lagging regions. They also had to devise strategies and policies to manage labor markets, financial markets, and external relationships.

The task of governing in any circumstance is immense. For new leaders without prior experience it is even more difficult. It is not surprising that they appreciated the support, which was offered by their counterparts in other countries, many of whom knew each other from earlier political struggles. So as they started to rebuild new bi-lateral relationships, they benefitted from an initial foundation of good will. The period 2002–2008 is filled with dozens of positive regional encounters, state visits, attendance at the inaugural ceremonies of respective presidents, and extensive communication among them. This good will, however, quite quickly encountered the fact in country after country that bi-lateral relations were heavily influenced by important economic and geopolitical factors. This situation cannot be ignored, because they dominated bi-lateral relations, in some cases, with positive results, but not always.

This was the context in which Argentina sought to redefine its bi-lateral relations. Argentina's most important Latin American relationship was with Brazil, its much larger neighbor to the north whose economic footprint was big and whose economy was in some cases complementary to Argentina while in other areas, such as agriculture and manufacturing of products such as automobiles, directly competitive. If the values of the real and the peso were stable and not excessively under- or over-valued, the two economies had enormous opportunities for collaboration and growth, individually and together. This situation was not altogether politically determined because businessmen and companies from both countries actively looked for opportunities in the other country. Brazilian investors had bought many companies and property in Argentina during the crisis of 2001–2002 and had benefitted considerably from the recovery. But the political tone was set by Nestor Kirchner and Brazilian President Lula, who mostly worked together from 2003 on in asserting Latin American opposition to a Latin American Free Trade Agreement, which was supported by the Bush administration.

Despite the traditional rivalry of the foreign ministries and foreign services of these two countries, and periodic worries about competition in trade, Argentina and Brazil supported one another internationally and within the region. Brazil's size and economic power, as well as Lula's political skill and interest in external relationships, also gave it a privileged position vis-à-vis the United States. It is interesting that, despite the ideological orientation of Lula's Workers Party in Brazil, as noted above, President Lula adopted a much more orthodox fiscal policy than Kirchner, adhering closely to IMF rules, keeping interest rates high, and assuring low inflation. Brazil was rewarded for following this path in early 2008 when it received an investment grade rating from Wall Street, something very much desired in Argentina but unlikely to occur given past history.

A second bi-lateral relationship for Argentina, which should have been equally friendly and collaborative, was with Uruguay, its Rio de la Plata neighbor. Uruguay had also elected a progressive government led by Tabaré Vasquez in November 2004. However, despite the very close economic, political, and cultural relations between the two countries, this relationship deteriorated sharply in 2005, with the announcement of Uruguay to build and operate two paper processing plants not far from the Rio de la Plata, thereby threatening to pollute the river from the chemicals used in paper processing. This announcement, which Kirchner described as having been "knifed in the back" led to continuing protests by Argentine environmentalists and groups living in Gualeguaychu on the Argentine side of the river. This led to the cutting of roads and bridges leading to Uruguay, threatened the economically-important Argentine tourist flow into Uruguay, and severely crippled bi-lateral relations. Presentations of the dispute by both sides to the International Court of Justice in The Hague did nothing to change the perception of both sides that they were being wronged by the other. This case illustrated how the perception of economic and subsequently political interests could so heavily influence a potentially important relationship for both countries.

The least expected, but the most watched bi-lateral relationship which Argentina established was with Hugo Chavez in Venezuela. After resuming power in 2002, Chavez reached out to Nestor Kirchner and offered to use some of oil-rich Venezuela's financial power to support Argentina. While various business deals were developed involving Argentine exports of food and Argentine private investments in Venezuela, the most significant single act was Venezuela's purchase of US$6 billion worth of Argentine bonds. In addition, Venezuela offered to supply cheap oil to Argentina to help meet the country's energy needs.

While the relationship with Venezuela had definite concrete benefits for Argentina, these benefits came at a high cost internationally as Chavez's growing rhetorical battle with the Bush administration led to Argentina being placed into the same category of Latin American "populist, leftist" regimes by the media. The Venezuelan conflict with the United States became very explicit in 2005 when Argentina hosted the Summit of the Americas in Mar del Plata. Chavez verbally attacked Bush from Argentina and furthered the impression that Argentina was closely tied to Venezuela. This situation continued into 2009 when, even after a harmonious hemispheric summit of leaders in April 2009, Chavez continued to attack the United States. He also surprised the Kirchners, following a visit to Argentina, by nationalizing Argentine private companies working in Venezuela.

Outside of Latin America, the country's closest bi-lateral supporter was Spain. With long historical origins and ties, not the least of which was the waves of Spanish immigrants coming to Argentina starting in the 1880s and continuing through the Spanish Civil War, Argentina and Spain also had the opportunity for closer political ties after the election of Nestor Kirchner in 2003. The Spanish Socialist Party government under Jose Luis Rodriguez Zapatero sought to improve Spain's political relationships with Latin America after the highly commercial relations that had dominated Spain's presence in the region during the Aznar government during the 1990s. Those political relationships, however, were also necessary conditions to advance Spain's continuing economic and financial interests with such major companies as Banco Santander and Repsol, the energy conglomerate. Nestor Kirchner and Cristina Fernandez de Kirchner visited Spain at least once a year from 2003 onwards and combined political relationships with commercial and financial deals involving Spanish holdings in the privatized public services in Argentina, such as *Aerolineas Argentinas* and others. Spain also played an important role in supporting Argentina in its dealings with the IMF and in other international arenas.

Other European relations were dominated primarily by economic issues. Italy, despite the election of the socialist Prime Minister Prodi, continued to be unhappy with the 2005 bond deal, in which many elderly Italian bondholders had refused to accept the reduced value of their bonds. France was unhappy with the termination of the contract for *Aguas Argentinas* held by Suez, one of France's biggest companies. Germany had some smaller outstanding issues, including an investigation of a Siemens contract involving bribes and a smaller but vociferous group of bondholders. Argentine relations with Britain were dominated by Britain's refusal to discuss the Malvinas issue.

The other major bi-lateral relationship, which was important, was with the United States. The "tough love" position of the Bush administration during the 2001 crisis had disappointed many Argentines after the country had been such an active ally of the United States during the 1990s, including sending troops for the first Iraq War. Argentina had even been placed into a special category of "non-strategic ally", which implied some shared interests between the two countries. The "carnal relations" of the 1990s—a term which had been used in the press to describe Argentine-US relations—had evaporated when Argentina was in trouble. The offensive comments of Treasury Secretary Paul O'Neill about Argentina during the economic collapse, saying that the crisis was their own fault, "They've been off and on in trouble for 70 years or more. They don't have any export industry to speak of at all. And they like it that way. Nobody forced them to be what they are."[34] This had further convinced the Kirchner government that it could not really rely on the United States.

Nevertheless, despite a prior history of inconsistency and imbalance in their relationship, the United States could not deny that Argentina's recovery after 2003 was remarkable. In a July 2004 interview, the then US ambassador to Argentina, Lino Gutierrez, said: "We understand where Argentina has been. We understand what happened here in 2001." As President Bush told President Kirchner, "We want you Argentina to succeed. And we want you, President Kirchner to succeed."[35] The ambassador nonetheless focused attention on the claims of the unsatisfied bondholders in the United States, at that time prior to the eventual deal, and to insisting that the government meet all of the demands of the IMF as the basis for going ahead for medium and long-term growth.

As more progressive leaders were elected in Latin America, and as Hugo Chavez continued to verbally provoke the Bush administration, the United States began to move a greater distance away from Argentina. This continued through 2006 and came to a head in late December 2007, a few days after the inauguration of Cristina Fernandez de Kirchner as president of Argentina. A Federal prosecutor in Miami brought charges against Venezuelans allegedly involved in illegally bringing US$800,000 into Argentina from Venezuela to support the election campaign of the newly-elected president. This public announcement of this news prompted a sharp retort from the President who referred to it as "garbage" and as an attempt to undermine a democratically elected leader. This led to sharp exchanges between the two governments, with the State Department saying that it had no control over the actions of a Federal prosecutor in Miami. The government of Argentina then announced it was curtailing the movements of the US ambassador within Buenos Aires and that he could only have official contacts with Foreign Ministry. The US retaliated by withholding approval of the new Argentine ambassador to the United States, Hector Timerman. This stalemate persisted for about a month and eventually was resolved, with Argentina agreeing to lift the restrictions and the US approving Timerman's appointment. The US went further, with Bush warmly receiving the new ambassador in the White House in March 2008 and sending a letter to the president praising the Argentine government for its efforts to punish those involved in prior human rights abuses. Timerman strengthened the relationship further by organizing a July 2008 bipartite working group meeting in Buenos Aires to work across of range of issues between the two countries.

Strengthening multi-lateral frameworks

The existence of many like-minded governments within Latin America seemed to offer many opportunities to strengthen efforts to build multi-lateral and regional cooperation. The first candidate was Mercosur, the common market for the Southern Cone, which had been created in 1991 by Argentina, Brazil, Paraguay, and Uruguay. While the organization initially had attracted some attention, it had been largely left behind in the tumultuous years of economic and crisis in Argentina. The election of Kirchner prompted Lula to raise the issue of strengthening Mercosur, whose headquarters was in Montevideo. Kirchner appointed Chacho Alvarez, the former Argentine Vice-President under Fernando de la Rua, in November 2005 as President of the Council of Permanent Representatives to Mercosur, replacing former President Eduardo Duhalde in this position.

The new government had led a major recovery from the crisis of 2002. Yet as President Kirchner noted repeatedly, the country was still in "purgatory," not having yet reversed many of the terrible consequences of the collapse of 2001–2002. A challenge was how to sustain the recovery. The next task was to strengthen the state.

6 Strengthening the state to manage at home

In 2005, Argentina was clearly on the road to economic recovery. Determined new political leadership and strong economic management had found a path for re-inserting Argentina into the global economy and into the community of nations and international organizations. The country's large external debt was under control and sustained economic growth had surprised even the most skeptical observers of Argentina. But how was the government managing at home? How was it dealing with the many problems and differences within the country itself — rich and poor, Buenos Aires and the rest of the country, the poor north versus the prosperous south, between labor and capital, and between short-term urgent matters versus medium- and longer-term strategy for sustained development? These questions, at their most fundamental level, involved redefining the role of the government in post-crisis Argentina.

Understanding the process and content of redefining government in Argentina in this period needs to be placed within the theoretical and comparative discussion of state performance and institutional capacity presented in Chapter 2. This includes addressing the issues of the role of the state in development, the relative emphasis of state functions on market-enhancing, versus growth-enhancing governance strategies, as suggested by Mustaq Khan,[1] the role of the state in what has been called regulatory capitalism, as well as judgments about the efficacy of specific public institutions in the executive, legislative, and judiciary branches, a subject which has been analyzed in some depth in the case of Argentina.[2]

Just as there is a large literature on this issue for other countries, there has also been a lengthy historical and academic debate and literature in Argentina itself about the role and efficacy of institutions in the country. While there is little controversy about Argentina's extraordinary natural resource endowments, many Argentines and external observers have long argued that the country has underperformed in its development trajectory, indeed has advanced, stalled, gone backward, and sometimes fallen into deep crisis.[3] Explanations of these episodes and the trajectory as a whole have largely focused on the weakness of democratic institutions to establish and enforce rules for making policies, laws, and development plans.[4]

This chapter will examine this strengthening of the state by addressing the following issues:

1 The redefinition of the role of government.
2 Strengthening the state as an agent of redistribution for social justice, including improving revenue collection to allow greater public expenditures, changing the composition of public expenditures to address poverty and social deprivation, and managing the labor market.
3 The state as protector of human rights, including reforming the Supreme Court, guaranteeing human rights, regulating and protecting rights, and managing the problem of security and the geography of fear.
4 The state as regulator of markets, including claims of hegemony and authoritarian national state power

1 Redefining the role of government

Prior to taking office in May 2003, Nestor Kirchner had described the Argentine government as an "absent state." This assessment was the result of the great contrast between the presence and activism of the Argentine government during many periods during the twentieth century and the "privatized" state, which resulted from the Menem policies in the 1990s. During Menem's tenure as president, Argentina had launched and completed the most extensive privatization program of any country in the world. Public services including water supply, sanitation, electricity, telephones, mail, urban transportation, railways, subways, airports, energy, gas, petroleum exploration, and others were placed into the hands of private concessionaires, mostly foreign, who were given long-term contracts for the management and operation of these activities.

The record of this privatization is mixed: on one hand, the long delays in the installation of telephones in private homes and apartments, in some cases for up to ten years, were reduced to days, thereby expanding the network of services and increasing the number of customers. A 1996 study of the privatization program concluded that Argentina had earned US$1.6 billion in efficiency gains from this approach.[5] A widely quoted study on water privatization concluded that infant mortality had declined as a result of increased access to water supply under privatization.[6] But many other observers noted that many of the tariffs for these services were considerably increased, thereby straining household budgets, and in some cases actually reducing the number of people served. An important result, however, was that "citizens were turned into customers,"[7] with little means to challenge the growing power of the privatized companies. It also meant that when the crisis of 2001–2002 led to the devaluation of the peso, the companies were more interested in protecting their own financial solvency and their stockholders' investments than in extending services to needy customers.[8]

Over time, partly through privatization and through the shrinking of the public service through fiscal contraction of the national budget, the Argentine state was greatly reduced from its earlier scale and power in, for example, the 1950s. The government of Argentina had been powerful and active at earlier times, most notably during the administration of Juan Peron when the state actively set policies, implemented programs, and redesigned Argentine society into a "welfare state" with many of the features which Franklin Delano Roosevelt had introduced in the 1930s with the New Deal in the United States. This activism had resulted in an extensive public health care system, social security, assistance for the poor, public housing, public education, and an extensive network of public infrastructure around the country. Extensive public employment, subsidies to various industries, tariff protection for national industries and many business sectors, and many regulations protecting labor, for example maternity leave, severance pay, or protection from arbitrary dismissal, all inserted government into the daily lives of all Argentines. These services and labor provisions were transformed into "rights" for all Argentines.[9]

The scaling back of the welfare state began actively in the 1970s, particularly during the military dictatorship, when Jose Martinez de Hoz was Minister of Economy. Following the growing rhetoric and ideology of free trade and improving competitiveness, Martinez de Hoz opened up the Argentine economy to foreign products and foreign investment by liberalizing trade rules and reducing the power of the unions. The consequences of these policies in the late 1970s was the de-industrialization of Argentina as many domestic industries were unable to compete with foreign companies that were not required to pay high salaries and benefits, as had been mandated by Peron. As noted earlier, thousands of small businesses closed down from the late 1970s to the mid-1990s.

This process had also been accompanied by a significant shrinking of the public sector in terms of numbers of employees and, most importantly, a decline in the capacity of public sector institutions to perform functions such as planning and policy analysis which had been relatively well-developed in earlier periods. This shrinkage contrasted to a more "capable" state which had existed during the administrations of Peron and later under Frondizi, where the developmentalism itself had led to active state intervention in the industrial sector and in public investment programs.

Partly on the basis of his own experience as mayor of Rio Gallegos and later as governor of the Province of Santa Cruz, Nestor Kirchner believed that the government could be effective and should be present in meeting people's needs and solving the country's problems. He, therefore, sought to rebuild the state or "*Nacion*" as it is known in Argentina, by expanding programs, hiring personnel, and issuing regulations, which asserted the authority of the state in many diverse sectors and activities.

Analytically, the areas in which the roles of the state would be redefined can be divided into three categories: the state as agent of redistribution for social justice, the state as protector of human rights, and the state as regulator of markets.

2 The state as agent of redistribution for social justice

One of the first issues, which the Kirchner government addressed, was the issue of the reach of the public sector itself through programs financed by public expenditures. This issue, however, depended very much on the magnitude and quality of resources which government controlled and therefore it immediately raised one of the most controversial and problematic issues in the history of Argentine government: tax collection.

Improving revenue collection to allow greater public expenditures

Despite 50 years of discussion in Argentina about poor tax collection and repeated international criticism, the post-crisis government committed itself to improving tax collection and actually achieved this objective. Tulio Halperin Donghi, the pre-eminent historian of Argentina, noted in 2002 that:

> The decadence of the state began in earnest in 1955, after the fall of the first Peronist regime, when the lifespan of regimes in power went from more than ten years to two to three years. While the consequences were felt everywhere, none was more important than the state's increasing inability to call upon the taxes it notionally raised. It was this inability, rather than excessive public expenditures, that encouraged governments to avoid bankruptcy by resorting to high inflation and later to foreign borrowing for much longer than prudent.[10]

This historical observation is quite important, because it linked this inability or unwillingness to collect taxes to the larger predicament which the country repeatedly found itself. It also relates to explanations of the crisis of 2001–2002 in which some external observers found that Argentina's overall level of public expenditure was not problematic in itself, the issue was that it was being financed by borrowing rather than by tax revenue. In fact, despite the obviously central role of government in the construction of modern Argentina throughout the twentieth century–whether in infrastructure, housing, education, health, the armed forces, or later in building an extensive social safety net through social protection and a pension system– there seemed to be a socially accepted notion that the obligation to pay taxes was less important than the personal and social approval to be gained by avoiding them.[11] Even though there had long existed a well-defined system of taxes on income, wealth, valued-added, as well as user fees for various public services, revenue collection was always far below what could have been reasonably expected.

Table 6.2 shows the major sources of public revenue.

Table 6.1 Tax evasion rates in Argentina, Brazil, and Chile, 2000 (%)

Tax	*Argentina*	*Brazil*	*Chile*
Value-added tax (VAT)	39	–	20
Payroll tax	43	55	17
Personal income tax	49	55	57
Corporate income tax	46	42	35
Informal economy as % of GNP	40	39	–

Source: Birdsall *et al.* 2007, op. cit., p. 62.

Table 6.2 Major sources of public revenue

- Income, profits and capital gains
- Property taxes
- Domestic goods and services
- Trade and international transactions
- Other
- Social security contribution

Source: Ministry of Economy and y Public Finances (MEyFP) 2010, "Secretaria de Hacienda."

Table 6.3 presents the historical evolution of performance for these taxes as well as total public revenue as a share of GDP. Interestingly, Argentina has had a higher GDP per capita than Brazil, but its ratio of taxes to GDP has been smaller than Brazil.

This earlier poor performance has been explained by both institutional instability over time and the structure of federalism itself. For example, from 1947 to 2002, Argentina had 49 directors of tax administration at the national level.[12] This problem is specific to taxing authorities, but also to the bureaucracy at large as argued by Barbara Geddes who has written that Argentina and Peru, which had the most political instability, had the least competent bureaucracies before 1980.[13] High instability in turn affected the composition of tax revenue as well, with more reliance on customs taxes and less on income or value-added taxes, which had more complicated political impacts.[14] Similarly, unstable and unreliable fiscal federalism, with high dependency of provincial and local governments on federal payments, which were nonetheless unreliable in amount and timeliness, also undermined incentives for taxation. This resulted in what Melo has

Table 6.3 Public revenue

Year	*Net total of tax collection* **1980-thousands of pesos* **1991–2010-millions of pesos*	*Net total of tax collection (% of GDP)*
1980	0.67	17.44
1991	30,562	18.40
2001	56,276	20.94
2002	62,218	19.90
2003	88,072	23.43
2004	117,977	26.36
2005	142,903	26.86
2006	179,547	27.44
2007	236,517	29.11
2008	317,578	30.75
2009	360,256	31.45
2010	480,828	33.66

Source: Ministry of Economy and y Public Finances (MEyFP) 2010, Secretaria de Hacienda.

described as "vertical fiscal imbalance," with the federal government accounting for about 60 percent of provincial spending.[15]

In contrast to this historically poor performance, at the end of 2006, the government announced that revenue collection had increased 26 percent more than in 2005 and had broken a new record of 150 billion pesos or US$50 billion.[16] This record was closely tied to the economic growth rate of 9 percent in 2006 in which taxes on profits and valued added could have reasonably been expected to grow. The Ministry of Economy commented that the high revenue was due to the overall level of economic growth, increased exports (including higher prices for agricultural commodities), higher profits, and the increase in formal sector employment as unregistered workers gradually moved into the formal sector. Higher payments into the social security system also contributed to increased revenue totals. The Argentine Chamber of Commerce reported that a survey of businesses had reported that 57.1 percent had higher profits than in 2005. Figure 6.1 shows this rising trend.

For the country as a whole, while national tax revenue reached a level of 23.5 percent of GDP, it nevertheless still left Argentina far below European countries that were in the 35–45 percent level, with Sweden at 50 percent of GDP. If provincial and municipal revenues were added to the 23.5 percent level, the overall tax level would have been about 30 percent of GDP.[17] Nevertheless, the 2006 performance of US$50 billion was a new record and exceeded the prior record of 1993.

This revenue performance translated into an overall primary fiscal surplus as shown in Table 6.4. Again, these data contrast sharply with historical data.

While the government was quite pleased with this much improved performance, and with the praise that it generated from the international institutions, the

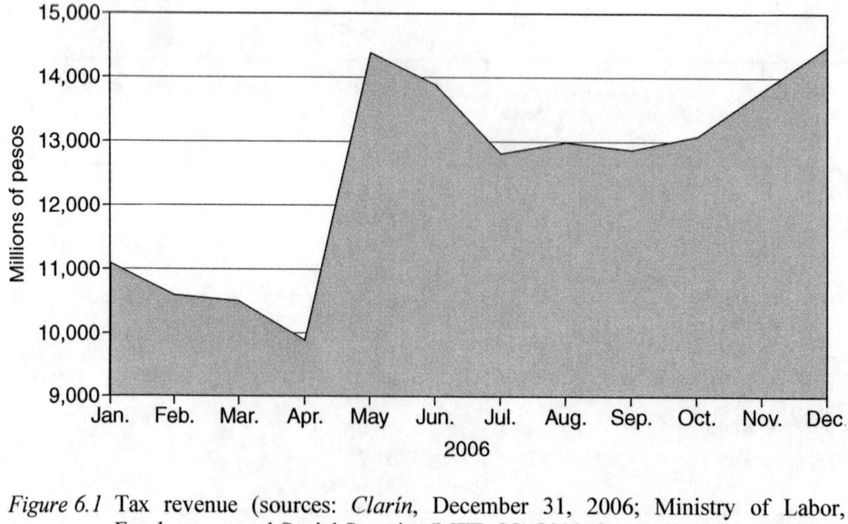

Figure 6.1 Tax revenue (sources: *Clarín*, December 31, 2006; Ministry of Labor, Employment and Social Security (MTEySS) 2010, Secretaria de Hacienda).

Table 6.4 Federal public sector, balance sheet and financing (millions of AR pesos and as % of GDP)

	2005		*2006*		*2007*		*2008*	
	AR$	*%*	*AR$*	*%*	*AR$*	*%*	*AR$*	*%*
Current revenues	125,594	23.9	140,349	23.6	154,838	23.5	171,135	23.5
Current expenditure	108,355	20.6	117,592	19.8	130,895	19.9	144,076	19.8
Economic deficit/surplus	17,239	3.3	22,757	3.8	23,943	3.6	27,059	3.7
Capital revenues	156	0.0	133	0.0	116	0.0	119	0.0
Capital expenditure	9,975	1.9	13,517	2.3	14,106	2.1	15,124	2.1
Total revenues	125,750	23.9	140,482	23.7	154,954	23.5	171,254	23.5
Total expenditure	118,330	22.5	131,109	22.1	145,001	22.0	159,200	21.8
Overall deficit/surplus	7,420	1.4	9,373	1.6	9,953	1.5	12,054	1.7
Primary deficit/surplus	18,326	3.5	19,349	3.3	22,045	3.3	24,759	3.4

Source: World Bank 2008, op. cit., p. 78.

politics of revenue generation proved to be much more complicated. Extensive discussions were held within the various economic sectors: industry, finance, agriculture, energy, and others about their respective level of taxation and how it cut into profits. While some of these discussions became quite contentious, for most the participants were so pleased with the rapid increases in profits from 2003 to 2006 that tax issues did not become major political debates during this period. As shown in Chapter 8, this changed dramatically when taxes were increased on profits from the exports of soya, wheat, corn, and sunflowers, as well as meat, in 2008. This increase led to major strikes and a period of intense political and economic instability as well.

Finally, one of the most interesting aspects of enhanced revenue performance is how various levels of government tightened their collection mechanisms. For example, the Province of Buenos Aires checked cars as they left the country for summer vacations from December to March. If the owners did not have proof that they had paid their taxes, the cars were impounded. This was a loud signal to the middle and upper-income groups who had cars and who could afford vacations. Similarly, the level of review by the tax authorities was also strengthened, as many individuals, households, and companies found themselves facing questions from auditors. The "culture of tax collection" was being changed.

Changing the composition of public expenditures to address poverty and social deprivation

As noted in Chapter 4, the Duhalde government had shifted public expenditures towards emergency programs benefitting the poorest households and regions in the country. While total public expenditure dropped in this immediate post-crisis period, its composition changed in what the World Bank called a "pro-poor" direction. This trend continued under the Kirchner government. Economy Minister Lavagna supported this orientation through public expenditures, rather than through across-the-board salary increases to address rising prices. In 2005, for example, when real incomes were in fact 12 percent below real incomes in 2001, Lavagna faced intense political pressure from the unions to allow upward salary adjustments. But because he was worried about the impact of increased wages on inflation, he used more targeted public expenditures to increase the real incomes of the most vulnerable groups. For example, in August 2005, the government increased the limit for family salary to 2,600 pesos for welfare payments. This was the third increase in this ceiling in two years, thereby targeting more money to poor families eligible for public assistance. Payments could increase, but only in small and well-studied increments.

Government investments were also targeted to generate employment for the poor. In 2007, the president announced a plan to build 250,000 low-income houses in the next three years. This was part of a government effort to improve housing but it was largely driven by the need to increase employment, particularly in the construction sector, which could absorb large quantities of labor. In 2007 alone, 100,000 houses were to be built.[18] Individual investment programs of this kind, in road-building and water supply, were carefully evaluated in terms of their broader economic impacts.

The most important of these programs was continuing government support for the *Jefes y Jefas* Program, although the latter eventually reduced its number of beneficiaries as the economy improved and later, evolved into another more stable medium-term program. The experience of the *Jefes* program is very instructive and helps to understand Argentina's recovery in relation to the efforts of other Latin American countries. As noted earlier, the program provided 150 pesos per month to eligible heads of household in return for certification of part-time work in municipalities. At its peak, in May 2003, the program had close to two million participants and was reaching about ten million family members, or about 30 percent of the Argentine population.[19] It was well-targeted and, according to the World Bank, "tilted the overall economic growth period from 2002 to 2003 in a pro-poor way."[20] It was similar to Brazil's *Bolsa* program and Mexico's *Opportunidades* program, pro-poor and similar in coverage. One study comparing programs across Latin American countries showed that *Jefes* program had the largest impact on poverty and inequality because of its careful targeting and wide coverage.[21]

While some questions were raised about the registration and eligibility of some people participating in the program, most of these were resolved following various local audits and program adjustments. For example, some registration of households was done through the *piqueteros*, some by unemployed groups, and non-governmental organizations. This was not illegal according to the original scheme. But questions were raised about increases in participation in some municipalities before the May 2003 presidential elections. The program never achieved its goal of having 90 percent of its participants working. But the overall performance of the program improved following the beginning of the Kirchner administration.

Specifically, the government took seven measures to improve targeting and eligibility within the *Jefes* program, including: closing the registration of new beneficiaries after May 2003, expansion of use of cross-checks for internal consistency, enhanced supervision of municipalities, improved handling of fraud accusations, dropping ineligible participants, improved transparency, and improving support to beneficiaries.[22] The World Bank had given the government of Argentina a loan for US$600 million in 2002–2003 in support of the *Jefes* program. But most of the financing of this program came from the government itself, with the Bank share reaching only 24 percent in 2002 and thereafter declining to 3 percent by 2005.

In February 2006, the World Bank approved another loan of US$350 million to Argentina to finance part of a Heads of Households Transition Project to support the government's shift of the *Jefes* program from an emergency program towards a medium/long term role in the country's social protection system. This transition strategy was announced on February 13, 2006, in the form of a new program called *Seguro de Capacitatión y Empleo*. It was intended to provide higher monthly payments for eligible beneficiaries, but limited only for two years. Its intention of linking training with employment was seen as critical, particularly as the government had become aware of a growing problem of high-school dropouts. A year later, the school dropout figures had reached 8.5 percent in the first few years and 19.8 percent in the last three years. By March 2007, the government reported that 270,000 adolescents had dropped out.[23] A late 2005 survey of 2,009 adolescents, representative of urban youth, in greater Buenos Aires, Neuquen, Posadas, and Salta, found that almost half of Argentine youths are exposed to important risks and that 25 percent of all youth are at high risk levels.[24] Risk factors included school dropouts, broken families, unprotected sex, and drugs. An October 2007 study concluded that 49.5 percent of minors under 14 years old were poor.[25]

While the picture of poverty and deprivation was improving year by year, the situation faced by the government was well-captured in a 2005 headline to a story in *La Nación*, "The social debt leaves very slowly after the default."[26] This article reported on a study entitled "*Barometro de la Deuda Social*" by the Catholic University of Argentina, which showed that, in 2005, 38.5 percent of the population was living below the poverty line. While the number was fewer than in 2002, it was still more than in 1998. Some 43 percent of adolescents were not in school; four of ten families had housing problems; 8.1 percent of families had been hungry that month; and 60.7 percent of families did not have enough money to purchase the basic food basket.

This message was repeated in a September 2006 news story about the numbers of people below the poverty line, "They are fewer, but still too many."[27] The article reported that the share of people living in poverty had declined to 31.4 percent, less than in earlier years but was still high. This national average also masked important regional differences, for example, 55.6 percent of people living in poverty in Chaco Province, but only 5.6 percent in Ushuaia-Rio Grande Province or 6.9 percent in Rio Gallegos. These differences will be discussed in more detail later in this chapter.

At the beginning of 2007, the government announced that the Ministry of Social Development, under the responsibility of Minister Alicia Kirchner, the president's sister, would increase its social spending by over US$500 million. It would spend $1.6 billion pesos more, with a total 2007 social spending budget of 5.1 billion pesos or US$1.7 billion in 2007.[28] The majority of this spending would fit within the *Plan Familias*, which was now the next generation *Jefes* program. Some share of the funds would also be directed to retirees of 70 years old and above. The Ministry of Social Development would also fund the *Plan Alimentario Nacional* and *Plan Manos a la Obra* through loans from the Inter-American Development Bank. Table 6.5 shows the growth in social spending from 2003 to 2007. By 2008, Ministry officials were stating publicly that 98 percent of their budget was going directly to needy families. They also described these outlays as "investment" in people, and not as expenditures.

The United Nations' Economic Commission for Latin American and the Caribbean concluded that Argentina's public expenditures had grown in this period, reaching 17 percent of GDP, placing it in eighth place among Latin American countries.

Table 6.5 Total public social spending in Argentina

	2002–2003	*2004–2005*	*2006–2007*
Per capita public spending *(in dollars 2000 Prices)*	1,301	1,531	2,002
Per capita public spending as % of GDP	19.5	19.6	22.1
Public social spending as % of total public spending	66.2	64.3	63.9

Source: ECLAC 2009, Trends in social spending, cash transfers and conditional transfer programs, pp. 113–114.

While this effort to increase public expenditures for the poor was a key component in the government's strategy–and also a central element in strengthening the role of the state itself– it should be noted that, by itself, this emphasis was not inconsistent with the earlier strategies implied by the Washington Consensus. What was different was the fact that the government had decided not to use scarce funds to repay foreign debt while those funds could be used for essential public social expenditures, which were targeted to unemployed and hungry people.

Managing the labor market

One of the biggest problems in managing domestic pressures, which faced the Kirchner government, was managing the labor market. While the economy was growing and unemployment and poverty were declining, albeit slowly, the pressures of creating employment and maintaining real wages were intense and felt by the government on a daily basis. Interest groups existed on all sides of these issues: from the chambers of commerce, industry, and construction, many unions from private industries and the public sector itself. On one side, more jobs and higher wages were clearly better, but a too, rapid increase in real wages would accelerate inflation, thereby generating price increases, particularly for food and basic goods consumed by the poor. Finding a balance was both difficult analytically within the government bureaucracy and politically within a highly transparent world of Argentine newspapers and television.

Three stages can be identified in the changes in the labor market during the recovery period. The first was from the second semester of 2002 to the beginning of 2003 when there was a strong increase in the numbers of hours worked, but few new jobs were created. As noted in earlier chapters, 2002 was the depth of the recession, where adjustments were being made by domestic enterprises to changes in relative prices resulting from the devaluation. As demand for goods and services grew by early 2003, a second stage began, with a large increase in employment through 2004. The third stage began in 2005 and has continued to the present with improvements in the quality and stability of employment, real wages, and benefits. These steps need to be understood in light of earlier changes in the labor market. Specifically, from 1991 to 2001, unregistered workers had grown by 52.8 percent while total employment only grew by 1 percent. The 1990s had seen the growth of the service sector, with increased flexibility in employment regulations, insisted upon by the IMF as a condition for financial support. The result was more precarious employment and a decline in job quality.

In contrast, as explained below, the Kirchner administration sought to improve both the quantity and quality of employment, ambitious objectives which were both achieved. Jobs in the formal sector grew by 33 percent, while unregistered jobs grew by only 8 percent.[29] In the first three years of the government, from May 2003 to May 2006, employment grew by 26 percent, at a rate of 7 percent a year. Figure 6.2 shows this rate of employment growth.

From 2003 on, two major changes became the focus of employment policy: employment growth in productive sectors and improving the quality of employment. The Ministry of Labor noted in 2005 that employment patterns in the 1990s showed that economic growth was a necessary but not sufficient condition to generate quality employment. The government saw the need to modify the pattern of economic growth itself, taking advantage of changed relative prices following the devaluation. This in fact occurred from 2002 to 2006, with big changes in job growth coming from the industrial sector, e.g., in 2002–2003, job growth was –1.2 percent while by 2005–2006 it had increased to 8.2 percent.[30]

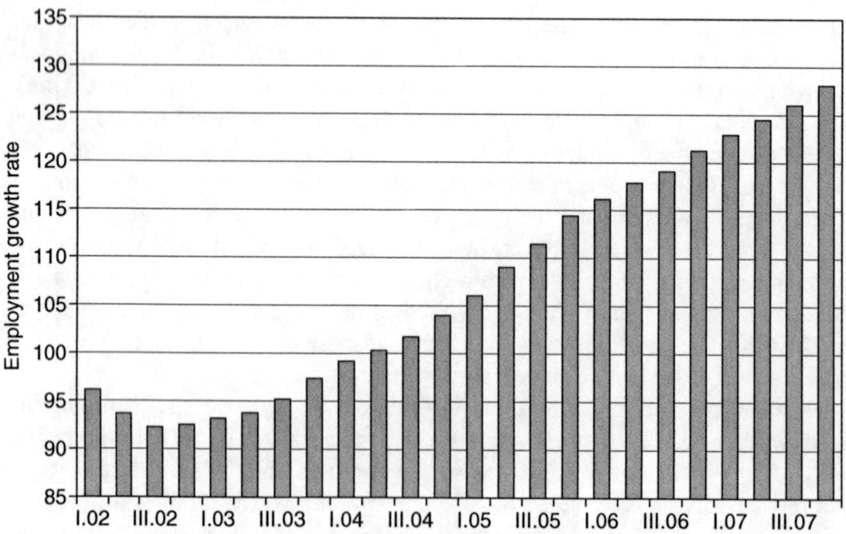

Figure 6.2 Rate of employment growth 2001–2007 (source: Ministry of Labor, Employment and Social Security (MTEySS) 2010. Survey of Labor Indicators).

Note
Base IV. 01 = 100.

The issue of changes in improving job quality was much more complicated than taking advantage of relative prices. Employment quality involves assuring social security if jobs are lost, health benefits, job safety, job stability, recognition of collective bargaining agreements, job training, and job mobility if needed within the same or different industries.[31] This growth of formal sector employment occurred not just in Buenos Aires, but also in many provinces throughout the country, as shown in Figure 6.3.

Particularly large increases in employment occurred, however in the four largest urban areas, as shown in Table 6.6.

Table 6.7 shows the sector composition of this employment growth, with very strong increases in manufacturing, construction, and services. Indeed in the construction sector employment grew by 78 percent in these three years.

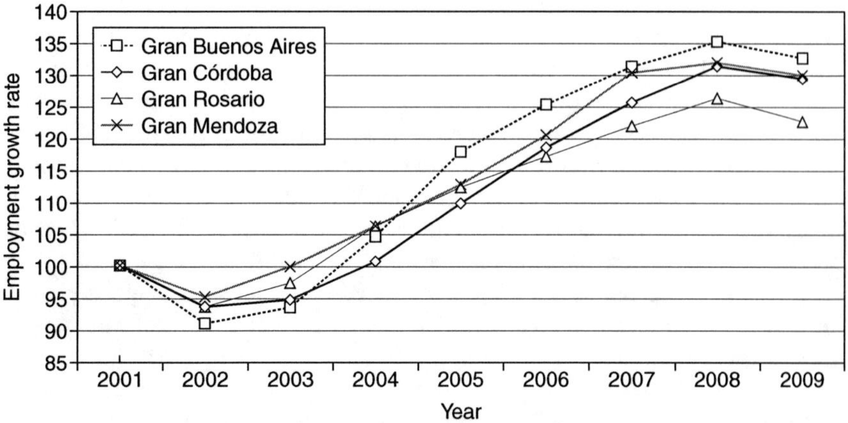

Figure 6.3 Employment growth: GBA vs Provincial Cities (source: Ministry of Labor, Employment and Social Security (MTEySS) 2010. Survey of Labor Indicators).

Note
Base IV.01 = 100.

Table 6.6 Urban employment growth, 2003–2006 (%)

Sector	*2003–2004*	*2004–2005*	*2005–2006*	*2003–2006*
Gran Buenos Aires	6.5	9.1	8.6	26.3
Cordoba	10.8	12.1	7.4	33.3
Rosario	9.4	5.7	4.1	20.3
Mendoza	4.8	7.4	7.5	21.0

Source: Government of Argentina 2006, p. 24.

Note
Variation calculated between first two quarters of each year.

Table 6.7 Sector composition of employment growth, 2003–2006 (%)

Sector	*2003–2004*	*2004–2005*	*2005–2006*	*2003–2006*
Manufacturing	10.8	8.2	7.5	28.9
Construction	13.0	29.6	21.9	78.5
Commerce and Services	4.5	7.8	7.2	20.7

Source: Government of Argentina 2006, op. cit., p. 25.

Note
*Variation calculated between first two quarters of each year.

Government data show that smaller- and medium-sized enterprises grew faster than bigger ones. While the distribution of employment in 2003 showed that small enterprises of 1–49 employees had 30 percent of jobs; those with 50–199 employees had 27 percent, and those with more than 200 employees had 43 percent, but three years later, the biggest firms had only added 28 percent of new jobs, while medium-sized firms had added 34 percent, while the smallest had added 38.8 percent.[32] Importantly, this job growth comes mostly for unqualified workers, with 39.7 percent, 20.6 percent for professionals, and 26.4 percent for qualified technical people. The result is that lower-level, untrained people were able to find employment. Starting from May 2003, there were 44 uninterrupted months of formal sector employment growth through 2006.[33] Newly formed businesses were important in contrast for example with the United States where some 79 percent of employment is in well-established companies; the figure is only 56 percent in Argentina. Importantly, salaries and real wages have also increased over time.

A leading question for government policy was the impact of the changing economic model on employment and how the profile of workers and firms were changing in response to new exchange rate incentives. Data from 2005–2006 on the demand for labor show more demand from big firms for qualified people and more demand for less qualified people from smaller firms.[34] A government survey in 2005–2006 showed that 65 percent of private firms surveyed were looking to hire during these years, with larger firms hiring more, particularly in financial services and construction.[35] Interestingly, the amount of training being provided by firms declined under the pressure to meet production and construction demand.

The character of formal sector employment is noteworthy in several respects. A 2005–2006 government survey of 7,815 workers representing 2.1 million workers in major cities and industries found that 46.5 percent of formal sector workers were covered by a collective bargaining agreement, 58 percent were affiliated to a health plan connected to a union, and 55 percent contributed to the union. But further questions demonstrated that in fact 80 percent of formal sector workers were covered by these agreements, an indicator demonstrating the political as well as economic importance of unions in Argentina.[36] Although only 37.6 percent indicated they were members of unions, two and half times that number were covered by agreements. Union membership also varied enormously by sector, for example, from 48 percent in transport and communications to 36 percent in construction to 25 percent in the financial sector, and 12 percent in education.[37]

How was this employment structure responding to new incentives for exports? From 1998 to 2005, Argentina had a 51 percent increase in exports in current dollars.[38] Table 6.8 shows export increases by firm size.

Table 6.8 shows a drop in exports in the recessionary period 1998–2001, then a big increase of 34.3 percent for 2003–2005, of which 32.7 percent are from big firms, 61.6 percent from medium size firms, and 51.7 percent from small firms. However, with a very high level of concentration of big firms in the export sector, actually 18.3 percent of the firms were responsible for 92.5 percent of exports and 54 percent of exporters were small and medium firms which account for only 3.3 percent of total exports. Further, 56 percent of total exports had low technological content and were mostly commodities. The result of the export boom, therefore, was that exports per se did not have much effect on employment because of their low technological component.

The problem, therefore, for government management of the labor market, was how to balance demands for wage increases in a growing and initially slightly inflationary economy with the need for profits and investment in creating new installed capacity. This has proven to be a serious challenge. For example, in 2006, there were 1,362 labor disputes of which 774 included strikes. The days lost from work amounted to 6,328,956, with average days not worked by strikers at 5.3 days. Of this total number of disputes, 810 were public and 552 were private, with lost days in public disputes reaching 5,453,779 days while losses reached 875,177 in the private sector labor disputes. The average days lost were 6.4 days in public disputes and 2.6 days in private disputes.[39] In this period, 61 percent of labor conflicts were about wages, particularly as inflation heated up.

The government's response to this situation was to actively participate in collective bargaining negotiations. In 2003 there were 406 such negotiations; by 2006, 930 negotiations were held. This government presence both helped to introduce some equity and consistency in individual settlements but also to demonstrate a strong government interest on a subject with immediate concern to many Argentines. For example, following April 2006 negotiations with the

Table 6.8 Export growth by firm size

Firm size	*1998/2005*	*2003/2005*	*2001/2002*	*1998/2001*
Large	59.3	32.7	–3.0	7.5
Medium	73.9	61.6	–12.7	7.8
Small	–22.1	44.6	–24.6	–40.5
Micro	–47.5	51.7	–25.7	–45.8
Total	53.7	34.3	–4.3	3.9

Source: Ministry of Labor, Employment and Social Security (MTEySS) 2007, p. 4.

powerful transport workers union where it was agreed on a 19 percent wage increase, this same level was then adopted by other unions as well. One aggregate result was that income from wages grew 32 percent in nominal terms in 2006, with the consequence that more profits were directed to labor in the form of wages. This produced a net redistribution towards lower income groups likely to spend rapidly, thereby also further increasing demand for goods and services and creating more employment.

By the end of 2006, the government claimed that 2006 had seen the creation of 693,000 new jobs, with about 100,000 unemployed finding jobs and another 270,000 changing their status from under-employed to employed. This was a major accomplishment of which Kirchner was proud. It did not, however, solve one of the most difficult issues in the labor market: the high proportion of the labor force working in the informal sector, or "*en negro*," meaning that they were not publicly registered, did not pay taxes, and did not have health insurance, nor public retirement benefits. Half of the labor market was beyond the effective control of the state.

In June 2005, it was reported that 47.5 percent of all employment in Argentina was "*en negro.*"[40] This amounted to some 4.7 million persons. The evolution of this unregistered labor force is presented below in Table 6.9, showing the period from 1990 to 2005.

The *2005 Human Development Report* for Argentina noted that 2004 studies concluded that 52 percent of all employment was non-registered. The Report

Table 6.9 Evolution of non-registered labor force, 1990–2005

	Total (%)	*Private sector*	*Private sector excluding domestic service*
May 1990	27.2	33.4	29.6
May 1991	31.0	37.9	33.3
May 1992	34.7	39.8	35.5
May 1993	33.4	37.7	33.1
May 1994	34.6	38.9	34.4
May 1995	32.4	37.6	32.8
May 1996	33.7	38.9	34.1
May 1997	38.4	43.8	39.4
May 1998	37.2	41.4	37.3
May 1999	37.8	43.0	38.6
May 2000	38.2	43.4	38.6
May 2001	38.2	42.7	37.4
May 2002	38.2	42.6	37.3
May 2003	44.8	46.1	41.4
Q2 2004	48.3	50.9	43.2
Q2 2005	47.7	50.1	41.3

Source: Government of Argentina 2006, op. cit., p. 150.

included the figure 51 percent for Buenos Aires province, but numbers varying from 78 to 61 percent for the nine north and northwestern provinces.[41] Table 6.10 presents this data by province.

Another critical dimension of informal sector employment was the large difference of 2.7 times in average salaries between registered and unregistered workers at the same skill level. This finding was reported in August 2006 and was larger than the difference in May 2003, when it was 1.7 times, thus confirming that the real wages of informal sector employment were declining.[42] Bringing people into the formal sector, therefore, was costly, but also represented an important step towards reducing poverty. Table 6.11 shows this difference in wages between formal and informal sector jobs.

In order to reduce informal sector employment, the government used its participation in collective bargaining negotiations to press for including more workers in legal arrangements. An impact of government presence in these negotiations was the slight reduction of about 4 percent of informal workers in metropolitan Buenos Aires from 2004 to 2007.[43]

Table 6.10 Unregistered employment by province, 2004

Province	*Unregistered employment rate[a] (%)*
Formosa	78
Corrientes	71
Chaco	70
Tucumán	67
Salta	66
Jujuy	65
Misiones	64
Santiago de Estero	63
Córdoba	61
Catamarca	61
Entre Ríos	59
La Rioja	58
San Juan	56
Mendoza	54
San Luis	53
National Total	52
La Pampa	52
Santa Fe	51
Buenos Aires	51
Neuquén	45
Ciudad de Buenos Aires	40
Tierra del Fuego	33
Santa Cruz	30
Chubut	26

Source: UNDP 2005, *Human Development Report*, p. 99.

Note
a First semester 2004.

Table 6.11 Salaries for formal and informal sector jobs

Category	*Q1 2006*	*% Change (2003)*	*% Change (2005)*	*Purchasing power*
Private worker	843.25	58.69	21.64	9.47
Formal worker	1,182.64	57.56	22.91	10.61
Informal worker	436.72	–2.23	19.26	7.32
Public worker	992.86	80.41	31.88	18.68
Self-employed	798.58	69.62	32.24	19.01
Averageincome	911.18	64.54	26.29	13.65
Non-primary school	442.96	72.67	23.65	11.27
Primary school	636.97	81.80	30.90	17.80
Non-secondary school	686.01	71.23	23.64	11.27
Secondary school	901.99	65.26	23.49	11.13
Non-university	1,021.65	53.61	23.29	10.95
University	1,599.95	47.49	23.24	10.91

Source: La Nación 2006.

Note

Average monthly income in AR$ pesos of principal worker occupations, along category and education level achieved and differences with May of 2003 and first quarter 2005.

In sum, government efforts to manage the labor market were largely successful in terms of increasing both the quantity and quality of employment, while reducing the number of paralyzing labor disputes. Active intervention by the Ministry of Labor under Minister Carlos Tomada proved to be quite effective. It should be noted that this type of successful engagement between government, the labor unions, and the employers' associations represents an important shift in this arena of state–society relations from the more conflictive interactions going back to the 1960s and thereafter. It also is a variant of the "embedded autonomy" argument of sociologist, Peter Evans, in his analysis of the developmental state. Clearly, improving both the quantity and quality of employment was a major achievement of the Kirchner administration.

3 The state as protector of human rights

A second broad area of strengthening the state was in the area of the state as protector of human rights. This involved not only reforming judicial institutions and establishing a new culture for the open discussion of the human rights abuses of the past, but also reconsidering the more general problem of strengthening regulatory institutions and procedures to assure that laws and rules were actually enforced in a fair and even-handed way. This issue became even more critical in 2004 as the growing incidence of crime and violence in various parts of the country became the leading issue of public discussion, often replacing employment as the issue of the day.

Reforming the Supreme Court

One of the major issues facing Argentina during the 1990s was the growing perception that the judicial system did not work. The weakness of judicial institutions meant that disputes could not be easily resolved, that matters of justice could not be addressed in either a timely or definitive manner, and that the absence of a fair judiciary meant that there was both growing cynicism about the role of government and a sense of impunity for those people and institutions violating the law.[44] While these problems are very complicated and involve the inner workings of specific judicial institutions, from investigators to prosecutors to lower and higher courts, there was also a perception that the weakness of the system was a desired political outcome of the political class.

In fact, in every regime since Peron, the justices on the Supreme Court had been changed. While the mechanisms of these changes differ across regimes, "the motivating force carrying out these sanctions against the Court has been the executive branch."[45] During the 1990s, "the Argentine judiciary was frequently criticized as an appendage of the executive branch."[46] The positive image of the court declined from an already low 27 percent in 1990 to only 13 percent by 1995.[47] Starting in 1990, Menem had a law passed in Congress, which changed the number of justices from five to nine. He then appointed close allies to the

Court, including his former law partner as Chief Justice and other political supporters, forming what was later known as "the automatic majority." When cases made their way to the Supreme Court, they were effectively squashed in the political and economic interests of Menem and his colleagues. Although there were repeated law suits against sitting justices, the majority stayed intact until they were asked to rule on Menem's effort to allow him to run for the presidency for a third term. The justices managed to avoid ruling on what would have been a politically difficult case.

The Court again became a central player in the immediate aftermath of the December 2001 crisis when it was asked to rule on the *corralito*, which was freezing savings accounts and limiting access of people to their bank accounts. Efforts to impeach the members of the Supreme Court had begun in January 2002. On February 1, 2002, the Court issued a ruling questioning the *corralito*. The Court managed to survive during 2002–2003, until shortly after the inauguration of Nestor Kirchner in May 2003, when the new president called on the Congress to reopen impeachment hearings for Supreme Court justices. This led to the resignation of Chief Justice Nazareno and over the next few months, the resignations of several other justices. A key strategic move by Kirchner in this process was to limit presidential discretion in appointing justices and to insist that the process be transparent and highly participatory, not just with the Congress but also announcing that any Argentine citizen who had a question about a proposed nominee could bring this question to the Congress. His wife, Senator Cristina Fernandez de Kirchner, was a major figure in this campaign in her role as Chair of the Senate Commission on Constitutional Affairs.

The results of this process were noteworthy. The new Supreme Court was reduced from nine back to the original five members, including a constitutional scholar, Raul Zaffaroni, and the first two women justices in the history of the Court, Carmen Aribgay and Elena Highton. The process of reforming the Supreme Court took several years, from June 2003 onwards to court reforms in 2006, but significantly strengthened a key institution and led to some major changes in Argentina's justice system. As one newspaper commentary described the Court: "The Supreme Court, with new air and less political profile."[48]

It is important to remember that the role of the Supreme Court had been critical in the recent history of Argentina, most notably in supporting the amnesty given to former military officers who had participated in human rights abuses, torture, and murder during the dictatorship from 1976 to 1982. The signal from the Court that these hundreds of cases would not be tried meant that the Court itself was a major contributor to a culture of denial of violation of human rights abuses in the country.

Guaranteeing human rights

The first major consequence of a reformed Supreme Court was the decision that the Amnesty Law introduced by President Carlos Menem was unconstitutional on June 14, 2005. This decision has opened the possibility for judicial trials of hundreds of former military officers involved in human rights violations during the dictatorship. The decision was warmly and very publicly embraced by President Kirchner, who sent very strong signals throughout the government that the leading human rights organizations, such as the Grandmothers of the Plaza de Mayo and the Mothers of the Plaza de Mayo were to be treated with the utmost respect. On March 24, 2004, the 28th anniversary of the military coup which established the dictatorship, he publicly took down the portrait of General Videla, the first head of state during the military period, at the military war college, stating that Videla had no place on a wall of honor. On the same day, Kirchner held a public ceremony opening up the *Escuela de Mecánica de la Armada (ESMA)*, a detention center and site of interrogation and torture, to the public and announcing that it would become a museum for memory. At this event he publicly apologized on behalf of the government of Argentina to the Argentine people for the acts of "state-sponsored terrorism," which had occurred during the military dictatorship.

These acts in the beginning of his presidency were widely acclaimed by international human rights organizations outside Argentina. They were followed by the initiation of trials within Argentina and active efforts to extradite former military officers charged with human rights violations from other countries as well. These have led to well-publicized trials and convictions.

However, these efforts to re-establish the rule of law, in this case human rights law, have not been fully supported within the country. After 30 years of public denial of these unresolved cases, many people are uncomfortable seeing these cases opened again. But more ominously, in one case, a leading witness of human rights abuses, Julio Lopez, disappeared in 2007 before he was to testify and was never found again. This kidnapping was obviously intended to intimidate potential witnesses for the prosecution in other cases. Two other potential witnesses were also kidnapped in 2007 and 2008 but were later released. Two other potential witnesses, both in prison, mysteriously died in 2007 before being called to testify.

Pursuing human rights violations has also opened up uncomfortable discussions about the role of important institutions during the dictatorship, such as the Catholic Church.[49] While there had been complaints against the Church for its silence on human rights abuses during the time of the dictatorship itself, these were reinforced by important trials, for example, which proved that priests and other Church officials had been personally involved in some cases of torture, such as the torture of the well-known journalist, the late Jacobo Timerman. In this case a priest who had been present during the torture of Timerman was sentenced to a long prison term for his involvement.

Regulating and protecting rights

One of the most important areas of state authority and power is in the area of regulation. While privatization of many public services during the 1990s was accompanied by the establishment of various regulatory agencies and authorities with the purpose of "regulating" the provision of services, the effective power of the state was substantially weakened. Many of these entities were highly dependent on the privatized companies and in fact developed close relations with the very institutions they were officially intended to regulate. The weaknesses of *Energía Argentina, Sociedad Autonoma* (ENARSA) and *Ente Tripartito de Obras de Servicios de Saneamiento (*ETOSS*)* have been evident in the many disputes between unhappy citizens, clients, and consumers of these services and the providing institutions.

The issue of regulation, however, did not really come into public consciousness until the December 2005 fire in the Cromanon discotheque in Buenos Aires, when 191 people, mostly teenagers, died. This tragedy revealed that there was a widespread practice of nightclubs receiving fire and other permits to operate, even if they had obvious violations, such as a lack of fire protection measures, sprinklers, and other methods in place to protect their clientele. This event led to a major public outcry, to large public demonstrations against the city government of Buenos Aires and specifically against Anibal Ibarra, the Mayor, for improperly performing their responsibilities in regulating nightclubs. The political reaction led to the impeachment of Ibarra as mayor in 2006 and the prosecution of city government officials for their failure to effectively regulate and to protect the public interest. While in the end there was no judgment of criminal or even civil liability for this failure, there clearly was political liability.

This episode led to an extensive debate in the Argentine press about the weakness of the regulatory functions of public institutions, at both the national and municipal levels. It led to many complaints on other regulatory issues and particularly equality before the law, whether enforcement of traffic violations, tax collection, and eventually even by random tests of drivers in the streets of Buenos Aires in 2008 for their alcohol levels. Enforcing rules—any rules—is an important indicator of institutional authority and capacity and this certainly seems to have changed in post-crisis Argentina, even if there is much more to be done.

Another interesting episode involved fires set by farmers in rural areas north of Buenos Aires to prepare their fields for later planting. This practice is long-standing, not only in Argentina but in many countries. But in April 2008, the winds brought the smoke from these fires to metropolitan Buenos Aires and even across the Rio de la Plata to Uruguay. Buenos Aires became "*malos aires.*" The air smelled of smoke for most of a week and led to hundreds of people going to hospitals complaining of respiratory problems. The smoke led to an immediate public outcry about why the national government allowed these fires in the first place and why now was the national government unable to stop the fires. This outcry is interesting in many respects, for example, why was the anger focused on the national government? Clearly a fire is a local, if not provincial, responsibility. Secondly, should not the remedy for this problem also been located at the local or provincial levels? Finally, even President Cristina Fernandez de Kirchner flew over the fire zone in a helicopter, thereby implicitly acknowledging that the national government had responsibility for a local fire. It was later revealed that the national government did not have the necessary equipment to fight such fires, but the key point is the presumption of national responsibility.

The problem of security and the geography of fear

If the episode of the smoke was perceived as unusual and unlikely to become a frequent condition in Buenos Aires, a far more serious issue was the growing level of crime after the events of December 2001. As people lost their jobs, as money became scarcer on the street, and as differences between rich and poor became more evident, crime increased, and with it, public media coverage of what was widely described as a major crime wave. While increased crime in metropolitan Buenos Aires did not compare statistically with the much more prevalent crime in cities such as Sao Paulo, Rio de Janeiro, or Mexico City, it nonetheless became increasingly urgent as more and more people reported their own stories of being robbed or threatened. Kidnappings for ransom increased.

Increasing crime came to a head in March 2004 with the kidnapping and murder of Axel Blumberg, a 24-year-old, in the suburbs of Buenos Aires. His father began to publicly criticize, first, the police for the handling of his son's case, and then the general response of the government of the Province of Buenos Aires to this alarming situation. Blumberg was treated with understanding and respect, but went further than the authorities expected and called for public marches to the downtown Plaza de Mayo to protest the growing security problem. His public march in April 2004 drew 150,000 people and represented the first serious popular challenge to the Kirchner government. It led to new efforts to strengthen police forces and crime reporting. What is interesting here again is whether the national government should have been asked to take on responsibility for local policing and crime-fighting, or whether these were essentially provincial and municipal functions. Blumberg became the most visible public advocate for crime prevention and the *mano duro* approach. He received growing attention for about eight months and later presented himself as a candidate for office in the provincial elections of 2007, but he was defeated.

4 State as regulator of markets

A third broad area of strengthening the state was as a regulator of markets. This has proven to be perhaps the most controversial area in which the Kirchner government asserted itself. One of the most obvious lessons of the Argentine recovery from 2001–2002 was that the markets for goods and services in Argentina actually could work in ways which once again generated incomes and productive growth for the economy as a whole. The economy recovered in large measure because the multipliers, which closed down as the economy contracted in 2001 and after the imposition of the *corralito* cut off the money supply for most consumers, began to operate once again. The World Bank has referred to this process as a "demand-led recovery."[50]

In fact, the Duhalde government played only a small role in this reactivation process, except to gradually help to build some confidence by reasserting the stability of public institutions and promising elections for the future. It had not been able to provide credit to finance the activities of small enterprises or to provide other forms to assistance to generate employment. As the economy recovered in 2002 and 2003, it nonetheless became apparent that some people had been able to profit from the crisis, partly by repatriating their dollars which were now worth three times more than when they had left the country, and partly by being able to rapidly provide domestic goods to replace now prohibitively expensive imported goods. The perception of unfair "profit-taking" was common, whether by privatized companies or by private sector companies.

This provided the background for Kirchner's decision to try to actually control prices on key consumption items such as meat and other foodstuffs starting in 2005 as inflationary pressures began to mount, in part from the high rate of growth of the economy as a whole. In this situation, it was not surprising that there would be shortages in the face of rapidly increasing demand from a population which had been deprived in 2002–2003 and which was now actively consuming all types of goods and services as they enjoyed the fruits of 8 and 9 percent growth of GDP. Some of the first efforts at price controls were to ban the export of meat, in order to keep domestic prices lower. Later, successive ministers of finance, following direct orders from President Nestor Kirchner, were meeting with the owners of supermarkets, later with key players along supply chains, and finally with the institutions responsible for production in the country, in order to urge price stability despite the fact that input prices were also increasing. This arm-twisting was hardly popular in the private sector, but the president used highly visible meetings with these commercial interests in the Casa Rosada to demonstrate the government's strong commitment to fighting inflation.

The president used the secretary of commerce, Guillermo Moreno, a trusted but increasingly hated political operative, to play the leading role in controlling prices. Despite the fact that Moreno worked under the authority of the minister of economy, he gradually accumulated growing power and trust from the president. He was widely regarded as a rough instrument for a tough and, at best controversial, policy, which might limit inflation in the short run, but with longer-term consequences might prove to be counter-productive in discouraging more production and hence actually increasing prices. These longer-term consequences have in some cases appeared and led to short-run shortages of various goods, leading to immediate remedial measures which themselves have further complicated the markets for these goods. Two examples are milk and tomatoes, both of which have had overly complicated management of their prices to assure availability to consumers in Buenos Aires.

A second arena in which the government sought to control prices was in utility tariffs. As mentioned in Chapter 4, the Duhalde government had frozen utility prices in order to soften the inflationary impact of the devaluation on consumers. All of the privatized companies expressed their strong need to increase tariffs in order to recoup their losses from the devaluation and improve their balance sheets, but also to allegedly generate the revenue needed to finance expansion of services, such as water supply into underserved settlements on the periphery of Buenos Aires. The Kirchner government, in this case personified by Julio De Vido, the minister of planning, refused to allow tariff increases on the grounds that such increases were unnecessary because the private operators had already repatriated excessive profits and that any increases would be inflationary. The most publicized dispute was between the government and *Aguas Argentinas*, the French-managed water company, which provided water to most of metropolitan Buenos Aires and had subsidiaries in other urban areas as well. Suez, the French concessionaire, eventually terminated its contract in 2006 with the government, saying that it was unable to meet its financial needs without tariff increases.

While most of the public discussion of government with the privatized utilities was about tariffs, there was a second level of discussion which reflected the deep skepticism of some people in government about the Menem legacy of privatization. Some key officials thought that some services, such as water supply, urban transport, and others should be brought back under public sector management and control. Privatization was regarded as one of the legacies of the Washington Consensus, which had promised great benefits but whose actual performance was less than expected, not just in Argentina but in other Latin American countries as well.

Another dimension of this problem concerned the efficacy of government regulatory agencies. As suggested earlier, many of these agencies were perceived as too close to the utilities they were supposed to supervise. These agencies usually had limited personnel, frequently without the technical skills to adequately follow the technical performance of the utilities. This became obvious in one the frequent summer electricity blackouts when the companies had either mishandled key equipment and repairs or whose operational decisions, even when approved by the regulators, had simply been wrong. In one case this led to a blackout lasting for more than three weeks in a large area of a lower-middle class residential district of Buenos Aires in the midst of very high summer temperatures where air-conditioning and refrigeration of food were critical, as well as elevators for tall buildings.

Regulating markets, therefore, was beyond simply trying to establish prices or even trying to guarantee adequate supply. In both cases, these technical and policy challenges involved other institutions, technical instruments, reliable information, and most importantly, an extremely astute and experienced understanding of the consequences of specific decisions.

Beyond these issues, the government further complicated the situation by attempting to change the calculation of inflation by changing the methodologies used by INDEC, the well-respected government agency responsible for data collection and analysis. While this move was interpreted as the government trying to "cook the figures" on inflation and to present reduced figures, the original decision to change the methodologies had some econometric justification. While

INDEC was nominally under the responsibility of the Minister of Economy, the Secretary of Commerce, Guillermo Moreno, aggressively took over responsibility for reforms in INDEC, with the support of President Kirchner. When ministers of economy such as Felisa Miceli, Miguel Peirano, and later Martin Lousteau sought to manage the reform of INDEC themselves by bringing new leadership, Moreno's role was further supported by Kirchner, contributing in the case of Peirano to his decision to resign his post. The mismanagement of the situation in INDEC has proven to have many far-reaching consequences for the credibility of the government, including the features of bonds tied to GDP growth, calculation of interest rates, and all-important tax rates on nominal and real profits.

Claims of hegemony and authoritarian national state power

One of the most interesting reactions arising from Kirchner's efforts to reassert the power of the national government was the repeated criticism by the political opposition that the Kirchner administrations, first Nestor Kirchner and later Cristina Fernandez de Kirchner, have sought to exercise "hegemonic" power. This criticism has resulted in part from the Kirchners' direct approach to governing, with relatively little attention given to consultation and public participation, but also by the use of presidential decrees for key policy areas, bypassing the Argentine Congress. Nestor Kirchner used these presidential powers extensively during his presidency. After seven months into her presidency, Cristina Fernandez de Kirchner proudly noted that she had not used emergency powers even once.[51] But the method of governing is hardly "authoritarian" if one considers the Soviet Union, China, or even Pinochet's Chile. In the case of the Kirchners, they were democratically elected and fairly defeated a divided opposition. The latter had been even further divided in 2006 and in the 2007 presidential campaign in which opposition parties and candidates vainly tried to build coalitions to defeat Cristina Fernandez de Kirchner's candidacy. Indeed, an effort was even made to unite the conservative right led by Ricardo Lopez Murphy with the allegedly progressive left led by Elisa Carrio of the ARI, but these candidates could not agree on anything except their opposition to the Kirchners.

The meaning of hegemonic power is clearly problematic in a society in which there are significant differences in economic and political interests. From 2003, the victory of Nestor Kirchner represented a version of Peronism, which sharply differed from the so-called Peronism of the 1990s under Carlos Menem. In fact, there are very few substantive policy similarities. Both relied on the support of the Peronist party and its affiliates and supporters such as the unions. But the assertion that Kirchner exerted "hegemonic power" is exaggerated.

What is true is that the Argentine state was significantly strengthened by Nestor Kirchner in his efforts to be "present" and not "absent" on the most important policy issues affecting the economic recovery of the country after the crisis of 2001–2002. The relative efficacy of the state in the period 2003–2007 was noteworthy in several respects in light of previous Argentine political history. First, the President had clearly indicated that a "present state" was needed to achieve important national goals. Secondly, presence meant the active use of policy instruments, public expenditures, restructuring of institutions such as the Supreme Court, and a major policy change in areas such as human rights. For the economy, the strengthening of the state has clearly helped to achieve key development objectives including promoting economic growth and investment, reducing unemployment and the poverty rate, targeting pro-poor social expenditures, and substantially increasing educational expenditures as a share of GDP.

7 A new government to address the geographies of inequality

On December 10, 2007, Cristina Fernandez de Kirchner, Senator and First Lady, was inaugurated as the first woman elected president of Argentina. Her husband, President Nestor Kirchner, had announced in July 2007 that he would not run for a second term and that his wife, Cristina, a long-time Argentine politician would be the candidate for the *Frente para la Victoria*. Kirchner's decision was not a surprise, even though it was a remarkable decision for a popular and successful president who had an approval rating of about 70 percent at that time. Kirchner announced that a presidency under Cristina would deepen the changes he had introduced during his term since 2003 and also herald a new period of strengthening institutions in a democratic Argentina.

Despite extensive critical comment by potential candidates from other political parties, from the left to the right, it was clear that the successes of the Kirchner administration would provide a solid basis of support for Cristina's candidacy. Public opinion polls indicated widespread support for the First Lady and scattered, but much less, support for other candidates.

The candidacy was formally announced in July and through a series of campaign events during August 2007. Cristina chose Julio Cobos, the governor of Mendoza Province and a member of the Radical Party, as her Vice-Presidential candidate and running mate. This choice represented an important effort to reach out beyond the Peronist political party and to widen her political base. She was challenged by three other candidates: former Economy Minister Roberto Lavagna, Congresswoman Elisa Carrio of the ARI party, and Ricardo Lopez-Murphy, representing the conservative party. While the national campaign was lively, it was clear from the outset that Cristina had a large and growing advantage. The only real unknown was whether she would win enough votes in the first round to be elected or whether her opponents could force a second round. The Argentine constitution stipulates that the winning candidate has to win either 50 percent of the vote, or receive 20 percent more votes than the other candidates.

On October 28, 2007, Cristina won a resounding 45.6 percent of the vote, with Roberto Lavagna trailing her, with 20 percent, followed by Elisa Carrio with 18 percent. This margin of victory was the largest in the electoral history of Argentina. While she had promised continuity with her husband's administration, it was also clear that some changes would be forthcoming. Both the national and international press commented on her interest in strengthening Argentina's ties to other countries.

In her inauguration speech in the Senate on December 10, attended by nearly all of the presidents of Latin America, the new president focused on continuing the economic recovery of the country with more attention to addressing poverty and inequality. She spoke about social justice and equality before the law, including payment of taxes by everyone. While describing her role as president of "all Argentines," she remarked that she would not be representing any specific group, neither business, labor, south, or north. But, as explained later in this chapter, she was entering a world of differences: geographic, demographic, political, economic, and social. How she would manage these differences while pursuing the objective of reducing poverty and inequality would be the major test for her government.

Buenos Aires versus the interior

A first geographic and also political, economic, and cultural difference was the enormous gap between Buenos Aires and the interior of the country. As noted in Chapter 3, a century ago, the world's vision of Argentina was as a rural "breadbasket for the world," sending vast and unlimited quantities of meat and grains to the Old World, to Europe. This was also reflected in Argentina's view of itself, romanticizing the *pampa* and its productive potential, and scattering settlements over a vast unpopulated hinterland. Two hundred years of development have reinforced the perceived dichotomy between the country's rural character with its agricultural wealth and the reality of Argentina being a country in which over 80 percent of its population lives in urban areas. The settlement of Buenos Aires grew from its first founding in 1536 to become the capital city and, within the settlements of the country, the center of one of the most concentrated urban systems in the world.[1]

The perception of Argentina as a rural country was complemented by a growing knowledge in Europe of the high standard of living in Buenos Aires at the beginning of the twentieth century when, in fact, Buenos Aires had been one of the richest cities in the world. The city had been the destination of millions of immigrants from Europe and had become the most developed cultural and technological city of the southern hemisphere. During the twentieth century, Argentina became a country of extremes, with great agricultural wealth and productivity along with urban sophistication in culture, infrastructure, and opportunity. In contemporary times this view of Argentina as a country of extremes is a frequently heard description.[2]

Argentina's self-definition evolved considerably during the post-World War II period. The government of General Juan Peron revised the vision of Argentina as a rural breadbasket by developing an "urban welfare state" with major investments in housing, infrastructure, health, education, and social services. The emphasis on urban investment was reflected in the growth of Buenos Aires, Cordoba, Rosario, and other secondary cities from 1945 to the onset of the dictatorship in 1976.[3] Urban investment complemented the import substitution strategy adopted in the 1950s as the country developed its industries for a wide range of consumer goods. Much of this industrial investment was located on the suburban periphery of Buenos Aires, where inexpensive land and subsidized infrastructure proved to be strong incentives for private entrepreneurs.

These were the days of the relatively easy life, as pre- and postwar immigrants were able to find jobs, build homes, and send their children to free public schools and universities. This life was captured in many images of happy workers in the period 1946 to 1955.[4] The Argentine version of "coming to America" fulfilled immigrants' hopes, and despite political instability from the 1940s onward, largely delivered on the promise of unlimited growth, which had been prevalent at the time of the Centennial in 1910.[5]

By the end of the twentieth century, Buenos Aires had become a vast metropolitan area, with more than nine million people living in 23 different municipalities surrounding the Federal Capital itself with three million residents. The standard of living of people living in the Federal Capital rivaled that of European and North American cities, with its preserved architecture, excellent food, sophisticated culture, and a sense that "life" meant "life in Buenos Aires." Indeed many of the city's population lived their entire lives in the city's neighborhoods. While there are many important differences in income, welfare, and opportunity between the residents of metropolitan Buenos Aires, as presented below, they nonetheless have higher overall incomes than much of the population living in the "interior" of the country. There has been, and still is a longstanding and now growing economic, social, and cultural gap between the *porteños* of Buenos Aires together with their neighbors in the *conurbano* and the rest of the Argentine population. Some of the indicators of these differences are presented in Table 7.1 below.

As noted in earlier chapters, the recovery of the economy has also benefitted from unprecedented harvests of soya and other commodities, favorable world prices, and a carefully managed low value of the peso, which together generated large profits to rural producers of these commodities. This resurgence of the rural economy also generated enormous tax revenues from exports for the national government to use for social expenditures and to meet some of its international financial obligations. The demand-led recovery in urban areas in 2002 and 2003 and rural commodity production from 2004 to the present together produced high aggregate levels of economic growth, economic confidence, and helped to re-energize urban investment and economic activities as well. Reduced unemployment figures and many indicators of economic activity were also reflected in growing levels of consumption, traffic in the streets, and a boom in the construction sector.

In the rural sector, it is apparent that regions of agricultural growth and high export revenues have generated a major overall increase in incomes and welfare. Residents of the small towns of the *pampa* also benefited as increased incomes for rural producers generated increased spending as well, thereby increasing the demand for services within these towns. This included purchase of consumer

Table 7.1 Dimensions of HDI index by province, 2009

Jurisdiction	*Life expectancy index*	*Education index*	*Income index*	*HDI score*
CABA	0.866	0.993	0.769	0.876
Tierra del Fuego	0.857	0.970	0.785	0.871
Santa Cruz	0.833	0.943	0.811	0.862
Córdoba	0.855	0.991	0.701	0.846
La Pampa	0.857	0.956	0.721	0.844
Neuquén	0.864	0.959	0.696	0.842
Chubut	0.820	0.947	0.732	0.833
Mendoza	0.856	0.964	0.677	0.832
Santa Fe	0.846	0.963	0.688	0.832
Río Negro	0.842	0.954	0.696	0.831
National Total	0.841	0.962	0.686	0.830
Tucumán	0.832	0.982	0.659	0.824
Entre Ríos	0.845	0.962	0.658	0.822
Buenos Aires	0.843	0.943	0.668	0.818
La Rioja	0.824	0.979	0.647	0.817
Salta	0.814	0.992	0.644	0.817
Catamarca	0.835	0.962	0.647	0.815
San Luis	0.845	0.953	0.647	0.815
San Juan	0.838	0.955	0.651	0.814
Corrientes	0.816	0.991	0.621	0.809
Jujuy	0.824	0.963	0.624	0.803
Misiones	0.827	0.944	0.634	0.802
Chaco	0.788	0.968	0.627	0.794
Santiago del Estero	0.809	0.938	0.606	0.784
Formosa	0.800	0.935	0.584	0.773

Source: UNDP 2010, *Argentina: Human Development Report*, p. 12.

durables, such as cars and other consumer appliances. Just as it was said that English towns were "eating sheep" during the enclosure period and industrial revolution, so too can be said that Argentina's cities and towns were eating soy beans.

Yet, despite this rural growth and prosperity, the first geography of differences is between Buenos Aires and the interior, which President Fernandez de Kirchner refers to as "*Argentina profunda.*"

Rural–rural differences

A second geography of differences is within rural Argentina itself, in which there are enormous disparities in income and opportunity. These disparities reflect the history of settlement in the country going back to the seventeenth century and the differences in the fertility of the soil, with the fertile *pampa* producing extraordinary agricultural yields and pastures for the grazing of livestock in contrast to the arid north of the Andes. Patterns of historical cumulative advantages and disadvantages had created geographies of differences unlikely to be overcome, even in the long term.

These disparities are most pronounced when comparing the three major regions of the country: the south with its rich deposits of oil and minerals, the agriculturally rich central regions, and the largely nine poorer provinces to the north and northwest, as presented in Figure 7.1. These poorer provinces include: Jujuy, Salta, Tucuman, Catamarca, Santiago del Estero, Chaco, Misiones, Formosa, and Corrientes.

Figure 7.1 The Provinces of Argentina (source: Ministry of Defense 2011).

While this pattern of differences has existed for a long time, it has received increasing attention in recent years as a development challenge in itself. In 2005, 21 percent of the national population, or about 7.5 million people, lived in this north/northwest region, which the UNDP described as "the challenging territories" and "the critical region."[6] Within the nine provinces, about 30 percent of this population or 2.4 million people lived in Tucuman and Salta. The population of the region grew by 20 percent in the last decade, twice the national average. It was a young population, with 41 percent of the total under 17 years of age, with the highest concentration of youth in Formosa and Misiones with 44 percent of the population.

In economic and social terms, there are a much larger proportion of people living below the poverty line in these nine provinces than elsewhere in the country. Table 7.2 presents these poverty levels for 2001, 2003, and 2007.

This poor population included high proportions of poor children and a higher level of illiteracy as well. Not surprisingly, some 1.7 million households from this region entered the *Jefes* Program in 2001. Four years later this number had declined to only 29 percent of that total or 511,675 households as of March 2005. This was nevertheless a larger proportion—almost twice as large—than the 15.5 percent or 1.56 million households who had left in the program by 2005.[7] In this region, poverty is deeper and persists longer, even if the economy in the rest of the country is recovering from the crisis of 2001.

Figure 7.2 shows the distribution of monthly income by province.

The distribution of income across the provinces is also a clear reflection of the productive base of these provinces. While rural, and in most cases highly agricultural, the natural quality of the land in the more mountainous provinces limits productivity and income. In some provinces such as Tucuman, crops such as lemons are produced with great intensity, in fact, making lemons from Tucuman the major source of lemons for the market in the United States, but more profitable crops such as soya and wheat have not been grown in quantity in these areas. Table 7.3 shows the differences in exports across the provinces. This has led to new efforts to diversify these provincial economies.

Table 7.2 Proportion of population living below the poverty line, 2001–2007—Buenos Aires versus Nine Provinces

Jurisdiction	*2 sem. 2001*		*2 sem. 2003*		*1 sem. 2007*	
	Households	*Ind.*	*Households*	*Ind.*	*Households*	*Ind.*
City of Bs As	8.2	10.9	14.3	21.7	7.7	11.6
Bs As metro region	21.4	29.0	37.3	46.3	15.6	21.8
Average for 9 provinces	40.5	51.9	57.6	67.9	28.5	38.8
Country	26.2	35.9	42.6	54.7	16.3	23.4

Source: UNDP 2010, op. cit., pp. 78–79.

Note
9 provinces: Catamarca, Jujuy, Salta, Santiago del Estero, Tucumán, Corrientes Chaco, Formosa, Misiones.

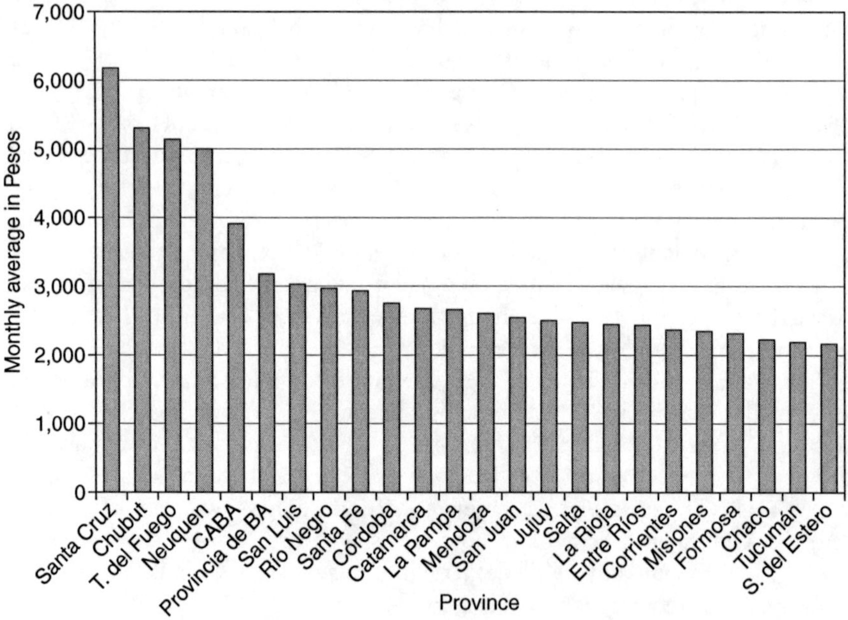

Figure 7.2 Average private sector wage by province. Monthly average in pesos, 2009 (source: INDEC 2010).

A big part of this problem has been the dearth of private investment. Table 7.4 shows the great historical differences between the levels of private investment per capita across provinces, with enormous investments in the south, for example in oil-rich Santa Cruz and within the city of Buenos Aires, compared to the north and northwest region.

To compensate for these differences, the government has directed substantial resources towards these lagging provinces. In 2003, almost 74 percent of total revenue in the nine provinces came from national government transfers for different programs.[8] This focus fit within the broader framework of relations between the national government and Argentina's 23 provinces, but also, as noted in Chapter 4, brought with it disincentives for revenue collection at the local level and other problems cited below.[9]

While a federal country, the national government has maintained close control over the policies and financial resources of the provinces. The most important law has been the Co-Participation Law of 1988, which defined the revenue-sharing formula between the national government and the provinces. This formula has been the subject of much attention, particularly as the financial resources of the state have fluctuated so much during the multiple economic crises and growth spurts. Both the magnitude of financial flows to the provinces and their timing have varied considerably, resulting in numerous provincial complaints about the difficulty of managing programs for which the funds are

Table 7.3 Exports by province, 2001–2003 (US$ millions)

Jurisdiction	*2001*	*2002*	*2003*
Group 1			
City of Buenos Aires	81.6	76.8	110.9
Group 2	**11,268.4**	**10,322.6**	**10,984.1**
Buenos Aires Metropolitan Region	11,268.4	10,322.6	10,984.1
Group 3	**7,875.1**	**7,837.7**	**9,893.2**
Córdoba	2,602.7	2,705.4	3,004.8
Mendoza	815.1	791.6	1,029.4
Santa Fe	4,457.3	4,340.6	5,859.0
Group 4	**913.6**	**833.1**	**1,171.2**
Entre Ríos	447.4	439.4	719.9
La Pampa	173.2	187.4	208.3
San Luis	293.0	206.3	243.0
Group 5	**4,189.7**	**3,595.5**	**4,100.6**
Chubut	1,360.4	1,210.9	1,501.4
Neuquén	1,213.9	1,028.1	1,244.4
Río Negro	380.2	312.1	355.4
Santa Cruz	882.7	756.0	724.3
T. del Fuego	352.5	288.3	275.2
Cuyo	**297.1**	**273.9**	**307.4**
La Rioja	185.5	150.2	185.6
San Juan	111.6	123.8	121.8
RC	**2,304.8**	**2,474.4**	**2,641.8**
N.O.A.	**1,699.1**	**1,864.0**	**1,959.0**
Catamarca	527.6	660.2	748.7
Jujuy	128.5	130.6	127.2
Salta	446.1	401.9	414.4
Stgo, del Estero	111.2	228.5	241.6
Tucumán	485.7	442.8	427.1
N.E.A.	**605.7**	**610.4**	**682.8**
Corrientes	90.0	94.7	77.2
Chaco	226.1	224.6	293.5
Formosa	23.5	14.7	12.2
Misiones	266.0	276.4	299.9
Country	**26,930.2**	**25,414.0**	**29,209.2**

Source: UNDP 2005, *Argentina: Human Development Report*, pp. 124–125.

frequently not available in a timely manner. Since much of the co-participation revenue is used to finance provincial salary expenditures, the unpredictability of the flows has heavy impacts on orderly administration as well. Together, while a central pillar of Argentine federalism, there is little doubt that the institutional arrangements for central government transfers to the provinces have weakened provincial and local government capacity and performance.

Table 7.4 Private investment per capita by province, 2002–2004 (US$)

Jurisdiction	*2002*	*2003*	*2004*
Group 1	256.17	633.39	1,318.70
City of Buenos Aires	256.17	633.39	1,318.70
Group 2	1,806.38	904.63	2,016.80
Buenos Aires Metropolitan Region	1,806.38	904.63	2,016.80
Group 3	575.72	710.25	2,408.45
Córdoba	108.52	187.18	455.24
Mendoza	333.55	228.96	914.16
Santa Fe	133.65	294.11	1,039.05
Group 4	12.24	58.16	75.16
Entre Ríos	4.00	24.66	48.76
La Pampa	0.20	9.20	3.75
San Luis	8.04	24.30	22.65
Group 5	506.65	1,421.24	3,820.40
Chubut	244.20	852.67	859.84
Neuquén	243.24	361.45	861.08
Río Negro	3.21	50.26	77.31
Santa Cruz	16.00	144.90	1,455.88
T. del Fuego	0.00	11.96	566.29
Cuyo	194.53	828.64	921.64
La Rioja	31.00	18.35	47.94
RC	158.16	395.76	1,566.79
N.O.A.	136.12	170.22	1,278.05
Catamarca	1.67	35.57	982.93
Jujuy	114.04	12.00	35.07
Salta	20.41	69.42	185.00
Stgo, del Estero	0.00	10.64	20.00
Tucumán	0.00	42.79	55.05
N.E.A.	22.04	225.54	288.74
Corrientes	15.00	1.07	0.44
Chaco	4.07	32.20	7.60
Formosa	2.62	3.41	20.00
Misiones	0.35	188.86	260.70
Country	3,509.85	4,952.07	12,127.94

Source: UNDP 2005, op. cit., pp. 122–123.

Table 7.5 and Table 7.6 show the growth of the amounts and uses of co-participation funds during 2009. The City of Buenos Aires receives 9.7 percent of federal funds as most of its income comes from its own provincial tax revenue. On the other hand, 77 percent of the income of Formosa comes from federal revenue.

One aspect of national–provincial financial relations has been the poor revenue performance of the provinces and the resulting large provincial budget

Table 7.5 Financial structure of provincial revenue funds (AR$ per capita) 2009

Jurisdiction	*Total income*	*Provincial taxes*	*Federal taxes*	*Transfers*	*Rest of income*
CABA	4,947	4,118	478	99	252
Buenos Aires	2,901	1,392	994	434	82
Corrientes	3,539	379	2,768	288	103
Santa Fe	3,553	1,038	2,041	358	116
Mendoza	3,801	909	1,778	404	710
Cordoba	3,831	1,144	1,942	499	246
Salta	3,929	615	2,341	527	446
Misiones	3,987	632	2,332	806	216
Tucuman	4,111	890	2,365	706	151
Entre Rios	4,812	831	2,849	836	295
S. Del Estero	5,084	413	3,506	1,058	107
San Juan	5,172	637	3,492	699	345
Jujuy	5,195	419	3,099	1,583	93
San Luis	5,364	1,002	3,784	372	206
Chaco	5,471	495	3,472	1,408	96
Rio Negro	5,800	1,103	3,138	656	904
Formosa	6,344	320	4,894	994	136
Catamarca	6,938	586	5,039	401	913
La Pampa	7,209	1,358	4,141	839	871
La Rioja	7,426	375	4,391	2,372	289
Chubut	8,944	1,431	2,698	811	4,004
Neuquen	11,179	1,770	2,447	570	6,392
T. del Fuego	15,065	2,381	7,323	1,943	3,418
Santa Cruz	22,577	2,304	5,440	5,710	9,123

Source: Fundación Mediterránea 2010 via Ministry of Economy and Public Finance.

deficits, which the national government is then expected to cover. This was a major source of dispute during the IMF's insistence on deficit reduction during the late 1990s and also during the crisis of 2001–2002. But the federal government has little recourse in this situation. If it holds back co-participation funds, it adds to the deficit and disables the provinces from performing their normal administrative functions, which includes revenue collection. This also has significant political implications, which have tended to concentrate power in the hands of provincial governors who become both political party bosses as well as the single largest channels of revenue for much of the country.

The issue of management of financial resources is exacerbated by the combination of natural resource constraints in most of the poorer provinces, particularly water and energy in some areas, infrastructure deficiencies such as passable all-weather roads, low education levels, serious health problems, and the cumulative consequences of having been left behind as the country developed in many sectors. It is not surprising that the human development indicators for these nine provinces are generally below the country averages and in some cases, far below, as shown in Table 7.7.

Table 7.6 Financial structure of provincial revenue funds (%) 2009

Jurisdiction	*Total income*	*Provincial taxes*	*Federal taxes*	*Transfers*	*Rest of income*
CABA	100	83.2	9.7	2.0	5.1
Buenos Aires	100	48.0	34.3	14.9	2.8
Cordoba	100	29.9	50.7	13.0	6.4
Corrientes	100	29.9	50.7	13.0	6.4
Santa Fe	100	29.2	57.4	10.1	3.3
Mendoza	100	23.9	46.8	10.6	18.7
Tucuman	100	21.6	57.5	17.2	3.7
Rio Negro	100	19.0	54.1	11.3	15.6
La Pampa	100	18.8	57.4	11.6	12.1
San Luis	100	18.7	70.5	6.9	3.8
Entre Rios	100	17.3	59.2	17.4	6.1
Chubut	100	16.0	30.2	9.1	44.8
Misiones	100	15.9	58.5	20.2	5.4
Neuquen	100	15.8	21.9	5.1	57.2
T. del Fuego	100	15.8	48.6	12.9	22.7
Salta	100	15.7	59.6	13.4	11.3
San Juan	100	12.3	67.5	13.5	6.7
Santa Cruz	100	10.2	24.1	25.3	40.4
Chaco	100	9.0	63.5	25.7	1.8
Catamarca	100	8.4	72.6	5.8	13.2
Jujuy	100	8.1	59.7	17.4	6.1
S. del Estero	100	8.1	69.0	20.8	2.1
Formosa	100	5.0	77.1	15.7	2.1
La Rioja	100	5.0	77.1	15.7	2.1

Source: Fundación Mediterránea 2010 via Ministry of Economy and Public Finance.

Intra-urban differences

The third major category of differences is within urban areas themselves. These differences reflect disparities in income, access to basic infrastructure, housing quality, and opportunities for social mobility. Table 7.8 shows some of these disparities within the major urban areas of Argentina: Buenos Aires, Cordoba, and Rosario.

These differences are largely metropolitan, reflecting the high degree of spatial and income segregation among groups, with many high quality gated communities, called "*countries*" or "*barrios cerrados*" in Argentina, close to growing area of slums called "*villas miserias.*" The case of metropolitan Buenos Aires illustrates this dramatically with three rings of settlement surround the Federal Capital. The third ring has expanded rapidly and now covers about 17,000 square kilometers. Since the 1980s, within the second and third rings, more than 500 private, gated communities have been established, with private homes, schools, and other facilities. This pattern of development fits within a broader pattern of privatization of urban space and infrastructure. The metropolitan area is now a mosaic of public and increasingly private spaces—also described as "insularities"—in which new forms of urban settlement and culture

Table 7.7 Human development index indicators

Jurisdiction	*% without healthcare 2008*	*Secondary graduation rate 2007*	*Level of infant mortality* 2008*
CABA	26	86.5	7.7
Santa Cruz	29	68.6	10.6
Tierra del Fuego	30	75.3	6.8
Chubut	40	78.0	10.4
La Rioja	41	74.9	15.0
Santa Fe	42	79.1	11.5
Catamarca	45	85.6	15.3
Córdoba	46	74.0	12.1
La Pampa	46	78.8	14.9
Tucumán	48	76.4	13.8
National Total	48	–	12.5
Neuquén	49	72.1	7.4
Entre Ríos	49	72.4	13.5
Buenos Aires	49	82.8	12.4
Río Negro	50	71.9	11.7
Mendoza	51	78.3	10.8
San Luis	52	76.7	13.1
San Juan	53	76.4	14.4
Jujuy	54	79.7	14.0
Misiones	58	75.6	13.9
Salta	60	83.4	14.4
Corrientes	62	81.2	17.1
S. del Estero	64	70.0	10.4
Chaco	66	78.5	18.0
Formosa	66	84.6	19.2

Source: UNDP 2010, op. cit., pp. 66, 145, 152.

Note
* For every 1,000 born.

have developed.[10] These patterns are consistent with global urban patterns seen in other countries and result from the impacts of globalization, infrastructure, technology, and information.[11]

Studies of the growth of gated communities show that the patterns in the late 1980s gained momentum and by 2000, there were 434 private communities in

Table 7.8 Intra-urban disparities

Urban Area	*Households below poverty line (2009)[a]*	*% Without healthcare (2008)[b]*	*Net secondary completion rates[b]*	*Employment growth rate[c]*
Buenos Aires	8.7	38.1	83.8	5.8
Cordoba	6.3	35.7	74.0	4.7
Rosario	9.7	25.7	79.1	4.1

Sources: [a]INDEC 2010, [b]UNDP 2010, [c]Ministry of Labor 2007.

metropolitan Buenos Aires (252 "*barrios privadas*," 139 "*countries*," 36 *chacras*, and seven mega-housing developments). By August 2000, some 500,000 people lived in an area of 323 square kilometers or an area 1.6 times larger than the Federal Capital.[12] Ten years later both the population and the area has expanded considerably.[13] This form of growth is more intense than similar developments in other Latin American cities, but shares common features.

Alongside the spread of gated communities has been the growth of shopping centers in the north and western sides of the Federal Capital, with dozens of stores, restaurants, movie theaters, special entertainment parks for children, and other services. Their design and appearance, with Burger King, McDonalds, Home Depot, Walmart, and other international brands, gives the feeling that they could be any place in the world. They have nothing to do with the Buenos Aires of the 1970s or 1980s, much less with earlier periods, and yet they are reflections on the penetration of global capital and global culture into Argentina.

In contrast to these ultra-modern settlement patterns, there are growing numbers of households without even minimal infrastructure. In contrast to the Federal Capital, where only 0.1 percent of households lacked access to potable water supply in 1991, these numbers were at 43.6 percent for the metropolitan municipalities and as high as 90.5 percent in General Sarmiento and 86.7 percent in Florencio Varela.[14] These low levels of service were ameliorated somewhat during the late 1990s, but continue to exist in the third ring of metropolitan Buenos Aires. Water supply is a good indicator of housing quality, which varies considerably within these municipalities, but remains, on average, quite poor.

More recent metropolitan studies demonstrate that the economic structure of the *conurbano* has shifted considerably from the zone of expansion of the 1960s. The liberalization of the economy after 1976 resulted in the closing of many of these metropolitan firms, which were producing goods for the Buenos Aires population. However, they were unable to compete with cheaper imported products. The economic collapse of these firms also meant the impoverishment of many of the 23 municipalities of the *conurbano*, which subsequently were pleased to sell land to private developers of gated communities. Not surprisingly, some of these gated communities are surrounded by informal settlements whose inhabitants may work in the gated communities.[15]

The *villas miserias* now house millions of people in the metropolitan area in the 23 municipalities outside the Federal Capital. Some of these, such as La Matanza, with a population of more than two million people, are large cities unto themselves. La Matanza has become the second largest municipality in the country. In 2004, La Matanza had an unemployment rate of about 34 percent, with 39.8 percent of the population classified as below the poverty line, 47 percent had no access to clean water, and 48.5 percent of the youth between 14 and 18 years lived in households below the poverty line.[16] Other large slums, such as La Cava, in the north of the metropolitan area, also lack infrastructure and social services and rival some of the worst slums in Latin America. The spread of these slums brings sharp contrasts to the metropolitan area with its gated communities. Polarization and social exclusion had become an important spatial reality.[17]

While earlier chapters have reported the drop in urban unemployment since 2002, the rate of unemployment for the municipalities around Buenos Aires stabilized around 13.6 percent in 2006. This was the highest unemployment rate of any region in the country, contrasting for example with a 9.1 percent rate in the Federal Capital.[18] High suburban unemployment had grown considerably throughout the 1990s, with for example, the *partido de Moreno*, with six *localidades* and 144 *barrios*, increasing unemployment from 5.7 percent in 1991 to 21.1 percent in 1999.[19]

More recent data support the general conclusions of many research studies of metropolitan Buenos Aires during the mid-1990s that urban poverty was increasing, that the share of the population without adequate water supply, sanitation, and housing was not being reduced very much, and that the spatial growth of the metropolitan area was leading to the growing exclusion of an increasing share of the population.[20]

Moreover, these trends were not changing even when the national economy was growing at reasonable rates. The economic crisis of 1995, following the Tequila Crisis in Mexico, and downturns after the Brazilian financial crisis of 1998–1999, led to further macro-economic adjustments, increases in unemployment felt most sharply in the poor neighborhoods of the *conurbano*, and cutbacks in public expenditures. Urban poverty was deepening and spreading further in metropolitan space.[21] This poverty has also been reflected in declining health status, increasing crime, and growing dropout rates in elementary and secondary schools in the *conurbano*.[22]

In addition to these intra-urban differences at the metropolitan level, there have also been important processes of transformation within the Federal Capital. These processes include greater differentiation among the various parts of the central city. As mentioned in Chapter 2, a study of public expenditure data from 1991 to 1997 examined the distribution of public investment in infrastructure according to the 21 school districts of the Federal Capital. This study showed there are five categories of districts of the city and that 11.5 percent of the population received 68 percent of public investment in infrastructure.[23] This pattern correlated closely with primary and secondary school dropout rates, rates of health care coverage, and the physical characteristics of housing and infrastructure. While correlation is not causation, this bundling of characteristics for different neighborhoods was also consistent with common sense perceptions.

Recognition of differences between the north and south of the Federal Capital was the basis of the decision of the city government in 1999 to establish special programs and institutions to develop a plan for the South. This led to investment incentives and an extensive planning exercise, but only a small level of either public or private investment has actually been devoted to this area. The plan had included a mix of improvements in infrastructure, incentives for private investment in manufacturing, training programs for residents, and a more spatial orientation to the allocation of municipal public investment.

The reality, however, is that there was deep and pervasive urban poverty in the metropolitan area as a whole. While open unemployment dropped considerably to

7 percent by December 2007, many Argentines were worried about finding or losing their jobs. The lack of urban job security is felt most acutely by young people, for whom the unemployment rate is considerably higher. In 2005, *Clarín* reported that there were 100,000 children working in the streets of greater Buenos Aires.[24] Real incomes and purchasing power dropped significantly following the devaluation of the peso in 2002. Prices for basic foods and other essential services have also increased with inflation since 2006. Tariffs for water supply, electricity, and telephones have increased considerably in this period.[25] Public expenditures for health and education dropped precipitously during the crisis of 2001–2003 and led to deteriorating services in both sectors, even though national expenditures for education were increased by the Kirchner administration after 2006.

Not surprisingly, these economic problems are reflected in growing social problems: in crime, particularly robberies and kidnapping, in rapidly rising rates of suicide among young people, and in the use of drugs, particularly in the vast slum areas of the *conurbano* of Buenos Aires. Most significantly, they are also reflected in the growing number of protests and demonstrations. Indeed, from December 2001 to February 2003, there were some 13,000 demonstrations in various parts of the country. The *piquetero* movement, which started in the late 1990s, has grown and split into those groups supporting the Kirchner government and those opposed. The demands of these groups focus mostly on jobs. It is noteworthy that even after an almost 35 percent increase in the minimum wage in early June 2005, a few days later there were still major *cortos*, or street barricades which stopped and diverted traffic, even on the major *Pan-Americana* highway leading out of Buenos Aires to the north.

Convergent demographies and geographies

The three types of geographical differences cited above also converge with growing differences for specific categories of people. The first distinction is according to age. On one hand, Argentina has large numbers of elderly retired people who require public retirement assistance as well as various services. The Kirchner administration was quite conscious of these needs and has substantially increased these payments since 2003. A second group, youth, still faces difficulties finding well-paying jobs. The level of youth unemployment is very high, particularly in the slums of metropolitan Buenos Aires where problems of violence and drugs have become rampant.

A second demographic category concerns employment itself, specifically whether people are working in the formal or informal sectors. As noted in Chapter 5, the share of the labor force working *en negro* has diminished since 2003, but it still remains very high in rural areas, reaching close to 50 percent. In some provinces this number is as high as 63 percent.[26] The 2010 national estimate for the share of informal employment is 35.8 percent.[27] Most of these people work in agriculture, for low wages, without any social benefits or job security. Informal rural employment is thus a significant part of the national and rural poverty problem.

One of the important aspects of this problem is that, by being informal it is deliberately kept out of sight by the large farmers and multi-national companies, which use this labor. Large agricultural profits rely in part on cheap labor. This issue was largely kept out of the public debate during the conflict over tax increases for agricultural exports, which will be discussed, in the next chapter.

An important conclusion of this analysis of differences is that maintaining such dichotomies is evidently functional for economic interests. The dichotomies between Buenos Aires and the interior, between regions, and within urban areas are important social constructed realities with both political meaning and economic content. They provide the context in which the politics of distribution take place.

8 The politics of redistribution

The conflict with *el campo*

The government of President Cristina Fernandez de Kirchner faced its first test three months after taking office when it announced its intention to increase the redistribution of income through taxing the large profits on agricultural exports. This episode, presented in some detail in this chapter, demonstrates the difficulties of the politics of distribution. It also represents the first major challenge to the government's strategy to reinforce the role of the state itself and particularly the role of the state as an agent of redistribution, as explained in Chapter 6. It also illustrates how the integration of a major sector, in this case agriculture, with the global economy presented an important opportunity for expanding revenue, but in so doing destabilized the government's position and power in its efforts to continue on the path from recovery from the crisis of 2001–2002 towards a sustainable path of growth for the medium term.

On March 11, 2008, the minister of economy, Martin Lousteau, presented a plan to introduce new rates for export taxes known as *retenciones* on soya, wheat, corn, and sunflower seeds. This system was a response to rising world prices for these commodities which were reaching historic levels and which promised to deliver enormous profits to Argentine farmers. The Ministry of Economy had developed a system of sliding tax rates for these agricultural exports depending on world prices. The proposed system was also intended to protect purchasing power for Argentine consumers, with subsidies for milk and cooking oils. global price increases of crops such as soya had seriously affected the prices of other foods in Argentina and other countries such as Brazil and Mexico as farmers substituted these high-priced crops for food crops.

The Government proposal involved a major increase—from 35 to 45 percent—in the export tax on soya, whose world price has increased from about $330 a ton in March 2008 to about $570 a ton in July. The objective of the tax increase was to raise funds to redistribute income from the rich to the poor, through subsidies, social services, and other programs. About US$1.2 billion or 0.04 percent of GDP was the expected revenue for this purpose.

Large farmers immediately objected to these measures, claiming that this level of taxation would be unfair and would cut into their projected incomes. Four major agricultural organizations joined together in the protest, including both older conservative organizations of large farmers with a federation of small producers—an unlikely coalition.

The conflict over taxes on agricultural exports in Argentina had its historical roots in the fact that most governments in the 200-year history of the country have taxed agricultural exports as a way of generating revenue for other purposes. As noted earlier, the country has a huge potential for producing food and grains; a 2008 report estimated that it can produce enough food for 450 million people, in contrast to its population of about 38 million. There has always been a significant group of powerful, wealthy rural landowners who appear on the political scene whenever they think their interests are being challenged.

This protest proved to be a cataclysmic episode in Argentine politics. This chapter presents the unfolding of these dramatic events over 130 days in four periods:

- the first reactions and negotiations from March 11 to April 1;
- the month-long pause in the conflict from early April to early May;
- the intensification through the events celebrating the May 25 anniversary of the 1810 revolution from Spain up until mid-June when the president decided to send the proposed legislation to Congress, and
- the surprising Congressional outcome through late July 2008 and its consequences

It also suggests that while the conflict was experienced inside the country as a particularly Argentine phenomenon, it has many characteristics, which can be understood through the lens of social science theory.

First reactions

In response to the criticism of the rural lobbies, Economy Minister Lousteau remarked on March 16 that, "The reaction of agriculture was exaggerated," noting that the projected revenues from the *retenciones* would account for more than half of the 2008 projected surplus. This form of tax and its revenue also lay outside the revenue allocated to the provinces under the co-participation law of 1988. A leading conservative journalist, Mariano Grondona, wrote an article entitled, "Nothing for society, all for the State."[1] Grondona cited Marx and attacked the appropriation of surplus value, in this case from inflated world commodity prices. He noted that there had been *retenciones* in 2002–2003 under President Duhalde and there had been little opposition during time of emergency. Under President Nestor Kirchner, the government had also financed higher public expenditures through revenue from the *retenciones* and this had some justification. But he strongly objected to the new tax rates saying that the revenue was for the state and not for the poor.

The immediate response by farmers was very striking because the ability to export such quantities of commodities did not just depend on favorable world prices but also on the government's management of the value of the peso in relation to the dollar, allowing Argentine exports to be cheap for foreign purchasers but providing huge profits for the exporters. The government's policies had very much been pro-farmer, including a wide variety of subsidies such as for fuel for trucks bringing crops to market.

Despite these policies and subsidies, the farmers groups had set up illegal blockades on forty highways around the country by March 18 and threatened to stop all shipments of food grains for export and also for consumption in urban areas. These actions coincided with newspaper attacks on the government, alleging that the first three months of the new administration had produced no accomplishments and that the President's authority had been undermined by a "*doble commando*" or shared command with her husband. *La Nación* charged that the "economy is on automatic pilot."[2] The media joined in trying to weaken the president.

A journalist more sympathetic to the government, Mario Wainfeld, observed that the protest was not a strike, as most of the media was describing it, but rather a "lockout" by owners seeking higher profits. Using the proletarian term, "strike," was an example of manipulation of language by large farmers for whom the 2002 devaluation and the elimination of foreign debts for farmers were *manna* from heaven.[3] Mario Rapoport, a leading economic historian supported the *retenciones* as a tool against inflation. He noted that the farmers objected to being called an oligarchy but their organizations were a structure of privileged interests.[4] Some of these organizations included people linked to the military dictatorship of 1976–1982.

In response to these attacks, the government sought to reassure the country. The Economy Minister noted that, "the local economy is healthy but is not isolated from the world."[5] Lousteau argued that Argentina needed to take advantage of the global demand for its products. For each one percent less of growth of the United States' economy, US$60 million of Argentine exports could be lost.

The media continued to keep the pressure on, predicting meat shortages for the following week.[6] The lockout was the largest rural protest in 30 years, with 51 cut highways, and in one small farming town, 1,000 protestors asked the four farmers' organization to keep the protest going on indefinitely. It is interesting to note that while the conflict was apparently about tax rates, even a conservative columnist such as Nestor Scibona for *La Nación* was noting that the conflict had political roots. The economy seemed to be growing, indeed the February 2008 budgetary surplus had grown by 61.6 percent over 2007, but the political opposition was growing to the government. On March 24 there were *cacerolazos* in the streets of Buenos Aires for the first time since 2002.

On March 25, the president spoke against the protestors, describing the cutting of roads as a form of extortion against the government and the country. By this time the major cities of Argentina were experiencing food shortages, with no meat having been delivered to the major wholesale market in Buenos Aires, leaving 70 percent of butchers without meat. Prices were going up, with lettuce up to 10 pesos per kilo (US$3.30 for 2.2 pounds). The newspaper, *Critica*, described this in its headline as the "sounds of silence."[7] It reported that if the *campo* did not give in, the government would apply the law of provisioning and militarize the conflict, which would allow arrests.

The next day, the president threatened to send force to unblock the roads, to which the urban middle class responded with more *cacerolazos*. On March 27, she gave a long speech explaining the situation and declaring, "I ask them to lift the strike to dialogue."[8] She described the *retenciones* as anti-inflationary measures and, attacking the Right, she said that among the rural protestors she saw faces involved in the genocides of Plaza de Mayo of 1955, a provocative historical reference and attack against the Right. A leading intellectual, the philosopher, Jose Pablo Feinmann, characterized the President's speech as speaking truth in face of an "institutional semi-coup" and class hatred.[9] The rural organizations had been given an invitation they could politically not refuse, so they positively responded to the president's invitation. The next day they suspended the blockades and began a process of negotiation with government representatives. These discussions failed to produce an agreement and the lockout began again.

On March 31, the government announced a set of measures and refunds for small agricultural producers, hoping to break apart the unified rural lobby, but while the measures were welcomed, the organizations claimed that these measures were not enough. The government had also introduced additional subsidies of various kinds for small farmers whose average small farm is about 200 hectares, which was worth over US$1 million. By focusing on "small farmers," however, the government was also approaching a complicated set of uncomfortable facts about the rural sector, including that small farms in Argentina are not really very small, and that there are many informal laborers working illegally at low wages and no benefits on the medium and large-scale farms. The underpayment of taxes by all categories of farmers: small, medium, and large, had been very obvious when export data from the Customs Department were compared with taxes paid by some of these farmers. Some were exporting large quantities but paying negligible tax.

By the end of March, the political stakes in the conflict seemed to be escalating and many informed observers began a series of lively commentaries in the press. A leading academic, Nicolas Casullo, published a long article about the conflict, noting that the government had made an error not to differentiate the various agricultural producers by their size and economic interests. He criticized the media avalanche for having distorted facts, for example making it look like 10,000 people were present at an event when only 100 people actually attended, or giving the impression that *campesinos* are being represented by the big agricultural lobbies. He noted that the lockout was "a savage, authoritarian strike affecting the provisioning of the country," holding the population hostage through a lockout orchestrated by big companies. He remarked that this conflict went back to the old battle between *Peronismo* and landowners in 1955 and thereafter.

Casullo observed that the *cacerolazos* had amplified the whole situation, evoking memories of 2001 and therefore clearly had a "*golpista*" or *coup d'etat* objective, which was not spontaneous at all. He characterized the attack on the government as anti-institutional, anti-republican, led by people in rich neighborhoods, and fed by the media, who gave the impression that the problem would be resolved if the Government resigned. He lamented the absence of a link between the redistributive policies of the government and a strategy to communicate them. He posed the important question of how to construct policies, which have democratic support in cultural terms as well as common-sense explanation of what was happening. Finally, he argued that this episode demonstrated the nature of capitalist reform supported by different forms of Peronism since the 1970s.[10]

These observations were also reflected in an article by Ernesto Tenembaum, "*Estamos todos locos*" (we are all crazy),[11] in which he argued that the conflict had become a dichotomous formulation in which the conflict was between a government perceived as wishing to tax the rich *campo* and producers vs. the *campo* defending itself from the voracious state. Tenembaum characterized this formulation as a classic Argentine response: too many people shouting, using ideological terms, using extreme means, taking out the flags, and too little real discussion about what is happening and why. He argued that another view is possible: that the *retenciones* were not so significant and would provide about US$1.5 billion in government revenue, a small amount for the state budget and less than a third of the rapid train being proposed between Buenos Aires and Rosario for which the government had announced it would invest US$4 billion.

On March 30 the lockout began again, leading the president to suspend her trip to London to meet Prime Minister Gordon Brown. A conservative columnist, Joaquin Morales Sola, remarked that, "a political cycle involving strong leadership by one person was over" and that multiple forces were now at play.[12] At this time, most of the newspapers began to publish detailed tables showing the proposed tax levels and their likely revenue amounts. Table 8.1 shows these figures.

This table shows the significant increases in taxes on soya and sunflower exports and decreases for corn and wheat. The increase in the tax rate for soya from 35 to 44.1 percent was expected to generate an additional US$1.756 billion. If the soya price rose above US$600 per ton, the tax rate would rise to 49 percent. The overall grain harvest was expected to be about 94 million tons, with an overall value of US$39 billion or about 13 percent of GDP. The expected revenue from taxes on grain exports was 43 billion pesos or roughly US$14.4 billion. These numbers need to be understood in relation to the high prices of grains, particularly soya which had already reached US$515 per ton by the end of March 2008, in contrast to the highest price a decade earlier, in 1997, when a ton of soya was US$281. Against this background, the producer organizations were asking the government for more "generosity."

One of the most sober voices on this subject was Aldo Ferrer, an internationally known Argentine macro-economist and a former minister of industry. Ferrer wrote that subsidies and *retenciones* were needed instruments for macroeconomic management and to overcome the distorting effects of great wealth

Table 8.1 Proposed tax rates and projected revenue

Exports	*Price F.O.B. (avg. US$, Feb. 08)*	*Existing export duty*	*Mobile export duty (avg. US$, Feb. 08)*	*Price range (US$/t)*	*Actual export duty (%)*	*New average export duty (%)*
Soy	515	35%	44.1	0–200	35	23.5
				201–300	35	23.5–28
				301–400	35	28–36
				401–500	35	36–43
				Actual 501–600	35	43–49
				600+	35	49+
Sunflower	569	28%	39.1	0–200	32	23.5
				201–300	32	23.5–25
				301–400	32	25–31
				401–500	32	31–37
				Actual 501–600	32	37–45
				600+	32	45+
Wheat	345	28%	27.1	0–200	28	20
				201–300	28	20–24
				Actual 301–400	28	24–30
				401–600	28	30–46
				600+	28	46+
Corn	217	25%	24.2	0–180	25	20
				Actual 181–220	25	20–25
				221–260	25	25–32
				261–300	25	32–40
				301+	25	40+

Source: Clarín, March 30, 2008, p. 20.

from natural resources in a country, the so-called "Dutch disease," whereby relative prices from a natural resource reduce the value of other products and services within an economy.[13] Ferrer defended the government's responsibility to manage prices.

Despite the publication of these various perspectives, the political situation was heating up. The children of producers and agronomy students issued a statement saying that they were not "*golpistas.*"[14] *La Nación* published an article equating the *retenciones* with the unpopular *corralito* of 2002, arguing that the taxes were confiscatory as was the freezing of bank deposits.[15] Another article argued that a model that kept increasing taxes to fund public expenditures was not sustainable.[16] The newspaper published a table showing that the government's projected surplus for 2008, indicating that public expenditures were going up by 43 percent in the first semester of 2008 in comparison to 2007, while income would only increase by 40 percent. Nevertheless, the overall surplus would increase from 3.2 to 4.8 percent of GDP.[17]

Under the headline, "Love or War," *Critica* reported that the President said there would be no meetings with the four rural organizations unless they accepted the government's last offer. She promised to "re-establish order."[18] On April 1, 2008, she gave another speech, this time in the highly symbolic Plaza de Mayo where Argentine presidents had historically called for popular support for their governments. In her third speech in six days, she announced large refunds to small producers and other measures and warned the big companies that "you are not the owners of the country."[19] She warned against the "soya-ization" of the economy, leading to higher prices for meat, corn, and wheat.[20] She said that in the 100 days since her inauguration, she had never witnessed such attacks and efforts to de-stabilize the government.

The president's concerns about the role of soya were supported several days later with the release of an independent report showing that the expansion of planting of soya had endangered the food security of the country: 200,000 hectares of fruit and vegetables had been lost, thereby increasing their prices. Similar trends were affecting wheat, corn, rice, sunflower oil, avena, and centeno.[21] This move towards higher-priced crops followed the devaluation of the *peso* in 2002 when there was a significant revaluing of agricultural land which was *Pagina/12* described as "spectacular." In the soya and corn-growing areas, land had increased from an average of US$3,950 per hectare in 2003 to US$9,167 by end of 2007, a 132 percent increase. In other areas, such as Trenque Lauquen and Rivadavia, land prices had increased from an average of US$1,525 per hectare in 2003 to US$4, 283 by end 2007, or a 181 percent increase. In contrast the fiscal value for tax purposes only increased 1 percent in this period. Rural incomes had soared, for example, breaking records for car sales as well. The report remarked that in 2002 farmers were unhappy with increases in *retenciones* from 10 to 20 percent by then President Eduardo Duhalde.

A pause

On April 2, the rural producers announced they would lift the lockout for 30 days to seek a negotiated settlement. *Critica* then published a balance sheet on the conflict on April 3, 2008. The article identified the losses as:

1 The government's proposal for the small producers was exactly what the *Federación Agraria* had asked for before the lockout.
2 There had been the first *cacerolazo* since 2001.
3 The government response had helped bring the rural sector together.
4 The episode had publicly shown differences within the Administration, notably between the president and vice-president, Julio Cobos.
5 The government had identified with verbal attacks of Luis D'Elia, leader of the *Federación de Tierra y Vivienda*, on the upper class.
6 There had been widespread criticism of the president for her attack on a widely-admired cartoonist, Ermengildo Sabat, who had published a cartoon showing the Ppresident with a bandage over her mouth, indicating that she should be silent.
7 The shortage of goods in urban centers.
8 The government had lost control of the "agenda" for its initiatives.

In contrast, there had been the following gains:

1 The government had shown its ability to resist the lockout without repression of the demonstrators.
2 The government had changed its discursive tone.
3 The government had developed a proposal, which helped the small producers and focused attention on the rich ones.
4 The government had disciplined the majority of its Peronist supporters.
5 The government had reaffirmed the authority of the Head of State.
6 The episode had shown the weakness of the political opposition.
7 The government had managed to fill the Plaza de Mayo with its supporters.[22]

Other newspapers also offered points for this balance sheet. *Clarín* noted that the country's economy had lost 300 million pesos in the previous 23 days. Despite the cease-fire agreed in Gualeguaychu, the president had been challenged by a new and previously unknown politics, different from what her husband had faced.[23]

An important result of this process was that the poor had been most affected by the conflict, as food prices had gone up during the shortages produced by the blockades of the highway and then had remained at levels higher than before the lockout.[24] These additional price increases were above the already substantial increases from 2001 to before the strike in 2008 for some fruits such as oranges (295 percent), grapefruits (299 percent), tomatoes (278 percent), and lettuce

(282 percent).[25] Not surprisingly, the image of government had dropped among different income groups after the first 23 days of the conflict.

On April 11, the government reopened negotiations with the four agricultural lobbies. The president met for three hours with the leaders of the four organizations who insisted publicly that the tax rates be lowered for all producers. The Chief of Cabinet, Alberto Fernandez, met with the leaders the following day and set an agenda for discussions, while at the same time limiting the exports of wheat and meat. This action actually tightened restrictions further, and directly attacked the interests of the rural exporters. A week later, the parties agreed to guarantee the provisioning of meat to the country as the government agreed to lift restrictions on beef exports. The Government also put into place a system of refunds for small- and medium-sized grain producers.

Through this period there was growing tension around the prices of food for consumers. On April 15, it was reported that a basket of basic food commodities was 23 percent higher than in February 2007. The first 12 days of April alone had seen increases of 4.46 percent according to consumer surveys.[26] Yet, the next day the farm organizations denounced the Secretary of Commerce, Guillermo Moreno, for the pressure he was exerting to lower the price of meat for consumers.[27] *Critica* reported on April 21 that the farm organizations were armed and ready to fight, raising the specter of violence.[28] The newspaper also presented an analysis of exports before the March 11, showing that there had been a boom in exports in February 2008, some 70 percent more than in 2007. The implication of this boom was that some of these multi-national companies had had advance notice of the tax increases and were seeking to avoid paying additional taxes by expediting exports during the month of February. These data are presented below in Figure 8.1.

The stakes in the conflict were raised considerably on April 24, 2008, when Economy Minister Martin Lousteau resigned. Lousteau had been having

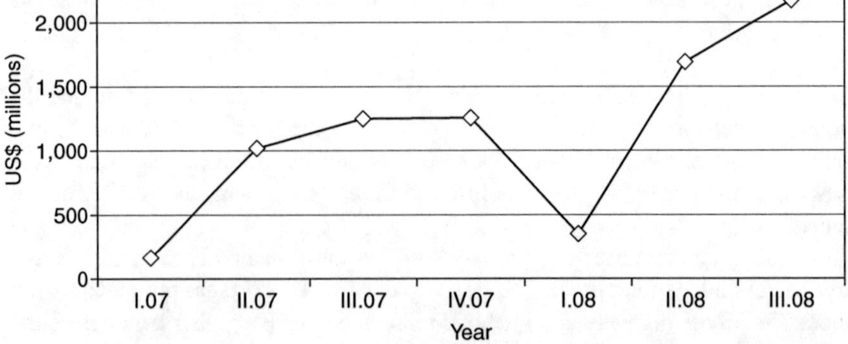

Figure 8.1 Export growth of seeds and oleaginous fruits, 2007–2008 (source: Ministry of Economy 2008).

disagreements with Commerce Secretary Moreno and with former president Nestor Kirchner. He had sent a letter to the President proposing a set of changes in economic policy, including an effort to address inflation, but his proposals were not accepted. While Lousteau's resignation was taken as a significant act at the time, he quickly became irrelevant to the conflict and his involvement was barely acknowledged by the press in the months which followed.

The conflict intensifies

By the end of April, an agreement was reached for both meat and wheat exports. But despite this progress, the protests started again on May 2, even though there were no blockades of highways. Five days later, following a meeting with the government, the agricultural organizations again blocked the roads, saying they would maintain the lockout against grain exports until May 15, but without blocking the roads. Both civic and industrial groups called on the government to reopen negotiations, which occurred during the third week of the month. While the government was optimistic, the rural groups were still unhappy with the lack of resolution to the dispute.

Public understanding of the conflict grew substantially during April and May. In early May, Horacio Verbitsky, one of the country's leading investigative journalists, published an article on "hidden actors," referring to the heretofore hidden role of the multi-national companies such as Monsanto and the association supporting mechanized farming of genetically-modified crops. He also noted that the leading newspapers, *Clarín* and *La Nación*, were partners in an organization, *Expoagro*, which was involved with hundreds of millions of dollars each year in agricultural exports.[29]

There were also growing concerns about effect of the lockout on the economy, as Argentines began to buy dollars as a hedge against a possible major crisis. This panic behavior was certainly exaggerated as some journalists began to suggest that the current crisis could result in a collapse as had occurred in 2001 and 2002. But some economists, including Daniel Marx, a former Secretary of Finance under President De la Rua, replied that buying dollars made no sense and that there was no parallel with the situation in 2001, when Argentina faced enormous external obligations, had growing unemployment and was in a deep recession. In contrast, the country had ample reserves in the Central Bank, high growth, and low unemployment.[30] In mid-May, the government agency, INDEC, issued a statement saying that the economy was growing in spite of the lockout. Growth in March 2008 had been 8.1 percent, equal to February 2007, with exports growing at 19 percent while imports grew at 22 percent. The numbers of tourists also grew by 11 percent over 2007, with 223,350 tourists in March alone. The economic importance of these figures is underlined by the fact that most tourists stay in the country for 13.7 days, with Europeans staying 22.5 days on average, thereby generating significant income for the country.[31]

Despite these positive signs, *La Nación*, continually critical of the government, published an article on its front page with the title, "Conflict affects all of the economy."[32] Some of the data on the slowdown included: a 50 percent drop in sales of agricultural machinery, worth more than US$20 million, 350,000 tons per day of grains not being exported, 160,000 trucks not working at a cost of US$2,600 a day per truck, an increase in the country risk from 490 on March 11 to 552 by May 16, US$1 billion per month lost in export taxes, and a drop in reserves of the Central Bank of US$590 million.[33] Clearly, there were some significant economic losses, which would eventually show up in the annual growth rate and in other macro-economic indicators.

An economic reporter, Jose Natanson, observed, however, in early May that not only was the macro-economy being affected by the lockout, but so was the micro-economy of the country.[34] He noted that while the macro-economy may go well, this is not necessarily the same for the micro-economy which is much more complicated. Macro-economic growth is tied to advantages from the exchange rate, including 85 percent of Argentina's exports. But what was missing was value-added of the kind, which Brazil has developed in sectors such as pharmaceuticals, oils, and technology. Changing macro-economic circumstances were also beginning to have an impact on economic decision-making at the firm level. This was being highlighted mostly by opposition economists writing in *La Nación*, with estimates that the country would lose from US$30 to US$40 million a day due to the economic slowdown resulting from the conflict.[35]

But what was most pronounced was the increasingly political character of the conflict. Producers inside Buenos Aires Province issued a statement saying that they would "resist until the end," as they cut the roads. In Cordoba Province the farmers pressured the governor to press more on the national government.[36] Even though producers were complaining about tax increases, by early May only 120 of 62,000 producers had asked for the refunds to which they were entitled. Commenting on the claim equating the *campo* with "*la patria*" by Mario Llambias, one of the rural leaders and a cousin of the former minister of economy during the military dictatorship, Horacio Verbitsky wrote an article entitled: "It's politics, stupid."[37] *Pagina/12* reported that the leaders of the *campo* had hired an advertising and media firm to manage its public relations. This firm, headed by a Colombian, Felipe Noguera, had previously been linked to former economy minister Cavallo, former president Menem, and former president Duhalde. The firm had used public opinion surveys, and had decided to link "*la patria*" with "*el campo*" as a slogan likely to generate support for the rural protest. Noguera's firm had worked with for conservative Nicaraguans in their electoral campaigns in the 1990s.[38]

Verbitsky observed that this strategy had also been linked to the military and the Church in earlier periods. He further raised the issue of external pressures against Latin American populism, whether against the policies and external posture of leaders such as Hugo Chavez, Evo Morales, Nestor Kirchner, or Cristina Fernandez de Kirchner. He noted that the claim of "populism" arises when there are proposals affecting the ownership, management, or taxation of natural resources.

Press criticism of the president remained constant during this period. On May 13, *Critica* published on its cover a picture of the president, with the headline, "Missing." The newspaper asked where she was, arguing that she was ignoring the rural lobbies. At the same time various governors were beginning to take sides, as their rural constituencies began to pressure them. The most notable defection from the government's position was Juan Schiaretti, the governor of the economically important Cordoba Province. Schiaretti, however, was countered by Daniel Scioli, the governor of Buenos Aires Province. The government sought to keep the governors out of the debate but this proved difficult. In mid-May, the president flew to Rome to participate in a meeting at the United Nations Food and Agriculture Organization on global food prices. In her speech, she strongly emphasized the need to protect the poor from the impacts of higher prices.

On her return, the president met with industrialists and asked for their support for the launching of an *Acuerdo de Bicentenario*, a Bicentennial agreement to identify a development path for the country. She continued to criticize the biased coverage by the media of the conflict. On May 15, she surprised the country by being the sole speaker at a ceremony installing her husband as the president of the Peronist party. In that speech, she also called for a dialogue with the rural lobbies if they lifted the blockades on the country's highways. This was well received by the press who noted that the ball was now in the court of the rural protestors. The government also received support from a group of influential intellectuals and academics who issued a "*Carta Abierta*" supporting the government, while noting that it nevertheless needed to resolve outstanding problems. The government also appeared to believe that being tough in its negotiations and refusing to meet with the rural lobbies while the lockout was going on would strengthen its own position. Governor Schiaretti and others questioned this position.

The political speculation about the position of the government versus the growing power of the *campo* continued in anticipation of two opposing events called for Independence Day on May 25, 2008: one called by the government in Salta in northern Argentina where the President would speak, and an opposing event scheduled in Rosario, organized by the farm lobbies and expected to be attended by opposition groups. One observer noted that no other Argentine historical case had occurred where farmers were doing so well economically and yet had staged a lockout. He commented that there were exaggerated claims about the role of the agricultural sector in the country's recovery from 2001–2002. He further argued that people should not confuse unhappiness with the government for other reasons with agricultural issues.[39] A philosopher, Ricardo Aronskind, wrote that the wave of rumors that were circulating were similar to how country risk had been used to whip up anxiety in 2001. The same process was occurring in May 2008.[40] An article appeared in *Critica*, saying, "The brand K is dissolving," noting that 77 percent of the population did not understand the President, Cristina Fernandez de Kirchner.[41] Eduardo van der Kooy, one of the most respected political commentators, wrote in *Clarín* that,

"Society was a hostage to the conflict." He asked, "Has Argentina lost its sense?" The journalist reported that there was growing criticism, confrontation, and unhappiness with the government and with the president. One survey showed that 79 percent of the population wanted an agreement. Van der Kooy concluded by asking, "How can the *campo* ask for an audience with Cristina Fernandez de Kirchner and then announce that it will prolong the lockout?"[42]

All of this was to come to a head on May 25, Argentina's Independence Day, when the rural groups had called for an anti-government demonstration in Rosario, challenging the government's annual official event, which this year would be held in Salta. The days before the planned Independence Day demonstrations saw intense efforts by both sides to legitimize their actions. The government referred to the rural protest in Rosario as an act of opposition, while its organizers described their actions as "defense of the interior."[43] The government had prepared its eight-page *Acuerdo de Bicentenario* or Bicentennial Agreement, identifying 56 lines of action under the subheading: "Bases for Economic Development with Social Inclusion and Territorial Balance." Its adherents included union groups such as the *Congreso Generale de Trabajadores*, business organizations such as the *Union Industrial*, the association of banks, and the chambers of commerce and construction, but the list did not include any agricultural organizations.

Observers were already anticipating that real progress towards resolving the conflict would only come after these opposing demonstrations. Former Economy Minister Lavagna urged both government and the rural lobbies to make concessions. The farmers warned that they would resume the cutting of the roads after Independence Day. The government announced that it would meet the rural organizations. *Pagina/12* humorously captured the mood in its headline, "Everyone to the 26th!" meaning that everyone was looking beyond the competing events to what would happen next.[44] One journalist referred to the event in Rosario as "a Sunday to put all the meat on the fire."[45] The rural organizations had adopted the slogan, "1810—*La Patria Somos Todos* (We are all the Homeland)—2008" for the Rosario event, again trying to link rural interests with the notion of "*la patria.*" In contrast, the government issued a not very different statement entitled: "We are all Argentina," a full-page advertisement in the newspapers referring to the country's history, to its favorable moment and favorable prices for exports, and the dream of a better country for everyone.[46]

The two events proved to be very different. The protest in Rosario drew some 200,000 people, including most of the country's opposition politicians such as Elisa Carrio from *Argentinos por una República de Iguales (*ARI*)*, Geraldo Morales from the Radical Party, and Juan Carlos Blumberg, the leader of a movement focused on security. The leader of the *Federación Agrícola*, Alfredo de Angeli, one of the leaders of the protest, spoke very aggressively about the government, saying: "*Señora Presidenta, no mienta mas*" (Senora President, don't lie anymore.) Another leader, Eduardo Buzzi, said: "The government of the Kirchners is an obstacle to development. We question the mechanism of export taxes."[47] This language was widely interpreted as being insulting and disrespectful of the president and led to a press criticism of the rural leaders.

In contrast, the president spoke for 14 minutes at the official event at Salta. She did not criticize the rural protest, but instead asked people to think about the country, rather than think about the interests of one sector. She stressed the need for national unity. This event was intended to be a show of support for the government, which provided 1,038 micro-buses to bring people to Salta from various parts of the country. An estimated 80,000 people attended.

In reaction to the speeches by the rural leaders in Rosario, the government announced on May 26 that it would not negotiate further with these groups. The farm groups then announced it would go back to blocking the transport of any grain for export. Former president Nestor Kirchner, as President of the Peronist party, called the rural protest "undemocratic," saying they were not elected by the people but they were taking unilateral action to disrupt the economy and the government. The opposition replied that the former president was "dividing the Argentines."

In fact the Government was studying possible changes in the taxes, mostly to benefit smaller producers. On May 29, the government announced some adjustments in the export tax proposal but these did not satisfy the rural groups. The lockout had now extended for more than 70 days and the government was consolidating its support, with key governors and industrial groups. *Critica* published an article saying the government was paying off politically important governors to assure their continued support.[48] A professor of media wrote an article entitled, "The immaculate conception of the media," arguing that the media act as if they are unbiased, which is not true.[49] But the government, nonetheless, presented proposed changes to the *retenciones* on May 27, most of which involved raising the ceiling on tax rates as prices rose. These proposals were immediately rejected by the rural lobbies who were perceived as "raising the bet" in their negotiations with the government. This rejection came despite the fact that it was now clear that the farmers would be earning considerably more than they expected when they had planted these crops for the current season.

The tension spilled over on May 31 when a judge decided that the blockade of national highways was illegal and he ordered the arrest of rural protestors in San Pedro. Included among those arrested was Alfredo de Angeli who was held for four hours. This led to *cacerolazos* in Buenos Aires and in many cities around the country. *La Nación* published an article the next day entitled, "Each time further from a solution."[50] The arrest of de Angeli was widely perceived as a mistake by the government, although it was not clear whether his arrest itself had been intended by the government.

On June 1, the respected journalist, Mario Wainfeld, wrote a critical article about the conflict. He reflected on the first six months of the presidency of Cristina Fernandez de Kirchner, saying that at the end of this period was:

> A storm which no one imagined. [The President] didn't take the initiative, did not propose an agenda, ran behind successes, and her team was not clear.... Closed inside its own logic, Kirchnerism has lost its privileged

> position it had had in public opinion. At times it seemed distant … In many points it was more right than its adversaries who were not characterized by good faith or democratic conduct. But the *campo* was a social sector which explains reasons and expressed to thousands of Argentines their rights and self-esteem. A single theme obsession is logical for a corporation but fatal for a government of everyone.
>
> To get out of this situation requires opening the game, receive reproaches which are floating in the air, acknowledge that this is a new stage, with new social requirements, with other modes and players, and another correlation of forces. If the *retenciones* are needed for redistribution and the present situation is unsatisfactory, it is important to be innovative in this field…
>
> Reader friend, do you think that the conflict is deescalating? This column recently gave up its crystal ball.[51]

The conflict continued to boil over the next few weeks. Former president Kirchner continued to attack the rural lobbies and the lockout, accusing them of being "*golpistas*" (coup plotters) and anti-democratic. These comments appear to have worsened the situation as governors and mayors began to question the firmness of the government's position. On June 9, the President announced in the Casa Rosada that the revenue generated from the *retenciones* would be used to finance hospitals, schools, and rural roads. She called this the National Distribution Plan.

Even after having explained the destination and uses of these funds, the President was unable to quiet down the political turmoil, even from her own supporters such as *piquetero* leader, Luis D'Elia, who declared that there was a plot being led by former President Eduardo Duhalde to overthrow the Kirchner government. On June 16, there were *cacerolazos* all over the country in response to the government statements. Protests were heaviest in the big cities of Buenos Aires, Cordoba, and Rosario. The urban upper class was clearly supporting the rural protestors, as was a sizable portion of the middle class. The Casa Rosada then announced it would hold a large mobilization of support at the Plaza de Mayo in Buenos Aires on June 18. Kirchner gave a news conference on June 17 and continued to attack *el campo*. Later that day, in a ceremony at the Casa Rosada, the president announced that she would send the *retenciones* legislation to the Congress for approval, to "defend democracy" and to strengthen democratic institutions. *La Nación* commented that the *cacerolazos* on June 16 had convinced the president to send the legislation to Congress.[52] On June 18 she declared, "In the name of democracy, free the roads."[53] The country had a collective sigh of relief with this decision, with many people commenting that the legislative route had been the correct decision from the beginning. Almost 75 percent of Argentines supported sending the proposal to Congress.

While the politics were intense in this period, the economic news was also revealing. On June 13, *Pagina/12* reported that, despite the lockout, agricultural exporters had exported more grain already in 2008 than they had in 2007. Exporters had already received US$10.399 billion in sales, 63 percent more than

Table 8.2 Export of selected products by main countries of destination, 2008

Crop	*Tons*	*US$ (thousands)*
Flour and Pellets from Extraction of Soybean Oil	23,293,511	7,118,166
Netherlands	3,112,650	916,762
Spain	2,961,366	858,782
Italy	2,079,607	634,301
Denmark	1,296,774	383,439
Poland	1,255,773	381,483
Philipines	969,109	299,452
Indonesia	909,373	285,791
Other	10,708,860	3,358,156
Crude Soybean Oil, Without Degumming	4,807,369	4,711,264
China	1,442,131	1,457,168
India	628,152	588,312
Egypt	402,349	402,783
Other	2,334,737	2,263,001
Soybeans Excluded for Planting	11,689,095	4,555,348
China	9,254,052	3,609,035
Other	2,435,043	946,313
Corn Grain	15,317,839	3,417,417
Spain	2,315,407	508,941
Iran	1,958,548	437,589
Algeria	1,264,199	280,983
Egypt	1,185,691	264,508
Chile	1,150,400	256,956
Other	7,443,594	1,668,440

Source: Ministry of Economy 2008.

2007, or US$4.028 billion more.[54] The explanation for this continued export activity was that the trading companies had stockpiled grains near the port even before the March 11 announcement. Table 8.2 shows the destinations of these crops.

At the same time, there was also evidence of significant tax evasions by rural producers. In an article entitled, “Men in Black,” it was shown that there were many tax irregularities in the rural areas, including the case of one producer who sent 21,000 trucks to the port (630,000 tons of grains) and only claimed 12,000 peso profits per month.[55] Alejandro Rofman, a respected economist, wrote about “The voice of those who have no voice,” referring to the 50 percent of farmers who had no land, but work as sharecroppers or renters, including some 200,000 family farmers of fruits, vegetables, and cotton.[56]

The congressional phase and its outcomes

As the congressional approval process got underway, the big question was whether there could be any changes in the government’s proposed bill. *La*

Nación reported on June 22 that more than half of the deputies wanted to change the bill, but the government firmly replied that it did not want any changes.[57] Indeed, the character of the communications with the government appeared to be "all or nothing" and the Right, which had supported blockades of highways, attacked the government with phrases such as "antagonism as strategy" from Hilda Sabato or "prison of the past" by Beatriz Sarlo.[58] The President met for almost two hours with the leaders of the four organizations on June 23 to discuss the issue and they asked for the suspension of taxes for 60 to 90 days to allow time to find a compromise. Economics writer, Alfredo Zaiat, later observed that such requests for suspension of taxes would allow large producers to make enormous profits during such period. He noted that, "Capital always wants more." The president turned down their proposal, saying that additional measures had already been introduced to protect small and medium-sized producers. *Pagina/12*'s coverage of that meeting was reported on its cover the next day with a picture of the president with the rural leaders under the caption: "We Hate Each Other So."[59]

At the other end of Avenida de Mayo in Buenos Aires, at the Congress, there were intense meetings and hot discussions going on in the seven tents set up in the Plaza de Congreso. Significantly, Vice-President Julio Cobos remarked at this time that the people had voted for more dialogue in the October 2007 elections. He met with 200 mayors who came to argue for some compromise. Cobos joined with leading governors as well, such as Hermes Binner from Santa Fe, Schiaretti from Cordoba, and Rodriguez Saa from San Luis, who were asking for an intermediate solution.

On June 25, the government took out a full page in *La Nación* under the title, "Each Argentine has the right to be informed," which included the following points:

- In the first five months of 2008 the country had exported 28.8 million tons of grains, or 893,000 more than in the same period in 2007. Exporters had earned 63 percent more than in 2007.
- By May 31, 2008, producers had exported 18 percent more soya than in 2007, and 80 percent of this had been exported during the conflict.
- Argentina remained the second largest exporter of corn in the world, having exported 7.4 million tons up to May 31, or 9 percent more than in 2007, with a 71 percent increase in earnings.
- The country had exported 144,000 tons of meat up to May 31, or 14 percent less than in 2007, but this had earned 13 percent more than in 2007.
- Export earnings were 175 percent more than 2007.
- Sunflower oil exports had increased by 25 percent but earnings had increased 144 percent.
- The government concluded that this lockout had not been for exports, but had created scarcity for Argentines. The exports showed that the times were good for the exporters. The lockout had been domestic, not external.
- The Argentine people and their representatives should know the truth.[60]

The next day it was reported that at least 33 congressmen in the ruling party would vote against the proposed law, including Felipe Sola, the former governor of Buenos Aires Province and previously an important supporter of the government.[61] Reports nevertheless circulated that former president Nestor Kirchner as head of the ruling party ordered that there be no changes in the proposed law. However, Cabinet Chief, Alberto Fernandez, and Agustin Rossi, the congressional leader, were reported to have introduced changes into the bill. The press in general was predicting that the *Frente para la Victoria* would win the congressional vote with 134 or 135 votes in the lower house. Nevertheless, many congressmen continued to search for a compromise. One of the leaders in this effort was Felipe Sola who proposed that the soya tax rate proposed by the Government be reduced from 47 percent to 39 percent and the maximum rate be set at 45 percent rather than the government-proposed rate of 57 percent. Some 60 deputies supported the Sola proposal.

The backdrop to this debate remained the issue of the health of the economy and the perception of growing inflation, unofficially estimated by various sources at around 25 percent in contrast to the Government's number of about 9 percent. *Critica* referred to the low profile of the new economy minister Carlos Fernandez and characterized his view of the economy as "no inflation, no recession, the house is in order."[62] The government was maintaining that it had the money required to pay the external debt for 2008, regardless of what happened in the global markets. The respected economist, Aldo Ferrer, said, "We have the luxury in the midst of an international crisis to create a serious domestic conflict and the economy continues to function."[63] Nevertheless, there were some signs of concern such as a reported growth in public expenditures cutting into the government's fiscal surplus and the apparent flight of some US$9 billion as reported by *La Nación*.[64]

On July 1, speaking in Tucuman at the summit of Mercosur presidents, Cristina Fernandez de Kirchner spoke about world food prices and the need for Mercosur leaders to find policy solutions which would protect the interests of their peoples. She mentioned the high price of soya at US$590 a ton on July 1, 2008, as unthinkable six months ago. While her message was well received by the presidents, there were protests in Tucuman.

On July 5, 2008, the *retenciones* bill passed the Lower House by 129 to 122, sending it to the Senate. Prior to the vote there had been intense lobbying, testimonies by experts on both sides, and even debates 24 hours a day in the Plaza outside the Congress building. While the *campo* had lost the vote, they argued that such a close vote had demonstrated widespread support for their protest. Most deputies from the interior of the country had supported the rural lobbies, including some important previous supporters of the government who were later called "traitors" by some government operatives. These defections further indicated the loss of political support for the government. The next step was to send the legislation to the Senate for a vote in mid-July. In the intervening period from March 11, the rise in world grain prices meant that the government would receive US$2 billion more in revenue than at the price level of March 11.[65]

The day after the vote, Vice-President Julio Cobos predicted that the *retenciones* bill would be passed by the Senate.[66] Nevertheless the rural organizations continued to lobby the senators very hard, particularly from their respective provinces. Many of the senators had agricultural holdings themselves. In addition, there was more discussion of the power of the large exporting companies who were profiting from Argentina's products. Table 8.3 shows some of these companies and their 2007 earnings.

Several days later *Pagina/12* published a list of the 40 largest landowners in the country, with 35 families each owning more than 20,000 hectares in Buenos Aires Province.[67]

These interests led to various proposals for changes in the draft Law 125, for example from Senator Carlos Reutemann of Santa Fe Province who suggested that there be a ceiling on the tax rates at 40 percent. This proposal certainly favored the important agricultural interests of Santa Fe Province, one of the most productive agricultural regions of the country. Other similar ideas were floated along this line, which had been suggested by Congressman Felipe Sola, but the government rejected these. Part of this hard line attitude from the government was a response to the threats of the rural protestors to bring chaos to the country if they lost in the Senate vote.[68]

The politics continued in the weeks leading up to the Senate vote, with former president Kirchner speaking of a new model for the country at a meeting of the *Carta Abierta* group of intellectuals, with the President speaking about "a new independence for Argentina," and efforts within the government to define a program which would help the middle class. But this pro-government activity was balanced by growing support for *el campo* among the urban middle class, governors and mayors, and all of this could be expected to have an important impact on the vote in the Senate.

In the days just before the vote there were very large demonstrations in Buenos Aires, with 100,000 people for the government's position assembling in the Plaza de Congreso at the same time that 200,000 people met in Palermo to

Table 8.3 Large exporting companies and earnings

Rank	*Company*	*Industry*	*2007 exports (US$)*	*Increase (%)*
1	Cargill	Oil	4,094.0	65.0
2	YPF	Petroleum	2,692.0	0.0
3	Bunge Argentina	Oil	2,686.6	31.1
4	LCD Argentina	Cereals	2,033.4	45.2
5	Aceitera General Deheza	Oil	1,805.4	20.4
6	Minera Alumbrera	Minerals	1,521.0	–4.0
7	Molimos Río de la Plata	Cereals	1,355.2	13.4
8	Vicentín	Oil	1,280.2	144.0
9	Tenaris Siderca	Iron and Steel	1,260.0	3.3
10	Nidera	Cereals	1,224.8	53.4

Source: Crítica, July 6, 2008, p. 12.

Table 8.4 Proposed bills

Initiatives	*Rate (US Soy $561)*	*Maximum deduction*	*Repayment*
Govt	47%	57%	Approximately 500 tn
Peronists	47%	57%	Approximately 500 tn (with automatic compensation)
Felipe Solá	39%	45%	Approximately 500 tn (with automatic compensation)
Opposition	35%	35%	According to productivity
Rural Lobbies	45%	45%	According to productivity

Source: Clarín 2008.

speak out against the *retenciones* and to show legislators the strength of the conflicting positions about the proposal to be voted upon.

On July 16, the formal debate on the law began, with 72 senators present in the chamber, including former president Carlos Menem, now a senator from La Rioja Province. The debate was intense and very lively, with almost every senator explaining his or her respective positions. Two very strong opposition speeches were delivered, one by Chiche Duhalde, the wife of former president Eduardo Duhalde and now senator from Buenos Aires Province, and Maria Essensoro, a senator of the *Coalición Cívica* party representing the city of Buenos Aires. Chiche Duhalde opposed the law and argued that the administration of the Kirchners lacked management and coherence. She reminded the senators and the country, on live television, that economic growth had not begun with the presidency of Nestor Kirchner in May 2003 but had started under her husband's term in 2002. In any case, she said that "growth without development" was useless and that the country needed more "*institutionalidad*" or institutional development and capacity and that the Kirchner governments had not worked in this direction, citing the lack of cabinet meetings and respect for congressional processes. She even argued that if the government was truly interested in redistribution it could easily do so without the revenue from the *retenciones*. She correctly observed that the proposed revenue was small in relation to the other budgetary resources of the government. Maria Essensoro argued in the same direction, saying that the proposed law could be better, and that there was a need for consensus. She also commented on the relatively small amount of revenue involved.

On July 17, at 4 a.m., the proposal was surprisingly defeated in the Senate 37 to 36. After the senators ended up with two tie votes, the Vice-President, Julio Cobos, from the Radical Party but still a member of the government and constitutionally president of the Senate, cast the deciding vote against his own government's proposal. This dramatic decision followed a long explanation by Cobos in which he stressed that his concern was to reach a consensus on the export taxes and not just to support a proposal that clearly was not supported by the majority of the country. He said he had asked for time to look for alternatives but this did not appear possible. He concluded his remarks with the comment, "history will judge me … my vote is not positive."

Cobos' unexpected decision led to an immediate celebration in Palermo by supporters of the rural organizations and consternation and shock on the part of the government. Many people commented that losing this vote was not expected by the government and this represented an important weakening of the President and her administration. Words such as "traitor" and "Judas" were used to describe Cobos, who spoke to the press later that morning, saying that he had no plans to resign from the vice-presidency and that he hoped that the president would understand his decision. He then quickly left Buenos Aires to return to his home town of Mendoza and then later escaped to a mountain retreat away from the press.

The next day, on July 18, the president announced that the government would follow the wishes of the Congress and would rescind the tax regulations, which had gone into effect on March 11. She personally drafted the resolution rescinding the law 125 and Chief of Cabinet, Alberto Fernandez, signed it. This action reduced the tax rate for soya exports from 45 to 35 percent, the rate before the March 11 announcement, and immediately handed a windfall gain to rich farmers and the multi-national exporting companies. This additional profit is estimated by *Critica*, an independent and anti-government newspaper, to be about US$530 million. The president also met with the 150 legislators who supported the government's intention to redistribute income to the poor. She pledged to continue this policy orientation and emphasized the importance of supporting democratic institutions and processes. The role of Vice-President, Julio Cobos, remained to be determined.

On July 22, the president announced the appointment of a new secretary of agriculture and implied that further changes were to come. The next day the chief of the cabinet, Alberto Fernandez, who had been the closest collaborator of the presidential couple since 2003, resigned, announcing that he had differences with the president and now was a time for a change. The president quickly appointed Sergio Massa, a former director of the national social security agency and then mayor of Tigre, in suburban Buenos Aires. Massa was sworn in on July 24.

While the government tried to contain the damage from losing the Senate vote, the rural lobbies woke up to some important realities. If they had won in the Senate, and the rate increases for the export taxes had been rescinded, they had at the same time lost all of the concessions, which the government had offered to small and medium producers. With the reversal of the law, the small and medium producers found themselves again having to pay tax rates of 35 percent on their soya exports and other taxes, which they had thought, had been eliminated. Moreover, important subsidies, which had been promised by the government, now disappeared as the bill had been defeated. This situation immediately provoked a reaction by the small and medium producers and began to threaten the coalition of rural protest groups. If the smaller groups had felt supported by the large producers and exporters during the 130 days of the protest, they now realized that they had different interests from the rich who were celebrating having defeated the tax increase, which, in the end, after months of negotiations, would only have affected them.

Toward some conclusions

This episode of 130 days clearly shows that the politics of redistribution are very tough and, given the history of Argentina, sometimes quite scary with the specter of military intervention looming in people's minds. As of the end of July 2008, it appeared that the Right had managed to stop this tax measure, and had seriously weakened a government with progressive intentions. But the government had many tools and means to continue to address the issue of inequality in the country.

Despite various efforts since March 11, 2008, to meet the demands of "*el campo*," the conflict had continued over 130 days, demonstrating that the protestors were not so poor and that they had some powerful economic backing. Only in the latter stages of the conflict was the importance of the large multi-national exporting firms such as Cargill and seed companies such as Monsanto acknowledged as having major interests which could be affected by the proposed tax increases.

While the government's policy orientation and intention was well-founded, it did not demonstrate the technical and political skill needed to effectively introduce the policy and to respond to the powerful rural farm groups supported by the media at key points during the conflict. These challenges included adequately explaining the measures at the beginning, as well as their objectives and the intended of the additional revenue. Furthermore, in the face of an aggressive and professional media campaign by the farm groups, the government was unable to distinguish between large, medium, and small farmers, with the result that it provoked more solidarity among farmers than should have been the case. Key unmentioned issues included the unequal distribution of land, with 40 families owning a substantial share of the best land in the country and wealthy foreigners such as Luciano Benetton, the Italian clothing magnate, owning 900,000 hectares. Even though 18 companies control about 80 percent of grain exports, which they sell through multi-national firms such as Monsanto, Cargill, Bunge, and others, this issue was largely overlooked in the discussion of export taxes.

The government also had difficulties sustaining a process of continuous dialogue with the farm organizations and allowed itself to be drawn into a conflict in which it did not demonstrate the asymmetrical character of the negotiations, i.e., that it was government and the farmers were only one segment of society. Here again, the government was very much hindered by the media, as the two largest newspapers, *La Nación* and *Clarín*, both have large agricultural holdings and interests themselves. The media, including most television channels, consistently sided with the farmers, and made it difficult for the government to explain its position. With these obstacles, the government was unable to find alternative ways to get out of the crisis.

With this disposition of forces, the Right, represented by the farmers, appears to have anyway been preparing to attack the government's intention to redistribute income towards the poor and, as the export tax blockades demonstrated, it was prepared to use non-institutional means to do so. The farmers' organizations severely disrupted the country from March through July 2008, limiting supplies of food, gasoline, medicines, and many other goods, which were needed by the population. While these actions were clearly extra-institutional and thus "anti-democratic," the government did not forcibly remove protesters from the more than 150 highways which were cut–not wanting to introduce violence into the situation, given Argentina's past history. There was much debate about whether this response was too lenient and allowed things to get out of hand.

Social theories, public policies, and politics

One of the questions arising from this episode is whether there is anything which can be generalized from the observed events and behaviors over the 130 days. While many Argentines would like to believe that their country is *sui generis*, in fact there are many aspects of this experience, which is consistent with theoretical social science frameworks developed outside of the country. A framework developed in 1964 by the American political scientist, Theodore J. Lowi, in fact not only helps to understand what happens but actually predicts some of the behaviors which arise in conflicts involving redistributive policies. In a 1964 review article of studies of the behaviors of American business in response to trade policies, Lowi proposed a threefold framework for understanding how specific kinds of policies structure the political responses they receive.[69]

Lowi suggested that there are three basic types of public policies: distributive, regulatory, and redistributive. He defined distributive policies as those which provide benefits or services to a number of people or groups and that these benefits can be almost infinitely sub-divided into smaller and smaller units, thereby reaching large numbers of people. The political response to distributive policies is to organize coalitions of groups, each seeking to assure that they receive their "fair" share of whatever is being distributed. The second type is regulatory policy, which fundamentally establishes a rule or law which applies equally, in principle, to everyone. Political behavior in response to regulatory policy change is to object to the change in rules in a way which represents everyone, such as a class action suit.

The third type is redistributive policy which, by definition, takes benefits or some material interests from one group and gives them to another, thereby creating two clear categories of actors: winners and losers. Lowi suggested that redistributive politics is by nature dichotomous and binary, with two groups–winners and losers–in conflict over the outcome. The introduction of proposed redistributive policies by government serves to represent in part the winners but also has an interest in assuring that its implementation of such policies reinforces its own legitimacy in representing the wider public interest. The most interesting aspect of this formulation–and most applicable to the Argentine experience with the *retenciones* as instruments for redistributive policies—is that Lowi argued that the form and organization of redistributive politics is hierarchical and dichotomous, with each group assembling various interests and smaller groups into a solid bloc of units which do not necessarily agree with each other but which, nevertheless, for the purpose of this redistributive conflict, function as a single bloc. The reason that otherwise hostile or competing groups would join together behind the leadership of stronger and richer groups is that they feel that these more powerful groups have a better chance of defending their interests, of winning the fight.

This process of forming a hierarchical bloc among previously competing groups is exactly what happened in the creation of the *mesa de enlace*, or coordinating group, of the four agricultural organizations which protested against the increases in export tax rates. The *Federación Agraria Argentina*, representing small farmers, joined with three organizations of large producers and exporters: *La Sociedad Rural Argentina*, *Confederaciones Rurales Argentinas*, and *Confederación Intercooperativa Agropecuaria Cooperativa Limitada.* While many observers in the press could not explain why the *Federación* had joined the other three groups, the Lowi framework helps to explain what happened. This dynamic supported the dichotomous character of the conflict, a dimension well-captured by journalist, Jorge Lanata, who described the political conflict in the most easily understood terms for his Argentine readers: it was like the battle between Boca and River, the arch-enemy soccer teams.[70]

This theoretical understanding converges with the framework developed by Ralf Dahrendorf in his book, *Class and Class Conflict in Industrial Society*, published in 1959, in which he showed how governmental authority and policy decisions create economic interests and thus also interest groups.[71] Insisting on the importance of the role of government, Dahrendorf demonstrated the consequences of public decisions, not only in terms of short-term political responses, but also for longer-term social stratification, income distribution, and social mobility.

An empirical example of this mode of analysis is found in the work of Argentine political scientist, Sebastian Etchemendy, who has studied how government behavior has shaped different coalitions in the steel, oil, and automotive industries in Argentina.[72] Government policies during the 1990s supported trade and financial liberalization, which had direct impacts on major economic interests in the country. But the government of President Carlos Menem was skillful in at the same time providing benefits, rents, and market opportunities to key economic interests, such as the powerful Argentine industrial conglomerates such as *Techint* and *Perez Companc*. Etchemendy argues that, "Menem's government managed to 'buy' the 'winners' in formerly protected industry and labor."[73]

Another useful concept in understanding this episode is what political scientists, Peter Bachrach and Morton Baratz, called "non-decisions" in the 1960s. Bachrach and Baratz sought to describe the differences between the impacts of explicit decisions and the impacts of relative neglect.[74] During the recovery period from 2002 to 2008, the governments of Nestor Kirchner and then Cristina

Fernandez de Kirchner did not focus much attention on agricultural policy. The rural sector was clearly benefitting from the 2002 devaluation of the peso and thus, able to dramatically improve its competitiveness in global grain markets. It was to some degree left alone. This approach can be considered an example of a "non-decision," leaving, in relative terms, a sector of actors and activity outside the continuous attention and direct intervention of government. The exception to this non-decision was the gradual increase of tax rates on exports, but this decision was not embedded within a longer-term policy framework for the agricultural sector.

These social science understandings are also supported by the empirical work of the leading historians of Argentina such as Tulio Halperin Donghi who has explained how the policies of successive governments of Argentina going back to the nineteenth century have contributed to the strength of a landed rural class in the country. They also support the historical interpretation of economic historians Enrique Arceo and Eduardo Basualdo in their Gramscian explanation of the economic transformation following the end of import substitution policies in the 1970s, and specifically how neoliberal economic policies reduced the power of organized labor in Argentina and reinforced the power of capital in the newly liberalized economy of the 1990s.[75]

Finally, probably the most dramatic dimension of the politics of redistribution was how both sides, winners and losers, perceived the conflict and how the media moved to define the representation of the conflict itself. The president and the government expressed their surprise at the violence, depth, and breadth of the opposition to the *retenciones*, coming only three months after the inauguration of a new democratically elected government with 45 percent of the vote, 20 points ahead of its closest contender. This opposition can be explained in part by the power of the media in constructing the "imaginary" of the conflict itself, invoking the image of "small" farmers standing up to the power of big government, despite the fact that the farm lobbies represented some of the biggest, most powerful economic and media interests in the country. But the refusal of the government to really negotiate with the farm organizations and its decision to oppose any modifications of the proposed law prior to the congressional votes stopped any effort to build consensus. The government, therefore, contributed to the creation of the dichotomy itself: either you were for or against the government. Indeed, both the president and former president attacked the farm lobbies suggesting that their real intention was to de-stabilize the new government, referring to them as "*golpistas*." The role and power of the media was thus a necessary but not sufficient factor to explain what happened.

Given the true economic interests at play in the conflict, it was no accident that the final political demonstration against the *retenciones*, in the name of all farmers, prior to the Senate vote in July 2009 was staged in Palermo, a middle- and upper-class neighborhood, and was attended by well-dressed, obviously wealthy supporters of large producers and farm interests.

In the end, the deciding factors in the conflict were less about what was really happening to grain producers and exporters, who, as shown above, continued to profit handsomely during the conflict despite the lock-out, than what people believed was happening and how they believed a settlement should be found through negotiation and consensus. These beliefs came first from how both sides spoke to the public and reacted to the conflict and second from how they deployed their forces in order to influence public opinion, the media, and through those channels, their legislative representatives. The arrival of 100 farmers on horseback in downtown Buenos Aires a few days before the Senate vote, trying to arrive at the Congress, exemplified the brilliant and effective construction by the farm organizations of an "imaginary" with whom the majority of the Argentine population could identify. If the conflict was between the government and a rural horseman being prohibited from riding his horse through the city, there was little question that Argentines would take sides against the government. By not effectively managing the political process, the government in effect left the field wide open for the farm organizations and their media supporters.

This episode is not the first time powerful imaginaries have been constructed in Argentina. The construction of powerful visions of social forces such as the poor and social inequality has been well shown by Argentine sociologist, Ana Wortman, in her study of how the media constructed the notion of social inequality during and after the crisis of 2001 and 2002.[76] While not the first, however, it marked an important turning point in strategy for the government.

9 Urban inequality

If the political and policy challenges of the *campo* proved to be difficult for the government to manage, the political complexity of urban inequality has proven to be even more persistent and growing. As introduced in Chapter 7, intra-urban differences in incomes, public services such as health and education, housing, and the overall quality of life have proven to be very sensitive to changes in the macro-economic fortunes of the country. When the economy grows, urban employment and incomes grow, affecting all levels of income and social status. But when the "crisis" returns, the urban poor stay poorer longer and more deeply than their upper and middle-class countrymen. This pattern has been observed throughout Latin America, but it also appears in North America and Europe.[1]

The "urban" also needs to be situated within the framework of theoretical issues that this book addresses, including the impact of neo-liberalism, state performance, and state capacity. The urban arena is particularly interesting from these three perspectives, in part because urban impacts of macro-economic policy, such as from monetary policy, trade liberalization, and privatization are visible and immediate, as presented in earlier chapters. At the same time, the historical weakness of institutions with the mandate to formulate and implement urban policy has inhibited explicit urban policy initiatives. This weakness shows up most dramatically in the absence of metropolitan institutions to govern metropolitan Buenos Aires. As a result, there is little coordination of infrastructure investment, industrial or social policy, environmental management, and, until recently, crime prevention and security. One foreign observer of the urban scene in Argentina has characterized this situation as "a ship without a captain."[2] This is most striking because Argentina is the most urbanized country in Latin America and greater Buenos Aires is equivalent to the city of New York in its scale.

The question, therefore, of state performance on urban issues is complicated and quite problematic. On one hand, urban problems are only partly the responsibility of the national government. They depend heavily on the performance of sub-national government, whether provinces, metropolitan institutions, or municipalities. Yet, the constitutional framework for sub-national policy and management must originate at the national level. Historical political differences between the leaders of the city of Buenos Aires and the surrounding Buenos

Aires Province and the gap between political leaders in secondary cities and national authorities helps to explain this institutional weakness, but it does not justify it, because over 70 percent of Argentina's GDP comes from urban-based economic activities. Hence the stakes in urban questions are quite high.

From this perspective, it is surprising that "scale" and "place" do not appear to have been publicly considered as important in the struggle for social and economic welfare. Yet, it is the level of differences between people in places at similar scale, which cause serious political problems. This chapter examines the differences in economic and physical welfare, which exist, between and within cities and towns in Argentina. It also identifies how current policies and programs might be strengthened to address these twin problems of poverty and inequality, starting not from the macro-economy, but from below. It is an assessment of sub-national institutions within the broader issue of helping the economy recover from the crisis of 2001–2002 and return to a path of more equitable economic growth. While the focus of the chapter is somewhat more technical than some other chapters, the urban issues facing political leaders are daunting and, for some, far from resolution.

The urban within the national economy

Table 9.1 shows the importance of urban-generated economic product within the national economy. As the most urbanized country in Latin America, it is not surprising that economic analysis shows that by 2005 almost 75 percent of GDP was being generated in the four most-urbanized provinces plus the Federal Capital. Even though the Federal Capital accounted for a large share of the loss of product during crisis periods, the second tier of cities: Cordoba, Mendoza, and Santa Fe, along with the Province of Buenos Aires, maintained positive growth when the size of the national economy was shrinking. Indeed, the urban share of the economy did not decline when GDP declined. The Argentine economy, like the population, is urbanized. While the economic importance of the Federal Capital receives most popular attention—by 1993, it alone accounted for 23.9 percent of GDP—the role of "the other urban Argentina" is considerable in industrial production, in servicing agriculture and other extractive industries. As shown in Table 9.1, by 2005, the Federal Capital and the Province of Buenos Aires together generated 58.8 percent of GDP.

These differences are not only found in the economic contribution of urban areas. Table 9.2 shows the considerable historical differences between individual towns and varying degrees of poverty as defined by the lack of infrastructure services and poor housing conditions, both of which are captured through the government's index of "unsatisfied basic needs" (UBN) and other indicators. While the population with unsatisfied basic needs was only 8.1 percent in the Federal Capital in the 1991 census, the average for the 25 largest urban areas was 16.5 percent or twice the level in the Federal Capital. Moreover, 14 of the 25 towns had UBN levels more than double this average. Secondary cities are twice as likely to be poor than the Federal Capital.

Table 9.1 Distribution of GDP within provinces of Argentina

Jurisdiction	*% GDP 1993*	*% GDP 2005*	*% Population 2005*
Province of Buenos Aires	34.3	33.9	38
Federal Capital	23.9	24.9	7.8
Córdoba	7.9	7.8	8.4
Santa Fe	7.8	7.7	7.7
Mendoza	3.9	3.9	4.3
Entre Ríos	2.2	2.2	3.2
Tucumán	2.0	2.0	2.0
Neuquén	1.7	1.8	1.4
Salta	1.5	1.4	3.0
Río Negro	1.4	1.5	1.5
Corrientes	1.3	1.2	2.5
Chaco	1.3	1.2	2.7
Chubut	1.3	1.4	1.2
Misiones	1.3	1.4	2.7
San Luis	1.3	1.0	1.0
San Juan	1.1	1.0	1.7
Jujuy	0.9	0.8	1.7
Santa Cruz	0.9	0.9	0.9
Santiago del Estero	0.9	0.9	0.9
La Pampa	0.8	0.8	0.8
Tierra del Fuego	0.7	0.6	0.6
Formosa	0.6	0.5	1.3
Catamarca	0.5	0.7	0.9
La Rioja	0.5	0.5	0.8
Total	100.0	100.0	100.0

Source: ECLAC, *Panorama del desarrollo territorial en América Latina y el Caribe*, 2009, p. 43.

These differences were also reflected in housing conditions between towns where 17 of the 25 towns had shares of their populations living in housing conditions worse than the national average. Fifteen of the towns had worse conditions regarding sanitation. A third of the urban population lacked health coverage, 14 percent could not read or write, 31 percent did not complete primary school, and 71 percent did not complete secondary school. While the scores on individual indicators vary considerably, the overall picture was of a country with enormous differences within and between its urban centers.

These data suggest that significant differences have existed between and within urban areas for many years. They also point to the fact that incomes tended to be higher in central Buenos Aires compared to the surrounding municipalities in the metropolitan area. The higher levels of welfare in central Buenos Aires reflected higher productivity and average wages as well. It is also not surprising that the population in large and medium-sized cities enjoyed levels of income and welfare, in the aggregate, considerably above the national average. The issue, however, is not so much what the averages portrayed, but rather, within a rich country with many thriving sectors of the respective urban economies, what were the differences among groups within cities and towns. Table 9.3

Table 9.2 Poverty and inequality in selected major cities and towns (%), 1991

*Urban area**	*Pop.*	*UBN*	*Pop. without health coverage*	*Illiteracy rate*	*Not completing sec school*	*Homes without toilet*	*Low quality home*	*Non-owner occupied*
Metro BA	7,924,424	18.9	38.1	14.5	77.1	71.5	8.8	30.8
Federal Capital	2,871,519	8.1	19.1	8.3	56.6	5.8	1.1	34.7
Córdoba	1,193,443	14.4	35.7	13.6	66.9	77.0	1.9	38.0
Rosario	1,108,917	17.2	25.7	14.3	70.6	54.0	6.6	29.4
Mendoza	766,454	13.3	35.5	15.0	72.3	40.6	4.1	31.4
Santa Fé	402,303	18.6	29.9	15.4	68.7	73.8	4.7	35.4
Salta	366,994	22.9	39.1	17.0	70.7	27.0	6.1	34.2

Source: SIEMPRO – based on the 1991 Population and Housing Census made by INDEC. *Metropolitan data.

Table 9.3 Inequality within selected cities and towns of Argentina—standard deviation (%)

District	*Pop.*	*UBN*	*Pop. without health coverage*	*Illiteracy rate*	*Not completing sec school*	*Homes without toilet*	*Low quality home*	*Non-owner occupied*
Metro BA	7,924,424	14	15	5	10	36	10	18
Federal Capital	2,871,519	11	7	2	11	9	6	10
Córdoba	1,193,443	10	11	4	16	35	3	12
Rosario	1,108,917	14	14	6	15	38	9	12
Mendoza	766,454	10	11	4	12	33	6	9
La Plata	627,927	10	11	4	15	38	6	10
Santa Fé	402,303	13	16	6	14	25	5	18
Salta	366,994	17	12	5	9	28	9	11
Sgo del Estero-Banda	260,997	10	9	5	8	24	6	11
Formosa	147,002	18	16	6	8	24	13	9
Concordia	115,699	14	8	5	8	28	11	5

Source: SIEMPRO – based on the 1991 Population and Housing Census made by INDEC.

presents historical data from 1991 on the distribution of scores on six indicators within Argentina's largest cities and towns.

As noted above, these data also allow these differences to be analyzed by location within urban areas, thereby demonstrating the importance of spatial location in explaining these differences. Table 9.3 presents the distribution of these data within the selected urban areas using standard deviations as a first indicator of the magnitude of differences. This table shows the degree of differences by variable for each of the towns. These data show that there were substantial differences within cities both in comparison to the city-wide average conditions, for example on UBN or housing, and with respect to national averages as well. This helps to distinguish what might be called "poor cities," versus those that on average had higher scores, and also, within each category, "unequal cities" with regard to the level of differences found within each city.

An initial breakdown of urban areas by level of inequality is presented in Table 9.4. This table presents inequality within cities using the degree of variation in UBN by presenting the percentage of population with UBN in top and bottom three deciles of districts. This table shows great differences in the proportion of UBN population at the top and the bottom deciles. In Santa Fe, the difference was ten times, and other big cities outside of Metropolitan Buenos Aires and Córdoba had great concentrations of poverty in the bottom. In contrast, there was greater homogeneity in Metropolitan Buenos Aires, which had, and still has, many poor districts.

Further analysis of the level of inequality within towns as well as between towns indicates that the degree of difference within towns was three times greater for infrastructure than for education and health. This finding reflects Argentina's historical investment in education and health in the past. The conclusion that differences in physical characteristics in infrastructure services and housing demonstrated even greater differences than in human capital challenges the frequently-heard neo-liberal observation that human capital investments are the most critical inputs needed to reduce poverty. While this may be appropriate

Table 9.4 Percentage of population with UBN in top and bottom 3 deciles of districts

Urban area	*% UBN population*		
	Top three deciles	*Bottom three deciles*	*Relation*
Santa Fé	3.2	34.5	10.8
Rosaro	3.2	31.3	9.8
Mendoza	3.1	24.4	7.9
Salta	7.8	39.7	5.1
Córdoba	5.1	24.7	4.8
Federal Capital	3.9	18.2	4.7
G.S.S. de Jujuy	18.6	57.3	3.1
Metro BA	10.8	25.3	2.3

Source: SIEMPRO – based on the 1991 Population and Housing Census made by INDEC.

in lower-income countries, it is not correct in upper middle-income countries such as Argentina with past histories of investment in education and health.

Further analysis also suggests that larger cities had greater inequality when measured by infrastructural differences. The exceptions to this finding were greater Rosario and greater Buenos Aires. Table 9.5 presents average coefficients of variation among the three groups of variables: infrastructure, education, and health. These summary "inequality scores" also tend to show that higher degrees of inequality existed in larger cities, with the exceptions of greater Rosario and greater Buenos Aires.

These historical data identify patterns that have persisted over the last two decades. More recent data demonstrate that there continue to be significant differences in the levels of income and infrastructure services between larger and smaller urban centers. Table 9.6 shows the quality of connection to the basic services of water and sewerage for the urban agglomerations in Argentina. Smaller cities in the northwestern and northeastern regions had a higher proportion of housing lacking at least one of the two services. However, Metropolitan Buenos Aires had the highest proportion, with 38.4 percent of housing having insufficient access to basic services. The largest and most populous urban area in Argentina continues to lack infrastructure services for a large percentage of its population. Much of this can be attributed to the migrations of the past two decades to Metropolitan Buenos Aires and patterns of irregular settlements.

Not surprisingly these physical differences also show up in differences between the average wage and income levels found in different size urban areas in the country. Within all the urban agglomerates, in 2010, the income per capita of the 90th percentile is on average nine-times more than the lower tenth percentile.[3]

Both the historical data and more recent analysis underline the conclusion that infrastructure is very important in terms of explaining levels of inequality and

Table 9.5 Average of coefficient of variation for infrastructure, education and health on largest cities of Argentina by decreasing average

City	*Population*	*Average coefficient of variation*
Mar del Plata	505,402	0.95
Santa Fé	402,303	0.85
Córdoba	1,193,443	0.70
La Plata	627,927	0.66
Mendoza	766,454	0.64
Federal Capital	2,871,519	0.61
Paraná	209,657	0.48
Santiago del Estero	260,997	0.46
Rosario	1,108,917	0.44
Metro Buenos Aires	7,924,424	0.31
AVERAGE 25 CITIES	776,290	0.56

Source: Author's elaboration.

Table 9.6 Housing per region by quality of connection to basic services. Population and Housing Census (EPH), Year 2006

Urban agglomerations	*Satisfactory*	*Basic*	*Insufficient*
Metro Buenos Aires	40.6	21	38.4
NOA	67.2	17.7	15.2
NEA	59.4	25.5	15.1
Pampeana	66.3	21.7	12
Cuyo	73.1	18	8.9
Patagonia	90.1	4.6	5.3
Federal Capital	98.1	1.1	0.8

Source: Ministry of Federal Planning, Public Investment and Services 2009, p. 18.

Notes

Satisfactory = water and sewerage Basic: water and septic tank. Insufficient: lacks at least one of the two services.

Cuyo: Gran Mendoza, Gran San Juan, San Luis – El Chorrill.

NEA: Corrientes, Formosa, Gran Resistencia, Posadas.

NOA: Gran Catamarca, Gran Tucumán – Tafí Viejo, Jujuy – Palpalá, La Rioja, Salta, Santiago del Estero – La Banda.

Pampeana: Bahía Blanca – Cerri, Concordia, Gran Córdoba, Gran La Plata, Gran Rosario, Gran Paraná, Gran Santa Fe, Mar del Plata – Batán, Río Cuarto, Santa Rosa – Toay, San Nicolás – Villa Constitución.

Patagonia: Comodoro Rivadavia – Rada Tilly, Neuquén – Plottier, Río Gallegos, Ushuaia – Río Grande, Rawson – Trelew, Viedma – Carmen de Patagones.

hence, place-based levels of welfare in urban areas. This conclusion is also supported by simple historical correlations between the variables across 25 urban areas. These data show that UBN scores were closely related to housing and unsatisfied infrastructure needs. UBN scores actually serve as the bridge between human capital and physical indicators.

As shown below in more detailed historical analysis of Metropolitan Buenos Aires and the Federal Capital, these variables tended to concentrate into distinct clusters, which can be considered as distinct "cities within cities." This study of urban inequality in Argentina leads to the following conclusions:

- First, at the aggregate level there was a high correlation between poverty and inequality, i.e. urban areas in which there were greater differences have higher levels of poverty.
- While some of the variables result from patterns of employment and disposable household income, others related to location. Neighborhoods reporting cumulative disadvantages with respect to their cities at large tended to have visible infrastructure problems. Whether these were affordable neighborhoods for the poor or these areas neglected by public expenditures, or both, the overall conclusion was that place matters.
- These data, covering half of the national population, suggested that much more attention was needed to address spatial differences in levels of economic welfare.

The debate about welfare was not only about employment, but how place-based variables affect levels of real income and quality of life.

Patterns of poverty and inequality in the largest secondary cities

Within this broader sample of urban areas, the six largest secondary cities (Cordoba, Rosario, Mendoza, Santa Fe, La Plata, and Tucuman) had patterns which deserve particular attention. In general, these cities were richer than the next tier of cities and their scores tended to be above the averages for the 25 towns. As shown in Table 9.7, they had fewer numbers of people and households with UBN and somewhat better scores for housing and education. And yet, about 15 percent of their populations were illiterate, a third had not completed primary school, and almost 70 percent of this population had failed to complete secondary school. Outside of the Federal Capital, most of the scores were surprisingly similar among the second and third tier of cities. While it was true that smaller towns tended to have higher shares of UBN population, these scores were not so different to the larger cities.

These numbers suggest that within these cities, as increasing shares of total employment opportunities require higher skills, there will be increasing differences within the incomes of the populations of these cities. The economic futures and the relative equality of living conditions in the secondary towns were at risk, unless urgent actions were taken to increase human capital investment in these centers. Moreover, the gap in economic opportunities and incomes between Buenos Aires and secondary towns was likely to increase. Even with higher costs of business in Buenos Aires, the Federal Capital was the locus of skills and therefore was most likely to attract higher-paying jobs.

2003–2010: change after the crisis

The incidence of poverty greatly decreased within the urban centers of Argentina from 2003–2009 as the country experienced high economic growth, as seen in Table 9.8. While Federal Capital had the lowest percentage of individuals living below the poverty line, the Metropolitan Buenos Aires had one of the highest percentages in 2009. The smaller cities with less than 500,000 people also experienced significantly decreased poverty levels compared to the larger cities.

While poverty has significantly declined since 2003, income inequality still remains an urban issue, as shown in Table 9.9. Within the urban centers of Argentina, the top 30 percent of the population receives 62.2 percent of total income as opposed to the bottom 30 percent who receive 9 percent. This demonstrates that, while the country did experience high economic growth, urban inequality did not change.

Table 9.7 Social indicators: secondary cities vs. the rest of the cities (%)

District	*Pop.*	*UBN*	*Pop. without health coverage*	*Illiteracy rate*	*Not completing sec school*	*Homes without toilet*	*Low quality home*	*Non-owner occupied*
Metro BA	7,924,424	18.9	38.1	14.5	77.1	71.5	8.8	30.8
Federal Capital	2,871,519	8.1	19.1	8.3	56.6	5.8	1.1	34.7
Sub-total	**10,795,943**	**13.5**	**28.6**	**11.4**	**66.8**	**38.7**	**5**	**32.7**
Córdoba	1,193,443	14.4	35.7	13.6	66.9	77	1.9	38
Rosario	1,108,917	17.2	25.7	14.3	70.6	54	6.6	29.4
Mendoza	766,454	13.3	35.5	15	72.3	40.6	4.1	31.4
La Plata	627,927	13.4	25.2	12.1	65.7	43.1	5.5	32.1
Tucumán	616,598	20.7	30.8	16.4	70.1	48.8	10.8	31.1
Santa Fé	402,303	18.6	29.9	15.4	68.7	73.8	4.7	35.4
2nd tier cities	**4,715,642**	**16.3**	**30.5**	**14.5**	**69.1**	**56.2**	**5.6**	**32.9**
3rd tier cities	**3,895,667**	**19**	**32.7**	**16.8**	**72.4**	**53.9**	**5.7**	**31.3**

Source: SIEMPRO – based on the 1991 Population and Housing Census made by INDEC.

Table 9.8 Percentage of households (HH) and individuals (Ind.) below the poverty line in the urban centers and regions, 2003 and 2009

	% 2003		*% 2009*		*% change (+/–)*	
	HH	*Ind.*	*HH*	*Ind.*	*HH*	*Ind.*
Federal Capital	17.1	22.1	4.5	6.1	–12.6	–16
Metropolitan BA	51.1	61.3	10.4	14.5	–40.7	–46.8
Cuyo	44.7	54.8	9.6	13.9	–35.1	–40.9
Noreste	63.7	73.4	16.7	23.5	–47	–49.9
Noroeste	54.3	64.8	12	16.6	–42.3	–48.2
Pampeana	39	50.3	7.7	11.5	–31.3	–38.8
Patagonia	32.5	39.3	4.9	6.4	–27.6	–32.9
Total urban centers with 500,000 or more people	41.2	52.5	10.8	15.8	–30.4	–36.7
Total urban centers with less than 500,000 people	49.6	60	8.6	12.5	–41	–47.5
Total urban centers	42.7	54	9	13.2	–33.7	–40.8

Source: INDEC, *Encuesta Permanente de Hogares Incidencia de la Pobreza y de la Indigencia*, 2010.

Table 9.9 Population by level of per capita income. Total urban centers. 3rd quarter of 2010

Deciles	*Min*	*Max*	*Pop. in thousands*	*% of pop.*	*Income in thousands of pesos*	*% of the sum of income*	*Avg.*	*Median*
1	0	300	2,493	10.0	489,779	1.5	196	213
2	300	470	2,492	10.0	963,015	2.9	387	390
3	470	625	2,492	10.0	1,353,438	4.0	543	540
4	625	800	2,491	10.0	1,771,975	5.3	711	705
5	800	980	2,492	10.0	2,193,261	6.5	880	880
6	980	1,197	2,492	10.0	2,682,488	8.0	1,076	1,073
7	1,197	1,500	2,492	10.0	3,301,603	9.8	1,325	1,317
8	1,500	1,900	2,492	10.0	4,164,799	12.4	1,671	1,667
9	1,900	2,800	2,491	10.0	5,701,893	16.9	2,289	2,250
10	2,800	81,200	2,492	10.0	11,073,865	32.9	4,444	3,750
Total	0	81,200	24,919	100.0	33,696,116	100.0	1,352	980

Source: INDEC EPH 2010.

Note
From the 3° quarter of 2006 the EPH incorporated 3 agglomerates (San Nicolás-Villa Constitución, Viedma-Carmen de Patagones y Rawson-Trelew), so the total surveyed clusters became 31.

The metropolitan area of Buenos Aires

This section reviews in more detail some historical and current data available for metropolitan Buenos Aires, which is divided into the Federal Capital and 24 surrounding municipalities within the Province of Buenos Aires. This section examines the area outside the Federal Capital, with the latter presented in the subsequent pages.

The averages

Looking at the metropolitan area in terms of average figures for the region as a whole, metropolitan Buenos Aires outside of the Federal Capital had a population in 1991 of approximately eight million people in some 2.2 million households inhabiting roughly 2.1 million housing units. According to SIEMPRO data, 19 percent of this population had unsatisfied basic needs, with 10.7 percent of this group reporting unsatisfactory housing conditions as measured by standardized indicators of quality and housing. Reflecting the widespread practice of squatter housing, some 69 percent of the households owned their housing. As mentioned earlier, the citizens of metropolitan Buenos Aires had similar educational characteristics to those of the second tier cities with 77 percent having not completed secondary school.

On the income side, 1998 INDEC data showed that the monthly income required for a minimum basket of goods and services in metropolitan Buenos Aires was 1,030 pesos.[4] While this number had changed since 1991, the share of the population below the poverty line had increased from 21.6 percent in 1991 to 26 percent in 1997, with absolute numbers growing from 2.36 million in 1991 to three million in 1997. As of August 1998, INDEC reported that 60 percent of households within the metropolitan area earned less than the required 1,030 pesos for four persons.[5]

Another important trend in the income data was that there had been an almost tripling of the percentage of women who were the principal income-earners within households, from 9.1 percent in 1991 to 25 percent in 1998.[6] This shift also indicated income differentials between men and women.

Between 2001 and 2010, the area of metropolitan Buenos Aires grew the most within the country as a whole, with its population increasing by 10.6 percent from the 2001 Census.[7] The country grew at an annual rate of 1.17 percent to reach 40,091,359 people. During this period, the share of the population living in poverty also dropped from 52 percent in 2003 to 12.6 percent by 2009.[8] Within the total population of 9,910,282 in the metropolitan area, by the first quarter of 2009, INDEC reported that families in Gran Buenos Aires required 3,015 pesos to cover the basic cost of goods.[9] Table 9.10 shows that 30 to 50 percent of the population earned less than 2,000 pesos and received 9.3 percent of total income while the top 30 percent received 59.1 percent of the total income.

Table 9.10 Total population by deciles in metropolitan Buenos Aires, 2006

Decile	*Scale of income*		*% per decile (thousands)*	*Total income per decile (thousands)*	*% of income*	*Average income per decile*
	From	*To*				
1	10	180	679	80,206	1.2	118
2	180	350	679	181,028	2.7	267
3	350	420	679	265,667	3.9	391
4	423	590	679	337,408	5.0	497
5	590	700	679	432,325	6.4	637
6	700	880	679	535,574	7.9	789
7	890	1,000	679	651,408	9.7	959
8	1,000	1,400	678	815,731	12.1	1,202
9	1,400	2,000	678	1,110,971	16.5	1,638
10	2,000	60,000	679	2,329,873	34.6	3,433
Total Pop.			12,625			

Source: INDEC 2006.

The differences within the metropolitan area

As shown in Table 9.11, enormous historical differences existed within metropolitan Buenos Aires, with 4.7 percent of the population of the municipality of Vicente Lopez in 2001 having unsatisfied basic needs compared to 31 percent for Florencio Varela. These differences were reflected as well in housing conditions, with poor housing varying from 1.5 to 21.6 percent between the two municipalities. If 90 percent of the households of Vicente Lopez had sewerage connections, the number was 5 percent in Echeverria-Ezeiza-Cañuelas. Similarly, in 2001, Vicente Lopez had 98 percent sewerage coverage as opposed to Florencia Varela, which was 28 percent. Strong differences also existed in access to water, with Vicente Lopez having 100 percent access, while Florencia Varela had reached 58 percent.[10]

Taking the 19 areas of metropolitan Buenos Aires as a group, it is possible, as shown in Table 9.12, to distinguish three "cities" within the suburban areas. Of the 19 areas, seven had scores above the metropolitan average, while eight had scores consistently below, with the remaining four having a mix of scores. These indicators for the three groups of communities differed significantly and are indicated in Table 9.12.

If these differences within the suburban areas of Buenos Aires were considerable, they take on a different significance when compared to the data from the Federal Capital itself. Average monthly household income within the metropolitan area differed significantly between the Federal Capital and the Province. These differences were reflected in social indicators, which include level of education, employment, family size, and length of residence of households within the metropolitan area. Families living in the Federal Capital were clearly better educated and enjoyed higher incomes than their counterparts in the Province.

Table 9.11 Differences within metropolitan Buenos Aires (%) 1991

District	*Pop.*	*UBN*	*Pop. without health coverage*	*Illiteracy rate*	*Not completing sec school*	*Homes without toilet*	*Low quality home*	*Non-owner occupied*
La Matanza—C. Paz—Gral. Las Heras	1,117,319	21.6	43.2	15.4	80.1	36.2	10.1	36.2
J.C. Paz—M.Arg.—SanMiguel	648,268	24.3	43.3	17.4	81.5	31.2	12.8	31.2
Hurlingham	637,307	12.3	32.9	12	72.7	29.4	5.2	29.4
L. Zamora	570,457	19.1	37	14.4	76.5	29.9	8.9	29.9
Quilmes	508,114	21	34.7	14.5	76.8	25.5	10.7	25.5
Lanús	466,393	14.5	33.8	11.8	76.8	38.9	5.8	38.9
Alte. Brown	447,805	20	40.5	16.4	79.5	22.9	9.5	22.9
San Martín	404,072	14.3	35.6	12.3	75.4	30.3	5.6	30.3
Merlo	390,194	23.5	44.7	16.7	82.1	36.6	12.3	36.6
Morón	348,343	10.7	33.4	11.3	74.4	29.9	3.8	29.9
Avellaneda	342,226	13.7	30.2	11.6	74.4	30.4	5.3	30.4
San Isidro	297,392	10.2	25.1	10.6	63.5	28.8	4.5	28.8
Vicente López	287,154	4.7	20.1	9.3	58.5	29.6	2.4	29.6
Moreno	286,922	26.4	49.4	18.5	82.4	28.9	12.7	28.9
Echeverría-Ezeiza-Cañuelas	273,740	25	44.3	17.4	81.4	28.4	11.7	28.4
Tigre	256,349	22.8	43.2	16.1	80.8	30.8	14.3	30.8
F. Varela	254,514	31	47.5	19.1	84	24.9	16	24.9
Berazategui	244,405	21.3	38.9	15.5	80.7	27.5	9.5	27.5
S.Fernando	143,450	23	38.8	14.6	76.1	31.1	11.4	31.1
Total	7,924,424	18.9	38.1	14.5	77.1	30.8	8.8	30.8
Average	417,075	18.9	38.1	14.5	77.1	30.8	8.8	30.8

Source: SIEMPRO – based on the 1991 Population and Housing Census made by INDEC.

Table 9.12 Historical grouping of districts within metropolitan Buenos Aires in relation to metropolitan averages* (%)

District	*UBN pop.*	*Pop without health care*	*Non-completion rate in secondary*	*Homes without toilets*	*Low quality houses*
Tier 1—Rich	11.9	31	71.8	59.7	5.5
Tier 2—Medium	20.2	37.5	77.9	73.8	14
Tier 3—Poor	23.9	44.2	81.1	81.4	23.3
Average G.B.A.	18.9	38.1	77.1	71.5	14.5

Source: SIEMPRO – based on the 1991 Population and Housing Census made by INDEC.

Notes
* Average weighted by district populations.
Tier 1: Vicente Lopez, Lanus, San Martin, Morón, Avellaneda, San Isidro.
Tier 2: Lomas de Zamora, Quilmes, Alte Brown, Berazategui.
Tier 3: La Matanza-Carlos Paz-Gral. Las Heras, Jose C. Paz, Malvinas Argentinas – San Miguel, Echeverria-Ezeiza-Cañuenlas, Tigre, Florencia Varela, San Fernando.

This pattern had been maintained historically: in 1980, families that lived in the Province of Buenos Aires had a three times greater chance to have unsatisfied basic needs than those in the Federal Capital.

High-income inequality still exists within the Province despite the small decrease in the income gap between 2001–2005, as shown in Table 9.13. The median income for persons in the fifth decile was 12 times greater than those in the bottom first decile in 2005.

These income gaps also reflected significant differences in access to employment. *Clarín* reported:

> Youth unemployment in the *conurbano* was the highest in the country, even higher than the northeast region of Argentina. Men were at 15 percent, while women were 21.2 percent. This is critical considering 40 percent of the national population lives in the *conurbano* ... 40.8 percent of the population works in the black market. With a population of 10 million, the *conurbano* had the greatest increase in population between 2001 and 2010 due to

Table 9.13 Evolution of the income per capita, income gap. Municipalities of Gran Buenos Aires, 2001–2005

	Median income of 5th decile (a)	*Median income of 1st decile (b)*	*Income gap (a)/(b)*
2001	740	52	14.3
2005	1,186	102	12

Source: INDEC, Encueste Permonente de Hogares 2005.

> internal and external migration, according to INDEC. The increase in population working in the black market indicates the increase in precarious working conditions and ultimately, conflicts with the subject of social inclusion. Thus, behind much of the production and sales activity emerges a reality in the principal region that helps explain the persistence of social conflicts.[11]

While the city did experience economic growth, the intra-urban inequality was evident through the physical concentrations of informal settlements within the city. Argentine urban sociologist Maria Cravino reported that, "between 2001–2006, for every 100 new inhabitants in metropolitan Buenos Aires, 60 entered an informal neighborhood while 40 entered into a formal structure."[12] In particular, 49.3 percent of that population settled in the southern part of the city, as shown in Table 9.14. In a study conducted by Universidad Naciónal de General Sarmiento in 2006, researchers found that there existed at least 819 informal settlements in the metropolitan region of Buenos Aires with an average of 1,300 people per settlement and 218 people living per hectare. This constitutes around one million people in total living in the GBA. However, government authorities recently stated there are at least two million people living in precarious housing conditions.[13]

Table 9.15 shows the surface area of these settlements in metropolitan Buenos Aires. From a physical point of view, informal settlements occupy a small percentage of the city which implies the high density of people living in precarious and overcrowded conditions. They are nestled within the formal neighborhoods on public or private land. To draw a comparison, gated communities or *barrios cerrados* occupy 40,000 hectares, double the size of the Federal Capital.[14] Researchers from the University of Buenos Aires School of Architecture, Design and Urban Planning refer to this spatial fragmentation in the Province as an "archipelago city," formed by isolated residential "islands."[15]

Within these informal settlements, access to basic services such as sewerage remains a fundamental problem. Table 9.16 shows the low level of service coverage in informal settlements.

Table 9.14 Population and spatial concentration of villas and informal settlements in metropolitan Buenos Aires (2001)

Zone	*Population*	*%*
South	292,956	49.3
West-Northwest	233,595	39.3
North	68,230	11.4

Source: Cravino 2008, op. cit. p. 134.

Note

South: Almirante Brown, Avellaneda, Berazatequi, Estaban Echeverria, Ezeiza, Lanus, Lomas de Zamora, Quilmes y Florencia Varela. ***West/NW:*** General San Martin, Hurlingham, Ituzaingo, Jose C. Paz, La Matanza, Malvinas Argentinas, Merlo, Moreno, Morón, San Miguel y Tres de Febrero. ***North:*** San Fernando, Tigre, y Vicente Lopez

Table 9.15 Surface area occupied by villas and informal settlements for selected municipalities

Municipality	*Surface area in hectares*	*% of territory occupied*
Vicente Lopez	3,900	0.50
Florencia Varela	19,000	1.44
Federal Capital	20,300	1.46
Total Metropolitan BA	278,900	2.32
San Isidro	4,800	2.64
La Matanza	32,300	3.63
Avellaneda	5,500	4.92
Lanus	4,500	5.89
Quilmes	12,500	6.64

Source: Cravino 2008, op. cit., p. 135.

Table 9.16 Public services that exist for homes and families in informal settlements (2006)

Service	*Coverage (%)*
Electricity	99.6
Running Water	60.6
Cellular phone	51.7
TV Cable	24.6
Telephone line	17.9
Sewerage	0.6
Natural Gas	0.0
Total	100.0

Source: Cravino 2008, op. cit., p. 181.

The statistics for school attainment levels also differ greatly from the national averages. Based on their fieldwork within informal settlements in Gran Buenos Aires, Jorgelina Hardoy and Florencia Almansi conclude that, "A youth between 13 and 17 years of age living within the poorest quartile of the population is ten times more likely to stop attending school than a youth of the same age living within the wealthiest quartile."[16] Table 9.17 shows the varying levels of education for heads of household within these settlements.

Table 9.18 demonstrates that the provincial government allocated more social assistance to the municipalities with higher concentrations of urban poor.

The major conclusion from the above metropolitan data is that a realistic perception of Buenos Aires must include appreciation of a spectrum of levels of income and welfare, which significantly vary in quantitative terms by orders of magnitude. If the Federal Capital was well-off in relative terms, its metropolitan neighbors were in some respects equal to or below national averages on critical social and economic indicators such as percentage with unsatisfied basic needs or secondary school dropout rates. If the economic opportunities of the metropolitan

Table 9.17 Level of education for heads of households in informal settlements

Education level	*Head of Household 1*		*Head of Household 2*	
	Frequency	*%*	*Frequency*	*%*
None (illiterate)	21	4.4	12	3.6
Primary incomplete	117	24.4	74	22.0
Primary complete	228	47.5	172	51.0
Secondary incomplete	58	12.1	52	15.4
Secondary complete	44	9.2	22	6.5
Tertiary incomplete	5	1.0	1	0.3
Tertiary complete	3	0.6	2	0.6
University incomplete	3	0.6	0	0.0
ns/nc	1	0.2	2	0.6
Without HH2			143	100.0
Total	480	100.0	480	

Source: Cravino 2008, op. cit., p. 164.

Table 9.18 Spending on social development and assistance within Gran Buenos Aires, selected municipalities. Year 2008

Municipality	*Pesos*
Vicente Lopez	462,260.85
Tigre	5,064,833.62
Quilmes	6,487,530.24
La Matanza	19,632,889.86
Florencia Varela	10,609,380.68
Morón	2,267,449.94
Total	224,098,898.27

Source: Ministry of Social Development 2008.

area had attracted rural migrants who largely live in the communities in the Province of Buenos Aires, these potential opportunities were not reflected in the social and economic data for these households. This view was supported by the 1998 INDEC study, which reported that 60 percent of the households of Greater Buenos Aires earned monthly incomes below the official poverty line of $1,000, required to purchase the minimum basket of goods and services. This process can be characterized as "the urbanization of poverty."

These economic differences were well-captured by Pablo Cicolella in an article in which he describes the different velocities of mobility of three households living in metropolitan Buenos Aires: one leaving their computer at home in a gated community, driving in their car along an *autopista* to downtown white collar employment probably in the financial sector, talking on their cell-phones; a second leaving their *barrio*, taking a bus or *collectivo* to work downtown in the service economy unconnected to computer technology; and a third not leaving their neighborhood at all.[17]

While the differences within the metropolitan area are another manifestation of the inequality and poverty presented in this chapter, they are particularly stark when compared to the patterns of the Federal Capital itself, as presented below.

The Federal Capital: the five cities of Buenos Aires

As briefly presented in Chapter 7, the differences in levels of welfare and quality of life within the Federal Capital of Buenos Aires itself, with 3.5 million people, were so great in the 1990s that it was possible to distinguish five broad levels of well-being or "five different cities." These differences correlated with spatial location.

Before examining these differences, it is important to appreciate the economic significance of the Federal Capital within the Argentine economy, which accounted for 25 percent of GDP in 1994.[18] It is important to note, however, that the composition of this activity changed considerably since 1970. Table 9.19 illustrates this change.

Table 9.19 shows that there was an important reduction of about 30 percent in industrial and manufacturing production from 1970 to 1994, with a corresponding tripling of production in financial services and other services. Some 54 percent of the product of the city changed sector over this period. Today, at least 60 percent of employment is within the services sector.

Table 9.20 shows the composition of employment and value of product.

Within this pattern, the process of economic restructuring also contributed to a substantial increase in unemployment from 2.3 percent in 1974 to 2.8 percent in 1985, to a 1996 level of 12.8 percent, roughly in the end 1998 range. City Government economists estimated that this growth of unemployment could be attributed to: some 4.3 percent from the hyperinflation up to 1990, increasing up to 8.7 percent as a result of the economic restructuring and opening up of the

Table 9.19 Economic structure of Federal Capital by sector

Sector	*% 1970*	*% 1995*	*% 2008*
Manufacturing industry	28.8	17.5	15
Electricity, gas, and water	2.5	1.6	1
Construction	6.2	1.3	3
Trade, restaurants, and hotels	31.6	21.6	20
Transport, storage, and communications	6.8	7.5	12
Financing, insurance, and immovables	10.9	32.9	30
Communal, social, and personal services	13.2	17.6	19
Total	100	100	100

Sources: Ciudad de Buenos Aires, Programa del Plan Estratégico DT N.2, Abril de 1998 and Anuario Estadístico 2008; Plan Estratetégico de Buenos Aires 2016, p. 74.

Table 9.20 Economic product and employment

Sector	*Added value 1994 (%)*	*Workers 1994 (%)*	*Added value 2010 (%)*
Manufacturing industry	27.7	20.3	14.4
Trade	28.1	25.4	14.3
Services	44.2	54.3	62.7
Other	–	–	8.6
Total	100	100	100

Sources: Ciudad de Buenos Aires, Estructura económica y posición de la ciudad frente al mundo, Technical Document Nr. 2 of Programa del Plan Estratégico based on data from Economic National Census 1994; Plan Estratégico de Buenos Aires 2016, p. 66.

economy, and later to 12.8 percent from the *tequila effect* and changes in economic policies.

With high economic growth following the crisis, unemployment rates fell by half, as seen in Figure 9.1. Compared to Gran Buenos Aires, the Federal Capital unemployment rates were lower by a few percentage points.

Table 9.21 shows this changing rate of national GDP growth produced in the City of Buenos Aires post-crisis. Compared to the national GDP, the Federal Capital has had a higher GDP growth rate since 2003.

Table 9.22 shows the growth of each sector from 2002–2007. The construction sector and trade sector led the economic growth of the city post-crisis. The growth of the construction sector grew mainly from the demand of high-income sectors.

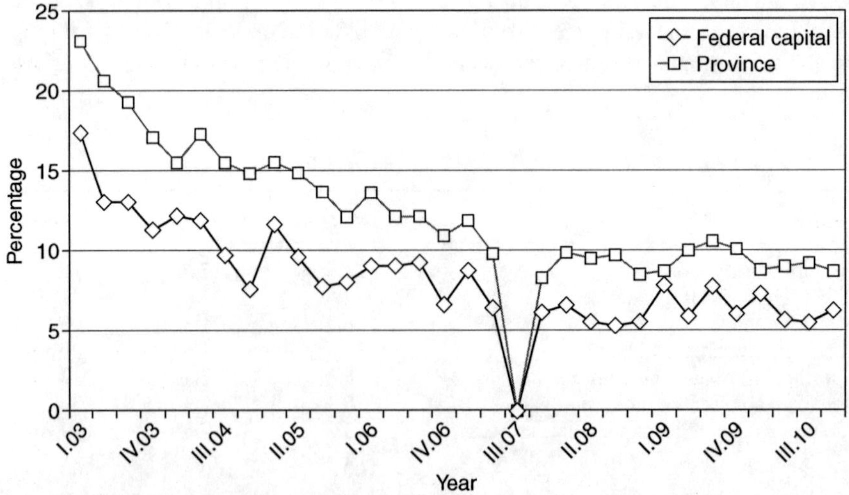

Figure 9.1 Unemployment rate: Federal Capital versus Province (source: INDEC 2010).

Table 9.21 GDP growth rate of federal capital vs. national GDP. (1993 prices)

	Fed. cap.	*National GDP*
2002	–16.4	–10.1
2003	5.3	7.5
2004	9.9	8.1
2005	13.3	8.9
2006	13	8.4
2007	9.7	8.6
2008	6.2	5.8

Source: Annual Household Survey (EAH) 2008, p. 107.

Table 9.22 Growth of sectors years 2002–2007 in city of Buenos Aires

Sector	*%*
Construction	364
Trade	107
Transportation	96
Industry	85
Total GDP	66
Hotels and restaurants	61
Real estate services	60
Electricity, gas, water	55
Education	33
Financial services	31

Source: City Government of Buenos Aires, *Plan Estratégico de Buenos Aires 2016*, p. 71.

While this chart shows the growth of the construction sector, in 2008–2009, residential construction permits fell by 65 percent and construction permits for economic activity fell by 59.1 percent due to the impact of the global financial crisis.

Despite the high growth in construction, the housing deficit remains a critical problem for the city as those in the lower income bracket lack access to basic credit.[19] As seen in Table 9.23, a significant proportion of the population does not either own or have tenancy to a home. Particularly, in the southern part of the city, 17.3 percent of the households lack tenure.

According the Annual Household Survey (EAH) 2009, 4.2 percent of houses and 4.6 percent of individuals live in precarious living conditions (tenement, illegal occupation, hotel, *pension*, *casilla*, *rancho*). 12.7 percent of this population lives in Commune 1, which includes Constitución, San Telmo, Retiro, San Nicolás, Montserrat, and Puerto Madero. Commune 4, which includes Barracas Boca, Nueva Pompeya, and Parque Patricios, holds 12.1 percent of this population, and Commune 3, which includes Balvanera and San Cristobal, with 9.3 percent.[20] The survey distinguishes that, "State intervention in the regulation of

Table 9.23 Percentage distribution of households by tenure of housing by area. Federal capital. Year 2009

	Total	*Owners of house and land*	*Renter or tenant*	*Other*
Total	100	61.7	27.5	10.9
North	100	62.5	27.8	9.7
East	100	49.8	37.4	12.8
South	100	54.0	28.7	17.3
West	100	72.5	19.5	8.0
Center	100	63.8	25.8	10.4

Source: EAH 2009, p. 7.

land distribution and other related markets (mortgage, rental housing development, alternative forms, such as leasing property, trusts) has a strong impact on access to housing for the low and medium income population."[21]

Alfredo Garay, a town planner and former provincial and city government official, highlighted that the city government does not have the same institutional capacity to deal with the social demand of housing as compared to the provincial government. "In Gran Buenos Aires, they built or repaired 60,000 houses in the last years. Most of the time, houses need renovation. In Federal Capital they only built 2,000 houses." He argued that the recent occupations such as in Villa Soldati are a result of the city's lack of institutional capacity to tackle the housing issue.[22]

According to the city government's *Plan Estratégico 2016*, the current tax system is highly regressive. Seventy-five percent of the city's tax revenue comes from consumer transactions, while 20.2 percent comes from property taxes. Much of the tax burden falls on the lower income population as a result.[23] The city government laments the difficulty in implementing investment plans as its budget mainly depends on the city revenue and income and also, it receives the least amount of transfers from the co-participation funds.[24]

Table 9.24 shows the growth in average monthly income for the city of Buenos Aires.

Table 9.24 Average monthly income for city of Buenos Aires, current pesos

Year	*Pesos*
2003	930
2004	1,011
2005	1,224
2006	1,399
2007	1,768
2008	2,160

Source: EAH 2008, p. 108.

The average monthly income of a *porteño* was nearly double the minimum wage as of 2008 ($1,075). From 2003 to 2008, the income of residents grew by 54.7 percent in real terms while minimum wage annual rate of variation grew by 202.4 percent.[25] Average real income decreased the level of actual purchasing power than what was observed in 2007.[26]

Table 9.25 displays the income inequality between formal and informal wages.

In 2008, 70.3 percent of the population worked in the formal sector as opposed to 29.7 percent in the informal sector.[27]

Public investment as a factor in inequality

If changes in employment structure and availability contributed significantly to the incidence of urban poverty and inequality, another important dimension of this process was public investment in infrastructure and social services. This section presents public investment data by individual sectors, identifies their spatial patterns, and correlates types of data to suggest the existence of patterns of cumulative inequality within the Federal Capital. Studies undertaken by the government of the city of Buenos Aires in 1997–1998 include data on infrastructure investment for the 21 school districts of the city.

Infrastructure

Data on investment in public infrastructure such as streets, sidewalks, public buildings, parks, playgrounds, and traffic lights over the period 1991 to 1997 show that some districts received more than 130 times the level of investment per capita than others. The study shows that through this period, a minority of population received a disproportionate share of this investment. For example, in 1991, 3.1 percent of the population received 45.1 percent of the investment. Over the 1991–1997 period, two districts with 6.2 percent of the population received 30.5 percent of total investment.

According to a study done by the *Defensoría del Pueblo de la Ciudad*, unequal real estate investment continues within the city. While the southern and

Table 9.25 Average monthly income formal vs. informal, current pesos 2003/2008

	Formal	*Informal*
2003	1,198	569
2004	1,300	608
2005	1,544	749
2006	1,749	851
2007	2,159	1,158
2008	2,638	1,320

Source: EAH 2008, p. 117.

southeastern areas have seen an increase in deteriorating living conditions, the northern part has experienced a real estate boom. In 2005, 25 percent of the real estate development projects were in Palermo and Puerto Madero.[28]

Public education

Similar patterns of investment in public education by school district within the Federal Capital existed in 1997. These data show that on a per capita basis, some districts received more than five times than others. Wide differences in public spending for education were also accompanied by wide differences in the percentages of student population who finish primary and secondary school. This resulted in different completion rates for the 21 districts, showing that while most, although not all, districts have high rates of completion of primary school, in 14 of 21 districts, more than half of the students did not complete secondary school. While the strict statistical relationship between educational expenditures and student performance was difficult to prove—and the correlation in this case did not exceed 0.35[29]—there was a correlation between districts above and below the city averages, both for expenditures and completion rates.

Although differences in health care coverage were less than in investment in infrastructure or education, 17 percent of the population of the Federal Capital did not have health insurance and that the percentages of uninsured varied from 11.6 to 25.2 percent of the population by school district. The concentration of hospital beds in the Federal Capital also reflected these patterns, with more than half of these beds (52.5 percent) concentrated in school districts #5 (23.6 percent), #2 (15.1 percent) and #1 (13.8 percent), which were situated in the east of the city. The concentration of hospital beds, partially explained by the growth dynamic of the city from East to West, resulted in only 10.3 percent of the population enjoying the benefits of the 52.5 percent of the hospital beds, even though people move around the city to seek better public health services.

When the geographic distribution of the hospital beds is related to the investment in public infrastructure and in primary and secondary education, the presence of the pattern of cumulative disadvantages was further strengthened: the inhabitants of the mentioned districts received the benefits of public investment in infrastructure and education superior to the average of the city in per capita terms.[30]

All of this was reflected in measurements of unsatisfied basic needs. Differences in investment in infrastructure and education were also reflected in the shares of population with unsatisfied basic needs. While 13 of the districts had less than 7.6 percent of their respective populations lacking basic services in 1991, 8 of the districts had more than 7.6 percent and four districts had more than two or three times that level. Indeed, two districts in the south of the city had 20.3 and 26.3 percent of their populations respectively with unsatisfied basic needs. This UBN index includes: housing type, sanitation, crowding, and presence of a child between six and 12 not attending school.

Patterns of cumulative inequality

Taken together, data on the distribution of public investment in infrastructure and education, health care coverage, and indices of unsatisfied basic needs, coupled with educational performance illustrate cumulative historical patterns of inequality. While the sample sizes of these data were small: only 21 districts and eight variables, there were nevertheless some high and significant correlations:

A between UBN and the rate of primary completion rates (–0.90)
B between per capita investment in infrastructure and per capita investment in education (0.73)
C between per capita investment in infrastructure and distribution of investment in infrastructure (0.92)
D between UBN and health care coverage (0.76)
F between UBN3 and secondary school completion (–0.59)

Districts with unsatisfied basic needs also had low levels of school attainment and lack health care. Districts, which receive low public investment in infrastructure, also receive low levels of public investment in education.

Table 9.26 displays the net enrollment rates in secondary school in the city of Buenos Aires.

In total, 88 percent of adolescents aged 13 to 17 years attended secondary school. In the North, the percentage was exceeded by nearly six percentage points. While 60.2 percent of the population is considered to have UBN in the South, 10 percent of the population has UBN in the northeastern part of the city.[31] One of the main conclusions under social development in the *Plan Estratégico de Buenos Aires* was that, "Education had deteriorated significantly as a result of public policy.... There remains a deficit of educational institutions in the southern part of the city due to a lack of fiscal resources."[32] The city government commits itself in its plan to further tackle the issue of "equitable integration for the southern zone," socially and economically.

Institutional change

The processes and disparities described in this chapter could not have occurred without the existence of many institutions in the public and private sectors, and

Table 9.26 Net enrollment in secondary school in Federal Capital, 2008

Total	87.9
North	93.8
East	83.1
South	81.5
West	88.7
Center	88.0

Source: EAH 2008, p. 58.

in some cases, working at cross purposes. The complicated overlapping and complementary processes of urban growth and expansion have been guided to some degree by institutions within a broad framework of public policies and active public and private investment. Yet, these policies and patterns of investment must be understood, however, within a broader process of the neo-liberal reform of the Argentine state since the early 1990s. The combination of policies of liberalization and privatization, discussed below, resulted in a considerable weakening of the national government.[33] These included the capacity of the state to provide basic urban services, regulate private sector activity, particularly private investment, and to guarantee a basic level of welfare for ordinary citizens. This process represents a sharp departure from the powerful and active presence of the state in urban policy during the decades of the 1940s and 1950s. This transformation operated at many levels: from macro-economic management, where the market was given a much larger role in the allocation of resources to the regulation of industrial development and to the management of urban growth itself. In the latter case, the combination of privatization of infrastructure services and the decentralization of responsibility for many services to municipalities dramatically changed the accessibility and costs of services to the population, and mostly the residents of the *conurbano*.

If national, provincial, and municipal institutions can claim responsibility for the many successes of the past two decades, so too do they deserve to be held accountable for many of the problems and negative impacts which the metropolitan area has felt. In contrast to most large cities around the world—in both developed and developing countries–Buenos Aires is one of the few cities, which do not have a metropolitan framework of governance. This institutional deficit is not a trivial matter.

The lack of metropolitan governance in Buenos Aires stems from many historical factors, including the federal structure of the country, the inertia of institutions, and political rivalries between the political leaders of the Federal Capital and the Province of Buenos Aires. After the creation of the Autonomous City Government of Buenos Aires in 1996, and the election as mayor of Senator Fernando de la Rua of the Radical Party, two parties governed Buenos Aires: the Radicals in the Federal Capital and the Justicialist or Peronist Party in the Province. Neither political leadership was prepared to cooperate with the rival party, much less to establish an institutional framework, which could in any way impinge on their respective political prerogatives. Both parties saw their political and administrative control—one had the capital city while the other had the largest and most populated province in country—as major components of their political power and possibilities for patronage.

A consequence of these factors is that metropolitan Buenos Aires in 2011 still does not have public agencies—with one major exception in solid waste management—to manage its environment, infrastructure services such as transport, water resources and water supply, liquid and toxic waste management, crime, public health, and many other sectors of municipal responsibility at a metropolitan scale.[34] Without a formal institutional framework, there is no guarantee much less likelihood that the individual policies and actions of 25 separate municipalities (the city government of Buenos Aires and 24 municipalities in the Province of Buenos Aires) will be mutually supportive, complementary, or even positive for the metropolitan area. This lack of institutional coordination is reflected in the difficulty, for example, of managing the cleanup of the La Matanza Riachuelo River Basin, even though the national government received a loan from the Inter-American Development Bank in the late 1990s to undertake this cleanup of the river basin so badly polluted with industrial waste[35] and then, a second major loan from the World Bank in 2009 to extend the cleanup efforts.

There have been a few exceptions to this pattern. The entity with the longest history has been the *Coordinación Ecológica Área Metropolitana Sociedad del Estado* (CEAMSE) which is a public agency overseeing solid waste collection, disposal, including several important landfills in the metropolitan area. CEAMSE works with 34 municipalities in the greater metropolitan area. This is obviously a big business, with the monthly cost for only the city of Buenos Aires at 13 million pesos.[36] It is interesting that while solid waste has proven to be the only service where a "metropolitan solution" has been found, it is also both formal CEAMSE and informal, with the *cartoneros*. Many of the latter used the *tren blanco* to enter and leave the city each day from 2002 to 2010. The city government mandated a set of regulations governing the *cartoneros*, including payments, which encouraged the school-age members of this group to attend school. Other entities, however, have been much less operational such as the *Ente para la Regulacion del Transporte en la Área Metropolitana* (ECOTAM) which was supposed to coordinate transport services among different jurisdictions, but this function has not provided effective control over private sector transport which dominates much of the service. An *Ente Tripartito de Obras y Servicios Sanitarios* (ETOSS) was also created to regulate the water supply concession, but which did not prove particularly effective.

The historically difficult relationship between the Federal Capital and the Province of Buenos Aires has led nevertheless to a series of ad hoc agreements, for example among four municipalities in April 2000: Vicente Lopez, San Isidro, San Fernando, and Tigre forming the *Región Metropolitana Norte* in the north and northwest of the city, with a combined population of 1.2 million persons, and among three municipalities south of the Federal Capital.[37] These groupings agreed, for example, to the coordination of policies governing social services, transport and traffic management, and public security. One specific example was opening access to emergency medical services in public hospitals among the four municipalities.

At the same time, some individual municipalities such as La Matanza, under the political leadership of then Mayor and National Congressman Alberto Balestrini, or Morón, under Mayor Martin Sabatella, demonstrated their own political weight in negotiating agreements with the national government. These areas have been characterized by a high level of political organization and clientelist politics.[38] The persistence and political importance of provincial and municipal politics in the metropolitan area was reflected in the Senatorial elections of

November 2005 in which First Lady, Senator Cristina Fernandez de Kirchner defeated the former First Lady, Congresswoman, Hilda "Chiche" Duhalde. What is also quite clear is that the municipalities of the *conurbano* are the spawning grounds for national political leaders, such as Anibal Fernandez, former Mayor of Quilmes, and later Minister of Interior in the government of President Nestor Kirchner.

These more recent political events have their origins in the important recognition of the *municipios* of the *conurbano* in March 1998 when mayors met with then President Carlos Menem to discuss the role of municipalities in the growing problems of unemployment and poverty. This led in 1999 to further decentralization of national social programs to the municipal level, with a particular focus on the *conurbano* which was both more politically significant but also the locus of serious problems. This followed earlier steps towards decentralization with the creation of new *municipios* in 1993–1994. The transfer of functional responsibility in 1999 covered many fields including health, food, education and training, and housing.[39] For example, by 2004, some 7,700 schools in the *conurbano* provided meals to school children from the ages of three to eight years old as well as other children from poor households, at a cost of 200 million pesos.[40] This process had several somewhat contradictory consequences: the municipalities were empowered to manage local problems under laws, which were referred to as *La Regimen Local de Implementación*. This led to additional financial resources from both the Province of Buenos Aires and the national government. It also offered municipalities and local authorities much more political power in managing these resources through the networks of the political parties known as the *manzaneras*.[41]

However, when the crisis of late 2001 to 2003 took place, these municipalities had new immediate social and economic responsibilities in the face of a national economic collapse. The structure of financial support, which they received from the Province of Buenos Aires and the national government, and the consequent level of financial autonomy differed considerably depending on the needs of their populations and the type of program for which they qualified. Detailed analysis of these differences across the municipalities helps to explain levels of poverty and the severity of socio-economic conditions and also highlights the growing political power of local mayors in the *conurbano*. [42] These studies also demonstrate the important, but also difficult and controversial roles of non-governmental organizations and community-based organizations in playing mediating roles between public resources and community needs. The growing presence of these civil society organizations represents a significant but complicated step towards democratization at the local level.[43] Local politics have developed around specific issues facing individual communities involving land, infrastructure and social services, but also the exercise of power and local control.[44] These processes were further complicated by the support provided by the World Bank for distinct social programs and the interaction of decentralization and different levels of local institutional capacity with the institutional requirements of the Bank. These experiences highlighted the growing metropolitan importance of inter-governmental financial relations, a subject that will be central to the evolution of the Buenos Aires metropolitan area.

It is important to appreciate the economic stakes involved in this issue. It is not just the outcomes at the municipal or even metropolitan levels, which are important. Even if there has been a growing role of local government in urban social policy in the *conurbano*, an institutionally-fragmented metropolitan area is a major liability for the country as a whole. As noted in Chapter 7, if the metropolitan area is to continue to generate a significant share of the national GDP as described below, while maintaining some equity in the level of income and quality of life for its inhabitants, it must face up to the institutional challenge of metropolitan governance.[45] This challenge involves the establishment of policies and institutions to manage the positive and negative externalities of urban scale, for example to help to mitigate negative environmental impacts, managing crime, maximizing coordination in infrastructure planning, design, and construction, as well as creating economic and financial multipliers for investment, employment, and income generation.

Despite these disappointments at the metropolitan level, it is interesting to note that institutional reform in Buenos Aires has essentially meant decentralization and reform on an urban scale. During the 1990s, important steps were taken to address the governance of the capital city. In 1994, the reform of the Argentine Constitution created the Autonomous City of Buenos Aires. Article 129 stated the following:

> The City of Buenos Aires shall have an autonomous system of government with power of legislation and jurisdiction, and its head of government shall be elected by the people of the city. One law shall guarantee the interests of the National Government while the City of Buenos Aires is the Capital of the Nation. Under the provisions of this Article, the National Congress will convoke the residents of the City of Buenos Aires so that they issue the Organizing Statute of their institutions through their representatives elected for that purpose.[46]

The reform provided for an elected mayor and an elected legislature to manage the affairs of the Federal Capital. The city of Buenos Aires was given the same autonomy as the 17 provinces of the country, including representation in the Congress and the Senate. The autonomy of Buenos Aires represents the ultimate step in consolidating the federal structure of the government. Until that time the Mayor had been a position appointed by the President of the Nation.

Elections were held in 1996 for the position of chief of the government of the city, or the Mayor, and Senator Fernando de la Rua was elected, along with Enrique Olivera as Deputy Mayor. The first two years of the De la Rua administration were characterized by some modest expansion of the capacities of the city government, of which the most important were the creation of 16 *Centros de Gestión Municipal (CGPs)*. These centers were distributed around the city and were organized to provide municipal services to citizens such as registry of property, marriages, and other ceremonies. The CGPs also had small budgets to support neighborhood activities and outreach for the city government. They were a welcome addition to a relatively centralized urban governance structure. It was interesting in 1998 to hear then Mayor de la Rua say that decentralization of the city government was his highest priority during his first term in order to strengthen Argentina's democracy.[47]

Starting in 1999, Mayor De la Rua began his campaign for the presidency, which he won in 2000. Despite the growing economic crisis in the city, the city government was not particularly active beyond its management of social services, schools, and infrastructure. Indeed at the time of handing over the city government to his deputy, Enrique Olivera, there was a surplus of unused funds in the budget. Elections were held in 2000 and Anibal Ibarra was elected Mayor.

This low level of municipal activity dropped further during the crisis of 2001–2002, when municipal revenues almost disappeared, municipal employees were being paid but, like all Argentine citizens, had no access to their bank accounts. Surprisingly, this situation changed quickly with the reactivation of the economy in late 2002 and thereafter, as municipal revenues from taxation on economic activities increased rapidly. The city government, therefore, began many infrastructure projects around the city, paving streets, fixing up parks, and various social facilities. The improvements were visible indicators of an active municipal government.

During this process, the further decentralization of the city government was underway, with preparations for the implementation of the constitutional provision that the Federal Capital should be divided into *communas.* These preparations included the convening of a municipal commission to recommend how the city's spatial area should be divided. This commission debated, for example, whether each *communa* should be drawn around "centralities" such as a major public square or shopping district, or whether there was some other legal criteria to be applied to defining *communas*. These debates led to extensive analytic work and discussions.[48] A proposal for 15 units was presented to the Municipal Legislature in 2005 and approved. The first elections for political leadership at this level were scheduled to take place in late 2006, but never happened.

A major political crisis, however, interrupted orderly political processes in late December 2004, in the midst of the end-of-the-year celebrations, when a tragic fire occurred in the overcrowded Cromanon nightclub in the Once district of Buenos Aires, killing 191 people, mostly youth. This event was presented in Chapter 6. A significant dimension of the Cromanon tragedy and its aftermath, however, was the demonstration of the growing role of civil society in public affairs. While there are political interpretations of the unseating of Mayor Ibarra, the Legislature's action reflected the power of political and civil society forces in the city calling for public accountability for an avoidable tragedy.

A second aspect of urban institutional performance has been the issue of crime and insecurity in the metropolitan area. By 2000, citizens of Buenos Aires were outraged by growing crime and later in 2004 by kidnappings and murder of young men and women. Crime in the Federal Capital had been growing steadily since 1995, at a higher rate than both the national and provincial rates. Interestingly, crimes against property were particularly high in the Federal Capital. In 2004, in response to the kidnapping and murder of a middle-class young man, Axel Blumberg, in the city, and his father's appeal for strong government action, more than 150,000 people marched on the Plaza de Mayo in central Buenos Aires to protest insufficient government attention to crime and insecurity, as noted in Chapter 6. A murder a month had captured the media, but the murder of Axel Blumberg further fed people's sense of insecurity.

It is interesting to note that at the same time, Washington, DC, a city of 600,000 people, or 5 percent of Buenos Aires, was experiencing 1.5 murders per day in the 1990s in contrast to one murder a month, yet the public outcry was much less in Washington than Buenos Aires. Perception and visibility of the problem is thus a major issue. It may also reflect who is being murdered; in the case of Buenos Aires, the victims were frequently middle-class people; while in Washington, the victims were almost always black, the crimes were usually drug-related, and they occurred in the poorer neighborhoods of the city, areas that received less coverage in the media.

Reducing the public institutional arena: the spread of privatization

A major transformation affecting metropolitan Buenos Aires since 1990 was the privatization of a wide range of urban services, including the water supply, electricity, telephones, public transport, including commuter trains, garbage collection, and sanitation. While privatization occurred in many developed and developing countries during the 1990s, Argentina went further than almost any other country.[49] Encouraged by the international financial institutions and private investors, the national government under President Carlos Menem accelerated this process and sold off national assets at often unjustifiably low prices. Privatization fit within a larger process of foreign direct investment in the country, with many countries, most notably Spain, taking advantage of stable exchange rates and no fear of inflation and gaining large profits from this process.[50]

Three areas of privatization deserve special comment because they had a particularly major impact on the metropolitan area. The first is the construction of a system of urban and suburban toll highways from 1990 to 1998, when some US$2 billion was privately invested.[51] These highways were necessary for the spatial expansion into the second and third rings of the metropolitan area. They include the 12-lane *Acceso Norte* or *Pan Americana*, as it is known, which channels traffic to the northwest of the city. These highways have dramatically improved the access of the suburban population to the Federal Capital. This has reduced the transport costs, in time, for the middle and upper income groups, but has increased the prices of land in the suburban rings for residential development for the gated communities described earlier. These price increases have contributed to a residential pattern of spatial segregation and fragmentation, polarizing suburban areas between middle and upper income groups in gated communities and the growing slums, which have proliferated as well.

A significant consequence of this process has been dramatically increased ownership of private cars and increased traffic. While Buenos Aires does not suffer from particularly high levels of air pollution from motor vehicles, it has now become a highly congested metropolitan area. Commuter trains bring mostly lower income people into the Federal Capital, with almost four million trips per day. Traffic management has become a subject of public debate and led to a "mobility pact" signed between the government of the city of Buenos Aires with private bus and taxi operators in 2005.

A second controversial aspect of privatization was the sale of a 30-year management concession for *Obras Sanitarios de la Nación*, the public company providing water and sewerage treatment to the Federal Capital and much of the metropolitan area. A French-led consortium of the French water company *Suez*, *Aguas de Barcelona*, and the *International Finance Corporation* of the World Bank Group, bought this concession in 1990. In addition to promising improvements in management, the consortium promised to make needed investments to rehabilitate the existing systems of water treatment and distribution, and most importantly, to extend water supply to the municipalities of the *conurbano*. While there is evidence that some of these promises were fulfilled, there were some important commitments, which did not particularly extend service on a large scale to unserved, mostly poor neighborhoods.

While *Suez* had developed an approach to participatory development in extending service to poor communities, particularly in La Matanza, this was not perceived as sufficiently large to be considered having met the commitments in the contract. As service lagged during the 1990s, non-governmental organizations tried to help communities meet their needs. Pilot projects at the neighborhood level demonstrated improvements,[52] but the problem of scale remained. The consortium argued that the government had not allowed needed increases in water tariffs to finance these investments, but the government complained that the consortium was able to take large profits from the company which should have been used for these investments. This was perceived as part of a larger phenomenon that the rate of investment by the privatized entities dropped from 62.7 percent annually in 1993 to 25.9 percent in 2000.[53]

In late 2005, after lengthy and contentious negotiations with the national government, *Suez* announced that it would break the contract and not continue after 2006. This led to further bad feelings, and in early 2006, the government rescinded the contract and announced it was seeking alternative private investors. By mid-2006, no private investors had agreed to take over the contract and in June 2006, the government decided to make the company a public entity once again. This decision was politically popular at a time when the impacts of economic liberalization and privatization of the 1990s had lost all credibility in the Argentine population.[54]

From the perspective of the metropolitan area, this 16-year experience actually contributed to creating further differences in the quality of life across the urban space. By focusing first on rehabilitating systems serving the Federal Capital and de facto giving the *conurbano* lower priority, the millions of people living in under served neighborhoods on the periphery of the city did not receive benefits in infrastructure investment, which the economic growth of the 1990s should have provided. While it is impossible to say that continued public water supply service during the 1990s would have reached a significant number of these people, a significant "opportunity cost" of privatization is that potential improvements never occurred. A strong critique of the privatization of water supply was that a public monopoly had been transformed into a private monopoly, without any of the effective regulation required to sustain performance.[55]

The third area of privatization with very large impacts on life in Buenos Aires was in telecommunications. At the beginning of the 1990s, it was commonly known that it could take up to ten years to get a telephone connection in a housing unit in the city. Privatization of the telephone system, with *Telefonica* of Spain and *Telecom* of France, dramatically changed the availability and quality of service. The wait of ten years was reduced to several days. This opening up of telecommunications became even more important with the arrival of cellular telephones in the late 1990s. Privatization resulted in widespread distribution and now ownership of cellular telephones, with benefits for people of all levels of income.

The spread of cellular telephones also presaged the arrival of inexpensive computers and Internet technology. Buenos Aires is now covered with call stations (*locutorios*) providing inexpensive access for the metropolitan population and providing the high density of communications needed for a growing economy.

As noted above, economic liberalization has resulted in a sustained and devastating process of de-industrialization in Argentina. The overall composition of the Buenos Aires economy has shifted substantially, away from industry and manufacturing towards commerce and financial services.[56] From 1970 to 1994, already 54 percent of the product of the Federal Capital had changed sector. These shifts continued over the following years, with increasing emphasis on real estate, transport, legal services, and financial management.[57]

While some of these economic processes have been beyond the effective control of the municipal or even the national government, others relate to the management of the metropolitan area and to what is clearly a metropolitan economy. If the productivity of a city is related to the management of its scale economies and externalities, in economists' terms, the absence of a policy and institutional framework to do so represents a major constraint to achieving that productivity. Indeed, this absence can undermine such economies of scale, particularly when, as in the case of Buenos Aires, there is no metropolitan policy with regard to management and development of needed infrastructure, nor to environmental problems, nor to the whole range of urban services and social problems found in the area. This lack of metropolitan framework is reflected in inefficient management of public finance, poor and uneven regulatory enforcement of all kinds, and threatens, in the end, to create a situation in which the "whole is less than the sum of its parts." Whether metropolitan Buenos Aires will be an under-performer in a country needing to develop medium- and long-term strategies for economic development remains to be seen.

The issue of efficiency in the Buenos Aires metropolitan area is not just an abstraction. Remy Prud'homme and his colleagues provided several insights into what efficiency actually means for Buenos Aires. First, they compared the level of economic productivity of all major cities in Argentina by analyzing product, wages, and incomes, and discover that for its size, metropolitan Buenos Aires was only 12 percent more productive than the un-weighted average of Argentine cities and is actually surpassed by some smaller cities. Thus, given its size, it is underperforming relative to what might be expected.[58] Secondly, this performance is related to the weakness of urban management, where they observe that municipalities are too weak while the Province of Buenos Aires is too strong in managing the finances and investment patterns for urban infrastructure and services.[59] In this regard, they note that metropolitan Buenos Aires is a socio-economic reality and even a statistical artifact, but it is not an administrative or political institution.[60]

A third and highly significant observation brings together the various processes outlined in this chapter: space, infrastructure, and employment. Using data on motorization and availability of public transport, employment, and spatial residential patterns, Prud'homme and his colleagues concluded that people using public transport have access to only 23 percent of the jobs available in the metropolitan area, while those with private cars have access to 87 percent of the jobs. This analysis assumed commuting times of 45 minutes. It demonstrates the "inefficient provision of public transport" and the "benefits of the good expressway system." Since many transport times and therefore costs are in fact much higher, the distribution of accessibility of employment was much worse, because the poor cannot afford either the financial costs of transport or the economic costs of time. Importantly, if the average speed of public transport increased by 20 percent, the size of the labor market for the poor would increase by 17 percent, suggesting the significant costs of inefficiencies in infrastructure. They concluded that this increase in the labor market would imply an increase in productivity and output of about 3 percent, or about 1 percent of the GDP of Argentina.[61]

Deciding to come to grips with these problems is above all a political project. It will require leadership and building coalitions among diverse interests and groups within the wider metropolitan and national community. Building coalitions and consensus take time and in Argentina, historically they have been too often disrupted by "exceptional moments."[62] For Buenos Aires, the challenge will be to make "metropolitan" more than simply a socio-economic reality or a statistical artifact. Rather its twofold challenge will be to create metropolitan institutions and policies to address these problems, and to foster the emergence of a metropolitan politics to assure that public institutions are democratically accountable to the citizens of the metropolitan area.

10 From crisis management to sustainable development

Extending the time horizon

As noted earlier, Argentina faces a severe problem of short-term vision. The medium and long term not only become blurred by the intensity of debate about the short-term, but are often neglected altogether as what appears urgent seems to replace what is really important. This problem of vision or perspective is not unique to Argentina, but it appears in many areas of public policy and discourse in the country, from economic policy, to a late recognition of the importance of environmental issues and conservation of the country's natural resources, to a historical lack of attention to research and development, with the consequence that many talented Argentines leave the country because they see no possibility of pursuing careers in science, technology, or similar professions that involve investment in longer-term discoveries and future benefits. The 2007 Brazilian discovery of oil deposits off their coast, after more than 15 years of exploration, reminds Argentines of the enormous stakes involved in investing in the long-term. As noted in Chapter 6, incoming president Nestor Kirchner noted in early 2003 that Argentina was one of the few countries in the world that did not control its own petroleum deposits.

This chapter addresses the specific issue of how Argentina has grappled with the challenge of extending its short-term vision. This is both a problem of government–of specific governments and the responsibility of specific holders of important jobs–and also of various segments of the society as a whole in actively raising their heads towards the horizon. It also necessarily involves weighing conflicting objectives and their opportunity costs. Three cases are presented in this chapter to illustrate the problem: managing inflation, investing in science and technology, and satisfying the growing demand for energy. The chapter then turns to various policy and strategic areas on which there have been public debates and around which some consensus seems to exist.

The issue of vision should be understood as a key aspect of state performance and institutional capacity. Even if the Argentine government has been very effective in leading the recovery from the crisis of 2001–2002, it is nonetheless fair to criticize its weakness in coming to grips with the medium- and longer-term development perspective.

The primacy of short-term factors

Managing inflation

The problem of inflation is part of the problem of accelerating economic growth, expanding domestic capacity, and managing monetary policy. In any process of rapid recovery from a downturn, recession, or depression, at some point there is excessive demand for the goods and services that the economy can provide. When demand exceeds supply, prices rise. The challenge is to manage the growth of demand in a way which is parallel to the growth of capacity to provide these goods and services. In a country such as Argentina, with considerable installed capacity to produce a wide variety of goods and services, there are relatively few problems in responding to the initial increase in demand. But as income increases, the demands and preferences of households and firms grow so that they want more and better goods and services. In the absence of focused investment in sectors where there are bottlenecks, there are likely to be price increases and hence inflationary pressures begin to build up.

This problem is significantly complicated by an open monetary policy, which allows the exchange rate to fluctuate in relation to changes in the global economy. As noted earlier in this book, Argentina faces the twin problems of not allowing the peso to appreciate too much in order to keep Argentine exports at competitive prices in the world market, while also managing the exchange rate to avoid flooding the domestic market with cheap goods from the outside.

The threat and impact of inflation has been growing in Argentina since early 2005, when inflation was estimated at below 10 percent. This was raised by many economic institutions, from the IMF to local and international banks, to economic commentators in the press and television. The government's initial response was to aggressively "jaw down" price rises by retailers by focusing public attention on them, followed by calls and visits from government officials. President Kirchner himself called in business leaders from different sectors and urged them to absorb price rises and not to pass on higher costs to customers in the hope that these actions would dampen inflation, at least for the short and medium term. In addition, the government decided on specific measures to fight inflation of prices of specific goods such as meat. In 2006, the government reduced and then prohibited the export of meat in an effort to stabilize domestic prices on a product consumed in great quantities in Argentina. These price control policies were criticized by many as creating distortions in the market and eventually producing inefficiencies and bad decisions in the economy.

Guillermo Moreno, as Secretary of Commerce, was given the task to closely monitor prices and to negotiate price rises for goods across the economy. While nominally reporting to the Minister of Economy, in fact Moreno reported directly to President Nestor Kirchner on a daily basis and carried out Kirchner's strategy of focusing on specific industries, such as supermarket chains and other mass consumer businesses. Over several years Moreno came to be known for his heavy-handed techniques and inability to demonstrate how individual decisions fit within a larger government economic model.

In 2006, Moreno was involved in changing the methodology by which the government's statistical office, INDEC, calculated inflation. Some INDEC officials resigned, saying they were being bullied by Moreno; others were fired for non-compliance with the new operating procedures. This led to serious fights between Moreno and several Economy Ministers including: Felisa Miceli, before she resigned in July 2007 over the discovery of a bag of money in the private bathroom of her office, Miguel Peirano, who resigned in November 2007 because President Kirchner would not support his plan to bring INDEC and Moreno more under his control, and Martin Lousteau, who resigned in April 2008 in part over disagreements with the president and former president Kirchner.

As noted in Chapter 6, this process led to the widely shared criticism of the government's handling of INDEC, to allegations that the government was trying to distort the official inflation statistics, and therefore all policies and programs to which price and GDP growth data were critical, including some government bonds whose dividends were tied to GDP growth rates. These criticisms severely undermined public confidence in the Government and its credibility on other matters as well. The press asked if the numbers were "cooked" on inflation and what else is being hidden by the government. The complete refusal of presidential candidate Cristina Fernandez de Kirchner to discuss inflation during the presidential campaign further fueled the criticism.

By the end of 2007, there was a widening gap between the government's official inflation number, 10.3 percent, and independent studies, which suggested the number was closer to 20 percent. Certainly individual consumer experience confirmed that the official INDEC numbers were too low. Over the first half of 2008 the INDEC problem and growing inflation contributed to growing criticism of the government of President Fernandez de Kirchner. In April 2008, there was a public discussion in the press and television about whether the economy should be "cooled down" to further reduce inflation. Former president Kirchner, in his capacity as president of the Peronist party, attacked this suggestion and, for example, proposals to reduce public expenditures, saying that any slowing down of GDP growth would increase unemployment and reduce the rate of poverty reduction. Kirchner repeatedly took this position and this was one of the ostensible reasons for the resignation of Economy Minister Lousteau in late April 2008.

While the story of managing inflation from 2006 through 2008 had many dramatic twists and turns, and indeed has continued through 2011 as well, it has provoked strong feelings by many professional economists. It can best be understood as a reflection of government efforts to assure achievement of short-term growth targets and the reduction of poverty and unemployment. These goals drove government policy and were repeatedly articulated by both Nestor Kirchner and Cristina Fernandez de Kirchner from 2006 to 2008. Where this approach failed was in the decision not to recognize that some slowdown in the short-run might mean more sustainable growth in the medium- and long-term. Instead, the government pursued what appear to be counterproductive efforts to control inflation. In fact, the economy did slow down during the 130-day conflict with *el campo*, with the result that even though some food prices increased during this period, the overall rate of inflation dropped according to most observers. Here the importance of INDEC is critical, because without a reliable statistical agency, any inflation figure is left open to question. If the government had been able to focus on the medium- term objective of creating conditions for sustainable growth, it would have been less worried about the short-term impact of inflation.

After the government recovered from the defeat of the *retenciones* bill in the Senate in July 2008, and Chief of Cabinet Alberto Fernandez resigned, new proposals emerged for the reconstitution of INDEC and the protection of its independence from the Ministry of Economy. These were being considered by the president and the then new chief of cabinet, Sergio Massa. Over the next few years these debates continued, resulting finally in a stalemate whereby the government has not acknowledged that the numbers were politically managed, but external critics challenge both the methodology and results of determining price increases. At the time of writing, this problem has not yet been resolved.

Investing in science and technology

One of the most disappointing legacies of various Argentine governments has been the continuing neglect of science and technology as a domain for public policy and investment. Although Argentina had invested in science and technological development during the 1950s as part of its import substitution strategy, starting in the 1960s there was a gradual and then sharp decline in public resources made available for this purpose. This came to a head during the 1990s during the rapid privatization of public services by the government of President Carlos Menem. Privatization of key sectors such as aviation, rail transport, water supply and sanitation, and communications all contributed to a reduction in any public money for research as the foreign, private sector managers of infrastructure focused on short-term profits and ignored investment in technological capacity. In this period, many well-trained scientists and technical people left Argentina.

A particularly telling example of this lack of public resources devoted to technology is the case of genetically modified (GM) crops and the use of pesticides to increase agricultural yields. In contrast to many countries, Argentina completely turned over responsibility for agricultural technology development to multi-national private firms such as Monsanto and Cargill.[1] Over 80 percent of its soya crop was of GM varieties. One of the unanticipated results of this decision was the strength of the reaction against the proposed export taxes in 2008 by a coalition of farm organizations, behind which were these powerful multi-national seed and agricultural technology firms. Over two decades, these companies had developed very sizable investments in Argentina's cultivation of soya and other grains for mass export into the world market. The process of extension and densification of soya cultivation and its displacement of food crops was actively supported by these multi-national companies who entered a society in which science and technology had been left to the private sector.

Another example has been in aviation where the privatization of *Aerolíneas Argentinas*, one of the world's 20 premier airlines in the 1980s, was followed by a complete neglect of the technological requirements in the rapidly changing field of air transport. Even though Argentina privatized its airports and generated substantial private investment in the rehabilitation of old facilities, this did not include the technical character of aviation, so that by mid-2008, when the government decided to re-nationalize the privatized company, more than half of its fleet of some 40 aircraft were unable to fly for various technical reasons. In addition, the country discovered in 2006 and 2007 that its radar was wholly inadequate to deal with an increasing number of incoming flights attracted by growing international tourism to Argentina. Air safety then became an issue, which scared away some tourists. These various issues all came to a head in January 2008 when thousands of foreign tourists were stranded in Ezeiza Airport in Buenos Aires after the cancellation of the flights of *Aerolíneas Argentinas* and other airlines. The same scene occurred in July 2008 during Argentina's winter vacation when thousands of people tried to travel to vacation sites around the country. Deferred maintenance in the short term led to medium-term disaster.

In 2006, the then Minister of Education, Daniel Filmus, announced that the government would be increasing funds allocated to education, up to 6 percent of GDP. This represented a major investment in human capital in the country and included more funds for science and technology. President Cristina Fernandez de Kirchner further strengthened this shift in her creation of a new Ministry of Science and Technology in December 2007 and the appointment of a respected scientist from the University of Cordoba to the position of Minister. It remains to be seen how successful this new ministry will be in shifting the government's attention towards the scientific frontier in the medium and long term.

Investing in energy

A third area in which a short-term vision has harmed medium- and longer-term development has been in the energy sector. One of the sectors most affected by the rapid economic recovery and growth averaging 9 percent from 2004 to 2008, was energy. Because the Government sought to maximize short-term growth, lower inflation, and low prices for consumers, it froze the tariffs in energy and infrastructure services. This meant that the privatized firms had reduced profits, given their increasing costs, and they failed to invest in developing new sources of supply. Energy production, therefore, stagnated and did not expand along with the growing demand for energy. Not surprisingly, there were shortages starting in 2005 and continuing through 2008. There were blackouts in the hot summer months as air conditioners strained existing capacity and shortages of natural gas in the winter when heating was needed. Public schools in Buenos Aires lacked heat for several months in the coldest times of the year. This dynamic continued in 2009 and 2010, with crises in both cold and warm weather seasons.

There are two features of this energy crisis that are noteworthy. First, Argentina had benefitted for many years from highly subsidized prices of natural gas imported from Bolivia. The election of President Evo Morales led to a re-evaluation of export prices for natural gas to Argentina and the decision to increase prices by a large margin, but still only reaching 55 percent of the world price. The privatized distributors of natural gas, therefore, had to pay a higher price for imported gas and were unable themselves to invest in exploration of possible domestic sources. This international dimension of provision of natural gas also affected Argentina's relationship with Chile to which the Argentine government had promised to deliver large quantities of natural gas to gas-poor Chile. When Argentina faced its own shortages, it simply announced it could not meet its obligations to Chile, leaving its neighbor with a major heating crisis.

The second dimension was that the government refused to publicly recognize the energy crisis until late in 2007, when then candidate Cristina Fernandez de Kirchner finally spoke about it during the presidential campaign. This denial was another example of behavior in which, for some short-term reason, a medium- and longer-term issue was not acknowledged. This was dangerous because it could potentially undermine the government's achievement of its own development objectives and particularly the GDP growth rate. This issue came to a head in the Senate in August 2009 when the Government sought higher tariffs for gas and other utilities and were pushed back by the opposition. The tariff issue remains to be resolved in a manner which will allow sufficient funds for reinvestment in the sector.

Components of a medium- and long-term development strategy

Each of the above examples illustrates, in different ways, how governmental decisions have not only prioritized perceptions of short-term urgencies, but in so doing have helped to undermine the likelihood of longer-term success. This bias in policy may be consistent with what Javier Santiso has referred to as "the political economy of the possible," which will be discussed in depth in the concluding chapter of this book.[2] But it also demonstrates some of the difficulties of sustaining development policies, which must balance the short-, medium-, and long-term.

This section examines the components of a medium- and long-term development strategy. Specifically, it focuses on recommendations coming from three sources of advice: academic and public debates on this question in Argentina, government discussion, and recommendations from international organizations. The comparison of these three perspectives reveals some of the different weights assigned to various economic and social objectives by these different kinds of actors and helps to identify the freedom of maneuver, which a government interested in improving income distribution actually has. The three arenas of debate on these questions include the following:

- Academic and public debates: the 2004 symposium of the *Centro de Estudios Politicos, Economicos, y Sociales*, (CEPES) led by Chacho Alvarez, the continuing debates of *Plan Fenix*, and the policy documents prepared for the electoral campaigns of 2007.
- Governmental discussion of medium and long-term strategy: available materials from the Ministry of Economy, Ministry of Labor, and other institutions.
- Development strategy recommendations of international organizations: including the Country Assistance Strategy of the World Bank, the program of the Inter-American Development Bank, the UNDP, and the United Nations Millennium Development Goals for Argentina.

These diverse discussions cover a wide range of strategic issues and problems, which any developing country faces as well as some which reflect the particular economic and political history of Argentina over the last two decades. While some participants refer to Argentine development trends as cyclical, others see them more as swings of a pendulum, reflecting the array of political forces at any given time, the current fashionable "advice" from the international institutions, the current media analyses of Argentine realities, and the most pressing real problems. Decisions taken in this context are less frequently abrupt changes in course than support for the current direction of the swing of the pendulum.

Nevertheless, a set of core issues emerged among the diverse participants of the 2004 CEPES seminar which include:

- sustaining the growth of exports;
- monetary policy to stabilize prices;
- fiscal solvency;
- promotion of science and technology;
- incentives for employment creation;
- integrated system for social protection and reduction of poverty;
- equal distribution of income between capital and labor;
- strengthening regulatory authorities and control over public services;
- active policies to reinforce the role of the state.[3]

Six of these areas stand out from these discussions during this period as well as the statements of the international organizations as foci for particular attention in formulating medium and long-term strategies: the role of the state, the need for sustaining macro-economic balances including fiscal and current accounts, increasing productivity within sectors and the economy as a whole, reducing poverty and inequality, with particular attention to the most vulnerable groups, whether the elderly on fixed incomes or impoverished groups in the critical region of nine northern and northwestern provinces, prioritizing the composition of public investment, and investing in human capital and intellectual capital to support growth and competitiveness for Argentina in its regional and global contexts. A seventh priority area that affects many of these is the need for urban policy and strategies, as suggested in the previous chapter, a subject which has been largely ignored in Argentina despite the fact that the country is the most urbanized in Latin America and more than half of GDP comes from urban-based activities.

The role of the state

As noted in Chapter 6, one of the priorities of incoming President Nestor Kirchner in May 2003 was the strengthening of the state. Kirchner had been critical of the "absent state" in the 1990s, with the lack of attention to many areas of economic development and society at large. In his inauguration speech on May 25, 2003, he conveyed his strong desire to bring the state into many arenas of national life which had been either turned over explicitly to the private sector during the 1990s, such as the mass privatization program affecting public infrastructure services, or which had simply been neglected. He commented on the lack of public regulatory authority over the private sector and the need to clarify the strength of the state. He referred to this orientation as building "national capitalism."[4]

Since May 2003, there has been considerable and growing agreement in Argentina that having a strong state is important for economic and social development. This is different from the criticism of the centralized style of administration of President Kirchner. Words such as "hegemonic" were used by the political opposition to describe the overwhelming political support that the Kirchner administration had from 2003 to 2007. But there were no objections to the functions which the government sought to perform, from re-negotiating the external debt, to providing cash assistance to the poor through the *Jefes* program, or even the re-nationalization of the water company, *Aguas Argentinas*.

Even the private sector acknowledged the importance of having effective state institutions to perform a wide variety of functions. This was well articulated by Luis A. Pagani, the chief executive of Arcor, a large food and candy producing company, in a 2004 seminar on development strategy. Pagani, representing the *Asociación Empresaria Argentina*, said:

> A modern society needs an effective State committed to the integrated development of society as well as solid market institutions to establish the framework for business activity.... The efficacy of the State and the capacity of the government to successfully lead the process of economic and social development of a country has a decisive impact on the environment in which businesses can develop.[5]

This consensus on the importance of the role of the state represents a significant difference from the neo-liberal philosophies and policies of the 1990s. It establishes the basic framework within which other components of strategy can be identified and specified. Not only is it not a subject of intense political debate, but it has also allowed more public attention, albeit critical attention, to the performance of these functions. What might have been considered a subject only for social science literature had in fact become an issue for public political debate.

This debate does not just apply to the presidency and the executive ministries but to the full range of institutions, including the judicial system, the Supreme Court, and the Congress. This issue of performance, for example, was raised by former president Kirchner in his repeated observation that the courts were not proceeding sufficiently rapidly with cases of human rights violations. The latter advanced significantly in 2008 with convictions in cases involving major figures responsible for various concentration camps and cases of torture. The issue of congressional performance was also raised during the battle over the *retenciones* as much more public attention was focused on individual legislators through the live television broadcast and on both chambers of the Congress.

One area which remains problematic is the effectiveness of regulatory authorities, particularly over previously public services such as water, energy, transportation, and aviation. Major failures in performance in blackouts, water shortages, traffic management, vehicle inspections, and infrastructure rehabilitation have focused public attention on the weakness of public institutions. While this is a common problem in most countries, it was particularly severe in Argentina, which had implemented the most extensive privatization program of any developing country during the Menem government of the 1990s. The politics of this regulatory capitalism is complicated and reflects the diverse and changing interests of both labor and capital.[6]

A second problematic area has been the performance of provincial governments, which vary tremendously in terms of capacity and dependence on the national government. As noted earlier in the discussion of the historically poor revenue performance of Argentina, provincial governments depend heavily on the Co-participation Fund to provide the majority of their annual revenue, without themselves making an effort to collect taxes. This is reflected in the weakness of regional public sectors as well as regional economies. In 2008 the majority of most provincial budgets consisted of salaries for provincial civil servants, including school teachers.

The need for sustaining macro-economic balances

All of the various organizations cited above agree on the need for Argentina to sustain its macro-economic balances. As suggested by the Argentine historian, Tulio Halperin Donghi, improved tax collection could have dramatic results in improving the possibilities of the state to undertake programs of distribution, investment, and even regulation. This has proven to be the case since 2003 as tax collection increased significantly. More effective performance depends on capacity, not just intention. Significantly improved revenue collection, beyond the increments received from export taxes, has allowed the government to be more active, "present," and important in promoting economic and social development.

The resulting fiscal deficit which has been kept within reasonable bounds has been a source of pride for the Government, contrasting sharply with the performance of the 1990s.

But the improvement of collection of existing taxes is not a substitute for reforming the tax structure itself, making it more progressive, and linking it more closely to the productive structure of the country. This problem has appeared throughout Latin America over the past decade as many governments have effectively improved revenue collection, but have not significantly reformed the structure and incidence of taxation. In some cases, the tax structure has become more regressive as the rich have avoided increased taxes on income and wealth. As suggested in Chapter 8, one of the underlying reasons for increasing the rates of export taxes for agricultural products was that while the rural sector produces many products in large quantities, it is significantly under-represented in total tax revenue.

The most controversial aspect of the macro-economic balances has been the size of the surplus itself and the role of the reserves of the Central Bank of Argentina. Here, the government of Nestor Kirchner clearly decided to build up a considerable fiscal surplus and the country's foreign exchange reserves. This was a confidence-building measure and signal in the domestic economy, but also a hedge against uncertainty. From 2003 to 2007, the Central Bank was able to significantly build up its foreign exchange reserves, a felicitous result of increased export earnings, selectively paying only its external debt to the IMF and the World Bank and not to bond holders, and monetary stability. It is interesting to reflect with hindsight on the IMF's advice in 2001–2002 that in good times Argentina needed to build up a fund "for rainy days," but when the government did so in 2003 and thereafter, the IMF criticized the size of the surplus, saying that funds should be used to pay off outstanding external debt. The error in this advice was particularly evident in 2007–2008 and thereafter when world financial markets trembled during the sub-prime mortgage crisis in the United States. Argentina's reserves allowed it to confidently withstand shifting pressures on interest rates, financial flows, and commodity prices in 2008–2009, resulting in an earlier return to growth in 2010 than the United States or many European countries.

One policy decision in this area was to keep the US dollar at a high value, above three pesos, in order to favor Argentine exports, particularly of agricultural commodities. This decision was also criticized by the IMF in 2002 and 2003 when it was argued that the Argentine currency should float and thereby find its true market value. This advice was rejected in order to generate a higher export volume and to take advantage of the domestic incentives, which would result from the relative price differences between the peso and foreign currencies. Full and effective control over monetary policy represented a sharp break from the policies during the Convertibility period of the 1990s when the hard peg of the peso to the US dollar eliminated the possibility of the Argentine governments using monetary policy as an instrument of adjusting to changing global economic and financial conditions.

Increasing productivity within sectors and the economy as a whole

As noted earlier, one of the key challenges facing Argentina is the problem of managing inflation. Part of this inflation arises from the difficulty of getting more production out of existing capacity. As a result, there are supply shortages and price rises. The constraints on existing capacity come from many sides: lack of new investment in technology, deteriorating infrastructure, energy shortages, and lack of incentives for firms to produce more if prices are controlled, among others. Resolving some of these problems could significantly improve the use of installed capacity. Despite these constraints, data from the Ministry of Labor show that employment growth from 2002 onward has occurred mostly in small and medium-sized enterprises, rather than the largest companies. The government has supported credit for small enterprises but in general it has not had an active industrial policy, for example, it only thought about supporting firms in the high technology sector in 2007. It has also not focused much public sector attention on pharmaceuticals or sectors with linkages to Argentina's well-developed health sector.

This lack of industrial policy contrasts sharply with Brazil and also suggests the historical difficulty of Argentine governments to develop shared perspectives with the industrial elite companies in the country. While some governments, such as during the presidency of Arturo Frondizi, had sought such agreements going back to the 1960s, the social and political distance between state and industrial leaders has frustrated efforts to develop sustained industrial policy initiatives.

This lack of effective industrial policy is also noteworthy in the agricultural sector, where the country's commodity exports have a very low level of value added. Aside from some production of vegetable and cooking oils, the agricultural sector is not known for producing products that would bring the country a higher level of profit. As a result the country has not benefitted as much as it could from the dramatically increased demand for agricultural commodities. President Cristina Fernandez de Kirchner highlighted this problem in speeches and news conferences during 2008, noting that the exports from the country's agricultural areas had the same profile as in 1910,[7] the centennial of the country's independence from Spain. It remains to be seen, however, what the government will actually do to invest in or promote such improvements in value-added.

Reducing poverty and inequality

Another area with a clear priority for the government and its progressive supporters is a stronger effort to reduce poverty and inequality. As noted in Chapters 7, 8, and 9, there are diverse geographies of inequality which require different responses, from the needs of both the elderly and the young, to the lower incomes and employment in the nine lagging provinces of the north, to the millions of people living in slums on the peripheries of Buenos Aires, and, to a lesser extent, Cordoba and Rosario. Both former president Nestor Kirchner and President Cristina Fernandez de Kirchner have called "trickle-down" approaches "theories of misery," dismissing the idea that market-driven policies by themselves will address the needs of the poorest and most vulnerable in society.

In this regard, the government has been quite successful since 2003 in reducing poverty from over 55 percent to around 20 percent by the end of 2007, before it later rose with inflation and the slowdown due to the conflict with the *campo* in the first half of 2008 and before the onset of the impact of the global economic crisis. By mid-2009 the poverty level reached closer to 30 percent. Unemployment had been in the 30 percent range and dropped, in mid-2008, to around 7 or 8 percent, a remarkable achievement, before rising again in 2009. However, the Government acknowledged that having 30 percent of the population still living in poverty in a country that has the potential to produce food for 450 million people, was not acceptable. The President herself repeated this on many occasions.

Going further in addressing poverty, however, will require more effective secondary and higher education and training of youth as well as improving the various constraints to productivity mentioned above. The experience of the *Jefes* program was promising in suggesting that the government was able to mount large-scale social programs through the provinces and municipalities of the country, as evidenced later in 2010 with the launching of a program of payments to all families with dependent children, including those in the informal sector.

The issue of further reducing inequality remains a longer-term objective. While the level of inequality in 2008 had much improved from 2002, it still reflected a structural shift in the financial returns to labor versus capital in the globalized economy of the 21st century. Finance, technology, and information-related industries all have advantages in generating profits and in establishing new products and services. This means that Argentina's youth will need increasing levels of technical skill to take advantage of these new markets. This is clearly an investment for the future but will not generate immediate benefits in the short-term for the Argentine economy.

Prioritizing the composition of public investment

Another area requiring attention for medium- and longer-term strategy is setting priorities for public investment. In the period 2003–2007, the Kirchner government announced many programs for school construction, housing, roads, and other infrastructure. Almost all of these projects have fallen under the responsibility of the Federal Minister of Planning, Julio de Vido. Most programs involve national financing but provincial responsibility for implementation. While there has been an impressive record of accomplishment, there appears to have been little effort to connect these efforts within regional development plans. An exercise by the Ministry of Economy to study the needs of different provinces generated data, but little progress was made towards articulating an overall vision of development strategy.

This situation is puzzling because, in many respects, the governments of Nestor Kirchner and later, Cristina Fernandez de Kirchner, have successfully undertaken many initiatives, but these have not been articulated as policies and plans which were communicated to the public in ways which has led to their recognition as the result of government effort. Part of this may be inattention to packaging public policies and programs for public consumption, but it is also a reflection of the lack of explicit strategic linkages between initiatives. It may thus be a case of the whole being less than the sum of its parts.

One critical component of determining the composition of public investment is focusing on infrastructure. Here there was a public outcry against a proposed fast train, "*la tren bala*," from Buenos Aires to Rosario, using older French technology, which would have cost close to US$4 billion, a sum equivalent to building some 80 hospitals and many schools around the country. While public objections were voiced about the cost of the project, the more serious issue was how it fit into a broader sense of national priorities over the medium and longer term.

Investing in human capital and intellectual capital

A sixth area requiring attention, as mentioned above, with regard to training for youth, is how the country can generally invest more in its people and in knowledge. Here, the critique voiced by the Swedish newspaper, *Dagens Nyheter* in 2002 is most relevant.[8] The newspaper argued that Argentina had a nineteenth century definition of wealth tied to commodity production and export, rather than a twenty-first century understanding that knowledge, information, and technology were the keys to wealth and income, as had been demonstrated by countries in East Asia or Finland. This seems clearly to be an issue for the medium and long term and one in which Argentina, with a generally high level of literacy and education and with many high-quality educational institutions, should be able to flourish. Kirchner's decision to increase the education budget to 6 percent of GDP goes in this direction, but it remains to be seen how these investments will be put in place and what human return they will achieve.

All of these issues fall within the problem of state performance and need to be considered from three analytical perspectives: state institutional capacity, state–society relations, and the impact of the legacy of neo-liberal ideology on the state itself even after a new regime is in power.

Clearly, many of the issues addressed in this chapter depend largely on how the Argentine government itself functions: how its leaders set strategic goals and priorities and how individual ministries and agencies develop and execute policies to achieve those goals. As shown by the case of intra-urban inequality in Buenos Aires, with local decisions for local public investment, intra-urban inequality is mostly a "local product." These outcomes are also not a result of the Washington Consensus or global forces. The many examples cited in this chapter are the results of internal, national decisions made by national leaders with the authority to make them. This underlines the importance of creating conditions and sufficient political space to allow better decisions.

The accountability of democratically elected leaders for their own decisions, however, does not depend entirely on the leaders themselves, but rather also on how well state–society relations function to hold leaders accountable and the degree of responsibility of political forces outside government. The case of Argentina is especially noteworthy in this regard because political life is intense in the extreme, with numerous television and newspaper media focusing on every daily detail of public policy, with second-guessing and aggressive criticism of any government initiative. This intense scrutiny is increased by the presence of much of national political life in one city, Buenos Aires, where most players live and work. Argentine politics is in every way as intense as Argentine *futbol*. This exacerbates the problem of the short-term, with national government leaders feeling the need to respond to the daily news. The urgent is the important in Buenos Aires, an unfortunate political perception that is held by almost all societal political forces.

This dynamic is in some sense independent of the external global environment with its critical policy recommendations coming from Washington or Wall Street. Yet, the relentless volatility of global economic forces and pressures invades the national context and permeates debates even at the local level. Neighborhood grocers are aware of changing global prices and the availability of global products and shifting numbers of restaurant patrons often reflect perceptions about whether global that of a implies less personal spending in Argentina. An extreme case is the woman in Buenos Aires who deferred going to the hairdresser in 2008 because of the possible coming of "*la crisis.*" When getting a haircut is conditioned by the daily perceptions of the global economy, the difficulty of extending the time horizons of government and society becomes very evident.

11 Argentina's experience and the search for alternatives

The book shows that history has not ended in Argentina. Writing the first draft of this book in Argentina during 2008 and 2009, including during the ongoing conflict with the *campo*, proved to be a very active and revealing time in which the questions raised in the Prologue were repeatedly asked by many people from diverse perspectives and interests. The conflicts between the reform goals of the government and its vocal and well-financed opposition will continue in the second mandate of President Fernández de Kirchner starts at the end of 2011.

The debate about the *retenciones* opened up a flood of analyses, commentaries and reflections on what had occurred since 2001. The discussion led to a fuller public assessment of what had been accomplished, what was lacking, and how political and institutional processes had affected policy and legislative outcomes. The debate also dramatically illustrated the enormous stakes in the redistribution of income, the power of vested interests and the media, and the need for the government to have well-developed and sophisticated strategies to overcome these constraints in the pursuit of its distributive and redistributive objectives. The obstacles to reform are formidable and deeply rooted.

The new pressures from the global economic crisis grew during the second half of 2008 and into 2009, as commodity prices fell, the total demand for commodities also dropped precipitously, with resulting effects on public revenue. As credit dried up, so did new investment, with its attendant effects on employment. If this process was not so rapid in Argentina as in Brazil or Mexico, it is probably a result of the policies that were put in place during the five years of recovery.

This book demonstrates that there had been "recovery and growth during a time of default." There was little doubt that economic and social indicators had improved enormously from 2002 to 2008 and that, contrary to the predictions of Wall Street, the world financial press, and many economists, Argentina did not fall off the southern tip of Latin America after it defaulted on its external debt in 2002. Contrary to the claims of advocates of the Washington Consensus, its economy grew, poverty and unemployment were significantly reduced, and its governments reached northwards to Brazil, Bolivia, Ecuador, and to Venezuela for political support and specific kinds of economic cooperation, demonstrating growing political confidence and economic strength. Its July 2008 disagreement with Brazil in the trade negotiations leading to the Doha Round was a strong indicator of Argentina's ability to articulate a different position and yet, retain strong and increasing political and economic ties with its larger and more powerful neighbor to the north.

This concluding chapter identifies lessons from the Argentine experience, which have implications for other developing countries. These lessons should also be considered when the global economic press, external advisors, external institutions, and academics formulate advice for developing countries. Before identifying some of these specific lessons, this chapter will first address one of the frequently heard observations made outside the country that Argentina was "lucky" because it was able to recover on the wave of high commodity prices.

The "Argentina was lucky" hypothesis

The "Argentina was lucky" hypothesis, while often used by external analysts to explain the country's recovery from the crisis of 2001–2002, coincides with one of the repeated claims of *el campo* during the conflict over export taxes that *el campo* played a central role in the economic recovery. Rural lobbyists argued that agriculture played a leading role in the recovery and is now central to the performance of the country's economy. They insisted that farmers and exporting companies must be allowed to keep the large profits earned from grain exports in order to increase investment in the rural sector and thus help the productivity of the economy as a whole.

As shown earlier, this claim was exaggerated. Semester economic data during the recovery showed that the economic recovery of Argentina was not led by agricultural exports, but rather was what the World Bank called in a 2006 report a "demand-led recovery." The installed capacity of the Argentine economy is considerable, supported by an educated and experienced labor force, which was further upgraded by government labor policies from 2003 to 2008. When the Convertibility period ended in 2002 and the peso was devalued, the prices of imports increased threefold and stimulated the production of domestic goods and services for consumers. This production in turn generated multiplying effects, which supported small and medium-sized firms and helped to create many new jobs. This process did not primarily take place in rural areas. It was mostly an urban phenomenon reflecting the fact that Argentina is one of the most urbanized countries in the world, the most urban in Latin America. Most Argentines live in cities and towns and buy goods and services produced in urban areas.

The contribution of *el campo* to the recovery came later in 2004 and thereafter, as the prices of commodities increased and the planting of larger and larger areas to grow soya and other crops had huge payoffs. These exports certainly helped build up the country's reserves and fiscal strength, but they cannot be credited with playing the key role in stimulating the recovery. This conclusion is supported by research by various Argentine economists such as Mario Damill, Roberto Frenkel, and Roxana Maurizio.[1]

This correction to the claims of *el campo* is important in many respects. First, the claim supports the perception of some Argentines and many foreigners that Argentina was "lucky" to escape from the crisis of 2001–2002 and that the recovery depended very much on external factors such as global prices for its products. This view gives too much weight to external factors in understanding how the economy recovered. It also under-values the inherent strengths of the economy including its educated labor force, decades of production experience in various sectors, the country's infrastructure, and what might be termed Argentina's anomalous position of being highly sophisticated and modern in some respects, while weak in others such as institutional development as shown in this book. This overly general and distant view comes from the same logic which operated when Argentina's country risk rating was considered in 2000 to be worse than Nigeria, a country lacking an educated populace, infrastructure, and effective institutions. Nonsensical logic, which generates such a conclusion, demonstrates that it is not being corroborated with realities on the ground.

Explaining the recovery through external factors such as global grain prices also under-values the role of effective economic management by successive governments, first under former president Duhalde and later, for an extended period by former president Kirchner, as shown in Chapters 3 through 6, and later continued by President Cristina Fernandez de Kirchner. The efforts of several ministers of economy to re-establish balance among economic factors over a seven-year period were largely successful.

It is interesting to note that in 2008 many Argentines also accepted this explanation of the recovery as an agriculturally-driven outcome. They were quick to forget how the government had managed to stabilize the economy in 2002, restart growth in 2003, reduce the weight of its debt by early 2005, cut loose from the intrusive and unproductive relationship with the IMF in 2006, and most importantly, reduce unemployment through this period beyond anyone's expectations. Even with the conflict over export taxes in 2008, there was no material equivalency between the *cacerolazos* of 2001–2002 with their reappearance in March 2008 and in the following months. By all economic and social indicators, Argentines were incomparably better off in 2008 than in 2002. Alarmist claims about the size of the Argentine debt in 2008 ignored that its size had been reduced considerably as a proportion of GDP when compared to 2001–2002. It is interesting that in 2009–2011 many Argentines still did not acknowledge that the relatively slight impact of the global economic crisis on the country might be a result of the economic policies of the previous seven years.

An interesting aspect of the claim by *el campo* was that farm leaders, and the public media, also did not acknowledge that Argentines had used many of their resources during the dark days of 2002–2003: financial, technical, human, and even spiritual, to dig out of the worst economic collapse that any country had ever experienced. Former president Kirchner had referred to the condition of the country in this time as being in "purgatory." *El campo* contributed to the recovery, but it was less important than it claimed.

Exaggerating the role of rural production obscured the fact that Argentina's economy is mostly non-agricultural, that production, jobs, and incomes come mostly from urban-based activities. Large export earnings from agriculture help economic growth, but without its urban base of manufacturing, services, and finance, those earnings would have nothing to buy or consume. Neither *el campo* nor its urban middle-class supporters should have believed too much in the rural rhetoric of the conflict. Argentina has an economy whose strength lies in its balance between urban and rural production, its productive capacity in manufacturing as much as its natural resources as stressed by former Minister of Economy Aldo Ferrer,[2] its educated people, and the ability of individuals and firms to find solutions to the problems they face. As suggested in Chapter 10, its challenge lies in extending the country's vision to its medium- and long-term future, avoiding too much dependence on short-term gains from inflated commodity prices. *El campo* was historically important, and continues to be important, but it is only one sector within a larger, mostly urban-based Argentine economy. The "Argentina was lucky" hypothesis has no basis in fact.

Lessons from the Argentine experience of 2002–2008

The real stakes in understanding the Argentine experience from 2002 to 2008 lie in their relevance not only to policies for Argentina in the future but for other developing countries as well. The lessons from this experience can be divided into three categories: fundamental premises for strategy and policy, policy orientation for the macro-economy, and approaches to problem solving. None of these categories are solely economic, political, institutional, or technical in nature. Rather they demonstrate how multiple perspectives can be brought to bear on different levels of strategy, policy, and operational decisions. While there has been some overall coherence to government decisions through this period, it cannot be termed "ideological" per se. But it does reflect a set of basic values, which have been translated into fundamental premises from which policy orientation and problem-solving approaches have emerged. After presenting these lessons within the three categories, the chapter will conclude by examining how this compares to the perspectives of other observers, including Javier Santiso's argument that Latin America has entered a period of "the political economy of the possible".

Fundamental premises for strategy and policy

The first premise of the government's orientation after May 2003 was that national needs were more important than international obligations. This premise may seem obvious, yet the histories of Argentina and many other developing countries have shown that many countries have undertaken huge fiscal adjustments and accepted heavy social and political costs in order to satisfy the requirements of international lending institutions. The decisions of the Menem government in the 1990s reflected a very rapid and almost unquestioning acceptance of a wide range of recommendations covering trade and financial liberalization, to privatization of public services, to tightening of fiscal policy, and ultimately to the composition of public expenditures. While many of the external recommendations were supported by the analysis and logic of these institutions, they nevertheless produced anomalies, which a more prudent national assessment might have identified. It is interesting, for example, to speculate on why the Menem government privatized so many different public services within a two-year period, when even the British government under Margaret Thatcher took a decade to do so. Clearly, the financial returns to these decisions were significant as private purchase of public assets helped to fill other financial holes in the country's fiscal condition, but who was determining the speed of the adoption of this program? Why were there not some cautionary notes sounded about the overall impact of a set of individual decisions concerning specific public services? What was the involvement of legislative institutions in ratifying decisions from the executive branch? These questions have both political and economic answers, but they also depended in the 1990s on the capacities of public institutions and civil society to assure some degree of accountability over public decisions.

The case of the adoption of the Convertibility Plan suggests similar dilemmas. While this plan was a response to the hyper-inflation of the late 1980s and an effort to use a hard currency peg to link the peso with the US dollar, and thereby assure monetary stability, there was surprisingly little questioning of the implications of this decision and later, when the economy was falling into recession after the Tequila Crisis in Mexico in 1994, no serious discussion took place about leaving this plan.[3] When the country faced volatility in prices and interest rates coming from the global economy, it had to resort to fiscal policy as its only instrument of adjustment and could not use monetary policy because the hard peg eliminated this possibility. This meant that cutting fiscal deficits through reducing public expenditures was the only clear route to maintaining solvency, with the attendant consequence that this implied the contraction of the State itself as well as the contraction of the economy.

While the early 2002 decision to default on its external debt was forced by the magnitude and terms of the debt, suggesting that the government did not really have a choice at that critical point, this step marked a turning point in several respects. First, it implied that the country would fail to meet its international obligations and that second this would necessarily cut off at least the short-term possibility of receiving official assistance from the public international institutions such as the IMF, the World Bank, and the Inter-American Development Bank. This situation then forced the following questions: Would the government seek to meet *any* external conditions to re-establish its worthiness to receive support or would there be some conditions that it would refuse to meet? The government of former president Duhalde sought to meet external conditions throughout 2002, as evidenced by repeated efforts to obtain IMF support, as described in Chapter 4. Only in January 2003 was this support finally agreed upon, but only after Economy Minister Lavagna put his foot down and refused to consider any further policy adjustments until the IMF financial support was approved.

Lavagna's step, after a lengthy series of efforts to meet the IMF's demands throughout 2002, and unfulfilled promises of support by the IMF management, helped to change the balance between national and international factors. It also provided a small precedent for what was to come much more forcefully with the administration of President Nestor Kirchner after May 2003.

Kirchner's approach to the balance between national versus international obligations became startling clear in the August 2003 proposal on the refinancing of Argentina's debt. After his Secretary of Finance, Guillermo Nielsen, announced the proposed "haircut" of 75 percent in the refinancing of Argentine bonds, Kirchner repeated his argument that the country could not afford to pay its debt and ethically should not pay its debt as long as people were hungry in Argentina. He remarked on several occasions that, "dead people don't repay their debts." He refused to accept any argument, which meant that the country would suffer more in the short run in order to satisfy externally approved concepts of justice and legal obligation. The welfare of the Argentine population–with some 57 percent living below the poverty line in 2002–was ethically more compelling than any international standard of good behavior. For a democratically-elected president, indeed any political leader of a country, this should have been understood as the correct ethical decision.

While the default on Argentine debt had shocked the international financial community in 2002, Kirchner's decision in August 2003 to seek a very favorable re-negotiation of Argentine bonds further infuriated many in this community. How did Argentina have the nerve to seek such debt-reduction? If Argentina was allowed to succeed in such debt reduction, what were the implications for other countries and other outstanding financial obligations? Kirchner's answer to these questions was very clear: national needs were of higher priority than international obligations.

The reaction of developing countries to Argentina's position on its debt was cautious, with many governments not wanting to upset the international financial community and thereby undermining their own access to financial support. Yet, some governments began to express begrudging admiration for the Kirchner administration and hoped that the Argentina case might helped to provoke a change in the policies of the Bretton Woods institutions.

The first premise for strategy and policy by the Kirchner government then was to privilege the national over the international. A corollary of this premise was that the national priorities and preferences were more important than global priorities set outside the country. A further corollary was that internal considerations were more important than external ones. While slightly different in their formulation, these premises were direct challenges to the neo-liberal power of globalization, to the institutions supporting the Washington Consensus, and the widely shared perception that this power was unstoppable, irreversible, and inevitable. Argentina's management of its own situation, once it had defaulted on its debt, demonstrated that governments could stand up to these assumptions about global neo-liberal power. If the collapse of Argentina in 2001–2002 was perceived as the country having fallen down a well, its recovery and high rate of growth after 2002 further challenged all of the apocalyptic warnings which the international financial community had issued in 2002, some of which are presented in Chapter 4.

This premise of prioritizing the national over the international not only asserted the country's own sovereignty in the face of the international financial community, but the country's outstanding economic performance from 2002 to 2008 demonstrated that initial reliance on domestic resources would not doom the country to low growth and continuing poverty and misery. While later benefitting from export earnings after 2004 as well as project lending from the World Bank, the government was clear and explicit in its intention to be rid of intrusive and inappropriate IMF commentary and questions about macro-economic policy. This same stance applied in relation to borrowing from the World Bank and the Inter-American Development Bank. Lending was acceptable, but not lending with macro-economic conditionality and policy requirements. In order to further assert its independence, the government pre-paid its outstanding debt of US$9 billion to the IMF in December 2006, thereby freeing it from any periodic interventions from the IMF.

A second fundamental premise of strategy and policy, which is derived from the first, was the importance of regional cooperation within Latin America. While Kirchner was described by many journalists as being more interested in domestic issues than international affairs, he in fact demonstrated through intensive engagement with Lula in Brazil, Chavez in Venezuela, and Morales in Bolivia that he understood the importance of having reliable and supportive regional partners. Even though Argentina has had a complicated relationship with Brazil and other neighboring countries at different times, and its Foreign Ministry has been known to support competition with Brazil, Kirchner strongly supported regional collaboration. This proved to be quite important to Argentina as Brazil has helped Argentina in various international issues and Venezuela had bought about US$7.5 billion worth of Argentine bonds by mid-2008. The election of many progressive governments in Latin America since 2002 facilitated a sense of collaboration and unity among these governments to which Argentina has contributed in a significant way. This perspective has been well-articulated by Marco Aurelio Garcia, the chief foreign policy advisor to Lula.[4] As shown below, it has also been strongly sustained by President Cristina Fernandez de Kirchner.

The third fundamental premise of strategy and policy was the assertion of the role of the State. As noted in several chapters in this book, Nestor Kirchner did not accept the notion of an "absent state." He had argued before assuming the presidency that many of Argentina's problems had stemmed from the absence of a state, either taking care of the poorest, regulating privatized services, or protecting human rights. His administration proved to be a surprise to many Argentines who did not know much about Kirchner's prior public career as a mayor of Rio Gallegos or later as governor of the Province of Santa Cruz, except perhaps that he had had a reputation of being a sound fiscal manager. But from his campaign speeches to his inauguration speech on May 25, 2003, he argued that the state had to play an active role to assure that the market worked in the interest of the country as a whole.

This third premise, the need to strengthen the role of the state vis-à-vis the market, also represented a significant departure from much of the conventional wisdom implied in the Washington Consensus. Kirchner accepted from the outset in his administration that the government had the responsibility to administer prices, even though many Argentines and almost all external observers believed that prices could be best determined by the market. This latter view, however, made no sense when the government perceived the urgent need to protect the purchasing power of the population, and particularly the poorest people. Arguments that the market would produce efficient and correct outcomes for the country have been met with great skepticism by both Nestor Kirchner and Cristina Fernandez de Kirchner. If the responsibility of government was to assure the welfare of the Argentine people, it (and they) could not leave decisions such as the price of milk or beef to the individual profit motives of Argentine and multi-national companies.

A fourth fundamental premise was that the government's objective should be to reduce poverty and inequality in the country. Longer-term growth was a necessary but not sufficient condition to assure economic welfare. The Kirchners repeatedly referred to "trickle-down" theories of poverty reduction as "theories of misery." This argument does not always meet with the approval of the middle class who worry about their position in this dynamic, and particularly as President Cristina Fernandez de Kirchner mentioned the question of income redistribution in every speech in 2008. But there is little doubt that this fundamental premise of strategy has had a huge influence on other decisions. One interpretation of the conflict with *el campo* over export taxes is that the rigidity and uncompromising character of the government's response was a function of the importance they assigned to the issue. On redistribution of income there was little room for backing down.

These four fundamental premises, therefore, were the guiding influences for all other policy: domestic needs were more important than international obligations, regional cooperation was essential for domestic success, a strong and present state was important to assure that national responsibilities to assure the welfare of the population, and the reduction of poverty and inequality were essential objectives to assure a more just and democratic society.

Policy orientation for the macro-economy

A second category of lessons from the Argentine experience of recovery since 2002 concerns the policy orientations for the macro-economy. These orientations cover the following areas: economic growth, monetary and foreign exchange management, fiscal policy including revenue growth to support higher public expenditures, public investment, trade and foreign direct investment, and employment policy.

Economic growth

One of the most interesting lessons from the Argentine experience is that there are important sources of growth within the domestic economy. As noted earlier, the urban economies of Argentina are highly productive and generate more than half of GDP. The Convertibility Plan had weakened these economies by over-valuing the peso against the US dollar and undermining domestic manufacturing and services. Monetary policy had in effect contributed significantly to de-industrialization. By devaluing the peso and bringing it more in line with its true value, and then keeping it relatively stable, three Argentine governments under Eduardo Duhalde, Nestor Kirchner, and Cristina Fernandez de Kirchner had created conditions under which domestic production could flourish.

This urban economic growth contrasted sharply with the gradual contraction of the urban economy from 1997 onward, as demand declined, reducing employment and incomes, which further reduced demand, resulting in an overall contraction of the Argentine economy. This contraction was also significantly affected by the continuous cutting of public expenditures under the guise of fiscal adjustment recommended by the IMF. A bad situation became worse and unbearable after the *corralito* was imposed in December 2001, freezing bank deposits and restricting people's access to their own savings. The limit of 250 pesos a week led to the disappearance of informal sector jobs such as coffee sellers who left the streets because no one could afford to use their scarce currency on anything less than essential items for themselves and their families. The devaluation changed relative prices and led to the reawakening of economic multipliers, which started to work again, eventually even bringing the coffee sellers and others back onto the streets of Buenos Aires.

It is interesting to remember that critics of the IMF's emphasis on reducing the fiscal deficit, such as Nobel Laureate Joseph Stiglitz, had observed that the IMF's advice ran counter to the conventional wisdom and sound judgment of every industrialized country that the Keynesian remedy to recession was more spending, not less. Yet the IMF told Argentina and other countries to reduce spending. Stiglitz had asked on more than one occasion, why was the IMF giving such bad economic advice?[5]

After the devaluation, sectors such as construction and manufacturing provided huge boosts for the economy as a whole. Small and medium sized firms expanded rapidly, hiring large numbers of unskilled laborers, which they needed to meet the demand for their goods and services. As shown in Chapter 6, the Ministry of Labor, Employment, and Social Security played an active role in improving the quality of employment, being present and resolving many labor disputes, and working with employers and labor unions to improve the minimum wage and working conditions. Improvements in labor conditions thus contributed to the overall performance in economic growth.

Monetary policy and foreign exchange management

The role of monetary policy proved to be central to the economy's strong record of economic growth from 2003 through 2008. Monetary policy helped "protect" domestic industry after the shock of devaluation in 2002. Stable relative prices allowed small and medium firms to re-establish their production lines, their work forces, and their capacity to produce more in response to growing consumer demand. In this sense, monetary policy served as an essential tool in import substitution. The main function of monetary policy then shifted from being a "defensive" instrument to becoming a more active support in allowing Argentina to export its commodities and manufacturing output into regional and global markets. Maintaining the value of the peso in relation to the dollar was a direct support from the Central Bank of Argentina to exporters. This strategy shifted in the second half of 2008 and into 2009 as new conditions in the global economy undercut Argentina's commodity exports. The Central Bank then allowed the peso to lose some value vis-à-vis the dollar, but only gradually, thus avoiding another major foreign exchange shock. The dilemma, which the Central Bank faces, is whether to maintain a high dollar and thus protect domestic industrial production, or allow a cheaper dollar and thereby make commodity exports more attractive.

One of the lessons of this experience is that again it contradicted the advice of the IMF in 2002 when Deputy Managing Director Anne Krueger repeatedly urged Argentina to float its currency, allowing the market to determine its real value. Instead, the government decided that an expensive dollar would help to stimulate domestic production and later make exports cheaper, thereby earning substantial foreign exchange. Resolving the issue of monetary policy was done through the lens of prioritizing national needs over international approval of its policy directions.

Fiscal policy

In the area of fiscal policy, the government did finally accept some of the external advice it had received over the years concerning the need to improve tax collection. From 2003 to 2008, tax revenue increased from 88,072 million pesos to 317,578 million pesos. This collection broke all records in Argentina and contributed both to strengthening the state, as noted earlier, and to allowing the State to be active in pursuit of specific objectives through public expenditures. In contrast to the commentary and expectations of many tax specialists such as Vito Tanzi,[6] a widely respected former tax expert at the IMF, Argentina managed to dramatically improve its overall collection effort.

But with this additional revenue, it shifted course and did not follow conventional external advice. It generated a large annual fiscal surplus for eight consecutive years and built up its reserves in the Central Bank. Rather than use its surplus to pay off portions of its outstanding debt, it built a fiscal shield which could protect it against global financial volatility of the kind generated earlier in the 1997 East Asian Crisis and more recently, first the sub-prime mortgage crisis in the United States and now, the wider global economic crisis. This surplus infuriated the IMF and the global financial community, which insisted that Argentina use its surplus to meet its over-due debt payments. As mentioned earlier, this is an interesting case of following earlier sound IMF advice–to build up a fund to cushion the country against unexpected global financial pressures–but then being castigated by the same IMF for maintaining this fund as an insurance policy against global surprises.

Public investment

One of the lessons from the Argentine experience is that public investment matters. While some governments regarded social measures simply as necessary public expenditures, the Argentine government used programs such as the *Jefes y Jefas de Hogares* program as a large-scale investment in people, not only to keep them alive during the crisis, but also to keep them connected to the labor force and the world of work. The World Bank credits this program as having played a major role in the country's impressive reduction of the population below the poverty line. The cash payments and work assignments provided to heads of households under this program are the kind of support frequently scorned by neoliberal economists as "make work," yet there is evidence that that is what this program did. It made work and it made people work, generating more income and multipliers in the economy.

In addition, the government undertook many investments in employment-intensive projects such as school-building, road-building, and other projects in which national funds were transferred to the provinces. It is interesting to note that the provinces, which have traditionally been politically difficult for national governments in Argentina, had been relatively "quiet" from 2003 to 2008, satisfied by payments through the Co-participation Fund and high agricultural incomes.

Declining local public revenues in poorer provinces have resulted in decreasing public investment as well. It has become much more difficult for the national government to transfer funds to the provinces to build and maintain these projects, particularly for infrastructure. This trend has worsened the employment situation significantly in some provinces, particularly those that also suffered from droughts in 2008–2009.

One aspect of public investment however has been the lack of government attention to spatial concentration and location. While individual municipalities have worked on their economic development plans, there has been surprisingly little focus by national authorities on how to capture the benefits from concentration of complementary economic activities such as smalls and medium-sized industries. Nor is it obvious that infrastructure plans have been designed to support expansion of industrial or agricultural productivity. The country lacks both metropolitan planning frameworks, with a few exceptions such as the plan developed, but not yet adopted, for metropolitan Buenos Aires by the Province of Buenos Aires without cooperation from the city government, and effective regional development plans which could focus investment on both needy areas as well as support areas with high economic potential.

Trade and foreign direct investment

As noted above in the discussion of monetary policy, in the post-crisis period since 2001–2002, Argentina did not withdraw from the global economy into itself as was predicted and assumed by many outside commentators. While the country recognized the primacy of national priorities versus international obligations, it also developed its trade of both manufactured goods and agricultural commodities. It used monetary policy to first protect domestic industry by making imports expensive and then to actively support exports, which were inexpensive in global markets. While it did not use tariffs and other forms of trade protection, the country nevertheless focused on how it could increase its foreign exchange earnings through active trade promotion and foreign direct investment (FDI).

An important component of its open external posture has been the attraction of FDI. As noted earlier, many observers predicted in the dark days of 2002 that defaulting on its debt meant that Argentina would not receive any FDI. This, however, was not the case. From 2002 to 2006, FDI increased at 26 percent annually and then later slowed down with the emerging global financial crisis. While the government has sought more, it is notable how wrong the naysayers proved to be. Clearly, the global economic crisis will have a longer-term impact on dampening the prospects for FDI, but this is not only for Argentina.

In this regard, about 30 percent of total FDI since 2002 has come from Brazil.[7] Brazilian involvement in the Argentine economy has grown considerably, for example, since 2004, imports of Brazilian products has grown from US$4 billion to US$10.3 billion in 2008, while exports grew from US$3 billion to US$7.3 billion, leaving a growing trade deficit which is 47 percent larger in 2008 than it was in 2007.[8] This deficit for Argentina builds on over 62 consecutive months of a trade deficit with its northern neighbor. Brazilian companies have invested heavily in the petroleum sector, cement, beer, and refrigeration. The Brazilian economy, with a GDP of some US$690 billion in 2008, compared to Argentina's GDP of US$230 billion, is also seeking to diversify further, producing planes for *Aerolíneas Argentinas*, military vehicles, and participating actively in public works projects.

An important part of this relationship with Brazil has been the concerted effort by both governments to support the efforts on the companies from their respective countries. This was agreed and further consolidated through an agreement in December 2007 between Presidents Lula and Cristina Fernandez de Kirchner in which they established working groups led by their respective foreign ministries to resolve obstacles to further integration of their two economies. In August 2008, Lula led a delegation of more than 200 Brazilian businessmen to Buenos Aires to continue this work and to close various negotiations on specific projects. Working groups of businessmen from both countries were organized by sector to advance this agenda. The political objective of building cooperation between the two countries has been concretized through increasingly dense economic relationships.

This approach is notable in both the global and Latin American contexts. It is also important to note that, while the countries are constructing shared economic interests, it also been possible to differ at key moments on policy questions. For example, Argentina joined other developing countries in their position on trade tariffs in the July 2008 meetings in Geneva on the Doha Round, even though Brazil actively supported the proposals of the industrialized countries. Argentina argued against the imbalanced approach of the industrialized countries to subsidize and protect their agriculture against imports from developing countries while at the same time pressing developing countries to reduce tariffs on imported goods from industrialized countries. Foreign Minister, Jorge Taiana, demonstrated that the Foreign Ministry was fully prepared to articulate a strong position in these global negotiations.[9] His argument was consistent with the argument that the industrialized countries have "kicked the ladder," not allowing the developing countries to climb up to their position after themselves having protected their own nascent industries in the past and continuing into the present.[10]

In contrast, Brazil was less concerned about opening its borders to industrial goods because it already had well-developed industrial and manufacturing sectors able to effectively compete with products from industrialized countries. Nonetheless, the two countries did not let this important policy and economic difference stand in the way of advancing their other shared interests. What remained to be determined was how these different interests could be reconciled within the institutional and political context of Mercosur.

An additional important dimension in the trade and FDI picture was the growing role of Venezuela in the Argentine economy. While Venezuela did not have the industrial weight of Brazil, it did have considerable financial weight from its oil revenues up to 2009, which proved to be helpful to Argentina. The government of President Hugo Chavez bought US$7.5 billion in Argentine bonds in 2008, thus helping the country refinance some portion of its external debt. Venezuela also provided oil to Argentina in exchange for food products, including milk, meat, and grains, and industrial machinery. From 2003 to 2008, Hugo Chavez had visited Argentina 14 times, had developed a working relationship with the Argentine government, and had launched numerous projects such as oil refineries and other industrial ventures. This trend, however, slowed down considerably after the drop in the oil price and Venezuela's own fiscal problems, which became more severe by late 2008 and into 2009.

Employment policy

Certainly one of the most successful features of the economic recovery since 2001–2002 was the rapid drop in unemployment. The growth of aggregate demand in response to the change in relative prices through the devaluation has generated many new jobs, most of which are in small and medium-sized industries, including the construction sector. Sustained economic growth has supported a growth in the number of new jobs created as well as the quality of employment through continuous increases in real wages, minimum wages, working conditions, and the determined resolution of labor disputes.

The active and effective involvement of the Ministry of Work, Employment, and Social Security under the leadership of Minister Carlos Tomada was a key factor in this process. The Ministry has also convened the National Council of Employment, Productivity, and Living Minimum Wage for five consecutive years. This Council, chaired by Tomada, brought together labor and business to work together on specific issues such as the regular adjustment of the minimum wage. Tomada referred to this Council as "*democracy par excellence*" during the announcement of a new minimum wage on July 28, 2008 at a time of concern about how wages might be controlled to not further inflationary pressures.[11] Not only was the Ministry able to obtain the agreement of the *Confederación General de Trabajo* (CGT), the largest grouping of Argentine labor unions, but it was also successful in receiving the support of the *Union Industrial Argentina*, the largest association of Argentine employers. It thus demonstrated effective state performance while also strengthening state–society relations.

Approaches to problem-solving

An assessment of Argentina's approaches to problem-solving since the crisis of 2001–2002 necessarily rests on how the government has been able to apply its fundamental principles and policy orientations to specific problems which arise. This assessment could include, among others, the following criteria: consistency in policy orientation, follow through in allocating funds behind policy initiatives and solutions to problems, identification of new arenas requiring attention, and success in solving significant problems.

Consistency

A perhaps surprising but also revealing assessment of consistency is found in a 2006 Country Assistance Strategy document of the World Bank concerning Argentina:

> When President Kirchner took office in May 2003 he outlined the principal goals of his administration in an address to the National Assembly. He stressed the need for continued economic stability with sustained growth in the order of 4–5 percent such that would generate employment and enable real incomes to double in the space of fifteen years. Mindful that the 2001 default on public debt was the result of excessive borrowing and faulty economic management, he pledged to follow prudent fiscal policies that would secure fiscal surplus on a consistent basis…

> At the same time, he envisaged a strong government role in guiding economic growth within a context of "national capitalism". Government would participate actively in the provision of infrastructure, broadly defined to include housing as well as health and education facilities ... while acknowledging the need for a robust social safety net, President Kirchner was quite explicit in stating that "the problems of poverty cannot be solved by social policies but rather by economic policies". The Government has been quite consistent in its pursuit of these goals and articulate in their elaboration in successive official documents and public speeches...
>
> The Administration has pursued many of these economic goals, although in a way consistent with its overarching principles of an assertive role for government and an emphasis on social considerations. With respect to attracting investment, for example, the President frequently reiterates that Argentina needs infrastructure investment, but that such investment must be different in nature and result from the investment patterns of the 1990s, and as he said recently, have a "clear Keynesian and heterodox" vision that generates growth, employment, social inclusion, and equity.
>
> The Administration has been similarly consistent in the area of social policy.

Finally, in its submission of its Economic Policy Guidelines to the World Bank, the government prepared a document in which it identified its "key challenges as ensuring adequate energy supplies, lowering inflation, strengthening the country's ability to withstand external volatility, and consolidating the social recovery."[12]

This lengthy quotation communicates the 2006 perspective of the World Bank, which had been quite critical of the Argentine government and the country's economic performance in earlier periods. This evaluation of the Government's consistency was noteworthy and worth some further reflection. If the crisis of 2001–2002 had been the result of a faulty approach by various Argentine governments to the management of what might be called economic fundamentals, this 2006 assessment seemed to endorse not only the guiding principles but also their application since 2003. To be fair, in its Country Assistance document, the Bank also expressed its concern about management of inflation, energy supplies, and improving the quality of governance of public institutions. But on balance, this was quite a positive assessment.

Beyond this evaluation, it can also be said that many of the government's key accomplishments have not occurred only through short-term decisions and actions. For example, the debt reduction strategy was launched in August 2003 and required sustained patience from the Ministry of Economy before it presented its final offer in January 2005. The government weathered a long and often insulting battery of commentary before it finally succeeded in obtaining the agreement of 76.1 percent of the bondholders to refinance their bonds as proposed by the government. This percentage was increased by subsequent bond offerings in 2009 and 2010. Other examples cited above, include the work of the

Council on Labor, Employment, and the Minimum Wage in securing agreements over five years between employers and labor unions, a notable accomplishment in a country known for extended labor conflict and disruption, and nurturing collaborative trade agreements with Brazil, also a subject upon which Argentina had a long history of rancorous disputes.

Follow-through on funding policy and program initiatives

Despite the range of its ambition in recovering from the crisis and finding a sustainable path for equitable growth, the government displayed some discipline in not launching too many new programs at the same time. The combined discipline first of Economy Minister Lavagna during Duhalde's term as president and then later with President Nestor Kirchner was noteworthy in its restraint, particularly until 2007. Their concern with financial prudence seems to have guided public expenditures. While the latter increased in 2007 leading into the presidential campaign and have continued to grow in 2008 under Cristina Fernandez de Kirchner, they have grown from a much larger revenue base than in previous years. The fiscal deficit therefore did not increase significantly.

In specific terms, the government's commitment to maintain real incomes for particularly the most vulnerable groups has been translated into successive increases in the minimum wage, pensions for retired people, and family allocations, and in 2010, for all children from poor families. The government did finally support salary increases for public sector employees. It also sought to limit the increases in tariffs for public services. While the latter increased for electricity, gas, and public transport in 2008, these increases were long overdue and necessary to meet the higher costs facing the providers of these services.

Identifying new areas requiring action

In contrast to this generally positive record in solving problems from 2003 to 2008, the governments of both Nestor Kirchner and Cristina Fernandez de Kirchner have been less quick to identify some specific high profile problems and to launch efforts to solve them. Despite their obvious intelligence, both presidents refused to acknowledge a growing energy shortage as early as 2005, when blackouts and shortages of natural gas seriously affected consumers and even disrupted manufacturing processes in some industries. Eventually, Cristina Fernandez de Kirchner spoke about an energy shortage and even launched a program in early 2008 to introduce low-consuming light bulbs in households, public buildings, and private businesses around the country. But this was surprisingly slow in coming.

A second and more controversial problem has been with INDEC, where management problems starting in 2006 undermined national and international confidence in the country's official statistics. As noted earlier, this problem has had significant implications for the management of inflation, salary agreements, dividends for the country's bonds, and other areas of the economy, as well as for the government's overall credibility as well. Several economy ministers including Peirano and Lousteau included INDEC as part of their reasons for resigning in 2007 and 2008.

Success in solving problems

If the government's capacity to solve the big problems of macro-economic management such as monetary policy and fiscal control, while making great headway in reducing unemployment, poverty, and inequality, is clear and a matter of public record, it is more perplexing how some other problems remain unresolved. The most evident was the bitter and lengthy dispute with Uruguay over the location of two paper plants near the Rio de la Plata and the possibility that these plants would pollute the river and the surrounding areas, including the Argentine side of the river.

The government of Nestor Kirchner seemed to accept the protests of environmentalists and residents of neighboring Gualeguaychu, accepting the cutting of bridges between the two countries, with its effect on commerce and tourism, but it did not focus very much political capital on solving the problem. Its technical response was delayed, its offer to use the good offices of third parties came late in the dispute, and finally it lost control over the domestic political process itself. Instead, the government sent the problem to the International Court of Justice at The Hague where it languished for months. Only in 2010 did the government finally reach some *modus operandi* with the new government of Uruguay of President Jose Mujica.

As noted in Chapter 8, a similar process occurred, with more drama and heavier political costs, in the context of the conflict over the *retenciones*. While there is little doubt that conservative economic and political interests—from the large farmers to the exporting companies to the large media conglomerates which owned both newspapers and television channels—were preparing to fight against any governmental efforts to redistribute income, it was surprising that the government of Cristina Fernandez de Kirchner had not anticipated the conflict in which it found itself. It responded to various thrusts by the farm organizations with different answers: small adjustments in tax rates, cash benefits and refunds for small producers, and eventually seeking legitimacy by sending the proposal to the Congress for an expected ratification. The sequence of 130 days included too many surprises for a government, which had been relatively consistent and competent in its pursuit of well-considered objectives in the process of economic recovery.

It may be that the forces of opposition simply proved to be too capable, well-organized, effective in securing wide political support, and above all, managing the media. The response of the government following the July 18, 2008 Senate defeat, however, demonstrated that the government could also, to some extent, shift its approach to the media, maintain continuity in asserting its legitimacy, shift its key personnel, and use various instruments of power, including allocations to the provinces and municipalities to reward loyalty while punishing defectors. The conflict with *el campo* suggests that if this situation was first perceived as a battle rather than a war, it proved in fact to be a war without final resolution, which may only come with the completion of the presidential elections of 2011. It was a bitter and politically very costly lesson for the government that has learned that it must be far more effective in winning against a well-financed, well-organized opposition.

This assessment is necessarily limited in scope and time. A fuller evaluation of the period of "recovery and growth during a time of default" will only be possible from a distance, when it is known whether the change in course introduced in this period was sustained and whether it produced the intended changes in the economy and the social welfare of the people of Argentina.

The political economy of the possible versus the search for alternatives

The story of Argentina from 2001 to 2008 demonstrates that there were alternative ways to think about the country's development and a range of policies and programs which could produce material changes in the lives of its people, particularly the poor who had been hurt most by the crisis of 2001–2002. This search for alternatives sought to address the widely acknowledged fact that market-led economic growth in Latin America in the 1990s had not reduced either poverty or inequality. The policies, which had been used to guide this growth, had been termed "disingenuous neo-liberalism" by the Chilean economist Ricardo Ffrench-Davis.[13]

But the forces of the status quo are persistent and, by definition, committed to maintaining themselves over the long term. Rather than simply insist on a simplistic triumphal victory as some authors such as Francis Fukuyama had asserted in his book, *The End of History*,[14] they turned the argument into an assertion of what was "realistic" or "possible" in the world, thereby re-affirming the inherent value of the status quo. This is the argument presented in the book, *The Political Economy of the Possible: Beyond Free Marketeers and Revolutionaries* by Spanish economist Javier Santiso.[15] The author argued that Latin American politics had changed, had become less ideological, and less focused on changing the framework of society, economy, and politics, and more directed towards managing smaller problems and achieving lesser objectives. He wrote of the end of the future as a dimension of this politics, with the short-term replacing the long-term as the time horizon for action and expectations.

Implicit in this argument were several key premises:

- that the big framework issues were in fact resolved to everyone's satisfaction,
- that the model of economic growth and development was effective in providing the incomes, jobs, goods, and services which are needed by Latin American populations,

- that the distribution of benefits from growth and development was acceptable, despite the existing and widening gaps between rich and poor in many Latin American countries, and
- that the "political economy of the possible" was sufficient to manage the risks and uncertainty of change in the medium and long term.

By not contesting these assumptions, Santiso's argument also accepted the basic prevailing de facto definitions of justice and political institutions in Latin American countries, which have long been characterized by inequality, and an absence of social and political consensus about how to address this inequality. In 1992, Fidel Castro had observed that these prevailing conditions were so extreme and problematic that, even with Cuba's great economic difficulties after the fall of the Soviet Union, there was little reason for Cuba to integrate into that social and political reality.[16]

Santiso's argument was, in effect, a sophisticated defense of a status quo which was adjusting to emergent needs but not changing in ways which might alter the basic distribution of economic and political power within Latin American countries. It was clothed in the language of realism and insider's knowledge of the world of economic policy choices and so-called "policy space," the area in which "real choices" are possible.

While policy space and real choices are relevant concepts for assessing development policies and their impacts, they need to be contextualized in larger frameworks as suggested by the fundamental premises which have been implicitly adopted by former President Nestor Kirchner and applied by his government and its successor to the most urgent problems facing Argentina. By adopting a strategy of "possibilism," Santiso is unable to explain the most important choices facing governments seeking to find better paths of development. These include being clear about:

- the priority of the national economy and basic needs of the national population, rather than giving priority to international advice and obligations;
- the role of government as an active and strengthened agent in development and in the management of national and local impacts of a volatile and largely unsympathetic global economy and international political system; and
- the overwhelming ethical imperative of reducing poverty and inequality as the topic agenda item for development policy.

The process of recovery and growth in Argentina demonstrates how a government learned to manage some, but clearly not all, of the dynamics of interaction between global and national/local forces to its own advantage. The case of Argentina illustrates the normative possibilities of expanding policy space and political choices in the face of what had been asserted by some to be fully determined frameworks at the end of the Cold War. The "political economy of the possible" was thus replaced by the active search for more effective, equitable, and sustainable development strategies within the region. As the Argentine case dramatically shows, this search can nonetheless run into powerful opposition. Even so, the Argentine crisis and recovery has contributed to a clearer understanding of the impacts of the Washington Consensus and to a rethinking of these policy choices and political alternatives.

This book has also shown, however, that the path from recovery to sustainable growth remains to be fully identified, much less completed. The pursuit of redistributive goals while shifting from recovery towards a path of sustainable growth proved to be politically risky in the face of well-organized protectors of the status quo. Indeed, despite the many achievements of 2002–2008, many Argentines seem to happily believe that the status quo has returned. They continue to criticize the Kirchners without acknowledging that their own material lives are immeasurably better.

Another part of this story is that recent experience in Argentina demonstrates that nationally defined development strategies offer greater chances of success than those imposed by external institutions. Reform efforts always face resistance. Not all policies of the post-crisis governments have been successful or even received political support. An active government inevitably runs into political constraints. As Theodore Lowi wrote many years ago, for every policy there is a politics. The crisis and recovery in Argentina, as well as the subsequent search for sustainable growth, demonstrates that government action necessarily must come to terms with political forces. The more ambitious is the policy vision, the more difficult will be the political road to its adoption.

In the end, this story is also about the strengths and weakness of democracy. Greg Grandin's historical observations were instructive about the legacy of the Cold War in Latin America when he argued that Latin America had adopted definitions of democracy in the 1990s, which did not include economic and social justice, but rather focused on political protection from authoritarian regimes.[17] Broadening those definitions to include economic and social justice is one of the most urgent tasks for political movements and their leaders.

Finally, the story of Argentina fits into the historical context of the beginning of the twenty-first century. Indeed, the country, along with many of its regional neighbors, began during the period 2002–2009 to undertake the complicated task of identifying a set of policies which could contribute towards building a new kind of country and society in which poverty, inequality, and social exclusion could be reduced amidst a democratic environment, and in which social justice and the rule of law could once again be fundamental values and shared objectives. Recent history suggests that this is not and will not be an easy goal to achieve, but recovering from the crisis of 2001–2002 was not easy either. The growing dark cloud of the global economic crisis affected Argentina in 2008 and 2009, and further complicated the search for a sustainable path and undermining some of the gains of the previous seven years. Nevertheless, it is apparent from the country's relatively rapid recovery from the global crisis that the experience of recovering and growing after the crisis of 2001–2002 provided some strength in facing the future.

Notes

Prologue

1 See, for example, Mario Rapoport, "*Mitos, etapas y crisis en la economia Argentina*," in Mario Rapoport and Hernan Colombo, eds, *Nacion-Region-Provincia en Argentina: Pensamiento politico, economico y social*, (Buenos Aires: Imago Mundi, 2007), Francisco Delich, *Sociedades Invisibles: La cultura de la ingobernabilidad en America Latina*, (Buenos Aires: GEDISA Editorial, 2007), Maria Seoane, *Nosotros: Apuntes sobre pasiones,razones y trampas de los argentines entre dos siglos* (Buenos Aires: Editorial Sudamericana, 2006), Jorge Todesca, El *mito del pais rico: Economia y politica en la historia argentina*, (Buenos Aires: Emece, 2006), Carl Waisman, *Reversal of Development in Argentina: Postwar Counterrevolutionary Policies and Their Structural Consequences*, (Princteon: Princeton University Press, 1987), Vito Tanzi, *Argentina. How one of the richest countries in the world lost its wealth: an Economic Chronicle*, (Washington: Jorge Pinto Books, 2007), Carlos Gabetta, *La debacle de Argentina: Una Argentina que muere y otra que bosteza*, (Buenos Aires: Icaria, 2002), Steven Levitsky and Maria Victoria Murillo, eds., *Argentine Democracy: The Politics of Institutional Weakness*, (University Park: Pennsylvania State University Press, 2005), Pablo Spiller and Mariano Tommasi, *The Institutional Foundations of Public Policy in Argentina*, (New York: Cambridge University Press, 2007).

2 F. Fukuyama, *The End of History*, New York: Penguin, 1992.

3 T. Friedman, *The Lexus and the Olive Tree: Understanding Globalization*, New York: Farrar, Straus, Giroux, 1999.

4 T. Friedman, *The World is Flat: A Brief History of the 21st Century*, New York: Farrar, Straus, Giroux, 2005.

5 J. Stiglitz, *Globalization and its Discontents*, New York: W.W. Norton, 2003.

6 S. Sassen, *Globalization and its Discontents*, New York: New Press, 1998.

7 H. Chang and I. Grabel, *Reclaiming Development: An Alternative Economic Policy Manual*, New York: ZED Books, 2004; M. Hardt and A. Negri, *Empire*, New York: 2000, L. Ramos, ed. *El Fracaso del Consenso de Washington: La caida de su major alumno: Argentina*, Barcelona: Icaria, 2003.

8 J. Gray, *False Dawn: The Delusions of Global Capitalism*, New York: The New Press, 1998.

9 S. Huntington, *The Clash of Civilizations and the Remaking of World Order*, New York: Simon and Schuster, 1996.

10 A. Appadurai, *Fear of Small Numbers: Essays on The Geography of Anger*, Durham: Duke University Press, 2006.

11 J.Williamson, "What Washington Means by Policy Reform," in: J. Williamson, (ed.): *Latin American Readjustment: How Much has Happened*, Washington: Institute for International Economics, 1989.

12 K. Polanyi, *The Great Transformation*, Boston: Beacon Press 1944.
13 S. Edwards, *Crisis and Reform in Latin America: From Despair to Hope*, New York: Oxford University Press, 1995.
14 S. Edwards, *Left Behind*, Chicago: University of Chicago Press, 2010.
15 J. Casteneda and P. Navia, "Elections and the State of Democracy in Latin America," *Americas Quarterly*, February 1, 2007, p. 4.
16 World Bank, *Argentina 2006–2008, Country Assistance Strategy*, Washington: The World Bank, 2006.
17 M. Gutman, "In Search of the (Lost) World to Come," in Michael Cohen and Margarita Gutman, eds., *Argentina in Collapse? The Americas Debate*, Buenos Aires: The New School, 2002, pp. 179–192.
18 UN Economic Commission for Latin America and the Caribbean, *The Time for Equality: Closing gaps, opening trails*, Santiago: ECLAC, 2010.

1 The emergence of neo-liberalism in Latin America: situating the Argentine experience

1 R. Thorp, *Progress, Poverty, and Exclusion: An Economic History of Latin America in the 20th Century*, Washington: Inter-American Development Bank, 1998, p. xi.
2 K. Polanyi, *The Great Transformation: The Political and Economic Origins of Our Time*, Boston: Beacon Press, 1944.
3 For example, see G. A. Cornia, "Income Distribution under Latin America's New Left Regimes," *Journal of Human Development and Capabilities*, Vol. 11, No. 1, February 2010, pp. 85–114; S. Edwards, *Left Behind: Latin America and the False Promise of Populism*, Chicago: University of Chicago Press, 2010; ECLAC, *Time for Equality: Closing gaps, opening trails*, 33rd session of ECLAC, Brasilia, 30 May to 1 June 2010, Santiago: ECLAC, 2010, J.M. Fanelli, ed., *Understanding Market Reforms in Latin America: Similar Reforms, Diverse Constituencies, Varied Results*, New York: Palgrave Macmillan, 2007; and J. A. Ocampo, Jomo K.S. and R. Vos, ed., *Growth Divergences: Explaining Differences in Economic Performance*, London: Orient Longman, 2007.
4 Ibid. pp. 3–4.
5 R. B. Collier and D Collier, *Shaping the Political Arena: Critical Junctures, the Labor Movement, and Regime Dynamics in Latin America*, second edition, South Bend: University of Notre Dame Press, 2002.
6 J. Casteneda, *Utopia Unarmed: The Latin American Left after the Cold War*, New York: Knopf, 1993.
7 G. Grandin, *The Last Colonial Massacre: Latin America in the Cold War*, Chicago: University of Chicago Press, 2004, and G. Grandin, *Empire's Workshop: Latin America, the United States, and the Rise of the New Imperialism*, New York: Metropolitan Books, Henry Holt and Company, 2006.
8 Thorp, op. cit., pp. 24–25.
9 S. Engerman and K. Sokoloff, "Colonialism, inequality, and long run paths of development," Working paper 11057, National Bureau of Economic Research, Cambridge, Mass., 2005.
10 Thorp, op. cit., p. 14.
11 R. Ffrench-Davis, ed. *Seeking Growth under Financial Volatility*, New York: Palgrave Macmillan and ECLAC, 2006; R. Caballero, *Macro-Economic Volatility in Reformed Latin America: Diagnosis and Policy Proposals*, Washington: Inter-American Development Bank, 2001, M. Pettis, *The Volatility Machine: Emerging economies and the Threat of Financial Collapse*, New York: Oxford University Press, 2001.
12 R. Prebisch, UNECLAC, 1950, p. 246, quoted in Kathryn Sikkink *Ideas and institutions: Developmentalism in Brazil and Argentina*, Ithaca: Cornell University Press, 1991.

13 R. Prebisch, *Economic Survey of Latin America 1949*, New York: Economic Commission on Latin America, 1951.
14 Thorp, op. cit., pp. 133–135.
15 R. Sidicaro, *Los Tres Peronismos: Estado y poder economic 1946–55/1973–76/1989–99*, Buenos Aires: Siglo XXI Editores Argentina, 2002; M. Gene, *Un mundo feliz: Imagenes de los trabadores en el primer peronismo 1946–1955*, Buenos Aires: Fondo de Cultura Economica y Universidad de San Andres, 2005.
16 E. Arceo and E. Basualdo, "Los Cambios de los Sectores Dominantes en America Latina Bajo el Neoliberalismo: La problematica propuesta", in E. Basualdo and E. Arceo, eds., *Neoliberalismo y sectores dominantes: Tendencias globales y experiencias nacionales*, Buenos Aires" CLACSO Libros, 2006, p. 16.
17 Thorp., op. cit., p. 138.
18 Ibid., pp. 159–161.
19 See, for example, Nora R. Libertun de Duren; "Growth and Poverty in the Urban Fringe: Decentralization, Dispersion, and Inequality in Buenos Aires", Ph.D. dissertation, MIT, June 2007.
20 C. Acuna, S. Galiani, and M. Tommasi, "Understanding Reform: the Case of Argentina", p. 34, in Jose Maria Fanelli, *Understanding Market Reforms in Latin America: Similar Reforms, Different Constituencies, Varied Results*; New York: Palgrave Macmillan, 2007.
21 Thorp, op. cit., p. 165.
22 Sikkink, op. cit., pp. 3–4.
23 Ibid., p. 31.
24 Ibid., p. 35.
25 Arceo and Basualdo, op. cit., pp. 18–19.
26 Thorp, op. cit., pp. 169–171.
27 Sikkink, op. cit., p. 98.
28 Ibid.,p. 108.
29 Ibid., p. 171.
30 G. O'Donnell, cited in Sikkink, op. cit., p. 171.
31 Ibid., pp. 172–175.
32 Ibid., p. 29.
33 O. Altimir, "Desigualdad, empleo y pobreza en America Latina: Efectos del ajuste y del cambio en el estilo de desarrollo," *Desarrollo Economico*, 17 (145), April–June 1997.
34 Thorp, op. cit., p. 208.
35 Ibid., pp. 216–217.
36 Cornia, op. cit., p. 87.
37 Ibid. pp. 87–89.
38 R. Ffrench-Davis, *Reformas para America Latina despues del fundamentalismo neoliberal*, Buenos Aires: CEPAL and Siglo Veintiuno Editores, 2005, p. 13.
39 N. Harris, "Structural Adjustment and cities: Three Papers," Working Paper No. 63, London: Development Planning Unit, University College, London, 1994; D. Cowan, "The World Bank, Urban Bias, and Structural Adjustment," Working Paper No. 67, London: Development Planning Unit, University College, London, 1994, C. Moser, "Confronting Crisis: A Comparative Study of Household Responses to Poverty and Vulnerability in Four Poor Urban Communities," Washington: The World Bank, 1996.
40 Center for International Development, Harvard University web-site, www.cid.harvard.edu/cidtrade/issues/washington.html April 2003.
41 Personal communication.
42 ECLAC, op. cit., p. 104.
43 Ibid., p. 111.
44 Ibid., p. 113.

45 These included well-known Latin American economists such as Domingo Cavallo, Carlos Rodriguez, Marcelo Selowsky, Sebastian Edwards, Roque Fernandez, Miguel Kiguel, and Pablo Guidotti.
46 See Jose Natanson, *Buenos muchachos: Vida y obra de los economistas del establishment*, Buenos Aires: Libros del Zorzal, 2005.
47 Arceo and Basualdo, op. cit., p. 22.
48 Thorp, op. cit., p. 218.
49 French-Davis, op. cit., p. 16.
50 To use Williamson's term from Kucynski and Williamson, op. cit.
51 J.A. Ocampo, "Overcoming Latin America's growth frustrations: The macro and meso-economic links," pp. 33–59, in Ffrench-Davis, 2006, op. cit., p. 33.
52 ECLAC 2003; Kuczynski and Williamson, 2003.
53 Ocampo, op. cit., p. 35.
54 Ibid., p. 40.
55 Ibid., p. 41.
56 Ibid., p. 42.
57 Ffrench-Davis, op. cit., p. 14.
58 Ibid., pp. 14–15, and Moser, op. cit.
59 Arceo, E., "El Fracaso de la Reestructuracion Neoliberal en America Latina: Estrategias de los sectores dominantes y alternativas populares," in Bausualdo and Arceo, op.cit., pp. 27–65.
60 Arceo and Basualdo, op. cit., p. 24.
61 J. Stiglitz, *Globalization and its Discontents*, New York: W.W. Norton, 2003, p. xiii.
62 Ibid., p. xiv.
63 Ibid., p. 7.
64 Ibid., p. 8.
65 C. Acuna, S. Galiani, and M. Tommasi, "Understanding Reform: the Case of Argentina", in Fanelli, op. cit., p. 32.
66 D. Rodrik, "Augmented Washington Consensus."
67 N. Birdsall, A. Torre, and R. Menezes, *Fair Growth: Economic Policies for Latin America's Poor and Middle Class Majority*, Washington: The Center for Global Development and the Inter-American Dialogue, 2008.
68 Ibid., pp. 3–4.
69 Ibid., p. 7.
70 Ibid., p. 8.
71 Ibid., p. 27.
72 J.A. Ocampo, "Overcoming Latin America's growth frustrations: The macro and mesoeconomic links", op. cit., p. 40.
73 Birdsall *et al.*, op.cit., pp. 12–15.
74 World Bank, *Argentina: Country Assistance Strategy 2006–2008*, Washington: The World Bank, 2006.
75 Ibid., p. 41.
76 Moser, op. cit.
77 Samuel Morley, *"Poverty during Recovery and Reform in Latin America: 1985–1995,"* Washington: Inter-American Development Bank, 1998.
78 W. Easterly and L. Serven, eds. *The Limits of Stabilization: Infrastructure, Public Deficits, and Growth in Latin America*, Washington: World Bank, 2003.
79 French-Davis, op. cit., p. 24.
80 Ibid., p. 29.
81 Edwards, op. cit.
82 Ibid., p. 1.
83 Ibid., p. 6.
84 Ibid., p. 7.
85 Ibid., p. 10.

86 Ibid., p. 9.
87 From Dornbusch and Edwards, *The Macroeconomics of Populism in Latin America (A National Bureau of Economic Research Conference Report*, Chicago: University of Chicago Press, 1992.
88 Ibid., pp. 72–73.
89 Ibid., p. 144.
90 Pettis, op. cit., *The Volatility Machine*, P. Salama, "Porque America Latina No Puede Alcanzar Un Crecimiento Elevado y Sostenido," in Basualdo and Arceo, op. cit., p. 95.
91 Ibid., p. 34.
92 J. Santiso, *Latin America's Political Economy of the Possible: Beyond Good Revolutionaries and Free Marketeers*, Cambridge: MIT University Press, 2006
93 F. Colburn, *Latin America at the End of Politics*, Princeton and Oxford: Princeton University Press, 2002, p. 4.
94 Ibid., p. 7.
95 Ibid., p. 35.
96 Ibid., p. 133.
97 G. Grandin, *The Last Colonial Massacre: The Legacy of the Cold War in Latin America*, Chicago: University of Chicago Press, 2004.

2 State performance and institutional capacity in development

1 World Bank, *The East Asian Miracle: Economic Growth and Public Policy*, New York: Oxford University Press, 1993.
2 See, for example, R. Wade, *Governing the Market: Economic Theory and the Role of Government in East Asian Industrialization*, Princeton: Princeton University Press, 1990.
3 A. Amsden, *The Rise of the "Rest": Challenges to the West from Late-Industrializing Economies*, New York: Oxford University Press, 2001; Atul Kohli, *State-Directed Development: Political Power and Industrialization in the Global Periphery*, New York: Cambridge University Press, 2004, or Vivek Chibber, *Locked in Place: State-Building and Late Industrialization in India*, Princeton: Princeton University Press, 2003.
4 S. Paul, *Institutional Reforms in Sector Adjustment Operations: The World Bank's Experience*, World Bank Discussion Paper 92, Washington: The World Bank, 1990, and Barbara Nunberg, *Public Sector Management Issues in Structural Adjustment Lending*, Working Paper 217, March 1990, Washington: The World Bank, Country Economics Department, March 1990.
5 P. Landell-Mills and I. Serageldin, "Governance and the External Factor," paper presented to *World Bank Annual Conference on Development Economics*, 1991, Washington: The World Bank, April 1991.
6 World Bank, "The State in a Changing World," World Development Report 1997, Washington: The World Bank, 1997 and World Bank, "Managing Development: The Governance Dimension: A Discussion Paper", Washington: The World Bank, August 1991.
7 See for example, World Bank Institute, *Improving Governance and Controlling Corruption: Towards a participatory andf action-oriented approach grounded on empirical rigor*, Washington: The World Bank, October 2001.
8 World Bank, "Attacking Poverty," *World Development Report 2001*, Washington: The World Bank, 2001.
9 World Bank, "Building Institutions for Markets," *World Development Report 2002*, Washington: The World Bank, 2002.
10 M. Khan, "Governance, Economic Growth and Development", in Jose Antonio Ocampo, Jomo K.S., and Rob Vos, eds. *Growth Divergences: Explaining Differences in Economic Performance*, New York: Zed Books, 2007, pp. 285–323.

11 Ibid., pp. 294–295.
12 Ibid., pp. 305–321.
13 H. Chenery, Development Strategies paper, 1970.
14 P. Evans, *Embedded Autonomy: States and Industrial Transformation*, Princeton: Princeton University Press, 1995.
15 Evans, citing Karl Polanyi, *The Great Transformation*, Boston: Beacon Press, 1957, p. 140.
16 Ibid., p. 30.
17 Ibid., p. 35.
18 Ibid., p. 37.
19 Ibid., p. 10.
20 Ibid., p. 8.
21 Ibid., pp. 228–229.
22 Ibid., p. 70.
23 Ibid., p. 249.
24 A. Montero, "Making and Remaking 'Good Government' in Brazil: Sub-national Industrial Policy in Minas Gerais," *Latin American Politics and Society*, Vol. 43, No. 2, Summer 2001, pp. 49–80.
25 B. Geddes, *Politician's Dilemma: Building State Capacity in Latin America*, Berkeley: University of California Press, 1994.
26 S. Stokes, *Mandates and Democracy: Neo-liberalism by Surprise in Latin America*, New York: Cambridge University Press, 2001.
27 A. Pereira, "Brazil's Agrarian Reform: Democratic Innovation or Oligarchic Exclusion Redux," *Latin American Politics and Society*, Vol. 45, No.,2, Summer 2003, pp. 41–65.
28 J. Burrity and L. Hallewell., "Reform of the State and the New Discourse on Social policy in Brazil," *Latin American Perspectives*, Vol. 33, No. 1, May 2006, pp. 67–88.
29 Ibid., p. 69.
30 Ibid., p. 71.
31 Ibid., pp. 75–79.
32 Ibid., p. 81.
33 E. Amann and W. Baer, "Neo-liberalism and Its Consequences in Brazil," *Journal of Latin American Studies*, Vol. 34, No. 4, Nov. 2002, pp. 945–959.
34 M. Kurtz, "State Developmentalism with a Developmental State: The public Foundations of the 'Free Market Miracle' in Chile," *Latin American Politics and Society*, Vo.43, No. 2, summer 2001; p. 19.
35 Ibid., p. 20.
36 P. Barrett, "Labour Policy, Labour–Business Relations and the Transition to Democracy in Chile," *Journal of Latin American Studies*, Vol. 33, 2001, pp. 594–595.
37 L. Tedesco, *Democracy in Argentina: Hope and Disillusion*, London: Frank Cass, 1999, p. 169.
38 A. Dinerstein, "The Politics of Unemployment: Employment policy, the Unemployed Workers Organizations and the State in Argentina (1991–2005)," London School of Economics, Non-Governmental Public Action Program, Working paper No. 9, Feb. 2008, p. 7.
39 M. Cleary and S. Stokes, D*emocracy and the Culture of Skepticism: Political Trust in Argentina and Mexico*, New York: Russell Sage Foundation, 2006.
40 S. Levitsky and M. Murillo, eds. *Argentine Democracy: The Politics of Institutional Weakness*, University Park, Pa.: Penn State University Press, 2005; and P. Spiller and M. Tommasi, *The Institutional Foundations of Public Policy in Argentina*, New York: Cambridge University Press, 2007.
41 Sikkink, op. cit.
42 Evans, op. cit.

43 C. Ramio and M. Salvador, "Civil Service Reform in Latin America: External Referents Versus Own Capacities," *Bulletin of Latin American Research*, Vol. 27, No. 4, p. 557, 2008.
44 O. Oszlak, "El Servicio Civil en America Latina y el Caribe: Situacion Actuel y Retos de Futuro", unpublished paper delivered at VI CLAD Congress on State and Public Administration Reform, Buenos Aires, 2001.
45 See, for example, M. Bergman, "Tax Reforms and Tax Compliance: The Divergent Paths of Chile and Argentina," *Journal of Latin American Studies*, Vol. 35, 2003, pp. 593–624 or Marcus Andre Melo, "Institutional Weakness and the Puzzle of Argentina's Low Taxation," *Latin American Politics and Society*, Vol. 49, No. 4, 2008, pp. 115–148.
46 Melo, op. cit., p. 117.
47 Ibid., pp. 119–124.
48 Levitsky and Murillo, op. cit., p. 21.
49 Ibid. pp. 27–31.
50 Spiller and Tommasi article in Levitsky and Murillo, op. cit., pp. 45–49.
51 P.T. Spiller and M. Tommasi, *The Institutional Foundations of Public Policy in Argentina*, New York: Cambridge University Press, 2007.
52 Ibid., p. 7.
53 M. Murillo, *Political Competition, Partisanship, and Policy Making in Latin American Public Utilities*, New York: Cambridge University Press, 2009, pp. 3–4.
54 R. Collier and D. Collier, *Shaping the Political Arena: Critical Junctures, the Labor Movement, and Regime Dynamics in Latin America*, second edition, South Bend: University of Notre Dame Press, 2002, p. 6.
55 Ibid., p. xi.
56 Ibid., p. 11.
57 Ibid., p. 30.
58 K. Weyland, "Neoliberalism and Democracy in Latin America: A Mixed Record," in William C. Smith, ed. *Latin American Democratic Transformation: Institutions, Actors, and Processes*, New York: Wiley-Blackwell, 2009, Ch. 3, p. 40.
59 S. Etchemendy, "Old Actors in New Markets: Transforming the Populist/Industrial Coalition in Argentina, 1989–2001," in Steven Levitsky and Maria Victoria Murillo, op. cit., pp. 63–65.
60 Weyland, op. cit., pp. 36–37.
61 J. Jordana and D. Levi-Faur, "The Diffusion of Regulatory Capitalism in Latin America: Sectoral and National Channels in the Making of a New Order," *Annals of the American Academy of Political and Social Science*, Vol. 598, March 2005, pp. 102–124.
62 Ibid., p. 116.
63 Ibid., pp. 117–118.
64 Ibid., p. 119.

3 The Argentine crisis: what happened?

1 M. Gutman, *Buenos Aires 1910: Memorias del Porvenir*, Buenos Aires: Gobierno de la Ciudad de Buenos Aires and the International Institute for Environment and Development–America Latina, 1999.
2 W. Lewis, *Growth and Fluctuations, 1870–1913*, London: George Allen and Unwin, 1978, p. 197.
3 R. Thorp, *Progress, Poverty, and Exclusion: An Economic History of Latin America in the 20th Century*, Washington: Johns Hopkins University Press, Inter-American Development Bank, European Union, 1998.
4 V.S. Naipaul, *The Return of Eva Peron*, New York: Vintage, 1980.
5 Lewis, op. cit., p. 223.

6 T.H. Donghi, "Why Did Argentina Adopt a Neoliberal Model?" in Michael Cohen and Margarita Gutman, eds., *Argentina in Collapse? The Americas Debate*, Buenos Aires: The New School and the International Institute for Environment and Development, 2002, p. 23.
7 Ibid., p. 24.
8 R.B. Collier and D. Collier, *Shaping the Political Arena: Critical Junctures, the Labor Movement, and Regime Dynamics in Latin America*, second edition South Bend: University of Notre Dame Press, 2002.
9 Ibid., p. 333.
10 Ibid., p. 485.
11 M. Melo, "Institutional Weakness and the Puzzle of Argentina's Low Taxation," *Latin American Politics and Society*, Vol. 49, No. 4, 2008, pp. 115–148.
12 Ibid., citing Barbara Geddes, *Politician's Dilemma: Building State Capacity in Latin America*, Berkeley: University of California Press, 1994.
13 This debt buildup has been criticized as an example of "odious debt", debt which was created by non-legitimate actors or was for non-legitimate purposes.
14 D. Azpiazu, "Ensenanzas del programa de privatizaciones desarrollado en la Argentina, 1990–1993," *Revista de CEPAL*, Number 54, December 1994.
15 D. Cecchini and J. Zicolillo, *Nuevo Conquistadores*, Madrid: Foca, 2002.
16 R. Frenkel, "Benefits and Costs of Convertibility," in Michael Cohen and Margarita Gutman, eds., *Argentina in Collapse?: The Americas Debate*, Buenos Aires: The New School and International Institute for Environment and Development—America Latina, 2002, pp. 33–50; Mario Damill, Roberto Frenkel, and Roxana Maurizio, "Argentina: A Decade of Currency Board: An Analysis of Growth, Employment, and Income Distribution," Buenos Aires: CEDES, February 2002.
17 Ibid., pp. 34–35.
18 Ibid., p. 36.
19 Ibid., p. 45.
20 W. Cline, "Restoring Growth in Argentina," Washington: Center for Global Development and Institute for International Economics, 2003, p. 7.
21 I. Bermudez, "*El reparto del ingreso: cada vez mas desigual*", *Clarín*, December 5, 1998, p. 22.
22 M. Svampa, *La Sociedad Excluyente: La Argentina Bajo el Signo de Neo-Liberalismo:* Buenos Aires: Taurus, 2005; Maristella Svampa, *Los Que Ganaron: la vida en los countries y barrios privadas*, Buenos Aires: Editorial Biblos, 2001; Carla Castelo, *Vidas Perfectas: Los Countries Por Dentro*, Buenos Aires: Editorial Sudamericana, 2007; and Michael A. Cohen, "*Convertibilidad, Crisis y Desafios 1992–2006*" in Margarita Gutman and Jorge Enrique Hardoy, *Buenos Aires: Historia del Area Metropolitana 1536–2006*, Buenos Aires: Ediciones Infinitos, 2007, pp. 270–313.
23 M. Cohen and D. Debowicz, "Las Cinco Ciudades de Buenos Aires: Pobreza y desigualdad urbana," *Medio Ambiente y Urbanizacion*, Buenos Aires: Instituto InterNaciónal de Medio Ambiente y Desarollo—America Latina, 2001, No. 56, July 2001, pp. 3–20.
24 S. O'Donnell, "*Villas, el nombre de la marginalidad*," *La Nación*, January 4, 2000, p. 11.
25 C. Palacios, "*Crece la poblacion en villas portenas*," *La Nación*, February 15, 2000, pp. 1 and 14.
26 World Bank, *Argentina: Poor People in a Rich Country*, Washington: World Bank, 1999, see also Inter-American Development Bank, *Facing Up to Inequality in Latin America: Economic and Social Progress in Latin America, 1998–1999 Report*, Washington: Inter-American Development Bank, 1998.
27 J.L. Machinea, "*La ausencia de un Estado compensador,*" *Clarín*, December 5, 1998, p. 25.

28 *Buenos Aires Herald*, August 10, 2000, p. 1.
29 *La Nación*, August 6, 2000, Section 7, p. 1.
30 Mirror on the Americas poll, 1999.
31 Ibid., p. 5.
32 *Buenos Aires Herald*, December 22, 2000, p. 1.
33 C. Krauss, "Argentina, Wobbly, Clears a Borrowing Hurdle," *New York Times*, November 9, 2000, p. C7.
34 Krugman, *New York Times*, November 22, 2000, p. A27.
35 H. Kohler, quoted in *Buenos Aires Herald*, December 27, 2000, p. 4.
36 *Pagina/12*, December 20, 2000, p. 2.
37 D. Marx, *Clarin Economico*, December 24, 2000, p. 4.
38 *Pagina/12*, op.cit, p. 4.
39 *Buenos Aires Herald*, December 22, 2000, p. 6.
40 *La Nación*, December 19, 2000, Section 2, p. 9.
41 *Buenos Aires Herald*, December 22, 2000, p. 12.
42 Ibid., p. 9.
43 *Buenos Aires Herald*, December 27, 2000, p. 12.
44 *Clarín*, December 24, 2000, *Economia* section, p. 16.
45 Ibid., p. 6.
46 Ibid., p. 22.
47 *Buenos Aires Herald*, December 24, 2000, p. 1.
48 IMF projections based on data from the Ministry of Economy, published in *Pagina/12*, February 20, 2001, p. 2.
49 P. Blustein, *And the Money Kept Flowing In (and Out): Wall Street, the IMF, and the Bankrupting of Argentina*, New York: Public Affairs, 2005; Michael Mussa, *Argentina and the IMF: From Triump to Tragedy*, Washington: Institute for International Economics, 2002; J. Stiglitz, "The Lessons of Argentina for Development in Latin America", in Michael Cohen and Margarita Gutman, eds., *Argentina in Collapse? The Americas Debate*, pp. 151–170; Rodolfo Terragno, *La simulacion: Argentina y el FMI: dos decadas de mentiras y autoenganos*, Buenos Aires: Planeta, 2005; Naum Minsburg, ed. *Los Guardianes del Dinero: Las politicas del FMI en la Argentina*, Buenos Aires: Grupo Editorial Norma, 2003; and Ernesto Tenembaum, *Enemigos: Argentina y el FMI, la apasionate discussion entre un periodista y uno de los hombres clave del Fondo en los noventa*, Buenos Aires: Grupo Editorial Norma, 2004.
50 J. Natanson, *Buenos Muchachos: Vida y obra de los economistas del establishment*, Buenos Aires: Libros de Zorzal, 2005.
51 G. Wilkinson, "Argentina's bark seen worse than its bite," *Reuters*, July 15, 2001, published in *Buenos Aires Herald*, p. 7.
52 S. Hanke, "Dollarize Argentina, Now," *Buenos Aires Herald*, July 14, 2001.
53 "Crunch Time: The United States needs to make up its mind about Argentina – and fast," *The Economist*, August 11, 2000, p. 10.
54 "Mixed Signals: Poor Argentina deserves better than confused messages from Washington," *The Economist*, August 9, 2001, pp. 56–57.
55 Reuters, "Fell asleep at the wheel," published in *Buenos Aires Herald*, July 12, 2001, p. 9.
56 Reuters, "No reason to default," published in *Buenos Aires Herald*, July 12, 2001, p. 8.
57 E. Yeyati and D. Valenzuela, *La Resurreccion: Historia de la Poscrisis Argentina*, Buenos Aires: Editorial Sudamericana, 2007, p. 23.
58 R. Navarro, "*Un viaje de ida: la lista de los que se llevaron la plata afuera en el ano del corralito,*" *Veintitres*, November 21, 2002, pp. 4–10.
59 Yeyati and Valenzuela, op. cit., p. 39.
60 E. Seman, "Political Dimensions of the Crisis" in Cohen and Gutman, op. cit., p. 120.
61 Frenkel, op. cit., p. 40.

62 Ibid., p. 48.
63 Margarita Gutman, "In Search of the (Lost) World to Come," in Cohen and Gutman, op. cit., p. 179.
64 Ibid., pp. 179–180.
65 Ibid., p. 182.
66 Cline, op. cit., p. 10.
67 Ibid., p. 11.
68 Idem.
69 Ibid., p. 12.
70 Ibid., p. 19.
71 Stiglitz, op. cit., pp. 160–161.
72 Cline, op. cit., p. 31.
73 Ibid., p. 32.
74 Ibid., p. 37.
75 Ibid., p. 38.
76 J. Fanelli, "Understanding Market Reforms in Latin America: Similar Reforms, Different Constituencies, Varied Results," in Jose Maria Fanelli, *Understanding Market Reforms in Latin America: Similar Reforms, Different Constituencies, Varied Results*, New York: Palgrave Macmillan, 2007, pp. 1–30.

4 Stabilization in 2002: stopping the free fall into poverty

1 S.Hintze, ed., *Trueque y Economia Solidaria*, Buenos Aires: UNDP, Universidad Nacional de General Sarmiento, Prometeo, 2003.
2 A. Fernandez and collaboradoras, *Politica y Subjetividad: Asambleas Barriales Y Fabricas Recuperadas*, Buenos Aires: Tinta Limones Ediciones, 2006, and Rafael Bielsa, Miguel Bonasso, y otros, *Que son las Asambleas Populares*, Buenos Aires: Pena Lillo Ediciones Continente, 2002.
3 E. Anguita, *Cartoneros*, Buenos Aires: 2004.
4 R. Hausman, "Argentina's route to salvation: A competitive exchange rate, a more open economy, and sound banks should be the priorities," *Financial Times*, January 4, 2002.
5 *Dagens Nyheter*, "Five Myths About Argentina," January 4, 2002.
6 J. Kahn and D. Sanger, "Bush's Policy on Argentina Signals Shift in Approach," *New York Times*, January 5, 2002.
7 M. Grondona, "One Last Chance for Argentina's Politicians," *New York Times*, January 6, 2002.
8 J. Sachs, "Duhalde's wrong turn," *Financial Times*, January 11, 2002.
9 L. Rohter, "Argentina's Crisis: It's Not Just Money," *New York Times*, January 13, 2002.
10 M. Wolf, "The mess Duhalde is making," *Financial Times*, January 16, 2002.
11 E. Yeyati and D. Valenzuela, *La Resurreccion: Historia de la Poscrisis Argentina*, Buenos Aires: Editorial Sudamericana, 2007, pp. 100–101.
12 D. Artana, quoted in Yeyati, op. cit., p. 103.
13 A. Ades, quoted in Yeyati, op. cit., p. 102.
14 T. di Tella, "*La Gran Coalicion: Que le paso a la Argentina?", Clarín*, January 13, 2002.
15 P. Kandel, "*El Presupuesto 2002 incluye una mayor presion impositiva," La Nacíon*, February 6, 2002.
16 M. Mulligan, "Fall of *peso* contained in Argentina," *Financial Times*, February 12, 2002.
17 A. Baron, "*EE.UU advierte:sin ajuste no apoyara la ayuda del FMI," Clarín*, February 22, 2002.
18 Yeyati, op. cit., p. 83.

19 *Clarín, Economico*, April 28, 2002, p. 5, and Peter Hakim, *The Washington Post*, March 5, 2002, quoted in Yeyati, op. cit., p. 153.
20 J. Stiglitz, "Lessons from Argentina for Latin American Development," in Michael Cohen and Margarita Gutman, eds., *Argentina in Collapse? The Americas Debate*, Buenos Aires: The New School and International Institute for Environment and Development, 2002, pp. 151–167.
21 I. Bermudez, "*La lista de deberes para Roberto Lavagna*," *Clarín*, April 28, 2002, pp. 2–3.
22 J. Godio, *Argentina: luces y sombras en el primer ano de transicion: Las mutacions de la economia, la sociedad, y la politica durante el gobierno de Eduardo Duhalde (enero-diciembre de 2002*, Buenos Aires: Editorial Biblos, 2003. pp. 99–101.
23 W. Cline, "Restoring Economic Growth in Argentina," Washington: World Bank Working Paper N.9/03, June 2003, pp. 42–43.
24 Ibid., p. 44.
25 Ibid., p. 46.
26 Ibid., p. 52.
27 *Clarín* article of May 15, 2000, cited in Cohen and Debowicz, "Las Cinco Ciudades de Buenos Aires: Pobreza y desigualdad urbana," *Medio Ambiente y Urbanizacion*, Buenos Aires: Instituto InterNaciónal de Medio Ambiente y Desarollo – America Latina, 2001, No. 56, July 2001.
28 World Bank, *Argentina: Crisis and Poverty 2003: A Poverty Assessment*, Report No. 26127-AR, Washington: The World Bank, July 2003, p. 9.
29 Godio, op. cit., p. 234.
30 L. Beccaria, "*El Mercado de trabajo luego de la crisis. Avances y desafios*," in Bernardo Kosacoff, (ed.) *Crisis, recuperacion y nuevos dilemmas: La economia argentina 2002–2007* Santiago de Chile: CEPAL-Naciones Unidas, 2007, pp. 359.
31 Godio, op. cit., p. 105.
32 Ibid., p. 105.
33 World Bank, op. cit., p. 10.
34 Godio op. cit., p. 113.
35 World Bank, op. cit., pp. 10–11.
36 Ibid., p. 12.
37 Ibid., p. 4.
38 Godio, op. cit., p. 363, quoted data from INDEC.
39 Ibid., p. 116.
40 Ibid., p. 103.
41 Ibid., p. 104.
42 A. Fiszbein, P. Giovagnoli, and I. Aduriz, "Argentina's crisis and its impact on household welfare," Buenos Aires: World Bank Working Paper N.1/02, November 2002, p. 4.
43 A higher number denotes a higher level of inequality in the distribution of income.
44 World Bank, op. cit., p. 6.
45 Beccaria, op. cit., p. 366.
46 Ibid., p. 388.
47 Godio, op. cit., p. 134.
48 World Bank, op. cit., p. 8.
49 Ibid., pp. 20–21.
50 Ibid., pp. 29–30.
51 Godio, op. cit., pp. 161–166.
52 Ibid., pp. 118–119.
53 *Clarín*, September 1–3, 2002, cited in Godio, op. cit., pp. 188–189.
54 Godio, op. cit., p. 188.
55 Ibid., p. 40.
56 R. Bielsa, M. Bonasso, and S. Calloni, *Que son las Asambleas Populares*, Buenos Aires: Pena Lillo, Ediciones Continente, 2002; and Ana Maria Fernandez and

collaborators, *Politica y Subjetividad: Asambleas Barriales y Fabricas Recuperadas*, Buenos Aires: Tinta Limon, 2006.
57 Godio, op. cit., pp. 38–39.
58 Ibid., p. 190.
59 Ibid., p. 209.
60 Ibid., pp. 153–157.
61 Ibid., p. 158.
62 *La Nación*, January 17, 2003, Section 2, p. 1.
63 *Pagina/12*, "*Los empresarios portenos opinan que estamos mal, pero vamos bien,*" January 2, 2003, p. 10.
64 M. Damill, R. Frenkel, and R. Maurizio, "Macroeconomic Policy Changes in Argentina in the Turn of the Century," mimeograph, December 21, 2006, pp. 13–15.
65 Idem.
66 R. Lavagna, quoted in *La Nación*, January 17, 2003, p. 1.
67 *La Nación*, January 17, 2003, Section 2, p. 2.
68 J. Todesca, quoted in *La Nación*, January 17, 2003, Section 2, p. 2.
69 "*Vivir sin el Fondo ya no es tan terrible*," *Pagina/12*, November 21, 2002, pp. 8–9.
70 A. Ferrer, "*Y si no les pagamos nada?*" *Veintitres*, November 21, 2002, pp. 14–17.

5 Electing a new government and facing the external world

1 N. Bar, "*Tiene anemia el 50% de los menores de 2 anos*," *La Nación*, p. 1 and p. 18.
2 M. Olivan, "*La Vida Perra,*" *Veintitres*, November 21, 2002, pp. 24–26.
3 R. Sietecase, "*Hambre: Chiche la sabia*"; *Veintitres*, November 21, 2002, pp. 20–23.
4 N. Kirchner, Inaugural Speech, May 25, 2003, quoted in World Bank, *Country Assistance Strategy 2006–2008*, Washington: World Bank, 2006, p. 21.
5 Ibid., pp. 21–22.
6 Conversations of Nestor Kirchner and Torcuato S. DiTella; *Despues del Derrumbe: Teoria y Practica Politica en la Argentina Que Viene*, Buenos Aires: Galerna, 2003.
7 Ibid., p. 22.
8 Ibid., p. 30.
9 Ibid., p. 33.
10 Idem.
11 Idem., p. 41.
12 Ibid., p. 151.
13 M. Damill, R. Frenkel, and R. Maurizio, "Argentina: A Decade of Currency Board: An Analysis of Growth, Employment, and Income Distribution," Buenos Aires: CEDES, February 2002. p. 16.
14 Ibid.
15 World Bank, op. cit., Annex B, p. 83.
16 Nestor Kirchner, remarks at The New School, New York, September 17, 2003 in response to a question from a correspondent from *Financial Times.*
17 Roberto Lavagna, cited in Damill, Frenkel, and Maurizio, op. cit., p. 20.
18 World Bank, op. cit., Annex B, pp. 83–84.
19 Ibid., p. 86.
20 Luis Cerlotto interview with Felipe Rovera, "*La recuperacion me permite pelear por mas inversions,*" *Clarín*, January 16, 2006, p. 16.
21 Damill, Frenkel, and Maurizio, op. cit., p. 18.
22 "*Historico: el riesgo pais cayo por debajo de los 200 punto,*" *Clarín*, January 19, 2007, and "*El riesgo pais bajo otro 4% y llego a su minimo en 10 anos,*" *La Nación*, October 26, 2006.
23 C. Zlotnik, "*La deuda externa, en baja,*" *Pagina/12*, March 23, 2007, p. 11.
24 I.Bermudez, "*Con mas inversion y consume, el crecimiento en 2006 fue de 8.5 percent,*" *Clarín*, March 16, 2007, p. 16.

25 Idem.
26 "Mediamap 2005: Los que mas invierten," *Noticias*, October 28, 2005, pp. 40–42.
27 World Bank, *Project Appraisal Document 32463-AR*, p. 1.
28 Idem.
29 Ibid., p. 3.
30 Ibid., p. 2.
31 UNCTAD, *World Investment Report*, Geneva: UNCTAD, 2006.
32 H.A. Mon, "*Preoccupa a Wall Street la economia argentina,*" *La Nación*, August 6, 2006, Section 2, pp. 1–2.
33 D. Cecchini and J. Zocolillo, *Los Nuevos Conquistadores*, Madrid: Foca, 2002.
34 P. O'Neill comments quoted in *Financial Times*, August 21, 2002, p. 13.
35 L. Gutierrez, quoted in *Buenos Aires Herald*, July 4, 2004, p. 3.

6 Strengthening the state to manage at home

1 M. Khan, "Governance, Economic Growth and Development", in Jose Antonio Ocampo, Jomo K.S., and Rob Vos, eds. *Growth Divergences: Explaining Differences in Economic Performance*, New York: Zed Books, 2007, pp. 285–323.
2 S. Levitsky and M. Murillo, eds. *Argentine Democracy: The Politics of Institutional Weakness*, University Park, Pa.: Penn State University Press, 2005 and Pablo Spiller and Mariano Tommasi, *The Institutional Foundations of Public Policy in Argentina*, New York: Cambridge University Press, 2007; and many others.
3 T. Donghi, *Revolucion y Guerra: Formacion de una Elite Dirigente en la Argentina Criolla*, Buenos Aires: Siglo XXI Editores, 1972; T. Donghi, *Vida y muerte de la Republica verdadera (1910–1930)*, Buenos Aires: Ariel, 1999, T. Donghi, *La Argentina y La Tormenta del Mundo: Ideas e ideologias entre 1930 y 1945*, Buenos Aires: Siglo veintiuno editores Argentina, 2003; Vito Tanzi, Argentina: *An Economic Chronicle: How one of the richest countries in the world lost its wealth*, New York: Jorge Pinto Books, 2007; Carlos H. Waisman, *Reversal of Development in Argentina: Postwar Counter Revolutionary Policies and Their Structural Consequences*, Princeton: Princeton University Press, 1987, Maria Seoane, *Nosotros: Apuntes sobre pasiones,razones y trampas de los argentines entre dos siglos*, Buenos Aires: Editorial Sudamericana, 2006.
4 See, for example, S. Levitsky and M. Murillo, eds. *Argentine Democracy: The Politics of Institutional Weakness*, University Park, Pennsylvania: Pennsylvania State University Press, 2005.
5 O. Chisari, A. Estache, and C. Romero, "Winners and Losers from Utilities Privatizations: Lessons from a General Equilibrium Model for Argentina," Universidad de la Empresa, Buenos Aires, and the World Bank, Washington, 1996.
6 S. Galiani, P. Gertler, and E. Schargrodsky, "Water for Life: The Impact of the Privatization of Water Services on Child Mortality." *Journal of Political Economy*, Vol. 113, No. 1.
7 Personal communication from Andrea Catannazi, Universidad Nacional de General Sarmiento.
8 D. Azpiazu and M. Schorr, *Cronica de una sumision anunciada: Las renegociaciones con las empresas privatizadas bajo la administration Duhalde*, Buenos Aires: Siglo veintuno editors argentina and FLACSO, 2003, and Karina Forcinito, "*Notas sobre el papel del Estado Argentino en la reestructuracion regresiva de la relacion entre el capital y la fuerza de trabajo: El caso de los sectores de infraestructura privatizados durante los anos noventa,*" pp. 83–106 en Carlos Vilas y otros, ed., *Estado y politica en la Argentina actual*, Buenos Aires: Universidad Nacional de General Sarmiento and Prometeo, 2005.
9 M. Gene, Un *mundo feliz: Imagenes de los trabajadores en el primer peronismo 1946–1955*, Buenos Aires: Universidad de San Andres and Fondo de Cultura Economica, 2005.

10 T. Donghi, "Why Did Argentina Adopt a Neoliberal Model?" in Michael Cohen and Margarita Gutman, eds., *Argentina in Collapse? The Americas Debate*, Buenos Aires: The New School and International Institute for Environment and Development – America Latina, 2002, p. 24.
11 The author once asked a 65-year-old Argentine professional if his pension amount was before or after taxes. The reply was "what are taxes?"
12 M. Melo, "Institutional Weakness and the Puzzle of Argentina's Low Taxation," *Latin American Politics and Society*, Vol. 49, No. 4, 2008, pp. 125–126.
13 B. Geddes, *Politician's Dilemma: Building State Capacity in Latin America*, Berkeley: University of California Press, 1994.
14 Melo, op. cit.
15 Ibid., p. 113.
16 A. Quiroga, "La recaudacion llega este ano a $150.000 millones y es record," *Clarín*, December 31, 2006, p. 18.
17 I. Bermudez, "*La presion tributaria marca un maximo de 23.5 percent del product,*" *Clarín*, December 31, 2006, p. 18.
18 *Clarín*, March 21, 2007, p. 3.
19 World Bank, *Project Appraisal Document on Proposed Loan to Argentina for Heads of Household Transition Project*, Report No. 32463-AR, Washington: The World Bank, February 21, 2006, p. 4.
20 Ibid., p. 5.
21 Ibid., p. 7.
22 Ibid., p. 9.
23 *La Nación*, March 17, 2007, p. 8.
24 M. Justesen, "Living on the Edge: Risk, Protection, Behavior, and Outcomes of Argentine Youth," World Bank Policy Research Working Paper No. 4485, January 2008.
25 L. Iurcovich, "Geografia de la probreza argentina," IEco, October 21, 2007, p. 5.
26 *La Nación, "La deuda social sale muy despacio del default,*" December 24, 2005, Sec.2, pp. 1–2.
27 R. Dellatorre, "*Son menos, pero tadavia son demasiados,*" *Pagina/12*, September 21, 2006.
28 M. Dinatale, "*Aumentara en $1600 millones el gasto social,*" *La Nación*, Jan.3, 2007, p. 1 and p. 7.
29 Gobierno de la Republica Argentina, *Trabajo, ocupacion y empleo: Salarios, empresas y empleo 2003–2006*, Serie Estudios/5, Buenos Aires: Ministerio de Trabajo, Empleo y Seguridad Social, September 2006, p. 7.
30 Ibid., pp. 19–20.
31 Ibid., p. 21.
32 Ibid., p. 26.
33 Ibid., p. 39.
34 Gobierno de la Republica Argentina, *Trabajo, ocupacion y empleo: Dimensiones del trabajo en el Nuevo modelo economic social, Serie Estudios/6*, Buenos Aires: Ministerio de Trabajo, Empleo y Seguridad Social, February 2007, p. 20.
35 Ibid., p. 40.
36 Ibid., pp. 80–81.
37 Ibid., p. 84.
38 Ibid., p. 90.
39 Gobierno de la Republica Argentina, *Trabajo, ocupacion y empleo: Los retos laborales en un proceso de crecimiento sostenido, Serie Estudios/7*, Buenos Aires: Ministerio de Trabajo, Empleo y Seguridad Social, November 2007, pp. 23–24.
40 I. Bermudez, "*El empleo en negro no cede: afecta al 47.5% de los asalariados,*" *Clarín*, June 11, 2005, p. 3.
41 UNDP, *Argentina Despues de la Crisis: Un Tiempo de Oportunidades, Informe de Desarrollo Humano 2005*, Buenos Aires: UNDP, 2005, p. 99.

42 S. Stang, "*Los salaries en negro, mas lejos de los formales,*" *La Nación*, August 6, 2006, Section 2, p. 7.
43 Ibid., p. 68.
44 See annual reports of the *Centro de Estudio Legales y Sociales* on the status of legal institutions in Argentina.
45 G. Helmke, "Enduring Uncertainty: Court-Executive Relations in Argentina in the 1990s and Beyond" in Steven Levitsky and Maria Victoria Murillo, eds., *Argentine Democracy: The Politics of Institutional Weakness*, University Park, Pennsylvania: Pennsylvania University Press, 2005, p. 141.
46 Ibid., p. 143.
47 Idem.
48 S. Boschi, "*La Corte Suprema, con nuevos aires y menos perfil politico,*" *Clarín*, December 31, 2006, p. 16.
49 H. Verbitsky, *The Silence: from Paulo VI to Bergoglio, the secret links between the Church and the Navy Mechanics School*, 2005.
50 World Bank, *Argentina 2006–2008: Country Assistance Strategy*, Washington: The World Bank, 2006.
51 Cristina Fernandez de Kirchner, June 18, 2008, speech at Plaza de Mayo, Buenos Aires.

7 A new government to address the geographies of inequality

1 M. Gutman and J. Hardoy, *Buenos Aires 1536–2006: Historia urbana del Area Metropolitana*, Buenos Aires: Ediciones Infinito, 2007.
2 M. Seoane, *N*, June 11, 2005.
3 N. de Duren; "Growth and Poverty in the Urban Fringe: Decentralization, Dispersion, and Inequality in Buenos Aires," Ph.D. dissertation, MIT, June 2007.
4 M. Gene, *Un mundo feliz: Imagenes de los trabajadores en el primer peronismo 1946–1955*, Buenos Aires: Universidad de San Andres and Fondo de Cultura Economica, 2005.
5 See Margarita Gutman, ed., *Buenos Aires 1910: Memoria del Porvenir*, Buenos Aires: Gobierno de la Ciudad de Buenos Aires, 1999.
6 UNDP, *Argentina Despues de la Crisis: Un Tiempo de Oportunidades, Informe de Desarrollo Humano 2005*, Buenos Aires: UNDP, 2005, pp. 62–63.
7 Ibid., p. 85.
8 Ibid., p. 148.
9 M. Melo, "Institutional Weakness and the Puzzle of Argentina's Low Taxation," *Latin American Politics and Society*, Vol. 49, No. 4, 2008, pp. 125–126, and Pablo Spiller and Mariano Tommasi, *The Institutional Foundations of Public Policy in Argentina*, New York: Cambridge University Press, 2007.
10 G. Tella, "*Rupturas y continuidades en el sistema de centralidades de Buenos Aires*" in Max Welch Guerra, ed. *Buenos Aires a la deriva: Transformaciones urbanas recientes*, Buenos Aires: Editorial Biblos, 2005, pp. 29–73.
11 E. Soja, *Postmetropolis: Critical Studies of Cities and Regions*, Oxford: Blackwell, 2000 and Stephen Graham and Simon Marvin, *Splintering Urbanism: Networked Infrastructures, Technological Mobilities, and the Urban Condition*, New York: Routledge, 2001.
12 M. Svampa, *Los Que Ganaron: la vida en los countries y barrios privadas*, Buenos Aires: Editorial Biblos, 2001, p. 57.
13 M. Cravino, ed., *Los mil barrios (in)formales: Aportes para la construccion de un observatorio del habitat popular del Area Metropolitana de Buenos Aires*, Buenos Aires: Universidad Nacional de General Sarmiento, 2008.
14 Ibid., p. 21.
15 Duren, op. cit.

16 M. Dinatale, *El Festival de la Pobreza*, Buenos Aires: La Crujia Ediciones, 2004.
17 The pattern of social exclusion had grown considerably in the 1990s. See Alberto Minujin, ed., *Desigualdad y Exclusion: Deafios para la politica social en la Argentina de fin de siglo*, Buenos Aires: Losada and UNICEF, 1996, and Cravino, op. cit.
18 INDEC, "*La Evolucion de la Desocupacion*," reported in *La Nación*, June 7, 2006, Seccion 2, p. 2.
19 F. Forni, ed., *De la Exclusion a la Organizacion: Hacia la integracion de los pobres en los nuevos barrios del conurbano bonaerense*, Buenos Aires: Ediciones Ciccus, 2002.
20 Ibid., p. 51, also Cravino, op. cit., and Adriana Clemente and Monica Girolami, eds., *Territorio, emergencia, e intervencion social: un modelo para desarmar*, Buenos Aires: IIED-AL, 2006.
21 P. Perelman, coordinador, *La Pobreza en el Area Metropolitana de Buenos Aires: Una Vision de sus caracteristicas y su evolucion*, Buenos Aires: Instituto Internacional de Medio Ambiente y Desarrollo – America Latina t Fundacion MAPFRE America, 1994; and Presidencia de la Nacion Argentina, *La Ciudad Para Todos: El Desafio de la Pobreza Para la Planificacion y Gestion Urbano Ambiental*, Buenos Aires: Comision de Tierras Fiscales Nacionales, 1994.
22 E. Stillwagon, *Stunted Lives, Stagnant Economies*, New Jersey and London: Rutgers University Press, 1998.
23 M. Cohen and D. Debowicz; "The Five Cities of Buenos Aires: An Inquiry into Poverty and Inequality in Urban Argentina," *The Encyclopedia of Sustainable Development*, edited by Saskia Sassen, Paris: UNESCO, 2004.
24 I. Bermudez, "*Mas de cien mil chicos trabajan en las calles del Gran Buenos Aires*," *Clarín*, June 13, 2005, p. 12.
25 K. Forcinito and C. Nahon, "La fibula de las privatizaciones: vicios privados, beneficios publicos? El caso de la Argentina 1990–2005," Observatorio Argentina, Grupo de Trabajo Economico, June 2005.
26 INDEC.
27 Annual Household Survey (EPH), INDEC 2010.

8 The politics of redistribution: the conflict with el campo

1 M. Grondona, "*Nada para la sociedad; Todo par el Estado,*" *La Nación*, March 16, 2008, p. 33.
2 *La Nación*, March 16, 2008, p. 10.
3 M. Wainfeld, Pagina/*12*, March 16, 2008, p. 8.
4 M. Rapoport, *Critica* March 16, 2008, p. 18.
5 *La Nación*, March 18, 2008, p. 16.
6 *La Nación*, March 19, 2008, Section 2, p. 1.
7 *Critica*, March 25, 2008, p. 1.
8 *Critica*, March 28, 2008, pp. 2–3.
9 J. Feinmann, *Pagina/12*, March 30, 2008, p. 40.
10 N. Casullo, *Pagina/12*, March 30, 2008, p. 12.
11 E. Tenembaum, "*Estamos todos locos*," *Pagina/12*, March 30, 2008, p. 13.
12 J. Sola, *La Nación*, March 30, 2008, p. 1.
13 A. Ferrer, "*Debate sobre el rumbo del desarrollo nacional*," *Cash*, March 30, 2008, p. 3.
14 "*No somos golpistas*," *La Nación*, March 30, 2008, p. 21.
15 J. Oviedo, "*Corralito para la soja*," *La Nación*, March 30, 2008, Section 2, p. 3.
16 *La Nación*, March 30, 2008, Section 2, p. 1.
17 N. Arganaraz, "Los desafios fiscales de 2008," *La Nación*, March 30, 2008, Section 2, p. 2.
18 *Critica*, March 31, 2008, p. 1.

19 *Critica*, April 2, 2008, pp. 1–3.
20 *Clarín*, April 1, 2008, pp. 3–4.
21 *Pagina/12*, April 6, 2008, p. 1.
22 *Critica*, April 3, 2008, p. 2.
23 *Clarín*, April 3, 2008, p. 6.
24 H. Tumini, "*Los aciertos y los errors*," *Pagina/12*, April 6, 2008, p. 10.
25 *Pagina/12*, April 6, 2008, p. 3.
26 *Clarín*, April 15, 2008, p. 5.
27 *La Nación*, April 16, 2008, p. 6.
28 *Critica*, April 21, 2008, pp. 1–5.
29 H. Verbitsky, "Actores ocultos," *Pagina/12*, May 4, 2008, pp. 4–5.
30 *Critica*, May 18, 2008, p. 10.
31 *Pagina/12*, May 16, 2008, p. 11.
32 *La Nación*, May 18, 2008, p. 1, p. 10.
33 Ibid., p. 10.
34 J. Natanson, "*Es la micro-economia*," *Pagina/12*, May 4, 2008, p. 6.
35 *La Nación*, May 11, 2008, p. 15.
36 *La Nación*, May 4, 2008, p. 9.
37 H. Verbitsky, *Pagina/12*, May 11, 2008, p. 4.
38 *Pagina/12*, May 18, 2008, p. 1.
39 J. Pierri, *Pagina/12*, May 16, 2008, p. 8.
40 R. Aronskind, *Pagina/12*, May 15, 2008, p. 10.
41 *Critica*, May 18, 2008, p. 9.
42 E. van der Kooy, *Clarín*, May 18, 2008, p. 31.
43 *Clarín*, May 24, 2008, p. 1.
44 *Pagina/12*, May 25, 2008, p. 1.
45 W. Pertot, *Pagina/12*, May 25, 2008, p. 3.
46 "*Argentina somos todos*," *Pagina/12*, May 25, 2008, p. 7.
47 *Clarín*, May 26, 2008, p. 1.
48 *Critica*, May 29, 2008, p. 1.
49 M. Becerra, *Pagina/12*, May 27, 2008, p. 6.
50 *La Nación*, June 1, 2008, Section Campo, p. 1.
51 M. Wainfeld, *Pagina/12*, June 1, 2008, p. 7.
52 *La Nación*, June 18, 2008, p. 3.
53 *Pagina/12*, June 19, 2008, p. 3.
54 *Pagina/12*, June 13, 2008, p. 1.
55 *Pagina/12*, June 1, 2008, p. 1.
56 A. Rofman, "*La voz que los que no tienen voz*," *Critica*, May 31, 2008, p. 8.
57 *La Nación*, June 22, 2008, p. 10.
58 Ibid., Section 6, p. 1.
59 *Pagina/12*, June 24, 2008, p. 1.
60 Presidencia de la Nación, "*Todo Argentino tien derecho a estar informado*" in *La Nación*, June 25, 2008, p. 11.
61 *Critica*, June 26, 2008, p. 1.
62 *Critica*, July 1, 2008, p. 1.
63 A. Ferrer, *Pagina/12*, July 3, 2008, p. 11.
64 *La Nación*, July 5, 2008, Section 2, p. 1.
65 *La Nación*, July 6, 2008, p. 19.
66 Quoted in *Perfil*, July 6, 2008, p. 1.
67 *Pagina/12*, July 13, 2008, pp. 1–4.
68 *Pagina/12*, July 10, 2008, p. 1.
69 T. Lowi, "American Business, Public Policy, Case Studies, and Political Theory," *World Politics*, Vol. 16, No. 4, July 1964, pp. 677–715.
70 J. Lanata, *Critica*, June 1, 2008, pp. 6–7.

71 R. Dahrendorf, *Class and Class Conflict in Industrial Society*, Stanford: Stanford University Press,1959.
72 S. Etchemendy, "Constructing Reform Coalitions: The Politics of Compensations in Argentina's Economic Liberalization," *Latin American Politics and Society*, Vol. 43, No. 3, Autumn 2001, pp. 1–35.
73 Ibid., p. 22.
74 P. Bachrach and M. Baratz, "Decisions and non-decisions: an analytical framework," The *American Political Science Review*, Vol. 57, No. 3, Sep. 1963, pp. 632–642.
75 E. Arceo and E. Basualdo, "*Los Cambios de los Sectores Dominantes en America Latina Bajo el Neoliberalismo: La problematica propuesta*," in Eduardo Basualdo and Enrique Arceo, eds., *Neoliberalismo y sectores dominantes: Tendencias globales y experiencias nacionales*, Buenos Aires" CLACSO Libros, 2006.
76 A. Wortman, *Construccion Imaginaria de la Desigualdad Social*, Buenos Aires: CLACSO, 2007.

9 Urban inequality

1 S. Morley, *The Impact of the Macroeconomic Environment on Urban Poverty*, Santiago: CEPAL, 1998.
2 R. Prud'homme, H. Huntzinger, P. Kopp, "Stronger Municipalities for Stronger Cities in Argentina," report for Inter-American Development Bank, January 2, 2004.
3 INDEC—Population and Housing Census 2010.
4 Clarín, September 7, 1998. According to INDEC, this is the amount of money required for the basic expenditures of a couple with two children.
5 See also *Clarín*, September 7, 1998.
6 See *Clarín*, October 10, 1998.
7 INDEC, op. cit.
8 INDEC 2009.
9 I. Bermúdez, "La mitad de los hogares vive con meons de $3.000 al mes," *Clarín*, June 29, 2010.
10 Atlas Ambiental de Buenos Aires, 2010, www.atlasdebuenosaires.gov.ar.
11 I. Bermúdez, "La decocupación golpea fuerte a los jóvenes del conurbano," *Clarín*, January 26, 2011.
12 M. Cravino, ed., *Los mil barrios (in)formales: Aportes para la construccion de un observatorio del habitat popular del Area Metropolitana de Buenos Aires*, Buenos Aires: Universidad Nacional de General Sarmiento, 2008, p. 105.
13 P. Morosi,"Vivien más de 2 millones en las villas bonaerenses," *La Nación*, April 5, 2010.
14 R. Wagner. "*No se explican la toma de Soldati sin entender el fenómeno de los barrios cerrados*," *Fundación Metropolitana*, December 2010.
15 Atlas Ambiental de Buenos Aires, op. cit.
16 J. Hardoy and F. Almansi, "Assessing the Scale of Urban Poverty in Buenos Aires," *International Institute for Environment and Development (IIED)*, Human Settelments Working Paper Series, 2011.
17 P. Cicolella, "Globalizacion y dualizacion en la Region Metropolitana de Buenos Aires. Grandes inversions y reestructuracion socioterritorial en los anos 90," *EURE*, Vol. 25, No. 76, Santiago de Chile: Instituto de Estudios Urbanos, Facultad de Arquitectura y Bellas Artes, Pontificia Universidad Catolica de Chile, 1999, pp. 5–28.
18 The relation between total wages of Federal Capital and Argentina is 25% (FADU-GCBA, Estudio de la Ciudad de Buenos Aires en el Sistema Metropolitano, 1999).
19 *Plan Estratégico de Buenos Aires* 2016, p. 72.
20 Encuesta Anual de Hogares de la Ciudad Buenos Aires (EAH) 2009, p. 3.
21 *Plan Estratégico* op. cit., p. 130.

22 "Usurpaciones y 'tomas', polémica y después," *Fundación Metropolitana.* January 2011.
23 *Plan Estratégico* op. cit., p. 75.
24 Ibid., p. 73.
25 Encuesta Anual de Hogares de la Ciudad de Buenos Aires (EAH) 2008 p. 109.
26 Ibid., p. 119.
27 Ibid., p. 114.
28 *Metropolitana* op. cit.
29 The correlation coefficient is 0.35 when correlating public investment per capita with primary completion rate, 0.24 when correlating public investment per capita with secondary completion rate, and –0.11 when correlating public investment per capita with secondary over-age rate.
30 Nevertheless, the linear correlation between percentage of beds and per capita investment in infrastructure and education results are low (0.49 y 0.40, respectively).
31 *Plan Estratégico de Buenos Aires*, 2010, p. 51.
32 Ibid. p. 79.
33 Rey and A. Lopez, eds., *Entre technocratas globalizados y politicos clientelistas: Derrotero del ajuste neoliberal en el Estado argentino*, Buenos Aires: Prometeo, 2005.
34 P. Pirez, "Buenos Aires: fragmentation and privatization of the metropolitan city," *Environment and Urbanization*, Volume 14, No. 1, April 2002, pp. 145–158.
35 The southern area of the city bordering the La Matanza-Riachuelo river receives 34.2 percent of the daily contamination of the city, according the city government.
36 E. Magnani, "El negocio de la basura, Buenos Aires," *Pagina/12*, March 26, 2006.
37 D. Cravacuore, S. Ilari, and A. Villar, *La articulacion en la gestion municipal: Actores y politicas*, Buenos Aires: Universidad Nacional de Quilmes Editorial, 2004.
38 M. O'Donnell, *El Aparato, Los intendentes del Conurbano y las cajas negras de la politica*, Buenos Aires: Aguilar, 2005.
39 This process is well documented in Magdalena Chiara and Maria Mercedes Di Virgilio, *Gestion social y municipios: De los escritorios del Banco Mundial a los barrios del Gran Buenos Aires*, Buenos Aires: Prometeo and Universidad Nacional de General Sarmiento, 2005, pp. 120–121; see also Serio Raul Ilari, "La gestion local de la politica social: los casos de Quilmes y Florencio Varela," in Alicia Ziccardi, ed., *Pobreza, Desigualdad Social y Ciudadania: Los Limites de la Politicas Sociales en America Latina*, Buenos Aires: CLACSO, 2002.
40 O'Donnell, op. cit., pp. 99–100.
41 Chiara and Di Virgilio, op.cit., pp. 125–138; See also Javier Auyero, *Poor People's Politics: Peronist Survival Networks and the Legacy of Evita*, Durham: Duke University Press, 2001.
42 Chiara and Di Virgilio, op. cit., see tables on pp. 132 and 134.
43 A. Clemente and C. Smulovitz, ed. *Descentralizacion, politicas sociales y participacion democratica en Argentina*, Buenos Aires: IIED and the Woodrow Wilson International Center for Scholars, 2004.
44 For an excellent study of the complexities of local politics in the *conurbano*, see Sabina Frederic, *Buenos vecinos, malos politicos: Moralidad y politica en el Gran Buenos Aires*, Buenos Aires: Prometeo, 2004.
45 Michael Cohen, "La construccion del territorio nacional: infraestructura y metropolis en el proximo siglo," Lecture, Buenos Aires: FADU, July 1999.
46 Constitution of the Republic of Argentina, Article 129, 1994.
47 Personal communication.
48 See chapters on the communas in Marcelo Escolar, Gastavo Badia, and Sabina Frederic, eds, *Federalismo y descentralizacion en grandes ciudades: Buenos Aires en perspective comparativa*, Buenos Aires: Banco Cuidad and Prometeo, 2004.
49 H. Shah, *Argentina Privatization Program: A Review of Five Cases*, Washington: The World Bank, 1996 see Lisa Guaqueta, *Public Services and Citizenship: The case of*

the privatizations of electricity, gas, and water in Buenos Aires, New York: The Argentina Observatory, 2006.

50 D. Cecchini y J. Zicolillo, *Los Nuevos Conquistadores, El papel del gobierno y las empresas españolas en el expolio de Argentina*, Madrid: Foca, 2002.

51 Ciccolella, op. cit.

52 Instituto Internacional de Medio Ambiente y Desarrollo-America Latina, *La Lucha por Acceder al Agua: La tierra, la expansion y prestacion de servicios de agua y saneamiento en barrios informales de Buenos Aires*, Buenos Aires: IIED, 2005.

53 D. Azpiazu y M. Schorr, *Crónica de una sumision anunciada*, Buenos Aires: Siglo XXI Editores Argentina SA, 2003.

54 A useful overview of the costs and benefits of privatization in Argentina is in Karina Forcinito and Cecilia Nahon, "La fibula de las privatizaciones: vicios privados, beneficios publicos? El caso de la Argentina 1990–2005," Observatorio Argentina, Grupo de Trabajo Economico, junio 2005. See also Eduardo Basualdo, Daniel Azpiazu, et al; *El proceso de privatizacion en Argentina: la renegociacion con las empresas privadas*, Buenos Aires: Pagina 12 and Universidad Nacional de Quilmes, 2002.

55 C. Vilas, "Privatization of the Water and Sanitation System in the Buenos Aires Metropolitan Area," A Report to the Globalization Research Center, University of South Florida, 2004.

56 M. Schorr, *Industria y nacion: Poder economico, neoliberalismo y alternatives de reindustrializacion en la Argentina contemporanea*, Buenos Aires: Edhasa y IDEAS, 2004.

57 CEPAL, Gobierno de la Ciudad de Buenos Aires, Producto Bruto Geografico de la Ciudad de Buenos Aires 1993/1998, Proyecto GCBA/CEPAL, 1999.

58 Ibid., p. 3.

59 Ibid., p. 45.

60 Ibid., p. 34.

61 Ibid., pp. 41–42.

62 M. Seoane, "Las marcas de la politica argentina: Un siglo de accion y excepcion", in Gutman, *Construir Bicentenarios*, pp. 109–117.

10 From crisis management to sustainable development: extending the time horizon

1 S. Fukuda-Parr, ed. *Gene Revolution: GM Crops and Unequal Development*, London and Sterling, Virginia: Earthscan, 2007.

2 J. Santiso, *Latin America's Political Economy of the Possible: Beyond Good Revolutionaries and Free Marketeers*, Cambridge: MIT University Press, 2006.

3 CEPES, *"Hacia un proyecto economico de mediano y largo plazo,"* in Chacho Alvarez, ed., *El desarrollo economic de la Argentina en el mediano y largo plazo: Hacia la construccion de consensus*, Buenos Aires: CEPES and Prometeo, 2005, pp. 17–18.

4 N. Kirchner and T. Di Tella, Despues del Derumbe: Teoria y Practica Politica en la Argentina Que Viene, Buenos Aires: Editorial Galerna, 2003.

5 L. Pagani, "Conclusiones," in Chacho Alvarez, ed., *El desarrollo economic de la Argentina en el mediano y largo plazo: Hacia la construccion de consensus*, Buenos Aires: CEPES and Prometeo, 2005, pp. 229–230.

6 M. V. Murillo, "Tango de un desencanto anunciado," *Foreign Affairs en Espanol*, Vol. 2, No. 2, Summer 2002.

7 President Cristina Fernandez de Kirchner, news conference at Olivos, August 2, 2008.

8 See Chapter 3, fn.5.

11 Argentina's experience and the search for alternatives

1 M. Damill, R. Frenkel, and R. Maurizio, "Macroeconomic Policy Changes in Argentina in the Turn of the Century," mimeograph, December 21, 2006.
2 A. Ferrer, speech to Congress, July 2008, and articles in *Sur.*
3 See Roberto Frenkel article 1996, and Frenkel chapter in Cohen and Gutman, eds., *Argentina in Collapse: America Debates*, Margarita Gutman, "In Search of the (Lost) World to Come," in Cohen and Gutman, op. cit.
4 M. Garcia, "Transition challenges in the Latin American context," in Michael Cohen and Margarita Gutman, eds., *Latin America on the Move: The Post Neo-Liberal Transition*, New York: The Observatory on Latin America, 2007, pp. 31–36.
5 J. Stiglitz, "The Lessons of Argentina for Development in Latin America", in Cohen and Gutman, op,cit., pp. 151–170.
6 V. Tanzi, *Argentina: An Economic Chronicle*, New York: Jorge Pinto Books, 2007.
7 *Clarín*, August 4, 2008, p. 4, presenting data from ABECES.
8 Ibid.
9 L. Corradini, "*Tension con Brasil por el comercio global*," *La Nación*, July 27, 2008, p. 15.
10 H. Chang, *Kicking Away The Ladder: Development Strategy In Historical Perspective*, Anthem Press, 2002.
11 C. Tomada, Remarks to "Consejo Nacional del Empleo, la Productividad, y el Salario Minimo Vital y Movil," July 28, 2008, quoted in *Pagina/12*, July 29, 2008, p. 3.
12 World Bank, *Country Assistance Strategy for the Argentine Republic 2006–2008*, Washington: The World Bank, 2006, pp. 21–23.
13 R. Ffrench-Davis, *Reformas para América Latina*, Buenos Aires: Siglo XXI Editores, 2005.
14 F. Fukuyama, *The End of History*, New York: Free Press, 1992.
15 J. Santiso, *Latin America's Political Economy of the Possible: Beyond Good Revolutionaries and Free Marketeers*, Cambridge: MIT University Press, 2006.
16 Fidel Castro, personal communication to the author, 1992.
17 G. Grandin, *The Last Colonial Massacre: Latin America in the Cold War*, Chicago: University of Chicago Press, 2004), and Greg Grandin, *Empire's Workshop: Latin America, the United States, and the Rise of the New Imperialism*, New York: Metropolitan Books., Henry Holt and Company, 2006.

Bibliography

Abal Medina, J., ed., *Evaluando el desempeno democratico de las instituciones politicas argentinas*, Buenos Aires: Prometeo, 2007.

—— ed., *Participacion y control ciudadanos: El functionamiento de los mecanismos institucionales electorales y societales de accountability en la Argentina*, Buenos Aires: Prometeo, 2009.

Acuna, C., Galiani, S., and Tommasi, M., "Understanding reform: the case of Argentina," in Jose Maria Fanelli, ed., *Understanding Market Reforms in Latin America: Similar Reforms, Different Constituencies, Varied Results*, New York: Palgrave Macmillan, 2007.

Aguiar de Medeiros, C., "Crecimiento e igualdad: los desafios de Brasil. Los politicas del Nuevo gobierno en perspective historica," *Toda Via: Pensamiento y cultura en America Latina*, Buenos Aires: Fundacion OSDE, 2004.

Ali, T., *Pirates of the Caribbean: Axis of Hope. Evo Morales, Fidel Castro, Hugo Chavez*, London: Verso, 2006.

Altimir, O., "Desigualdad, empleo y pobreza en America Latina: Efectos del ajuste y del cambio en el estilo de desarrollo," *Desarrollo Economico*, 17 (145), 1997.

Alvarez, C., ed., *La Argentina de Kirchner y el Brasil de Lula*, Buenos Aires: Prometeo y CEPES, 2003.

—— *El desarrollo economic de la Argentina en el mediano y largo plaza: Hacia la construccion de consensus*, Buenos Aires: Prometeo y CEPES, 2005.

Amann, E. and Baer, W. "Neo-liberalism and its consequences in Brazil," *Journal of Latin American Studies*, 34 (4), 2002: 945–959.

Amsden, A., *The Rise of the "Rest": Challenges to the West from Late-Industrializing Economies*, New York: Oxford University Press, 2001.

Appadurai, A., *Fear of Small Numbers: An Essay on the Geography of Anger*, Durham, NC: Duke University Press, 2006.

Arza, V., "Contexto macroeconomico y comportamiento de largo plazo de las empresas: la inversion en I+D y en maquinaria en Argentina durante los años 90," *Desarrollo Economico*, 47 (187), 2007: 459–486.

Auyero, J., *Poor People's Politics: Peronist Survival Networks and the Legacy of Evita*, Durham, NC: Duke University Press, 2001.

Azpiazu, D., "Ensenanzas del programa de privatizaciones desarrollado en la Argentina, 1990–1993," *Revista de CEPAL*, 54, 1994.

Azpiazu, D. and Schorr, M., *Cronica de una sumision anunciada: Las renegociaciones con las empresas privatizadas bajo la administracion Duhalde*, Buenos Aires: Siglo veintuno editors Argentina and FLACSO, 2003.

Bachrach, P. and Baratz, M., "Decisions and non-decisions: an analytical framework," *The American Political Science Review,* 57 (3), 1963: 632–642.

Barrett, P., "Labour policy, labour–business relations and the transition to democracy in Chile," *Journal of Latin American Studies*, 33, 2001: 594–595.

Barrett, P., Chavez, D., and Rodriguez-Garavito, C, eds., *The New Latin American Left: Utopia Reborn*, London: Pluto Press, 2008.

Basualdo, E., *Estudios de Historia Economica Argentina: Desde mediados del siglo XX a la actualidad,* Buenos Aires: FLACSO/Siglo XXI Editores Argentina, 2006.

Basualdo, E. and Arceo, E., eds., *Neoliberalismo y sectores dominantes: Tendencias globales y experiencias nacionales,* Buenos Aires: CLACSO Libros, 2006.

Basualdo, E. and Azpiazu, D., *et al.*, *El proceso de privatizacion en Argentina: la renegociacion con las empresas privadas*, Buenos Aires: Pagina 12 and Universidad Nacional de Quilmes, 2002.

Basualdo, E., Nahon, C., and Nochteff, H., "La deuda externa privada en la Argentina (1991–2005): trayectoria, naturaleza, y protagonistas," *Desarrollo Economico*, 47 (186), 2007: 193–224.

Bear Stearns, *Emerging Markets: Sovereign Quarterly*, April 18, 2006.

Beccaria, L., "*El Mercado de trabajo luego de la crisis: Avances y desafios*," in Bernardo Kosacoff, ed., *Crisis, recuperacion y nuevos dilemmas: La economia argentina 2002–2007*, Santiago de Chile: CEPAL-Naciones Unidas, 2007.

Beccaria, L. and Maurizio, R., eds., *Mercado de trabajo y equidad en Argentina*, Buenos Aires: Universidad Nacional de General Sarmiento and Prometeo, 2005.

Bergman, M., "Tax reforms and tax compliance: the divergent paths of Chile and Argentina," *Journal of Latin American Studies*, 35, 2003: 593–624.

Bielsa, R., Bonasso, M., *et al.*, *Que son las Asambleas Populares*, Buenos Aires: Pena Lillo, Ediciones Continente, 2002.

Binetti, C., and Carrillo-Florez, F., eds., *An Unequal Democracy? Seeing Latin America through European Eyes,* Washington, DC: Inter-American Development Bank and the European Union, 2005.

Birdsall, N., *From Social Policy to an Open-Economy Social Contract in Latin America*, Working Paper 21, Washington, DC: Center for Global Development, 2002.

Birdsall, N., Torre, A., and Menezes, R., *Washington Contentious: Economic Policies for Social Equity in Latin America*, Findings of the Commission on Economic Reform in Unequal Latin American Societies, sponsored by the Carnegie Endowment for International Peace and the Inter-American Dialogue, 2001.

Birdsall, N., Torre, A., and Menezes, R., *Fair Growth: Economic Policies for Latin America's Poor and Middle Class Majority*, Washington, DC: Center for Global Development and the Inter-American Dialogue, 2008.

Blustein, P., *And the Money Kept Rolling in (And Out)*, New York: Public Affairs, 2005.

Bordegaray, S. and Flores, T., ed., *De la culpa a la autogestión: Un recorrido del Movimiento de Trabajadores Desocupados de la Matanza*, Buenos Aires: MTD de la Matanza, 2002.

Bril Mascarenhas, T., "El colapso del sistema partidario de la ciudad de Buenos Aires: Una herencia de la crisis Argentina de 2001–2002, *Desarrollo Economico*, 47 (187), 2007: 367–400.

Burrity, J. and Hallewell, L., "Reform of the state and the new discourse on social policy in Brazil," *Latin American Perspectives*, 33 (1), 2006: 67–88.

Caballero, R., *Macroeconomic Volatility in Reformed Latin America: Diagnosis and Policy Proposals,* Washington, DC: Inter-American Development Bank, 2001.

Campos, R.,"Ayer y hoy: las ideas sobre el desarrollo en America Latina," *Toda Via: Pensamiento y cultura en America Latina*, Buenos Aires: Fundacion OSDE, 2004.

Castaneda, J., *Utopia Unarmed: Latin America's Left After the Cold War*, New York: Alfred Knopf, 1993.

Castaneda, J., "Latin America's left turn," *Foreign Affairs*, May–June 2006: 28–43.

Castaneda, J. and Navia, P., "Elections and the state of democracy in Latin America," *Americas Quarterly*, February 1, 2007.

Castelo, C., *Vidas Perfectas: Los Countries Por Dentro*, Buenos Aires: Editorial Sudamerica, 2007.

Cecchini, D., and Zicolillo, J., *Nuevo Conquistadores*: *El papel del gobierno y las empresas españolas en el expolio de Argentina*, Madrid: Foca, 2002.

Chalmers, D., Vilas, C., Hite, K., Martin, S., Piester, K., and Segarra, M., eds., *The New Politics of Inequality in Latin America: Rethinking Participation and Representation*, New York: Oxford University Press, 1997.

Chang, H.J., *Kicking Away the Ladder: Development Strategy in Historical Perspective*, London: Anthem Press, 2002.

Chang, H.J. and Grabel, I., *Reclaiming Development: An Alternative Economic Policy Manual*, London: ZED Books, 2004.

Chavez, D., "Hacer o no hacer: los gobiernos progressistas de Argentina, Brasil, y Uruguay frente a las privatizaciones," *Nueva Sociedad*, 207, Enero–Febrero 2007: 63–79.

Chenery, H, "Alternative strategies for development," World Bank Staff Working Paper 165, Washington, DC: World Bank, 1973.

Chiara, M. and Di Virgilio, M., *Gestion social y municipios: De los escritorios del Banco Mundial a los barrios del Gran Buenos Aires*, Buenos Aires: Universidad Nacional de General Sarmiento and Prometeo, 2005.

Chibber, V., *Locked in Place: State-Building and Late Industrialization in India*, Princeton, NJ: Princeton University Press, 2003.

Chisari, O., Estache, A., and Romero, C., "Winners and losers from utilities privatizations: lessons from a general equilibrium model for Argentina," Universidad de la Empresa, Buenos Aires, and the World Bank, Washington, 1996.

Cicolella, P., "Globalizacion y dualizacion en la Region Metropolitana de Buenos Aires. Grandes inversions y reestructuracion socioterritorial en los anos 90," *EURE*, 25 (76), 1999: 5–28.

Cimoli, M., Dosi, G., and Stiglitz, J., *Industrial Policy and Development: The Political Economy of Capabilities Accumulation*, New York: Oxford University Press, 2009.

Citigroup, *Prospects for Latin America: Opportunities and Challenges for 2007 and Beyond*, New York: Global Economic and Market Analysis, 2006.

Cleary, M. and Stokes, S., *Democracy and the Culture of Skepticism: Political Trust in Argentina and Mexico*, New York: Russell Sage Foundation, 2006.

Clemente, A. and Girolami, M., eds., *Territorio, emergencia, e intervencion social: un modelo para desarmar*, Buenos Aires: Institute for Environment and Development-America Latina, 2006.

Clemente, A., Girolami, M. and Smulovitz, C., eds., *Descentralizacion, politicas sociales y participacion democratica en Argentina,* Buenos Aires: IIED and the Woodrow Wilson International Center for Scholars, 2004.

Cline, W., "Restoring economic growth in Argentina," Working Paper 9/03, Washington, DC: World Bank , 2003.

Cohen, M. "Argentina: a season of hope," *Challenge,* September 2003: 37–58.

Cohen, M. "Hacia una nueva definicion de la riqueza y geografia en la Argentina" (Towards a new definition of wealth and geography in Argentina), in Margarita Gutman, ed., *Construir Bicentenarios: Argentina*, Buenos Aires: The New School and Caras y Caretas, 2005.

Cohen, M. "Convertibilidad, Crisis y Desafios: 1992–2006," in Jorge Enrique Hardoy and Margarita Gutman, eds., *Buenos Aires: Historia del Area Metropolitana*, Buenos Aires: Ediciones Infinito, 2007.

Cohen, M. and Gutman, M., eds., *Argentina en Colapso? America Debate*, Buenos Aires: Instituto Internacional de Medio Ambiente y Desarrollo y New School University, 2002.

Cohen, M. and Gutman, M., eds., *Latin America on the Move: The Post Neoliberal Transition*, Buenos Aires: Ediciones Infinito, 2007.

Cohen, M. and Debowicz, D., "Las Cinco Ciudades de Buenos Aires: Pobreza y desigualdad urbana," *Medio Ambiente y Urbanizacion*, Buenos Aires: Instituto InterNaciónal de Medio Ambiente y Desarollo – America Latina, 2001.

Cohen, M. and Debowicz, D., "The five cities of Buenos Aires: an inquiry into poverty and inequality in urban Argentina," *The Encyclopedia of Sustainable Development*, edited by Saskia Sassen, Paris: UNESCO, 2004.

Colburn, F., *Latin America at the End of Politics*, Princeton, NJ and Oxford: Princeton University Press, 2002.

Collier, R. and Collier, D., *Shaping the Political Arena: Critical Junctures, the Labor Movement, and Regime Dynamics in Latin America*, 2nd edition, South Bend, IN: University of Notre Dame Press, 2002.

Cornia, G., "Income distribution under Latin America's new left regimes," *Journal of Human Development and Capabilities*, 11 (1), 2010: 85–114.

Cowan, D., "The World Bank, urban bias, and structural adjustment," Working Paper 67, London: Development Planning Unit, University College London, 1994.

Cravacuore, D., Ilari, S., and Villar, A., *La articulacion en la gestion municipal: Actores y politicas*, Buenos Aires: Universidad Nacional de Quilmes Editorial, 2004.

Cravino, M., ed., *Los mil barrios (in)formales: Aportes para la construccion de un observatorio del habitat popular del Area Metropolitana de Buenos Aires*, Buenos Aires: Universidad Nacional de General Sarmiento, 2008.

Cravino, M., *Entre el arraigo y el desalojo: Derecho a la ciudad, capital immobiliario y gestion urbana*, Buenos Aires: Universidad Nacional de General Sarmiento, 2009.

Dahrendorf, R., *Class and Class Conflict in Industrial Society*, Stanford, CA: Stanford University Press, 1959.

Damill, M., Frenkel, R., and Maurizio, R., *Argentina: Una Decada de Convertibilidad: Un Analisis del Crecimiento, el Empleo y la Distribucion del Ingreso*, Geneva: International Labor Organization, 2002.

Damill, M., Frenkel, R., and Maurizio, R., *Argentina: A Decade of Currency Board: An Analysis of Growth, Employment, and Income Distribution*, Buenos Aires: CEDES, 2002.

Damill, M., Frenkel, R., and Maurizio, R., "Macroeconomic policy changes in Argentina in the turn of the century," paper prepared for the Institute for Labor Studies, International Labor Organization, December 21, 2006.

Davidson, P., *The Keynes Solution: The Path to Global Economic Prosperity*, New York: Palgrave Macmillan, 2009.

DeFerranti, F., Perry, G., Gill, I., and Serven, L., *Securing Our Future in a Global Economy*, Washington, DC: World Bank, 2000.

DeFerranti, D., *et al.*, *Beyond the City: The Rural Sector in Latin America*, Washington, DC: World Bank, 2004.

Delich, F., *Sociedades Invisibles: La cultura de la ingobernabilidad en America Latina*, Buenos Aires: GEDISA Editorial, 2007.

De Luca, M., "Elecciones y cambio en Bolivia," *El Debate Politico: Revista Iberoamericana de Analisis Politico*, Año 3/Numero 4/5, Buenos Aires: Fondo de Cultura Economica, 2006.

Dessein, D., ed., *Reinventar la Argentina: Reflexiones sobre la crisis*, Buenos Aires: Ediciones Sudamericana, 2003.

Devlin, R., Estevadeordal, A., and Rodriguez-Clare, A., eds., *The Emergence of China: Opportunities and Challenges for Latin America and the Caribbean*, Washington, DC: Inter-American Development Bank and David Rockefeller Center for Latin American Studies, Harvard University, 2006.

Di Mauro, J., *Cristina K: La Dama Rebelde*, Buenos Aires: Editorial Sudamericana, 2004.

Dinerstein, A., "The politics of unemployment: employment policy, the unemployed workers organizations and the state in Argentina (1991–2005)," London School of Economics, Non-Governmental Public Action Program, Working Paper 9, 2008.

Domingues, J., "Modelos de desarrollo y retos latinoamericanos," *El Debate Politico: Revista Iberoamericana de Analisis Politico,* Año 3/Numero 4/5, Buenos Aires: Fondo de Cultura Economica, 2006.

Dornbusch, R. and Edwards, S., *The Macroeconomics of Populism in Latin America (A National Bureau of Economic Research Conference Report)*, Chicago, IL: University Of Chicago Press, 1992.

Dubois, L., *The Politics of the Past in an Argentine Working-Class Neighborhood*, Toronto: University of Toronto Press, 2005.

Easterly, W. and Serven, L., eds., *The Limits of Stabilization: Infrastructure, Public Deficits, and Growth in Latin America*, Washington, DC: World Bank, 2003.

Economist, The, "The return of populism," April 15, 2006.

Edwards, S., *Crisis and Reform in Latin America: From Despair to Hope*, New York: Oxford University Press, 1995.

Edwards, S., *Left Behind: Latin America and the False Promise of Populism*, Chicago, IL: University of Chicago Press, 2010.

Eicher, T. and Garcia-Peñalosa, C., eds., *Institutions, Development, and Economic Growth*, Cambridge, MA: MIT Press, 2006.

Eissa, S., Gorgal, L., and Tedeschi, K., *Hacia un a political integral de seguridad: Consensos y disensos*, Buenos Aires: Prometeo, Grupo Sophia, y Fundacion Konrad Adenauer, 2006.

Engerman, S. and Sokoloff, K., "Colonialism, inequality, and long run paths of development," Working paper 11057, National Bureau of Economic Research, Cambridge, MA, 2005.

Escolar, M., Badia, G., and Frederic, S., eds., *Federalismo y descentralizacion en grandes ciudades: Buenos Aires en perspective comparativa,* Buenos Aires: Banco Cuidad and Prometeo, 2004.

Etchemendy, S., "Construir coaliciones reformistas: la politica de las compensaciones en el camino argentine hacia la liberalizacion economica," *Desarrollo Economico*, 40 (160), 2001: 675–706.

Etchemendy, S., "Constructing reform coalitions: the politics of compensations in Argentina's economic liberalization," *Latin American Politics and Society*, 43 (3), 2001: 1–35.

Etchemendy, S., "Repression, exclusion, and inclusion: government–union relations and patterns of labor reform in liberalizing economies," *Comparative Politics*, 36 (3), 2004: 273–290.

Etchemendy, S., "Old actors in new markets: transforming the populist/industrial coalition in Argentina, 1989–2001," in S. Levitsky and M. Murillo, eds., *Argentine Democracy: The Politics of Institutional Weakness*, University Park, PA: Penn State University Press.

Evans, P., *Embedded Autonomy: States and Industrial Transformation*, Princeton, NJ: Princeton University Press, 1995.

Fanelli, J.M., ed., *Understanding Market Reforms in Latin America: Similar Reforms, Diverse Constituencies, Varied Results*, New York: Palgrave Macmillan, 2007.

Fay, M., ed., *The Urban Poor in Latin America*, Washington, DC: World Bank, 2005.

Feinmann, J., "Apuntes para una ontología de la periferia," in Margarita Gutman, ed., *Construir Bicentenarios: Argentina*, Buenos Aires: The New School and Caras y Caretas, 2005.

Fernandez, A. *et al.*, *Politica y Subjetividad: Asambleas Barriales y Fabricas Recuperadas*, Buenos Aires: Tinta Limon Ediciones, 2006.

Fernandez, A., ed., *Estado y relaciones laborales: tranformacions y perspectives*, Buenos Aires: Prometeo, 2005.

Fernández de Kirchner, C., "El Bicentenario: una oportunidad histórica para repensar la Argentina," in Margarita Gutman, ed., *Construir Bicentenarios: Argentina*, Buenos Aires: The New School and Caras y Caretas, 2005.

Fernández de Kirchner, C., *Pensando en la Argentina*, Buenos Aires: Planeta, 2007.

Ferrer, A., *La Economia Argentina desde sus origins hasta principios del siglo XXI*, Buenos Aires: Fondo de Cultura Economica, 2008.

Ffrench-Davis, R., *Reforming the Reforms in Latin America: Macroeconomics, Trade, and Finance*, London: Macmillan Press Ltd, 2000.

Ffrench-Davis, R., *Seeking Growth under Financial Volatility*, New York: Palgrave Macmillan, 2006.

Ffrench-Davis, R., "El contexto de la privatizaciones y la situacion actual: Entre el Consensos de Washington y el crecimiento con equidad," *Nueva Sociedad*, Numero 207, Buenos Aires, 2007.

Fiszbein, A., Giovagnoli, P., and Aduriz, I., "Argentina's crisis and its impact on household welfare," World Bank Working Paper N.1/02, Buenos Aires, 2002.

Foer, F., "The Talented Mr. Chavez," *The Atlantic*, May 2006.

Forcinito, K., "Notas sobre el papel del Estado Argentino en la reestructuracion regresiva de la relacion entre el capital y la fuerza de trabajo: El caso de los sectores de infraestructura privatizados durante los anos noventa," in Carlos Vilas *et al.*, eds., *Estado y politica en la Argentina actual*, Buenos Aires: Universidad Nacional de General Sarmiento and Prometeo, 2005.

Forcinito, K. and Nahon, C., "La fibula de las privatizaciones: vicios privados, beneficios publicos? El caso de la Argentina 1990–2005," Observatorio Argentina, Grupo de Trabajo Economico, 2005.

Forni, F., ed., *De la Exclusion a la Organizacion: Hacia la integracion de los pobres en los nuevos barrios del conurbano bonaerense*, Buenos Aires: Ediciones Ciccus, 2002.

Franco, R. and Lanzaro, J., eds., *Politica y politicas publicas en los procesos de reforma de America Latina*, Buenos Aires: CEPAL y FLACSO, 2006.

Frederic, S., *Buenos vecinos, malos politicos: Moralidad y politica en el Gran Buenos Aires*, Buenos Aires: Prometeo, 2004.

Frenkel, R., "Benefits and costs of convertibility," in Michael Cohen and Margarita Gutman, eds., *Argentina in Collapse? The Americas Debate*, Buenos Aires: The New School and International Institute for Environment and Development – America Latina, 2002.

Fretes-Cibils, V., Guigale, M., and Luff, C., eds., *Bolivia: Public Policy Options for the Well-Being of All*, Washington, DC: World Bank, 2006.

Fukuda-Parr, S., ed., *Gene Revolution: GM Crops and Unequal Development*, London and Sterling, VA: Earthscan, 2007.

Fukuyama, F., *The End of History*, New York: Free Press, 1992.

Fukuyama, F., ed., *Falling Behind: Explaining the Development Gap Between Latin America and the United States*, New York: Oxford University Press, 2008.

Fukuyama, F., *La brecha entre America Latina y Estados Unidos: Determinantes politicos e institutionales del desarrollo economico*, Buenos Aires: Fondo de Cultura Economica, 2006

Galiani, S., Gertler, P., and Schargrodsky, E., "Water for life: the impact of the privatization of water services on child mortality," *Journal of Political Economy*, 113 (1), 2005: 83–120.

Gallegos, F., "Mucho mas que dos izquierdas," *Nueva Sociedad*, 205, 2006: 30–45.

Garcia, M., "Transition challenges in the Latin American context," in M. Cohen and M. Gutman, eds., *Latin America on the Move: The Post Neo-Liberal Transition*, New York: The Observatory on Latin America, 2007.

Garreton, M., "Modelos y liderazgos en America Latina," *Nueva Sociedad*, 205, 2006: 102–113.

Geddes, B., *Politician's Dilemma: Building State Capacity in Latin America*, Berkeley, CA: University of California Press, 1994.

Gene, M., *Un mundo feliz: Imagenes de los trabajadores en el primer peronismo 1946–1955*, Buenos Aires: Universidad de San Andres and Fondo de Cultura Economica, 2005.

Ghani, A. and Lockhart, C., *Fixing Failed States: A Framework for Rebuilding a Fractured World*, New York: Oxford University Press, 2009.

Giordano, P., Lanzafame, F., and Meyer-Stamer, J., eds., *Asymmetries in Regional Integration and Local Development,* Washington, DC: Inter-American Development Bank, 2005.

Gobierno de la Republica Argentina, Ministerio de Desarrollo Social, *La Bisagra: Memoria, Verdad, Justicia, Organización Social*, Buenos Aires: Ministerio de Desarrollo Social, 2007.

Gobierno de la Republica Argentina, Ministerio de Economia y Produccion, Secretaria de Politica Economica, *Patagonia: Mapa Productivo Regional*, Buenos Aires: Ministerio de Economia y Produccion, 2006.

Gobierno de la Republica Argentina, Ministerio de Economia y Produccion, Secretaria de Politica Economica, *Nuevo Cuyo: Mapa Productivo Regional*, Buenos Aires: Ministerio de Economia y Produccion, 2007.

Gobierno de la Republica Argentina, Ministerio de Economia y Produccion, Secretaria de Politica Economica, y Gobierno de Entre Rios, *Entre Rios: Dinamica y perspectivas de la Region de Salto Grande en la Economia Provincial*, Buenos Aires: Ministerio de Economia y Produccion, 2007.

Gobierno de la Republica Argentina, Ministerio de Trabajo, Empleo, y Seguridad Social, *Revista de Trabajo: Instituciones del mundo del trabajo (II): Negociacion colectiva*, Año 3, Numero 3, Nueva Epoca 2006.

Gobierno de la Republica Argentina, Ministerio de Trabajo, Empleo, y Seguridad Social, *Trabajo, ocupacion y empleo: Salarios, empresas y empleo 2003–2006*, Serie Estudios/5, Buenos Aires: Ministerio de Trabajo, Empleo y Seguridad Social, Septiembre de 2006.

Gobierno de la Republica Argentina, Ministerio de Trabajo, Empleo, y Seguridad Social, *Revista de Trabajo: Pensar el Trabajo: debate y actualidad*, Año 3, Numero 4, Nueva Epoca, 2007.

Gobierno de la Republica Argentina, Ministerio de Trabajo, Empleo, y Seguridad Social, *Trabajo, ocupacion y empleo: Dimensiones del trabajo en el Nuevo modelo economic social*, Serie Estudios/6, Buenos Aires: Ministerio de Trabajo, Empleo y Seguridad Social, Febrero de 2007.

Gobierno de la Republica Argentina, Ministerio de Trabajo, Empleo, y Seguridad Social, *Trabajo, ocupacion y empleo: Los retos laborales en un proceso de crecimento sostenido*, Serie Estudios/7, Buenos Aires: Ministerio de Trabajo, Empleo y Seguridad Social, Noviembre de 2007.

Gobierno de la Republica Argentina, Ministerio de Trabajo, Empleo, y Seguridad Social, *Estructura productive y empleo: Un enfoque transversal,* Buenos Aires: Ministerio de Trabajo, Empleo, y Seguridad Social, Noviembre 2007.

Godio, J., *Argentina: luces y sombras en el primer ano de transicion: Las mutacions de la economia, la sociedad, y la politica durante el gobierno de Eduardo Duhalde (enero-diciembre de 2002)*, Buenos Aires: Editorial Biblos, 2003.

Goni, E., Lopez, J., and Serven, L., *Fiscal Redistribution and Income Inequality in Latin America,* Policy Research Working Paper 4487, Washington, DC: World Bank, 2008.

Gorelik, A., "Modelo para armar: Buenos Aires, de la crisis al boom," *Punta de Vista: Revista de Cultura*, 84, Buenos Aires, 2006.

Graham, S. and Marvin, S., *Splintering Urbanism: Networked Infrastructures, Technological Mobilities, and the Urban Condition*, New York: Routledge, 2001.

Grandin, G., *Empire's Workshop*, New York: Metropolitan Books, 2006.

Grandin, G., *The Last Colonial Massacre: The Legacy of the Cold War in Latin America*, Chicago, IL: University of Chicago Press, 2004.

Grimson, A. and Jelin, E., eds., *Migraciones regionales hacia la Argentina: Diferencia, desigualdads y derechos*, Buenos Aires: Prometeo, 2006.

Guaqueta, L., *Public Services and Citizenship: The Case of the Privatizations of Electricity, Gas, and Water in Buenos Aires*, New York: The New School, The Argentina Observatory, 2006.

Guillen, M., *The Limits of Convergence: Globalizatiobn and Organizational Change in Argentina, South Korea, and Spain*, Princeton, NJ: Princeton University Press, 2001.

Gutman, M., *Buenos Aires 1910: Memorias del Porvenir,* Buenos Aires: Gobierno de la Ciudad de Buenos Aires and International Institute for Environment and Development – America Latina, 1999.

Gutman, M., "In search of the (lost) world to come," in M. Cohen and M. Gutman, eds., *Argentina in Collapse? The Americas Debate*, Buenos Aires: The New School and International Institute for Environment and Development – America Latina, 2002.

Gutman, M., ed., *Construir Bicentenarios: Argentina*, Buenos Aires: The New School and Caras y Caretas, 2005.

Gutman, M., *Buenos Aires: El poder de la anticipación. Imágenes itinerantes del futuro metropolitano en el primer Centenario*, Buenos Aires: Ediciones Infinito, 2011.

Halperin Donghi, T., *Revolucion y Guerra: Formacion de una Elite Dirigente en la Argentina Criolla*, Buenos Aires: Siglo XXI Editores, 1972.

Halperin Donghi, T., *Vida y muerte de la Republica verdadera (1910–1930)*, Buenos Aires: Ariel, 1999.

Halperin Donghi, T., "Why did Argentina adopt a neoliberal model?" in M. Cohen and M. Gutman, eds., *Argentina in Collapse? The Americas Debate*, Buenos Aires: The New School and International Institute for Environment and Development, 2002.

Halperin Donghi, T., *La Argentina y La Tormenta del Mundo: Ideas e ideologias entre 1930 y 1945*, Buenos Aires: Siglo veintiuno editores Argentina, 2003.

Hardoy, J. and Almansi, F., "Assessing the scale of urban poverty in Buenos Aires," *International Institute for Environment and Development (IIED)*, Human Settlements Working Paper series, 2011.

Harris, N., "Structural adjustment and cities: three papers," Working Paper 63, London: Development Planning Unit, University College London, 1994.

Harris, R. and Nef, J., eds., *Capital, Power, and Inequality in Latin America and the Caribbean*, Lanham, MD: Rowman and Littlefield Publishers, Inc., 2008.

Helmke, G., "Enduring uncertainty: court-executive relations in Argentina in the 1990s and beyond," in Steven Levitsky and Maria Victoria Murillo, eds., *Argentine Democracy: The Politics of Institutional Weakness,* University Park, PA: Pennsylvania University Press, 2005.

Helpman, E., ed. *Institutions and Economic Performance*, Cambridge, MA: Harvard University Press, 2008.

Hernandez, V., "El fenomeno economic y cultural del boom de la soja y el empresario innovador," *Desarrollo Economico*, 47 (187), 2007: 331–366.

Hershberg, E. and Rosen, F., eds., *Latin America After Neo-liberalism: Turning the Tide in the 21st Century?*, New York: The New Press and NACLA, 2006.

Hintze, S., ed., *Trueque y Economia Solidaria*, Buenos Aires: UNDP, Universidad Nacional de General Sarmiento, Prometeo, 2003.

Ilari, S., "La gestion local de la politica social: los casos de Quilmes y Florencio Varela," in Alicia Ziccardi, ed., *Pobreza, Desigualdad Social y Ciudadania: Los Limites de la Politicas Sociales en America Latina*, Buenos Aires: CLACSO, 2002.

Inter-American Development Bank, *Facing Up to Inequality in Latin America: Economic and Social Progress in Latin America, 1998–1999 Report*, Washington, DC: Inter-American Development Bank, 1998.

International Crisis Group, "Venezuela: Hugo Chavez's Revolution," *Latin America Report No. 19*, Washington, DC: ICG, 2007.

Johnson, C., *Arresting Development: The Power of Knowledge for Social Change*, New York: Routledge, 2009.

Jones, M.P., "Assessing the public's understanding of constitutional reform: evidence from Argentina," *Political Behavior*, 18 (1), 1996: 25–49.

Jones, M.P., "Federalism and the number of parties in argentine congressional elections," *The Journal of Politics*, 59 (2), 1997: 538–549.

Jones, M.P. and Hwang, W., "Party government in presidential democracies: extending cartel theory beyond the U.S. Congress," *American Journal of Political Science*, 49 (2), 2005: 267–282.

Jones, M.P., Saiegh, S., Spiller, P., and Tommasi, M., "Amateur legislators – professional politicians: the consequences of party-centered electoral rules in a federal system," *American Journal of Political Science*, 46 (3), 2002: 656–669.

Jordana, J. and Levi-Faur, D., "The diffusion of regulatory capitalism in Latin America: sectoral and national channels in the making of a new order," *Annals of the American Academy of Political and Social Science*, 598, 2005: 102–124.

Justesen, M., "Living on the edge: risk, protection, behavior, and outcomes of Argentine youth," World Bank Policy Research Working Paper 4485, Washington, DC: World Bank, 2008.

Karush, M. and Chamosa, O., eds., *The New Cultural History of Peronism: Power and Identity in Mid-Twentieth-Century Argentina*, Durham, NC: Duke University Press, 2010.

Khan, M., "Governance, economic growth and development," in Jose Antonio Ocampo, K.S. Jomo, and Rob Vos, eds., *Growth Divergences: Explaining Differences in Economic Performance*, New York: Zed Books, 2007.

Kiguel, M., "It's the politics, stupid," *Econviews*, 49, 2008.

Kiguel, M. "Goodbye penguinomics: what's next?," *Econviews*, 50, 2008.

Kirchner, N. and Di Tella, T., *Despues del Derumbe: Teoria y Practica Politica en la Argentina Que Viene*, Buenos Aires: Editorial Galerna, 2003.

Kliksberg, B., *Mitos y realidades sobre la criminalidad en America Latina*, Madrid: FIIAP, 2007.

Kliksberg, B. "Bajar la desigualdad impacta mas en la pobreza que el crecimiento," *Pagina/12*, September 3, 2007.

Kohli, A., *State-Directed Development: Political Power and Industrialization in the Global Periphery*, New York: Cambridge University Press, 2004.

Kosacoff, B., ed., *Crisis, recuperacion y nuevos dilemmas: La economia argentina 2002–2007*, Santiago de Chile: CEPAL-Naciones Unidas, 2007.

Kuczynski, P. and Williamson, J., eds., *After the Washington Consensus: Restarting Growth and Reform in Latin America*, Washington, DC: Institute for International Economics, 2003.

Kulfas, M., ed., *Postales de la Argentina productiva*, Buenos Aires: Libros de Zorzal, 2009.

Kurtz, M., "State developmentalism with a developmental state: the public foundations of the 'free market miracle' in Chile," *Latin American Politics and Society*, 43 (2), 2001: 1–25.

Laclau, E., "La deriva populista y la centroizquierda latinoamericana," *Nueva Sociedad*, 205, 2006: 56–61.

Landell-Mills, P. and Serageldin, I., "Governance and the External Factor," Paper presented to World Bank Annual Conference on Development Economics, Washington, DC: World Bank, 1991.

Levitsky, S. and Murillo, M., eds., *Argentine Democracy: The Politics of Institutional Weakness*, University Park, PA: Pennsylvania State University Press, 2005.

Lewis, W.A., *Growth and Fluctuations, 1870–1913*, London: George Allen and Unwin, 1978.

Libertun de Duren, N., "Growth and poverty in the urban fringe: decentralization, dispersion, and inequality in Buenos Aires," PhD dissertation, MIT, June 2007.

Lin, Justin Yifu, "New structural economics: a framework for rethinking development," Washington, DC: World Bank, 2010.

Lowi, T., "American business, public policy, case studies, and political theory," *World Politics*, 16 (4), 1964: 677–715.

Lustig, N., "Poverty, inequality, and the new left in Latin America," Woodrow Wilson Center Update on the Americas, 5, October 2009.

Mahon, J., "Tax reforms and income distribution in Latin America," Paper presented at XXVIII Congress of the Latin American Studies Association, Rio de Janeiro, June 2009.

Mainwaring, S. and Scully, T., eds., *Democratic Governance in Latin America*, Stanford, CA: Stanford University Press, 2010.

Masiello, F., *The Art of Transition: Latin American Culture and Neoliberal Crisis*, Durham, NC and London: Duke University Press, 2001.

Meller, P., "Chile: de la economia semi-cerrada a la economia globalizada. Los puntos de partida de la actual politica commercial," *Toda Via: Pensamiento y cultura en America Latina*, 8, Buenos Aires: Fundacion OSDE, 2004.

Melo, M., "Institutional weakness and the puzzle of Argentina's low taxation," *Latin American Politics and Society*, 49 (4), 2008: 115–148.

El Mercurio, "Nuevo progresismo," April 9, 2008, p. A3.

Migdal, J., *Strong Societies and Weak States: State–Society Relations and State Capabilities in the Third World*, Princeton, NJ: Princeton University Press, 1988.

Mignolo, W., *The Idea of Latin America*, Malden, MA: Blackwell, 2005.

Minsburg, N., ed., *Los Guardianes del Dinero: Las Politicas del FMI en la Argentina*, Buenos Aires: Grupo Editorial Norma, 2003.

Minujin, A., ed., *Desigualdad y Exclusion: Deafios para la politica social en la Argentina de fin de siglo*, Buenos Aires: Losada and UNICEF, 1996.

Montero, A. "Making and remaking "good government" in Brazil: sub-national industrial policy in Minas Gerais," *Latin American Politics and Society*, 43 (2), 2001: 49–80.

Morley, S., "The impact of macro-economic environment on urban poverty," United Nations Economic Commission on Latin America and the Caribbean, Santiago: ECLAC, May 1998.

Moser, C., "Confronting crisis: a comparative study of household responses to poverty and vulnerability in four poor urban communities," Washington, DC: World Bank, 1996.

Moser, C., *Reducing Global Poverty: The Case for Asset Accumulation*, Washington, DC: Brookings Institution, 2007.

Murillo, M. "Tango de un desencanto anunciado," *Foreign Affairs en Español*, 2 (2), 2002: 1–17.

Murillo, M., *Political Competition, Partisanship, and Policy Making in Latin American Public Utilities*, New York: Cambridge University Press, 2009.

Mussa, M., *Argentina y el FMI: Del triunfo a la tragedia*, Madrid: Planeta, 2002.

Natanson, J., *Buenos muchachos: Vida y obra de los economistas del establishment*, Buenos Aires: Libros del Zorzal, 2005.

Natanson, J., *La Nueva Izquierda: Triunfos y derrotas de los gobiernos de Argentina, Brasil, Bolivia, Venezuela, Chile, Uruguay y Ecuador*, Buenos Aires: Debate, 2008.

Navarro, R., "*Un viaje de ida: la lista de los que se llevaron la plata afuera en el ano del corralito*," *Veintitres*, November 21, 2002.

Navia, P.,"La eleccion presidencial de 2005 en Chile," *El Debate Politico: Revista Iberoamericana de Analisis Politico,* Año 3/Numero 4/5, Buenos Aires: Fondo de Cultura Economica, November 2006.

Nouzeilles, G. and Montaldo, G., eds., *The Argentina Reader: History, Culture, Politics*, Durham, NC and London: Duke University Press, 2002.

Novick, M., Tomada, C., Damill, M., Frenkel, R., and Maurizio, R., *Tras la crisis: el nuevo rumbo de la política económica y laboral en Argentina y su impacto,* Geneva: ILO Institute for Labor Studies, 2007.

Nun, J., "El Bicentenario como festival," in Margarita Gutman (ed.), *Construir Bicentenarios: Argentina*, Buenos Aires: The New School and Caras y Caretas, 2005.

Nunberg, B., *Public Sector Management Issues in Structural Adjustment Lending*, Working Paper 217, Washington: World Bank, Country Economics Department, 1990.

Ocampo, J.A., "Overcoming Latin America's growth frustrations: the macro and meso-economic links," in R. Ffrench-Davis, *Seeking Growth under Financial Volatility*, New York: Palgrave Macmillan, 2006.

Ocampo, J.A. "Has economics failed the challenge of development," Speech at New School conference, April 20, 2006.

Ocampo, J.A., Jomo, K., and Vos, R., eds., *Growth Divergences: Explaining Differences in Economic Performance*, London: Orient Longman, 2007.

O'Donnell, M., *El Aparato, Los intendentes del Conurbano y las cajas negras de la politica*, Buenos Aires: Aguilar, 2005.

O'Donnell, M., *Propaganda K: Una Maquinaria de Promocion con El Dineiro del Estado*, Buenos Aires: Planeta, 2007.

Oszlak, O., "El Servicio Civil en America Latina y el Caribe: Situacion Actuel y Retos de Futuro," unpublished paper delivered at VI CLAD Congress on State and Public Administration Reform, Buenos Aires, 2001.

Oszlak, O., *Gobernar el Imperio: Los Tiempos de Bush*, Buenos Aires: Capital para Todos, 2006.

Palermo, V. and de Souza Telles, H., "El scenario politico brasileno: la matriz institucional y la dimension representative en el gobierno de Lula de Silva," *Umbrales de America del Sur*, 1, Buenos Aires: CEPES, December 2006–March 2007.

Parry, R., "The role of fiscal transparency in sustaining growth and stability in Latin America," IMF Working Paper WP/07/220, Washington, DC: IMF, 2007.

Paul, S., *Institutional Reforms in Sector Adjustment Operations: The World Bank's Experience*, World Bank Discussion Paper 92, Washington, DC; World Bank, 1990.

Pereira, A., "Brazil's agrarian reform: democratic innovation or oligarchic exclusion redux," *Latin American Politics and Society*, 45 (2), 2003: 41–65.

Perelman, P., Coordinador, *La Pobreza en el Area Metropolitana de Buenos Aires: Una Vision de sus caracteristicas y su evolucion*, Buenos Aires: Instituto Internacional de Medio Ambiente y Desarrollo – America Latina, 1994.

Perry, G. and Serven, L., *The Anatomy of a Multiple Crisis: Why Was Argentina Special and What Can We Learn From It*, Washington, DC: World Bank, 2002.

Petras, J. and Morley, M., *Latin America in the Time of Cholera: Electoral Politics, Markets Economics, and Permanent Crisis*, New York and London: Routledge, 1992.

Pettis, M., *The Volatility Machine: Emerging Economies and the Threat of Financial Collapse*, New York: Oxford University Press, 2001.

Pirez, P., "Buenos Aires: fragmentation and privatization of the metropolitan city," *Environment and Urbanization*, 14 (1), 2002: 145–158.

Polanyi, K., *The Great Transformation*, Boston, MA: Beacon Press, 1957.

Portes, A., *El Desarrollo Futuro de America Latina: Neoliberalismo, clases sociales y transnacionalismo*, Bogota: Instituto Latinoamericano de servicios legales alternatives, 2004.

Prashad, V. and Ballve, T., eds., *Dispatches from Latin America: On the Frontlines Against Neoliberalism*, Cambridge, MA: South End Press, 2006.

Prebisch, R., *Economic Survey of Latin America 1949*, New York: Economic Commission on Latin America, 1951.

Prud'homme, R., Huntzinger, H., and Kopp, P., "Stronger municipalities for stronger cities in Argentina," Report for the Inter-American Development Bank, January 2004.

Ramio, C. and Salvador, M., "Civil service reform in Latin America: external referents versus own capacities," *Bulletin of Latin American Research*, 27 (4), 2008: 557.

Rapoport, M., *Historia economica, politica, y social de la Argentina (1880–2003)*, Buenos Aires: Emece, 2007.

Reato, C., *Lula: La Izquierda al Divan: Un biografia no autorizada y la dificil relacion con Kirchner*, Buenos Aires: Catalogos, 2006.

Regalado, R., *Latin America at the Crossroads: Domination, Crisis, Popular Movements, and Political Alternatives*, Melbourne: Ocean Press, 2007.

Rey, M. and Lopez, A., eds., *Entre technocratas globalizados y politicos clientelistas: Derrotero del ajuste neoliberal en el Estado argentino*, Buenos Aires: Prometeo, 2005.

Robinson, W., *Latin America and Global Capitalism: A Critical Globalization Perspective*, Baltimore, MA: Johns Hopkins University Press, 2008.

Roth, L., "Acerca de la independencia judicial en Argentina: la creacion del Consejo de la Magistratura y su desempeno entre 1994 y 2006," *Desarrollo Economico*, 47 (186), 2007: 285–318.

Santiso, J., *Latin America's Political Economy of the Possible: Beyond Good Revolutionaries and Free Marketeers*, Cambridge, MA: MIT University Press, 2006.

Schmitter, P., "Los vicios y virtudes de los 'populismos': un balance general," *El Debate Politico: Revista Iberoamericana de Analisis Politico,* Año 3/Numero 4/5, Buenos Aires: Fondo de Cultura Economica, November 2006, pp. 208–214.

Schorr, M., *Industria y nacion: Poder economico, neoliberalismo y alternatives de reindustrializacion en la Argentina contemporanea,* Buenos Aires: Edhasa y IDEAS, 2006.

Schuster, F., "Izquierda politica y movimientos socials en la Argentina contemporanea," in Cesar A. Rodriguez Garavito, Patrick S. Barrett, and Daniel Chavez (eds.), *La Nueva Izquierda en America Latina: Sus origenes y trayectoria futura*, Buenos Aires: Grupo Editorial Norma, 2005, pp. 239–282.

Schuster, F., Naishtat, F., Nardacchione, G., and Pereyra, S., eds., *Tomar la palabra: Estudios sobre protesta social y accion colectiva en la Argentina contemporanea,* Buenos Aires: Prometeo, 2005.

Seman, E., "Political dimensions of the crisis," in M. Cohen and M. Gutman, eds., *Argentina in Collapse? The Americas Debate*, Buenos Aires: The New School and International Institute for Environment and Development – America Latina, 2002.

Seoane, M., "Las marcas de la politica argentina: Un siglo de accion y excepcion," in M. Gutman, *Construir Bicentenarios: Argentina*, Buenos Aires: The New School and Caras y Caretas, 2005.

Seoane, M., *Nosotros: Apuntes sobre pasiones, razones y trampas de los argentines entre dos siglos*, Buenos Aires: Editorial Sudamericana, 2006.

Shah, H., *Argentina Privatization Program: A Review of Five Cases*, Washington, DC: World Bank, 1996.

Shifter, M., "In search of Hugo Chavez," *Foreign Affairs*, May–June 2006: 45–59.

Sidicaro, R., *Los Tres Peronismos: estado y poder economic: 1946–55/1973–76/1989–99*, Buenos Aires: Siglo XXI editors Argentina, 2002.

Sikkink, K., *Ideas and Institutions: Developmentalism in Brazil and Argentina*, Ithaca, NY: Cornell University Press, 1991.

Silletta, A., *Salir del Infierno: Estrategia de un piloto de tormenta. La Transicion Duhalde 2002/2003*, Buenos Aires: Editorial Biblos, 2005.

Skidelsky, R., "Gloomy about globalization," *New York Review of Books*, April 17, 2008: 60–64.

Smith, W., ed., *Latin American Democratic Transformation: Institutions, Actors, and Processes*, New York: Wiley-Blackwell, 2009.

Smith, W., Acuna, C., and Gamarra, E., eds., *Democracy, Markets, and Structural Reform in Latin America: Argentina, Bolivia, Brazil, Chile, and Mexico,* New Brunswick: Transaction Publishers, 1993.

Spiller, P. and Tommasi, M., *The Institutional Foundations of Public Policy in Argentina*, New York: Cambridge University Press, 2007.

Soja, E., *Postmetropolis: Critical Studies of Cities and Regions*, Oxford: Blackwell, 2000.

Stiglitz, J., *Globalization and its Discontents*, New York: W.W. Norton and Company, 2002.

Stiglitz, J., "The lessons of Argentina for development in Latin America," in M. Cohen and M. Gutman, eds., *Argentina in Collapse? The Americas Debate*, Buenos Aires: The New School and International Institute for Environment and Development – America Latina, 2002.

Stiglitz, J., *Making Globalization Work*, New York: W.W. Norton and Company, 2006.

Stiglitz, J., *Free Fall*, New York: W.W. Norton and Company, 2009.

Stillwagon, E., *Stunted Lives, Stagnant Economies*, New Brunswick, NJ and London: Rutgers University Press, 1998.

Stokes, S., *Mandates and Democracy: Neo-liberalism by Surprise in Latin America*, New York: Cambridge University Press, 2001.

Svampa, M., *Los Que Ganaron: La vida en los countries y barrios privados*, Buenos Aires: Editorial Biblos, 2001.

Svampa, M., *La Sociedad Excluyente: La Argentina Bajo el Signo de Neo-Liberalismo*, Buenos Aires: Taurus, 2005.

Tangelson, O., *Argentina frente al Siglo XXI*, Buenos Aires: Universidad Nacional de Lanus, 2003.

Tanzi, V., *Argentina: An Economic Chronicle. How One of the Richest Countries in the World Lost its Wealth*, New York: Jorge Pinto Books, 2007.

Taylor, L., ed., *After Neoliberalism: What Next for Latin America?*, Ann Arbor, MI: University of Michigan Press, 1999.

Tedesco, L., *Democracy in Argentina: Hope and Disillusion*, London: Frank Cass Publishers, 1999.

Teichman, J., *The Politics of Freeing Markets in Latin America: Chile, Argentina, and Mexico*, Chapel Hill, NC: University of North Carolina Press, 2001.

Teichman, J., "The World Bank and policy reform in Mexico," *Latin American Politics and Society*, 46 (1), 2004: 39–74.

Tella, G., "Rupturas y continuidades en el sistema de centralidades de Buenos Aires" in Max Welch Guerra, ed., *Buenos Aires a la deriva: Transformaciones urbanas recientes*, Buenos Aires: Editorial Biblos, 2005.

Tendler, J., *Good Government in the Tropics*, Baltimore, MD: Johns Hopkins University Press, 1997.

Tenembaum, E., *Enemigos: Argentina y el FMI, la apasionate discussion entre un periodista y uno de los hombres clave del Fondo en los noventa*, Buenos Aires: Grupo Editorial Norma, 2004.

Terragno, R., *La simulacion: Argentina y el FMI: dos decadas de mentas y autoenganos*, Buenos Aires: Planeta, 2005.

Terry, D. and Wilson, S., eds., *Beyond Small Change: Making Remittances Count*, Washington, DC: Inter-American Development Bank, 2005.

Thomas, V., *From Inside Brazil: Development in a Land of Contrasts*, Washington, DC: World Bank and Stanford University Press, 2006.

Thorp, R., *Progress, Poverty, and Exclusion: An Economic History of Latin America in the 20th Century*, Washington, DC: Johns Hopkins University Press, Inter-American Development Bank, and the European Union, 1998.

Todesca, J., *El mito del pais rico: Economia y politica en la Historia argentina*, Buenos Aires: Emece, 2006.

Torrado, S., ed., *Poblacion y bienestar en la Argentina del primero al Segundo Centenario: Una historia social del siglo XX,* 2 volumes, Buenos Aires: Ensayo Edhasa, 2007.

Torrado, S., ed., *El costo social del ajuste, Argentina 1976–2002*, two volumes, Buenos Aires: Ensayo Edhasa, 2010.

Touraine, A., "Entre Bachelet y Morales, existe una izquierda en America Latina," *Nueva Sociedad,* 205, 2006: 46–55.

Umbrales de America del Sur, December 2007–March 2008.

United Nations Commission for Trade and Development, *World Investment Report*, Geneva: UNCTAD, 2006.

United Nations Development Program: Argentina, *Informe de Desarrollo Humano 2005: Argentina Despues de la Crisis: Un Tiempo de Opportunidades*, Buenos Aires: UNDP, 2005.

United Nations Economic Commission for Latin America and the Caribbean (ECLAC), *Time for Equality: Closing gaps, Opening Trails,* 33rd session of ECLAC, Brasilia, May 30 to June 1, 2010, Santiago: ECLAC, 2010.

Vilas, C., "Privatization of the water and sanitation system in the Buenos Aires metropolitan area," a report to the Globalization Research Center, University of South Florida, 2004.

Vilas, C., Lazzetta, O., Forcinito, K., and Bohoslavsky, E., *Estado y politica en la Argentina actual*, Buenos Aires: Prometeo y Universidad Nacional de General Sarmiento, 2005.

Vos, R., Taylor, L., and Paes de Barros, R., eds., *Economic Liberalization, Distribution, and Poverty: Latin America in the 1990s*, Northampton, MA: Edward Elgar, 2002.

Wade, R., *Governing the Market: Economic Theory and the Role of Government in East Asian Industrialization*, Princeton, NJ: Princeton University Press, 1990.

Wagner, R. "No se explican la toma de Soldati sin entender el fenómeno de los barrios cerrados," *Fundación Metropolitana*, December 2010.

Waisman, C., *Reversal of Development in Argentina: Postwar Counter Revolutionary Policies and their Structural Consequences*, Princeton, NJ: Princeton University Press, 1987.

Weyland, K., "Neoliberalism and democracy in Latin America: a mixed record," in W. Smith, ed., *Latin American Democratic Transformation: Institutions, Actors, and Processes*, New York: Wiley-Blackwell, 2009.

World Bank, "Managing development: the governance dimension. A discussion paper," Washington, DC: World Bank, 1991.

World Bank, *The East Asian Miracle: Economic Growth and Public Policy*, New York: Oxford University Press, 1993.

World Bank, *Argentina: Argentina's Poor. A Profile*, Washington, DC: World Bank, 1995.

World Bank, *The State in a Changing World, World Development Report 1997*, Washington, DC: World Bank, 1997.

World Bank, *Building Institutions for Markets, World Development Report 2002*, Washington, DC: World Bank, 2002.

World Bank, *Argentina: Crisis and Poverty 2003. A Poverty Assessment*, Washington, DC: World Bank, 2003.

World Bank, *El Desafio de Argentina: Crecimiento, Inclusion Social y Gobernabilidad: Notas de Politica*, Buenos Aires: World Bank, 2003.

World Bank, *Argentina: A la Busqueda de un Crecimento Sostenido con Equidad Social. Observaciones Sobre el Crecimento, la Desigualdad y la Pobreza,* Washington, DC: World Bank, 2005.

World Bank, *Argentina 2006–2008: Country Assistance Strategy*, Washington, DC: World Bank, 2006.

World Bank, *Project Appraisal Document on Proposed Loan to Argentina for Heads of Household Transition Project*, Washington, DC: World Bank, 2006.

World Bank, *Argentina: Institutional and Governance Review*, Washington, DC: World Bank, 2006.

World Bank, *Agricultura y Desarrollo Rural en Argentina: Temas Claves*, Washington, DC: World Bank, 2006.

World Bank, *Argentina: Facing the Challenge of Ageing and Social Security*, Washington, DC: World Bank, January 2007.

World Bank, *Infrastructuras Rurales en Argentina: Diagnostico de Situacion y Opciones para su Desarrollo*, Washington, DC: World Bank, April 2007.

World Bank, *Fragmentacion Territorial y Desarrollo Rural: Nuevas interpretaciones y propuestas para el desarrollo de los territories rurales en un context de globalizacion*, Sustainable Development Working Paper 1, Washington, DC: World Bank, October 2007.

World Bank Institute, *Improving Governance and Controlling Corruption: Towards a Participatory and Action-oriented Approach Grounded on Empirical Rigor*, Washington, DC: World Bank, 2001.

Wortman, A., *Construccion Imaginaria de la Desigualdad Social*, Buenos Aires: CLACSO, 2007.

Yeyati, E. and Valenzuela, D., *La Resurreccion: Historia de la Poscrisis Argentina*, Buenos Aires: Editorial Sudamericana, 2007.

Zalles, A., "Bolivia y Chile: los imperatives de una nueva epoca," *Nueva Sociedad*, 207, 2007.

Zanetta, C., *The Influence of the World Bank on National Housing and Urban Policies: The Case of Mexico and Argentina during the 1990s*, London: Ashgate, 2004.

Index

Page numbers in *italics* denote tables, those in **bold** denote figures.